Studies in Russian and East European History and Society

Series Editors: **R. W. Davies, E. A. Rees, M. J. Ilič** and **J. R. Smith**, Centre for Russian and East European Studies, University of Birmingham

Recent titles include:

Lynne Attwood
CREATING THE NEW SOVIET WOMAN

Edwin Bacon and Mark Sandle (*editors*)
BREZHNEV RECONSIDERED

John Barber and Mark Harrison (*editors*)
THE SOVIET DEFENCE-INDUSTRY COMPLEX FROM STALIN TO KHRUSHCHEV

Vincent Barnett
KONDRATIEV AND THE DYNAMICS OF ECONOMIC DEVELOPMENT

R. W. Davies
SOVIET HISTORY IN THE YELTSIN ERA

Linda Edmondson (*editor*)
GENDER IN RUSSIAN HISTORY AND CULTURE

James Hughes
STALINISM IN A RUSSIAN PROVINCE

Melanie Ilič
WOMEN WORKERS IN THE SOVIET INTERWAR ECONOMY
WOMEN IN THE STALIN ERA (*editor*)

Peter Kirkow
RUSSIA'S PROVINCES

Maureen Perrie
THE CULT OF IVAN THE TERRIBLE IN STALIN'S RUSSIA

E. A. Rees (*editor*)
DECISION-MAKING IN THE STALINIST COMMAND ECONOMY
CENTRE–LOCAL RELATIONS IN THE STALINIST STATE 1928–1941

Lennart Samuelson
PLANS FOR STALIN'S WAR MACHINE
Tukhachevskii and Military-Economic Planning, 1925–1941

Vera Tolz
RUSSIAN ACADEMICIANS AND THE REVOLUTION

J. N. Westwood
SOVIET RAILWAYS TO RUSSIAN RAILWAYS

Stephen G. Wheatcroft (*editor*)
CHALLENGING TRADITIONAL VIEWS OF RUSSIAN HISTORY

Galina M. Yemelianova
RUSSIA AND ISLAM
A Historical Survey

Studies in Russian and East European History and Society
Series Standing Order ISBN 0–333–71239–0
(*outside North America only*)

You can receive future titles in this series as they are published by placing a standing order. Please contact your bookseller or, in case of difficulty, write to us at the address below with your name and address, the title of the series and the ISBN quoted above.

Customer Services Department, Macmillan Distribution Ltd, Houndmills, Basingstoke, Hampshire RG21 6XS, England

Brezhnev Reconsidered

Edited by

Edwin Bacon

and

Mark Sandle

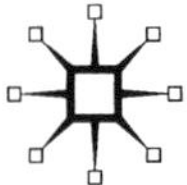

First published 2002 by
PALGRAVE MACMILLAN
Houndmills, Basingstoke, Hampshire RG21 6XS and
175 Fifth Avenue, New York, N.Y. 10010
Companies and representatives throughout the world

PALGRAVE MACMILLAN is the global academic imprint of the Palgrave Macmillan division of St. Martin's Press, LLC and of Palgrave Macmillan Ltd. Macmillan® is a registered trademark in the United States, United Kingdom and other countries. Palgrave is a registered trademark in the European Union and other countries.

ISBN 0–333–79463–X

This book is printed on paper suitable for recycling and made from fully managed and sustained forest sources.

A catalogue record for this book is available from the British Library.

Library of Congress Cataloging-in-Publication Data

Brezhnev reconsidered / edited by Edwin Bacon and Mark Sandle.
p. cm. — (Studies in Russian and East European history and society)
Includes bibliographical references and index.
ISBN 0–333–79463–X
1. Brezhnev, Leonid Il§'ch, 1906– 2. Soviet Union—Politics and government—1953–1985. I. Bacon, Edwin, 1966– II. Sandle, Mark. III. Studies in Russian and East European history and society (Palgrave(Firm))

DK275.B7 B74 2002
947.085'3'092—dc21

2002072321

10 9 8 7 6 5 4 3 2 1
11 10 09 08 07 06 05 04 03 02

Printed and bound in Great Britain by
Antony Rowe Ltd, Chippenham and Eastbourne

Contents

Acknowledgements

The editors would like to thank several people whose assistance in the preparation of this work was very much appreciated – namely, Marea Arries, Professor Bob Davies, Melanie Ilič, Bettina Renz, Jeremy Smith and Bill Tompson.

Notes on the Contributors

Edwin Bacon is Senior Lecturer in Russian Politics in the Centre for Russian and East European Studies, the University of Birmingham. Between 2002 and 2005 he is on secondment as Director of Research at Bishop Grosseteste College in Lincoln. He is the author of *The Gulag at War* (1994) as well as a number of articles and book chapters in the field of Russian politics.

Mike Bowker is currently Lecturer at the University of East Anglia, Norwich. He has written extensively on Russian foreign policy and the cold war. His publications include: *Superpower Détente: A Reappraisal* (1988) with Phil Williams; *Russian Foreign Policy and the End of the Cold War* (1997); and *Russia After The Cold War* (2000, co-editor with Cameron Ross).

Ben Fowkes was until recently Senior Lecturer in History at the University of North London. He previously taught at Sheffield University. He is the author of a number of books related to the theme of communism, including *Communism in Germany under the Weimar Republic* (1984), *The Rise and Fall of Communism in Eastern Europe* (1995), *The Disintegration of the Soviet Union* (1997) and *The Post-Communist Era* (1999). He has done archival research in a number of central and eastern european archives, and in Moscow.

John Gooding is Reader in History at the University of Edinburgh. His most recent books are *Rulers and Subjects: Government and People in Russia, 1801–1991* (1996) and *Socialism in Russia* (2001).

Mark Harrison is Professor of Economics at the University of Warwick. He is currently working on the economics of innovation in the Soviet aircraft industry. Recent publications include *The Soviet Defence Industry Complex From Stalin to Khrushchev* (2000, with John Barber) and *The Economics of World War II* (1998).

Mark Sandle is Principal Lecturer in Russian and Soviet History at De Montfort University. His most recent work is *A Short History of Soviet Socialism* (1999). He is currently working on a book on Mikhail Gorbachev.

Ian D. Thatcher is Senior Lecturer in Modern Russian History at the University of Leicester. The author of many articles and several books, he is currently completing a political life of Leon Trotsky, to be published by Routledge in 2002–3.

Mark Webber is Senior Lecturer in Politics in the Department of European Studies, Loughborough University. He is the author of *The International Politics of Russia and the Successor States* (1996), editor of *Russia and Europe: Conflict or Cooperation?* (2000), and joint author of *Foreign Policy in A Transformed World* (2002).

1
Reconsidering Brezhnev

Edwin Bacon

Leonid Ilyich Brezhnev was leader of the Soviet Union between 1964 and his death at the age of 76 in November 1982. During this time the Soviet Union was, with the United States, one of two superpowers dominating global affairs. The entire international system was based around this bifurcation of power and influence between the USSR and the United States. At any given time during his eighteen years in power, Leonid Brezhnev was one of the two most powerful people in the world.

Where then are the great works devoted to this man and his times? A bibliographical search for works on Brezhnev will reveal scarcely anything written in English on the subject of Brezhnev or the Brezhnev years – and not much more in Russian – since the days when the topic was current affairs. Twenty years on since his death it is time for this gap in history to be filled. A sufficient period has now passed for a sense of perspective in considering an era which in many ways was the high point of Soviet power. In this book, we begin the process of re-evaluation. Contributors deal with Brezhnev himself and with the era over which he presided. They consider the central aspects of the politics, ideology, international relations and economics of these years. First though, let us address more deeply the question of why Leonid Brezhnev is one of history's forgotten men.

Let Gorbachev judge

One of the primary reasons why Brezhnev and his era in power have attracted so little posthumous analysis is that a consensus on these years was formed early on and has remained remarkably resilient. The reforming discourse of the political project known as *perestroika* and overseen by the last Soviet leader Mikhail Gorbachev (1985–91), declared the Brezhnev years to be 'an era of stagnation', and this discourse became the overwhelmingly dominant conceptualisation of the almost two decades during which Brezhnev oversaw the Soviet state.[1]

What though was meant by 'an era of stagnation'? Gorbachev's own view was that Brezhnev pursued 'in essence a fierce neo-Stalinist line'.[2] During this time dissidence was dealt with brutally, the arms race increasingly gathered pace, Eastern Europe was tied by force to the Soviet Bloc – as witnessed most dramatically in the crushing of the Prague Spring in 1968 – and the ill-fated invasion of Afghanistan was launched.

In particular, though, the Gorbachevian discourse blames Brezhnevism for failing to change with the times. The leadership team which took power from Khrushchev in 1964 grew old in office, so that by the beginning of the 1980s the average age of a Politburo member exceeded 70. According to Gorbachev, these men 'overlooked the far-reaching changes that were taking place in science and technology . . . and they ignored the transformations that were occurring in other countries'.[3] While the 1960s meant youthful radicalism and social transformation in much of the West, in the Soviet Union the *shestidesyatniki,* as the young generation of the 1960s was known, for the most part had to confine their radicalism to kitchen table discussions as it was stifled by an authoritarian Communist Party and its 'blind adherence to old dogmas and obsolete ideas'.[4] While high-tech industry developed in the West – from smart weapons to smart washing machines – the USSR lagged behind. While by the end of the 1970s a renewed confidence in the international sphere became apparent under the resurgent Right of the Reagan–Thatcher–Kohl era, Soviet socialism appeared to be declining in health along with its leaders. In the end, the Gorbachevian discourse neatly suggests, the leader and his team were a metaphor for the country – conservative, decrepit and incoherent. Stagnation was seen to have taken hold across all spheres of public life. In the political arena the low level of personnel changeover, known as Brezhnev's 'stability of cadres' policy, led not only to a log-jam of increasingly elderly men in positions of power across the country, but also promoted corruption and a lack of forward planning. In the economic sphere, as Mark Harrison points out in Chapter 3, the Soviet economy slowed down, particularly when compared with western Europe, and absolute declines in output became more frequent. According to Moshe Lewin, 'at the heart of the malfunctions in the economy, in politics and in other areas was the long-standing phenomenon . . . "departmentalism"'.[5] This administrative behaviour undermined the theoretical logic of the centralised system, that an all-seeing state would allocate resources and goods optimally. Instead, departmental and sectoral interests prevailed, at the lowest levels allocation was as likely to be based on *blat* as on entitlement.[6] Shortages, bottle-necks, hoarding and the production of unwanted goods became increasingly commonplace. In the social sphere, as Mark Harrison points out, this translated into a perceived decline in living standards, and a cynicism about privilege and corruption.

If Brezhnev himself was a metaphor for his country then the cameo played out after his death on 10 November 1982 was perhaps fitting.

Two days later, as the coffin containing the deceased leader was lifted into place for its lying in state, Brezhnev's body fell through the bottom. A new coffin – this time metal-plated – was made for the funeral itself. As this metal casket was lowered into the grave, one of the funeral attendants could not bear its weight and it fell with a loud crash into the hole.[7]

The impression of a decaying superpower prevailed, and of course was not helped by the fact that in the less than two and half years between Brezhnev's death and Gorbachev's accession to the General Secretaryship of the Communist Party of the Soviet Union, there were two further leaders – Yurii Andropov and Konstantin Chernenko. Both of these were elderly men who spent most of their leadership fighting against terminal illness. Andropov died a few months short of his seventieth birthday in February 1984, Chernenko died in March 1985 aged 73.

Whatever the reality – and we will discuss that further both below and throughout this volume – the atmosphere at home and the impression abroad is summed up in the memoirs of Aleksandr Lebed, who by the mid-1990s was to become a candidate for the Russian presidency and subsequently President Yeltsin's National Security Adviser. In the early 1980s Lebed studied at the Frunze Military Academy in Moscow, where his particular duty was as a member of the Funeral Detachment:

> Remember that I studied at the academy from 1982 to 1985. In this period, in terms of General Secretaries alone, three died. And then there was Marshal of the Soviet Union Bagramyan, Ustinov [Defence Minister], Politburo member Pel'she. And many more less well known but no less important people. We weren't short of work.[8]

A political and economic malaise appeared to have settled on the Soviet Union by the early 1980s as the superpower found itself ruled by a gerontocracy which was slowly dying out. As any passing regime, the Brezhnev leadership attempted to confirm its contribution to history, and in particular to the great project of building communism. Chernenko used his funeral address to describe the late Soviet leader as 'the most consistent successor of Lenin's cause'. Gorbachev is scathing in his memoirs when criticising these 'grandiloquent words' where 'stagnation of cadres . . . is presented as a great achievement of Leonid Ilyich'.[9] Gorbachev is, however, being a little disingenuous here, on two counts. First a funeral is hardly the place to launch swingeing criticism of the deceased, and second, Gorbachev himself had regularly talked of Brezhnev in the same vein. Only five years previously, in October 1977, the Communist Party newspaper, *Pravda*, carried a speech by Mikhail Gorbachev given to the Supreme Soviet, in which he praised Brezhnev's contribution to that meeting of the Supreme Soviet, declaring that, 'the report of Leonid Ilyich Brezhnev is a significant contribution to the treasury of Marxism–Leninism'.[10]

Clearly Gorbachev's agenda was to pave the way for his reforms, and to justify them retrospectively by letting stagnation stand for the Brezhnev years. In discourse theory terms, 'stagnation' became the 'key signifier' whose function as 'speech act' was to create the political environment in which only radical reform of some sort would answer the needs of the Soviet state. According to this discourse, the bureaucracy and conservatism of the Brezhnev years produced what Gorbachev termed a 'pre-crisis situation' founded on low growth rates.[11] Radical reform was thereby justified as the appropriate solution, the aim of which was – ironically given its end result – to prevent a full-blown crisis arising in the Soviet Union.

Let the people judge

Having established the generally accepted 'stagnation view' of Brezhnev and his era, let us begin our questioning of that approach. We will not by any means claim that the stagnation approach is wholly unfounded and mistaken; it is not without good reason that this view has been widely accepted as an appropriate shorthand for perceptions of the Soviet Union particularly in the latter part of Brezhnev's leadership. However, a shorthand approach is by definition not the full picture. There are many nuances which need drawing out. Any serious assessment of the stagnation hypothesis must distinguish between Brezhnev the leader and developments in Soviet life during the Brezhnev years, and between different periods within 'the Brezhnev years'. Similarly, comparative approaches bring differing interpretations. Temporal comparisons of the Brezhnev era with the rule of Stalin, of Khrushchev, or of Gorbachev will all provide their own emphases, and each of these will in turn be different from a systemic comparison with the West during the 1960s and 1970s. There is too the question of sources – different interpretations come from archival documents, memoirs and academic writings. Each chapter of this volume will provide a more detailed assessment of its particular topic. This Introduction will develop different perceptions of the Brezhnev era as a whole. Let us begin with a perception which provides an indictment of the stagnation hypothesis from what is perhaps a surprising source: the Russian people.

A public opinion survey carried out in Russia by the respected Moscow-based polling organisation VTsIOM in January 2000 asked its respondents to evaluate on a positive/negative basis the leadership periods of their country's twentieth-century history. The results of this survey are set out in Table 1.1.

The most highly regarded leadership period is clearly that of Leonid Brezhnev. Nor is VTsIOM's January 2000 poll a statistical one-off. Rather it confirms the findings of other polls throughout the 1990s. A VTsIOM poll of November 1994 similarly asked respondents to choose the best period since the 1917 revolution, and again the Brezhnev era was most favoured, in this case by 36 per cent, compared with the 33 per cent who chose the

Table 1.1 'Was a given period more positive or more negative for the country?'

Period	*More positive*	*More negative*
Nicholas II	18	12
Revolution	28	36
Stalin	26	48
Khrushchev	30	14
Brezhnev	51	10
Gorbachev	9	61
Yeltsin (March 1999)	5	72
Yeltsin (January 2000)	15	67

Source: The All-Russian Centre for the Study of Public Opinion (VTsIOM), January 2000.

Khrushchev era.[12] A poll by the Public Opinion Fund in September 1999 similarly chose the Brezhnev period as the time in the twentieth century when 'ordinary people lived best of all'.[13]

As noted above, however, the distinction between Brezhnev the leader, and life in the Brezhnev era, is worth making. Archie Brown points out, in relation to an opinion poll of 1994, that though the Brezhnev era rated high and the Gorbachev era low in terms of the best time in which to live, when it came to regard for the leaders themselves, Gorbachev rated slightly higher than Brezhnev in terms of playing a positive role in history.[14] Nonetheless, this poll was in 1994, and between then and the end of the century, evaluations of the Brezhnev era became ever more positive among the Russian people (see Table 1.2). By 1999 it was not just the Brezhnev era which was being rated highly but Brezhnev the leader. Respondents in the same Public Opinion Foundation poll cited above chose Leonid Brezhnev above all other contenders, as the man for whom they would vote were any twentieth-century

Table 1.2 Evaluations of periods of twentieth-century Russian history

Period	*1994 poll results (positive/negative)*	*1999 poll results (positive/negative)*
Nicholas II	–	18/12
The Revolution	27/38	28/36
Stalin	18/57	26/48
Khrushchev	33/14	30/14
Brezhnev	36/16	51/10
Gorbachev	16/47	9/61
Yeltsin	–	5/72

Source: *Monitoring obshchestvennogo mneniya*, No. 3(41), May–June 1999, p. 11.

Russian leader or contemporary Russian politician to run for the presidency then.

What explains this positive evaluation of the Brezhnev years? It is possible to answer that by questioning the scientific value of 'historical' polls. Affection for the Brezhnev era – so the argument would go – increased as standards of living in post-Soviet Russia declined. The impact of the economic collapse of 1998 in particular awoke in respondents an overly rosy remembrance of the 1960s and 1970s, where stability in prices and incomes was the norm, and the state heavily subsidised the essentials of life. This view is backed up to an extent by the fact that positive evaluations of the Brezhnev years were higher among the older generation, who suffered more than most in the economic collapse of the 1990s.[15] Nonetheless, this explaining away of the poll results goes only so far. Evaluations of the era may have been more positive among older respondents, but they were also positive, in comparison with other eras, among younger respondents. That there may be a measure of 'mis-remembering' when setting the past against immediate contemporary difficulties may likewise be the case, but this is both unavoidable, and irrelevant to our task of reassessing Brezhnev. The fundamental fact to be drawn from these surveys is that to the Russian people as a whole the Brezhnev years are considered as something of a golden era, rather than an era of stagnation. The almost ubiquitous acceptance of the stagnation hypothesis in the West represents a triumph for the Gorbachevian discourse over the realities of life as lived in Russia. There are arguments on both sides of the debate, but these need to be made. Too often in the past the stagnation hypothesis has simply been stated rather than argued.

Having considered the stagnation hypothesis against the views of the Russian people, as revealed in opinion polls, let us now analyse how academic and political observers have assessed Brezhnev and his era. First, Brezhnev as a man and a leader, for which the memoirs of his contemporaries provide a rich source of material, then the Brezhnev years as whole, where the development of academic assessments will be traced.

Remembering Leonid Ilyich

Leonid Brezhnev was born in 1906 in Ukraine, the son of a steel worker. At different times in his life he would describe himself as Ukrainian or, later on as he moved through the ranks of the Communist Party, Russian.[16] His biography (see Box 1.1) indicates a man who made the most of the social and political upheaval through which he lived. Noted as a hard worker and good organiser, rather than an intellectual, he joined the Party in 1929, and took his first steps up the political ladder in 1937–9 in Dnepropetrovsk, when Stalin's 'Great Terror' created many vacancies in party and government positions. The war years saw his continued advancement through the Political Administration of the Red Army, and thereafter he resumed his career as a Party boss, first in Zaporozhe, and then back in Dnepropetrovsk. His rise into the higher echelons of the Party began with his appointment in 1950 as First Secretary of the Party in Moldavia, and two years later he was named a candidate member of the Presidium (Politburo).

Having all but achieved membership of the Presidium in 1952, Brezhnev was removed from this position the next year and appointed Head of the Political Directorate of the Army and Navy. His fortunes continued to change rapidly with the times, within a year or so he was given responsibility for overseeing Khrushchev's prestigious 'Virgin Lands' campaign in Kazakhstan, and by 1957 he became a full member of the Presidium. By 1963 he was the senior Central Committee Secretary, and from there launched – with Presidium colleagues – the overthrow of Khrushchev in 1964.

Box 1.1 Biography of Leonid Ilyich Brezhnev – his rise to power

Leonid Ilyich Brezhnev was born on 19 December 1906 in the town of Kamenskoye (from 1936 renamed Dneprodzerzhinsk) in Ukraine. His background was industrial working class (both father and grandfather worked in the local iron and steel plant) and in 1915, Leonid Ilyich was one of only six workers' children, out of 45 students, to be admitted to the Kamenskoye Classical Gymnasium.

In 1921, Brezhnev graduated from the Classical Gymnasium – which had been renamed the First Labour School following the Bolshevik revolution of 1917 – and he moved with his family (parents, younger brother Yakov, and younger sister Vera) to Kursk, where he began factory work. The first steps of his political career were taken when he joined the Komsomol (Communist youth organisation) in 1923, the same year in which he enrolled in the Kursk technical school to study land management. He graduated from the technical school in 1927.

In 1929 and 1931, Brezhnev's political career advanced further as he was admitted to the Communist Party of the Soviet Union, first as a candidate member and then as a full member. He spent the academic year 1930–1 in Moscow at the Kalinin Institute of Agricultural Machinery before returning in 1931 to his home town of Kamenskoye. With the exception of a period of national service in the Chita region in 1935, Brezhnev remained in Kamenskoye until 1936, steadily rising through the party ranks while working as an engineer and supervising the technical and political training of other workers. This pattern continued after he moved to Dnepropetrovsk in 1936 to become director of a technical institute. By the time war broke out in June 1941, Brezhnev had risen to the position of regional party secretary for the defence industries.

Box 1.1 *Continued*

Throughout the war years, Brezhnev served as a political officer, in 1943 becoming the Head of the Political Department of the 18th Army. By the end of the war he was in charge of the Political Administration of the 4th Ukrainian Front. Back in civilian life Brezhnev's Party career gathered pace. Between 1946 and 1950 he was appointed in rapid succession to Party First Secretaryships in Zaporozhe, Dnepropetrovsk, and then the Republic of Moldavia. In 1952 Brezhnev was elected to the Party's Central Committee, and in the same year Stalin nominated him as a candidate member of the Communist Party's highest body, the Presidium (Politburo).

Brezhnev's first candidature to the Presidium was short-lived, ending after the death of Stalin in 1953. Nonetheless, he was not discarded by the Party leadership. Having proved himself in Moldavia, he was then appointed to the larger Republic of Kazakhstan – as Second Secretary in 1954 and First Secretary in 1955 – with a main task being to oversee the prestigious 'Virgin Lands' agricultural policy of Stalin's successor as Soviet leader, Nikita Khrushchev. He was once again made a candidate member of the Presidium in 1956, and became a full member in 1957, having returned to Moscow to head the Central Committee's department for defence, heavy machine-building, and capital construction.

In 1960 Brezhnev was elected to what was, *de jure* at least, the position of head of state, namely the Chairman of the Presidium of the Supreme Soviet. He held this position until July 1964, and in October 1964, following Khrushchev's removal from power, was elevated to the *de facto* highest position in the Soviet Union, General Secretary of the Communist Party of the Soviet Union. He was to lead the Soviet Union until his death in November 1982.

Brezhnev was an organisation man rather than a policy man. He was no great theorist, and indeed was described by his former Politburo colleague Petro Shelest as 'a dim-witted fellow'.[17] Shelest's removal from office by Brezhnev perhaps gave him reason to denigrate his former boss, nonetheless, even those without such reason would recognise Shelest's view that Brezhnev 'loved power and honours'. The General Secretary's vanity was legendary, and in particular he liked to receive decorations. On his 60th birthday in 1966 he was awarded the Hero of the Soviet Union medal. In the subsequent years of his leadership he received three more Hero of the Soviet Union medals, the Order of Lenin with Gold Star for bravery during the Second World War, the Lenin Prize for literature, and innumerable medals from other socialist states and international organisations – so many in fact that carrying over 200 decorations at his funeral proved a problem, only resolved by having several medals pinned to most of the 44 cushions carried in the parade.

In addition to these medals, Brezhnev had himself created a Marshal of the Soviet Union – the highest military rank in the Soviet army – in 1976. After this award he attended the next meeting of 18th army veterans in a long coat, and, saying 'Attention! Marshal's coming!', he took off the coat and proudly showed off his new uniform.[18] This weakness for undeserved military glory was reflected too in the memoirs which Brezhnev 'wrote' of his service in the Second World War.[19] The memoirs concerned his part in the battle around Malaya Zemlya, Novorossiisk in 1943. As Zhores Medvedev puts it, 'until Brezhnev transformed it into a major battle 30 years later, it was a minor episode of the war'.[20] Despite their poor literary quality, these memoirs were published in large numbers, received the Lenin Prize for Literature, and were widely praised within the Soviet Union.[21]

Brezhnev's vanity made him the butt of many jokes in the Soviet Union, at a time when political jokes were one form of dissention with which citizens could get away. Similarly, jokes were made about Brezhnev's other character traits, notably his love of western cars of which there were reportedly over thirty in the Kremlin garages after his death.[22] Alongside his love of cars, and of driving them at some speed, Brezhnev was a sports fan. He regularly swam and had a passion for hunting, he played chess, and often attended football and ice hockey games. This apparently healthy lifestyle was balanced by the fact that for much of his life he was a chain smoker and, according to his Foreign Minister Andrei Gromyko, he had a serious drink problem.[23]

The late Russian historian Dmitrii Volkogonov had access to the diaries of Leonid Brezhnev in the 1990s, and notes the mundanity of their content, and Brezhnev's apparent obsession with minor, personal issues, rather than the great issues of state:

> *16 May 1976.* Went nowhere – rang no one, likewise no one me – haircut, shaved and washed hair in the morning. Walked a bit during the day, then watched Central Army lose to Spartak (the lads played well)... *7 August.* 19th day of holiday. Swam in sea 1.30 – massage pool 30 minutes. Washed head – with children's soap...
> *16 June [1977]* 86.00 [kilograms]. 10 a.m. Supreme Soviet session. Appointment of Com. Brezhnev as chairman of the Presidium of the Supreme Soviet (a lot of congratulations).[24]

There is no escaping the conclusion that in many ways Brezhnev was a simple man. He could, in later years, be easily moved to tears by a sentimental film or a laudatory speech in his honour. Whether these characteristics made him a poor leader, however, is another matter. Was he an unimaginative leader, promoted above his abilities to head a superpower, and yet unable to grasp the great issues of his time even before the ravages of age and ill health set in? Or did his simple, cautious approach bring much-needed stability to the Soviet Union and to the international relations of his day?

Brezhnev the politician

In Chapter 2 in this volume, Ian Thatcher provides a provocative assessment of Brezhnev as leader, considering him from the perspective of the system which he oversaw. His view that Brezhnev was one of the most successful exponents of the art of Soviet politics seems on the face of things to be at odds with the familiar image of Brezhnev presented in the stagnation view, that of a decrepit and vain man, barely able to stand under the weight of undeserved medals, and scarcely capable of coherent speech let alone the wise governance of a superpower. Of course the latter view – like much in the stagnation hypothesis – applies most appropriately to the final years of Brezhnev's life. For a more rounded consideration, a longer time-frame is needed. How did Brezhnev come to power? And how did he manage to remain in power for eighteen years, longer than any other Soviet leader with the exception of Josef Stalin? Brezhnev's part in the removal of his predecessor, Nikita Khrushchev, from power in 1964 reveals a picture of a decisive man with clear views on how the Communist Party should be run. Since the late 1950s, Brezhnev had been dissatisfied with Khrushchev's leadership style.[25] He was not alone in this, as Khrushchev's impulsiveness and nascent cult of personality were increasingly alienating Politburo colleagues and other influential groups. Nonetheless, when it came to the removal of Khrushchev from office, recent memoirs make clear that it was Brezhnev, assisted by Podgorny, who planned and executed the ouster. According to Gennadii Voronov, Brezhnev carefully planned his move for some time in advance, talking to all of the key people and keeping a list of the Central Committee members who could be relied upon to support the Kremlin coup.[26] Furthermore, Khrushchev himself was apparently wary of Brezhnev's ambition, seeing his arduous speaking schedule as a dangerous sign.[27] Although he experienced a last-minute panic before eventually moving against the incumbent First Secretary, it was nonetheless Brezhnev who acted decisively in telephoning Khrushchev at his Black Sea resort and calling him back to Moscow, where his removal from office was confirmed by the Central Committee.

Once installed as Soviet leader, Brezhnev showed himself adept at operating within the Soviet machine. According to Anatolii Dobrynin, former Soviet ambassador to the United States,

> Brezhnev was a political actor who knew well the 'corridors of power', was used to 'playing in a team' and not separately. He was careful, unhurried, willing to listen to the opinions of his colleagues, wary of

> sudden turns or sharp new directions, preferring the aforementioned stability... He didn't concern himself much with problems of ideology and didn't show much interest in them.[28]

This commitment to stability applied equally in personnel policy and in broader policy directions, as exemplified in Dobrynin's report of Brezhnev's attitude to relations with the United States at the height of the Cold War: 'the main thing is that there is peace'.[29] Against the background of the upheavals of the preceding fifty and following twenty years of Russian and Soviet history, the nuclear brinksmanship of the Khrushchev years, and the international crises of the 1960s and 1970s, what Fedor Burlatsky described as Brezhnev's '18 years without any terrors, cataclysms, and conflicts' can arguably be seen as an achievement of great historical import.[30] A more ideologically driven leader might well have brought to his policy-making more fundamentalist goals and reactions.

Of course, stability is the flip-side of stagnation. Burlatsky hinted at this when, having lauded Brezhnev for the absence of catastrophe during his time in office, continued, 'and the people immediately surrounding him desired only one thing – that this man live for ever, so good was he to them'.[31] Indeed the contribution of the policy of 'stability of cadres' to the development of stagnation is undeniable. The Politburo grew old together, the younger generation of leaders was held back, and corruption was encouraged by the job security enjoyed by high-ranking officials, most infamously in the veritable fiefdoms of a number of regional leaders.[32]

Brezhnev was, however, not so wedded to the stability of cadres that he would endanger his own position. On numerous occasions regional leaders and Politburo colleagues were removed from their posts. In his early years in office, Brezhnev oversaw the removal of half of the regional leaders in the Soviet Union.[33] This installation of his own team was the typical move of a man familiar with the machinations of Soviet politics. Nor was he afraid to remove competitors – or simply those whom he deemed misplaced – from the Politburo, with the high-level careers of Polyansky, Voronov, Podgorny, Shelepin, and Shelest all coming to an end at Brezhnev's behest. In the latter two cases at least, it appears that strong potential rivals were removed from the scene by the same sort of decisive action which had seen an end to Khrushchev's leadership of the Soviet Union.[34] In fact, far from 'stability of cadres' being a marked feature of the Brezhnev era as a whole, many western observers writing in the first decade or so of Brezhnev's period in office devoted themselves to the 'science' of Kremlinology, a large factor within which involved the close scrutiny of every personnel move for hints of policy changes.

Canadian academic, Teresa Rakowska-Harmstone, writing in 1976, identified four stages in the personnel policy adopted by Brezhnev in order to secure his unchallenged personal ascendancy over the party.[35] First, in 1965

Brezhnev's principal immediate rival for power, Nikolai Podgorny, was removed from his position as Secretary of the Central Committee and 'promoted' to become the nominal head of state, as Chairman of the Presidium of the USSR Supreme Soviet. His position as Central Committee secretary for personnel policy was taken by Andrei Kirilenko, whose links with Brezhnev went back to 1946 when Kirilenko was Second Secretary during Brezhnev's First Secretaryship of the Communist Party in Zaporozhe, Ukraine. At the same time, a second rival Central Committee secretary, Aleksandr Shelepin, was removed from the chairmanship of the Party-State Control Commission and the deputy chairmanship of the Soviet government (the Council of Ministers). Rakowska-Harmstone's second stage came in 1967 when Shelepin was removed as a Central Committee Secretary altogether.

The third stage in Brezhnev's consolidation of power was the early 1970s which saw the 'retirement' of Gennadii Voronov and Petro Shelest, and the demotion of Dmitrii Polyansky to become Minister of Agriculture, having previously been first deputy to the prime minister Aleksei Kosygin. Both Polyansky and Voronov were considered part of the Kosygin 'faction', which was thus weakened by these moves. The fourth stage of the 'further gradual consolidation of Brezhnev's power' noted by Rakowska-Harmstone came in 1973 as the representation of the 'power ministries' in the Politburo was increased. Minister of Defence Andrei Grechko, Minister of Foreign Affairs Andrei Gromyko, and KGB Chairman Yurii Andropov, were all elected voting members of the Politburo at the Central Committee plenum in April 1973, thereby balancing the influence of the Party apparatus, and decreasing Brezhnev's vulnerability to opposition from that quarter.

These manoeuvres certainly give the lie to the idea that 'stability of cadres' was the norm at the highest level of Soviet politics for most of the Brezhnev era. It could be argued though, that the events outlined here laid the foundations for later stagnation. It took Brezhnev a decade to fashion a Politburo within which there was no real threat to his position. However, the caution which prompted such astute management of the Soviet political system also provided reason for the preservation of the Politburo which had thereby been created. Furthermore, the balancing of the 'power ministries' (defence, foreign affairs, and the security services) against the Party apparatus arguably reflected, or perhaps created, Brezhnev's willingness to give economic priority to the 'defence sector' in its broadest sense – a willingness which contributed substantially to the economic decline of the early 1980s, and the creation of the 'pre-crisis' situation identified by Mikhail Gorbachev.

Brezhnev and the collective

It is apparent that when we begin to look in more depth at the Brezhnev years, then the shorthand summations of an 'era of stagnation' and 'the stability of cadres' become less accurate and less useful. Much depends on the perspective of our observation and various 'perception altering' criteria in particular have been noted so far. It makes a difference whether one is looking at Brezhnev himself or at wider phenomena such as society, international relations, or the economy. As noted above, the temporal perspective is also important. Perceptions of Brezhnev and his era were different in the mid-1980s from those in the mid-1970s, and these were different again from those of a decade earlier.

In the mid-1960s appraisals of Brezhnev centred on the new leadership of the Soviet Union as a whole. Just as in the early Khrushchev years, it was not immediately apparent after 1964 who wielded how much power in the Soviet hierarchy. The immediate talk was of a triumvirate of Brezhnev at the head of the Communist Party, Kosygin as prime minister (Chairman of the Presidium of the Council of Ministers), and – after December 1965 – Podgorny as the head of state, the Chairman of the Supreme Soviet. This then was a reaffirmation of collective leadership. On Stalin's death in 1953, the Presidium of the Central Committee of the Communist Party had decided that no single individual should inherit the powers accrued by Stalin. In particular, the Party and the government should be under separate men – at the time, Khrushchev and Malenkov. As the Khrushchev years progressed, so it became clearer that the true location of power in the Soviet system was in the Party rather than in the government or the Supreme Soviet. By the early 1960s Khrushchev's position was apparently secure, and the 22nd Party Congress of 1961 saw the beginnings of a 'cult of personality' emerging around the leader. It was this tendency to accrue too much personal power, or more particularly, to disregard the interests of key groups within the political elite, which lay behind Khrushchev's eventual removal by Brezhnev and his colleagues in 1964. The accusation, albeit circumlocutory, was that Khrushchev had acted in a 'voluntarist' manner. In other words, his personal power had prevented the objective, and therefore collective, development of policy.

For the first years after Khrushchev's removal from power, this collective leadership continued to act as such, and indeed it might be argued that, despite the undoubted consolidation of power by Brezhnev himself as the '*primus inter pares*', in terms of leadership style the Soviet Union was ruled by a collective leadership throughout the Brezhnev era. Certainly, through to the end of the 1960s, the consensus view was that collective leadership prevailed. The economic reforms of 1965 were clearly identified with the prime minister, and referred to as the 'Kosygin reforms'. By the end of the decade, T. H. Rigby argued that a stable oligarchic system had developed in the Soviet Union, centred around Brezhnev, Podgorny and Kosygin, plus Central Committee secretaries Mikhail Suslov and Andrei Kirilenko.[36] Accurate though this assessment was at the time, its publication coincided with the further strengthening of Brezhnev's position by means of an apparent clash with Suslov.

At a Central Committee plenum in December 1969, Brezhnev gave a frank speech on economic matters, which had not been agreed with other Politburo members in advance. This independent line both surprised and angered colleagues, particularly Suslov, Shelepin, and first deputy prime minister Kiril Mazurov, who wrote a joint letter critical of the speech which they intended to be discussed at the next Plenum in March 1970. Brezhnev, however, exerted pressure on Suslov and his colleagues, the Plenum was postponed, the letter withdrawn, and the General Secretary emerged with greater authority and pledges of loyalty from his erstwhile critics.[37]

The balance of the collective leadership was being upset, as had happened in the Khrushchev years, by the increasing power of the Party leader. This was confirmed in true Kremlinological style after the promotion of Andropov, Grechko and Gromyko to the Politburo in April 1973 (see above). Under Khrushchev, as a mark of the collective leadership system, the practice had been established that any list of Politburo members was published alphabetically. (This was in contrast to the ranking list which had previously been employed.) By happy alphabetical coincidence Brezhnev was top of the list, and had been since the removal of Averky Aristov and Ivan Belyaev from Khrushchev's Politburo in 1960. The promotion of Andropov upset this fortunate literal coincidence, and when the first list of the new Politburo was published, it was in alphabetical, rather than ranking, order – with the exception of Brezhnev's name which remained at the head of the list. The assertion of his supremacy could not have been clearer.

This rather convoluted means of communicating who ruled a global superpower served its purpose, in that the formal position of Brezhnev's leadership was confirmed. Nonetheless, the argument that the Soviet leadership remained collective in style and practice throughout the Brezhnev years is not necessarily undone by this assertion that Leonid Ilyich headed the leadership line. In other words, although Brezhnev's hold on power increased through his term in office, the way in which this power was exercised did not approach a one-person dictatorship owing to factors such as his leadership style, the existence of networks of political patrons and their clients, and the physical and mental decline of Brezhnev particularly from around 1977 onwards.

Memoir materials repeatedly suggest that Brezhnev was, in contrast to his predecessor Khrushchev, content to delegate responsibilities to his subordinates, so long as his position of power was not challenged. One contemporary noted that,

> In contrast to Khrushchev, Brezhnev didn't consider himself an expert on agriculture, however, as in other policy areas, he listened to advice and allowed people to argue with him. However, he soon gently pulled into line V. V. Matskevich (USSR Minister of Agriculture), saying, 'You, Volodya, do not contradict me in front of people, I'm the General Secretary,

> this is the office in which Stalin sat. Hold on until later, when I'm alone, and then tell me what you think I should know.'[38]

Anatolii Dobrynin confirms this contrast, arguing in his memoirs that whereas Khrushchev, when he wanted, would force his will on Foreign Minister Andrei Gromyko, Brezhnev declined to do this, considering that in the day-to-day conduct of international relations, his minister was the expert.[39]

Although laudable to an extent, in the relatively 'hands-off' leadership style of Leonid Ilyich can once again be seen the beginnings of stagnation. In particular, in relation to the Soviet regions, the attitude of 'autonomy with loyalty' increasingly took hold, with a subsequent slide towards corruption and mismanagement in many areas. Mikhail Gorbachev, himself a First Secretary in Stavropol region from 1970 to 1978, claims that 'first secretaries were given almost unlimited power in their regions, and they, for their part, had to support the General [Secretary]...this was the essence of the "gentleman's" agreement'.[40]

As Brezhnev aged, he became increasingly incapable of exercising the power which he had accrued, and a 'hands-off' leadership approach was born of necessity rather than choice. Without a culture of resignation among Soviet leaders, however, the General Secretary continued in office, and key decisions had to be made by him. Cordovez and Harrison's work *Out of Afghanistan* provides a fine illustration of the momentous decisions being made by a man scarcely, by this stage, capable of coherent speech and action. The decision to invade Afghanistan in 1979 was made at a meeting of around half of the Politburo. Gromyko chaired the meeting, and Brezhnev joined them after half an hour or so. Hardly able to walk he made his painstaking way to his seat, sat in silence for three or four minutes, then, at Gromyko's prompting, muttered, in relation to Afghan prime minister Amin, 'indecent man', and left the room.[41]

Beyond totalitarianism

The leadership style of Leonid Brezhnev played a part in the attempts made by western academics, chiefly in the 1970s, to establish new approaches which might explain the Soviet system. The traditional model had been that of totalitarianism, which posits single-party, dictatorial control over the totality of life in a given state. Political, economic, intellectual, spiritual, social, and family life would all be legitimate objects of state control. Under Brezhnev, the authoritarian aspects of totalitarianism were increasingly evident in, for example, treatment of dissidents, banning of literature and the grip of the KGB (security service) on everyday life. However, there were other aspects of life, particularly the mode of political leadership outlined above, which did not fit the totalitarian model. Brezhnev, despite promoting the partial rehabilitation of Stalin, was himself no Stalin-esque dictator, and the within-system autonomy enjoyed in many areas by members of the policy elite led to discussion of how best to describe Brezhnev's system of government. In particular, the question was, to what extent could it be termed a pluralist system?

Clearly, a one-party state dominated by the 'dictatorship' of even a collective leadership and by a single ideology, is not pluralist *per se*. Nonetheless, in comparison with the dictatorship of the Stalin era, and the 'voluntarist' rule of Nikita Khrushchev, the Brezhnev regime had moved *in a pluralist direction*. H. Gordon Skilling developed an 'interest group' approach in his study of the Soviet Union in a situation of 'post-totalitarianism'.[42] Skilling and his contributors identified specific groups, usually by profession, such as the military, heavy industry, light industry, the media, the KGB and the agricultural sector. These groups, to varying degrees, brought their own agenda and lobbying powers to the policy-making process. Although not without fault, Skilling's argument was credible in many aspects, and contributed to the further development of two approaches which provoked much debate in academic circles, namely corporatism and convergence.

The corporatist approach was very much of its time, and saw similarities between the profession-based, or institutional, interest groups in the Soviet Union and the question of the power balance between trade unions, bosses and politicians in the western industrialised countries. Corporatism is not so much about fundamental competition between the groups concerned, but more to do with an acceptable compromise, or consolidation of interests between them.

The concept of compromise and agreement is familiar to those who study the Brezhnev era and can be perceived not only in the compromises and agreements among the leading institutional actors which are emphasised in the corporatist discourse, but also in relations between the regime and society. As associated with the Brezhnev era as the phrase 'stability of cadres' is the phrase 'social contract', and the old joke that on the workers' part this contract could be summed up as 'we pretend to work, they pretend to pay us'. The idea of a social contract between the people and the regime was summed up slightly more seriously by Boris Kagarlitsky as, 'if you shut up, don't ask for more rights and accept the rule of the bureaucracy then we will supply you with consumer goods'.[43] The social contract thesis argues that the Soviet leadership under both Khrushchev and Brezhnev privileged consumer spending, particularly among blue-collar workers, to foster stability at the expense of civil and political freedoms.

T. H. Rigby, while not embracing the corporatist argument, came up with the term 'mono-organisational society' to describe the way in which the various interests within Soviet society were brought together under the umbrella of the Communist Party of the Soviet Union.[44] Faced with a rapidly changing society, Brezhnev's attitude seems to have been similar to that he took in relation to the Cold War with the United States, 'the main thing is that there is peace'.[45]

If corporatism saw similarities between trends in the capitalist West and those in the Soviet Union, the convergence model took these apparent similarities a stage further and argued, from a socio-economic perspective, that both the capitalist and the communist worlds were moving towards each other as they developed in such a way as to balance social welfare with economic production in a modern, industrialised world. This was not just about industrialisation, but also about the growth of modern bureaucracies and similarities in the ways that economic, political and social systems responded to the problems of governance, irrespective of ideological leaning.

A variety of versions of convergence theory existed, but underlying them all was the undeniable fact that underneath the apparent conservatism and stability of the Brezhnev regime, a social revolution was taking place in the USSR. The 'maturing of Soviet society', as noted by scholars such as Moshe Lewin, David Lane and Geoffrey Hosking, saw an increasingly 'modern' society develop which was urbanised, educated and professionalised. None of these phenomena were new to the USSR, having increasingly been features of Soviet development since the revolution. However, two additional factors particularly came into play from the 1960s onwards. First, unlike in the preceding decades, the process of modernisation continued without interruption by 'terrors, cataclysms, and conflicts'.[46] Second, these features had reached critical mass, so that the modern now dominated. Under Brezhnev these phenomena were becoming the norm, a second-generation experience, rather than the social upheaval of the 1920 and 1930s. Between the 1950s and the 1980s there was a four-fold growth in higher education in the Soviet Union. The phrase 'scientific-technological revolution' became a common feature of official discourse, and within this new intellectual 'class' women made up more than half of the USSR's educated specialists.

Academic debates surrounding pluralism, corporatism and convergence indicate at the least that to gain a full picture of the Brezhnev era – and so make a more reasoned judgement on the stagnation hypothesis – it is essential to consider socio-economic developments. Again though, in our attempts to see something beyond the usual discourse, we see too the seeds of stagnation. Attempts by academic observers to come up with new political models for the Soviet Union had a sound basis as outlined above, but talk of 'pluralism', 'corporatism' and 'convergence' foundered on some of the fundamental givens of the Soviet system. As T. H. Rigby's work noted, the dominance of the Communist Party of the Soviet Union (CPSU) was the most central feature of the Soviet regime. How then could there be talk of pluralism or corporatism, when any 'interest group' existed only under the control of and enveloped by the almost omnipresent CPSU? Let us consider Skilling's largely profession-based concept of interest groups. That they existed and lobbied after a fashion there is little doubt – although there are questions about the unity of opinion within each of the groups identified – but to move from here to pluralism would mean contending with the fact that scarcely a single high position in the land was filled without the permission of the Party. Consequently too, if we are to talk of corporatism within the Soviet system under Brezhnev, then it is clearly 'state corporatism' of which we are talking, with the state in the form of the Party deciding on the representatives of any particular group.

Convergence theory likewise worked up to a point, but led on to other questions. Similarities between modern industrialised societies are evident. However, to build on these a deterministic theory which paid little attention to the distinctive political systems of individual states seemed a step too far for most observers. Indeed, arguing for the move of history in particular ways is always difficult to do without loading the argument with unsustainable assumptions. Surface similarities can be explained relatively easily, but converging social and political systems was a rather large leap from these observations. At the height of the Cold War the issue was further complicated by *ad hominem* considerations of the politics behind the theorising. To emphasise the similarities between the democratic West and the Communist East, and to suggest ways in which each might learn from the other, was usually the preserve of the political left. Any emphasis on similarities between the opposing systems could be accused in particular of downplaying the lack of democracy and the multi-faceted disregard for human rights within the Soviet state.

In noting the social revolution which had taken place in the Soviet Union by the middle of the Brezhnev era, convergence theory also pointed towards some of the central arguments behind the stagnation thesis. Historians such as Lewin and Hosking emphasised the mismatch between social revolution and political conservatism.[47] Increasingly educated citizens sought an outlet for their intellectual and material ambitions, only to be frustrated by the lack of free speech in the Soviet system, the often insurmountable official barriers to international travel and the lack of career opportunities in a country where the leadership, at many levels, grew old but never retired. An increase in urbanisation made easier the spread of ideas and dissident discontent. The experience and expectations of the younger generations differed greatly from those of the Brezhnev generation, who had lived through and – to varying degrees – participated in the founding of the Soviet state, the upheavals of collectivisation and industrialisation, the Stalinist terror and the cataclysmic Second World War. The formative years of 'the Gorbachev generation' had instead been the post-war world where higher education, urban living, culture and steadily increasing living standards were the norm. For the privileged few, like Gorbachev himself, an awareness of the world beyond the Soviet bloc brought a wider perspective.

Conclusion

This view of Brezhnev from the perspective of the end of his era and of the rising generation is where we began our introductory chapter. In this chapter, we have briefly considered Brezhnev and his era from the point of view of academics, contemporaries, and Russians today. We have noted the social revolution which occurred in the Soviet Union during his tenure of office, and have argued that, certainly at the beginning of this period, Leonid Brezhnev was an astute politician within the Soviet system. He brought an unprecedented stability to that system, oversaw a continuing rise in living standards for his people, consolidated the USSR's position as a global superpower, and played a part in the prevention of the global nuclear conflict which many observers considered likely during those years. He stands as the most popular leader of the USSR/Russia in the twentieth century.

Brezhnev also oversaw a one-party dictatorship with little regard for human rights and a security police (the KGB) whose brutal treatment of dissidents included forced psychiatric treatment. Under his leadership, Soviet invasions of Czechoslovakia and Afghanistan destabilised the delicate international balance, and the people of Eastern Europe were denied democratic freedoms by their Soviet hegemon. By the time of his death, the Soviet economy had stopped growing, and the country's highest political leadership was a 'gerontocracy' increasingly lacking physical and intellectual vigour.

It is clear from this Introduction that, not surprisingly, the eighteen years during which Leonid Ilyich Brezhnev led the Soviet Union give opportunity for a range of perspectives and opinions. That there was stagnation is not in doubt. That there was much more besides is elucidated in the remainder of this volume.

Notes

1. M. Gorbachev, *Zhizn' i reformy*, Vol. 1 (Moscow: Novosti, 1995), p. 218.
2. M. Gorbachev, *Zhizn' i reformy*, Vol. 1 (Moscow: Novosti, 1995), p. 218.
3. M. Gorbachev, *Memoirs* (London: Doubleday, 1995), p. 138.
4. M. Gorbachev, *Memoirs* (London: Doubleday, 1995), p. 138.
5. M. Lewin, *The Gorbachev Phenomenon: A Historical Interpretation* (London: Radius, 1988), p. 104.
6. 'Blat' is the Russian word used to describe a combination of connections, corruption, and informal exchanges which served as a distribution system in the Soviet shortage economy. The most concise definition of 'blat' is provided by the title of Alena Ledeneva's book on the subject, *Russia's Economy of Favours: Blat, Networking and Informal Exchange* (Cambridge University Press, 1998).
7. Z. Medvedev, *Andropov* (Oxford: Blackwell, 1983).
8. A. Lebed, *Za derzhavy obidno . . .* (Moscow: Moskovskaya pravda, 1995), pp. 176–7.
9. M. Gorbachev, *Zhizn' i reformy*, Vol. 1 (Moscow: Novosti, 1995), p. 221.
10. *Pravda*, 6 October 1977, p. 5.
11. Gorbachev report to the 27th Party Congress, 25 February 1986.

12. A. Brown, 'The Russian Transition in Comparative and Russian Perspective', *Social Research*, 63/2 (1996).
13. Interfax press release, 24 September 1999.
14. A. Brown, 'The Russian Transition in Comparative and Russian Perspective', *Social Research*, 63/2 (1996).
15. *Monitoring obshchestvennogo mneniya*, 6/44, November–December 1999, p. 27.
16. D. A. Volkogonov, *The Rise and Fall of the Soviet Empire: Political Leaders from Lenin to Gorbachev* (London: HarperCollins, 1998), p. 265.
17. A. Adzhubei, *Krushenie illyuzii* (Moscow, 1991), p. 307.
18. *Far-East Russian Magazine*, No. 2–4, September–November 1995 <http://vladivostok.com/rus_mag/eng /N_4/>.
19. L. I. Brezhnev, *Malaya zemlya* (Moscow: Politizdat, 1978).
20. Z. A. Medvedev, *Gorbachev* (Oxford: Blackwell, 1986), p. 217.
21. Mikhail Gorbachev wrote of them, in *Stavropolskaya Pravda*, 6 May 1978, 'not long ago we opened the pages of Comrade L. I. Brezhnev's remarkable book *Malaya Zemlya*, in which the legendary heroes of the battles of the North Caucasus are portrayed in letters of gold. A short time has elapsed since its publication, but the memoirs have provoked wide, truly national interest... In its number of pages, the book *Malaya Zemlya* is not very large, but in the depth of its ideological content, in the breadth of the author's generalisations and opinions, it has become a great event in public life. It has evoked a warm echo in the hearts of the Soviet people, a delighted response by front-line soldiers at readers' conferences and in the press. Communists and all the workers of Stavropol are boundlessly grateful to Leonid Ilyich Brezhnev for this truly party-spirited, literary work in which the sources of the great feats of our heroic nation, its spiritual and moral strength, its steadfastness and courage are depicted with deep philosophical penetration' (reported at <http://artnet.net/~upstart/brezhnev.html>).
22. R. A. Medvedev, *Lichnost' i epokha: Politicheskii portret L. I. Brezhneva*, Kniga 1 (Moscow: Novosti, 1991), p. 308.
23. D. Cordovez and S. S. Harrison, *Out of Afghanistan: The Inside Story of the Soviet Withdrawal* (Oxford University Press, 1995), p. 48.
24. D. Volkogonov, *The Rise and Fall of the Soviet Empire: Political Leaders from Lenin to Gorbachev* (London: HarperCollins, 1998), pp. 315–17.
25. D. Volkogonov, *The Rise and Fall of the Soviet Empire: Political Leaders from Lenin to Gorbachev* (London: HarperCollins, 1998), p. 178.
26. G. I. Voronov, 'Nemnogo vospominanii', *Druzhba Naroda*, 1, 1989, p. 182.
27. A. Aleksandrov-Agentov, *Ot Kollontai do Gorbacheva* (Moscow, 1994), p. 120.
28. A. F. Dobrynin, *Sugubo doveritel'no: Posol v Vashingtone pri shesti prezidentakh SShA (1962–1986)* (Moscow, 1997), p. 121.
29. A. F. Dobrynin, *Sugubo doveritel'no: Posol v Vashingtone pri shesti prezidentakh SShA (1962–1986)* (Moscow, 1997), p. 121.
30. V. Shelud'ko (ed.), *Leonid Brezhnev v vospominaniyakh, razmyshlenniyakh, suzhdeniyakh* (Rostov on Don: Feniks, 1998), p. 175.
31. V. Shelud'ko (ed.), *Leonid Brezhnev v vospominaniyakh, razmyshlenniyakh, suzhdeniyakh* (Rostov on Don: Feniks, 1998), p. 175
32. A. Vaksberg, *The Soviet Mafia* (New York: St Martin's Press, 1991).
33. V. Shelud'ko (ed.), *Leonid Brezhnev v vospominaniyakh, razmyshlenniyakh, suzhdeniyakh* (Rostov on Don: Feniks, 1998), p. 141
34. Z. Medvedev, 'Russia Under Brezhnev', *New Left Review*, September–October 1979, pp. 6–7.

35. T. Rakowska-Harmstone 'Soviet Leadership Maintenance', in P. Cocks, R. V. Daniels and N. Whittier-Heer (eds), *The Dynamics of Soviet Politics* (Cambridge, Mass.: Harvard University Press, 1976).
36. T. H. Rigby, 'The Soviet Leadership: Towards a Self-Stabilising Oligarchy', *Soviet Studies*, 22/2, 1970, pp. 167–91.
37. <http://www.anet.net/~upstart/suslov.html>.
38. V. Shelud'ko (ed.), *Leonid Brezhnev v vospominaniyakh, razmyshlenniyakh, suzhdeniyakh* (Rostov on Don: Feniks, 1998), p. 152.
39. A. F. Dobrynin, *Sugubo doveritel'no: Posol v Vashingtone pri shesti prezidentakh SShA (1962–1986)* (Moscow, 1997), p. 122.
40. M. Gorbachev, *Zhizn' i reformy*, Vol. 1 (Moscow: Novosti, 1995), p. 180.
41. D. Cordovez and S. S. Harrison, *Out of Afghanistan: The Inside Story of The Soviet Withdrawal* (Oxford University Press, 1995), p. 48.
42. H. G. Skilling and F. Griffiths (ed.), *Interest Groups In Soviet Politics* (Princeton University Press, 1971).
43. Interview with Boris Kagarlitsky, *L.A. Labor News*, 25 November 1999 <http://www.LALabor.org>.
44. T. H. Rigby, 'Politics in the Mono-Organisational Society', in A. C. Janos (ed.), *Authoritarian Politics in Communist Europe* (Berkeley: University of California Press, 1976), pp. 31–80.
45. A. F. Dobrynin, *Sugubo doveritel'no: Posol v Vashingtone pri shesti prezidentakh SShA (1962–1986)* (Moscow, 1997), p. 121.
46. V. Shelud'ko (ed.) *Leonid Brezhnev v vospominaniyakh, razmyshlenniyakh, suzhdeniyakh* (Rostov on Don: Feniks, 1998), p. 175.
47. M. Lewin, *The Gorbachev Phenomenon: A Historical Interpretation* (London: Radius, 1988); G. Hosking, *The Awakening of the Soviet Union* (London: Heinemann, 1990).

2
Brezhnev as Leader

Ian D. Thatcher

Introduction

Leadership is a central component of communist politics. As early as 1848 Marx and Engels noted that communists have over the working class the advantage of knowing the general march of history. It was this knowledge that enabled communists to 'always represent the interests of the movement as a whole'.[1] The centrality of leadership given by socialist intellectuals in communist politics was also recognised by Russian Social Democrats, and is a well-known aspect of Lenin's thought. According to Lenin, workers left to their own devices would develop only trade union consciousness. To attain socialism workers would have to be guided by Bolsheviks.[2] Lenin's view of the relationship between vanguard communist leaders and the rank-and-file acquired a special prominence following the October Revolution. Both admirers[3] and detractors[4] have claimed that without Lenin's guidance one of the key events of the twentieth century would not have happened.

In Soviet political discourse Lenin's leadership was beyond criticism. Each successive leader, from Stalin to Gorbachev,[5] paid homage to Lenin, showing how their politics were Leninist in content. In the context of establishing their own Leninist credentials Soviet leaders would however criticise their predecessors for deviating from Leninism. If alive Stalin was the greatest Leninist of his times, for example, once dead Khrushchev denounced him for abandoning Leninist norms of party life.[6] Khrushchev considered as one of his achievements the fact that his contemporaries were able to make a similar case against him while he was in power, and remove him as head of party and state in 1964.[7] The denunciation of Brezhnev's leadership had to wait until after his long period of rule came to an end following his death in 1982. No Soviet leader was rejected so thoroughly by a successor as L. I. Brezhnev. If Gorbachev remained convinced that Stalin's rule had positive aspects (collectivisation, industrialisation),[8] he had no such kind words for Brezhnev's leadership. This, Gorbachev claimed, had resulted in nothing other than stagnation and a pre-crisis situation.[9]

Indeed, perestroika-inspired critiques of the Brezhnev era deny that Brezhnev possessed leadership qualities. The image created is that of a vacuous,[10] hedonistic playboy who occupied the top leadership positions only because he allowed the Soviet elite to enjoy the full fruits of their power, building personal wealth in a corrupt manner. Any inspiring acts of bravery and courage in Brezhnev's life, as in heroism and leadership in the Second World War, had to be invented by his 'Soviet' biographers.[11] A notable example of this interpretation is Roi Medvedev's projected two-volume account of Brezhnev's political life, only the first volume of which appeared before the USSR collapsed in 1991. This begins by renouncing any claims its subject may have had to the title 'leader':

> Brezhnev was not a great political leader. Indeed, one cannot call him a leader in the strict sense of the word. Neither in his youth, nor as an adult did Brezhnev have any clear political aims, to the achievement of which he wanted to devote his whole life. He almost always followed others, accepting their aims, their ideas, and their leadership. He was a second- or even third-rate man who did not seek the top job, and certainly not unlimited power... Brezhnev did not climb the greasy pole, using fair and unfair means. He was pushed by others.[12]

Doubts about Medvedev's view of Brezhnev arise immediately one considers the barest facts of Brezhnev's career. Could a man devoid of all ambition for power really have become head of state in 1960, head of the party in 1964, achieved a successful combination of the two roles in 1977, and maintained his position at the top for nearly twenty years? Medvedev's interpretation also turns a long-established current of Western writings on Brezhnev upside down. Several commentators have portrayed Brezhnev as a seasoned and skilful manager of power, able to insist on his own programme and head off any challenges.[13] The most enthusiastic case, put by Valerie Bunce and John M. Echols, III, argues that Brezhnev had constructed a form of corporate politics that would offer the USSR long-term political stability, economic growth, and social harmony. It concludes:

> Brezhnev will leave office a hero rather than a nonperson... [he] has been much more of an innovator than many scholars have argued; like his predecessors he has ushered in a new system. But, unlike his predecessors, this system may even outlive his founder.[14]

We now know that history has not justified Bunce and Echols' hopes, but their positive evaluation of Brezhnev cannot simply be written off as poor scholarship or wishful thinking. While the Gorbachev-critique of Brezhnev is wholly negative, *glasnost'* did at least enable a range of first-hand accounts of high politics under Brezhnev to be published.[15] This trend has continued to a certain extent in post-Soviet Russia.[16] These sources contain contradictory versions and evaluations, but they do enable us to place old and new, positive and negative, interpretations in a new perspective. This will become clear as we examine various aspects of Brezhnev's career as leader, beginning with the question of how he took over the job of First Secretary from Khrushchev in the unprecedented circumstances of October 1964.

Brezhnev and Khrushchev's fall

The thesis that Brezhnev was not a leader begins by claiming that he had minimal influence in the events that led to Khrushchev's downfall. One of the strongest advocates of this interpretation is Fedor Burlatsky, one-time adviser to Khrushchev and Gorbachev.[17] According to Burlatsky, generational conflict lay behind Khrushchev's removal. The key plotters were a group of younger communists based in Komsomol networks, headed by Central Committee Secretary Aleksandr Shelepin and KGB chief V. Semichastny. Brezhnev, drawn in only during the final stages, became the plot's chief beneficiary out of accidental and negative reasons. 'Power came to Brezhnev,' claims Burlatsky, 'like a gift from the Gods.' Since no-one saw him as a leader, the decision to appoint Brezhnev First Secretary was 'hypocritical'. Brezhnev was considered a temporary figure, suitable as such because he fell in the middle of the conflict between the pre- and post-war leadership factions, and because he lacked the ambition and qualities to become a more permanent fixture.

Unfortunately for Burlatsky his version of the events of October 1964 has been refuted by none other than the man he cites as leading the plotters, Shelepin.[18] According to Burlatsky the 'young Turks' had hatched their anti-Khrushchev plot in football stadiums, a fact he states he discovered shortly after October 1964 from one of those involved, Candidate Politburo member, Petr Demichev. Shelepin recounts reading out this claim to Demichev, who then denied ever having spoken on this theme to anyone, or, indeed, ever having attended a football match! Shelepin also rejects the notion that Brezhnev became leader out of an accident of fate. On the contrary there were several good reasons to elect Brezhnev as the new First Secretary. Together with fellow Politburo member Nikolai Podgorny, it was precisely Brezhnev that had taken a leading role in organising Khrushchev's removal. Second, one could not ignore Brezhnev's vast experience of party and state positions, including Chairman of the Presidium of the Supreme Soviet and Second Secretary of the Central Committee. Finally, at a time when comrades were upset with Khrushchev for not consulting with them over endless changes to party norms and state policy, Brezhnev stood out for his 'calmness, accessibility and democratism in communications with comrades, the ease with which he established good relations, and his kindness'.[19]

Indeed, several other primary source accounts confirm that Brezhnev helped win power for himself, and that he seemed to be the ideal candidate for leader at that time. Politburo member, Gennady Voronov,[20] First Secretary of the Ukrainian Party, Petr Shelest,[21] and trades union chief Viktor Grishin[22] all testify that it was Brezhnev who recruited them to the anti-Khrushchev plot, which was obviously in preparation for at least a year before Khrushchev's fall. Moscow party chief, Nikolai Egorychev,[23] head of the Belorussian Party, Kirill Mazurov,[24] and V. Vrublevsky[25] all state that they preferred Brezhnev for his political experience, including the skill and bravery he had displayed in removing Khrushchev. Furthermore, there was a consensus that Brezhnev had the best interests of the party at heart; indeed, he was supported and trusted from below.[26]

In considering this evidence one should keep in mind both the unique nature of the change of leadership and the problems a new First Secretary would face. Never before had a Soviet leader been removed from office; both Lenin and Stalin had died in-post. It would be wrong to draw far-reaching conclusions about Brezhnev's general leadership style from accounts that focus upon his moments of doubt over the plot's likely success. For example, Egorychev portrays Brezhnev becoming more nervous in early October 1964, frightened by news that Khrushchev had discovered the plot. In particular Brezhnev was afraid to return to Moscow from the GDR, and had to be calmed by Egorychev on the eve of the vital Plenum.[27] Shelest also paints a particularly unflattering picture of a trembling Brezhnev, phoning Khrushchev to recall him early from his holiday to attend the Plenum that would remove him from office.[28] Against these versions, one can construct a gambling Brezhnev, willing to take the risk of asking the KGB to assassinate Khrushchev.[29] Furthermore, Brezhnev was not alone in worrying about whether Khrushchev could be removed smoothly.[30] In the last analysis Brezhnev did return from the GDR, he did phone Khrushchev, and he was rewarded with the post of First Secretary. A post-Khrushchev leader would have to address a difficult situation in the party, in the country, and internationally. In these circumstances it would be unlikely that the CPSU's leadership broadly defined would select his successor lightly. Surely that candidate would have to be distinguished in important respects. The years following October 1964 would provide some stern tests.

Brezhnev as leader

Elected First Secretary, Brezhnev displayed many talents as a Soviet leader. He built up and secured his own power base, partly through the appointment process, and partly by appealing to important constituencies in the party, state and society. He reconciled different tendencies within the leadership, synthesising advice and recommendations from various sources. He formed a stable and trusted team of advisers and leading ministers, quietly demoting potential rivals for power or those who had the potential to upset unity at the top. Brezhnev took a particular interest in foreign policy. He successfully projected an image of a powerful, stable, and responsible superpower. Foreign statesmen found in Brezhnev a leader with whom they could do business.

Brezhnev's political programme sought moderate improvements through incremental change. As a leader he possessed the skill of knowing what to prioritise, taking into account the errors of the recent past. Shortly after his election he noted that, 'under Stalin people were afraid of repression, under Khrushchev of reorganisations and rearrangements...Soviet people should receive a peaceful life so that they can work normally'.[31] A key aspect of Brezhnev's leadership was the avoidance of extremism. Georgii Arbatov, who worked in the Central Committee apparatus from 1964 to 1967, for example, has written an interesting account of how Brezhnev resisted the demands of a group of right-wing Politburo members in the immediate post-October 1964 period.[32] These demands included, among others, Stalin's full rehabilitation and a much firmer course in relations with the West. However, a 'cautious' Brezhnev took advice from others, particularly his personal assistants A. M. Aleksandrov and G. E. Tsukanov, and orchestrated a compromise at the 23rd CPSU Congress of Spring 1966. The evaluation of Stalin was more positive, but there was some continuity of policy from the Khrushchev era, most notably that of peaceful coexistence. Medvedev has criticised the 23rd Congress as being 'the most boring Congress in the whole of the Party's history'. Specifically,

> Brezhnev's report said nothing not only about recent disagreements in the Presidium, but also about many other important events of the recent period, especially Khrushchev's replacement. Yes Brezhnev and other delegates spoke briefly about 'subjective mistakes' and 'unjustified changes' and the huge significance of the October Plenum. But this amounted only to hints, not a serious political analysis.[33]

Here Medvedev clearly asks the impossible of Brezhnev's leadership. It was important to portray an image of calm, to preserve party unity, and to avoid the negative fallout caused by Khrushchev's fiery speeches of recent party congresses.[34] In achieving this, Brezhnev displayed good leadership qualities.

If Brezhnev did not make an explicit and detailed critique of Khrushchev's leadership style at the 23rd Congress, he did seek to overcome Khrushchev's 'voluntarism' in several important respects. Brezhnev did not claim to be an expert in everything. He gave due consideration to greater knowledge and experience. Drafts of speeches were circulated to colleagues for comments before they were finalised. The role and status of policy advisers grew to new heights. Burlatsky has ridiculed this trait in Brezhnev's leadership, describing in a briefing session of February 1965 how the new First Secretary admitted that he could not follow Burlatsky's 'fountain of eloquence'.[35] Of course, Burlatsky does not consider the possibility that his report may indeed have been lacking in clarity. However, most colleagues preferred Brezhnev's respectful and listening ear, a leader who, in Gromyko's opinion, pursued policies adopted through consultation and negotiation rather than personal 'originality',[36] over Khrushchev's assertion of his own righteousness. Certainly, more modesty on Khrushchev's part may have led to better policy decisions, for instance if scientific advice had been followed in the 'Virgin Lands' Campaign.[37]

Brezhnev's 'democratic' leadership style also won him crucial support from regional leaders, with whom he maintained close contact. This vital layer in the party's power structure and in its management of society had been threatened by Khrushchev's organisational changes, especially the ruling on limited tenure introduced at the 22nd Congress. Brezhnev sensibly reversed this policy, emphasising instead 'stability of cadres'. Brezhnev seems to have taken a particular interest in the regional functionaries, taking care to appoint good candidates to these important positions. He then reassured, encouraged and consulted. Even the critical Gorbachev mentions Brezhnev's personal role in his appointment as first secretary of the Stavropol kraikom, before which the First Secretary vetted Gorbachev's understanding of key issues. Remembering a conversation that probed issues local, national, and international, Gorbachev notes that 'Brezhnev was nothing like the cartoon figure that is made of him now'.[38]

Gorbachev's account of his encounters with Brezhnev while a regional first secretary is at odds with his general characterisation of the First Secretary's relationship with the regional first secretaries. According to Gorbachev, Brezhnev bought the latter's support for his leadership by allowing them 'almost unlimited power in their regions'.[39] Indeed, some interpretations portray Brezhnev as nothing other than the tool of the regional functionaries.[40] But as in the case of Trotsky's characterisation of Stalin as merely the 'spokesman of the bureaucracy',[41] such an analysis underestimates the leader's role. If this were the case why, one wonders, did Gorbachev have to seek Brezhnev's approval for a development of the canal system in Stavropol? We are informed that only after a close perusal of Gorbachev's proposals did Brezhnev successfully see them through the next meeting of the Politburo. Here he referred to Gorbachev as one of the 'new young leaders who address issues of national importance [and] who deserve our support'.[42] When, later in his career, Gorbachev clashed with the more senior Kosygin over agricultural policy, Brezhnev took the trouble to telephone Gorbachev to reassure him. When Kosygin then contacted Gorbachev to arrange a compromise, the impression is formed that it was precisely Brezhnev who brokered it behind the scenes.[43] Gorbachev's testimony of an open-minded, caring, and yet independent leader is not unique. There are similar cases in much of the memoir literature.[44] It is of little surprise then that in his regional tours, it has been noted that local leaders greeted Brezhnev with a warmth lacking in Khrushchev's regional forays.[45]

A similar picture of a leader concerned to create a good working atmosphere with trusted and able colleagues also emerges when Brezhnev's approach to the key ministries is considered. It is surely a gross oversimplification to claim, as Shelepin has done, that Brezhnev sought to block the careers of the young and talented, preferring to promote mediocrity and family members.[46] Views over who formed Brezhnev's inner team differ,[47] but it is not difficult to find positive evaluations of their skills, and of Brezhnev's wisdom in his use of the power of appointment. This is particularly so in the case of the key ministries of Foreign Affairs and Defence, and the KGB. Allowing his ministers to represent their departments and taking their advice appropriately, Brezhnev cultivated in them both independence of viewpoint and loyalty. Certainly Brezhnev was not betrayed by his colleagues as Khrushchev was before him, and Gorbachev was to be afterwards.[48] So close was Brezhnev's working relationship with his leading colleagues and advisers from the Central Committee apparatus that some complain that the Politburo was increasingly by-passed as the Brezhnev era wore on.[49] Here, of course, Brezhnev was not an innovator. Mazurov's criticism that all the leading questions had been resolved before being put to the Politburo is reminiscent of Trotsky's account of Soviet politics post-Lenin.[50]

Brezhnev's skills as leader were revealed not only in his approach to the party's internal structures and in his dealings with the key offices of state. Brezhnev designed policies and adopted attitudes to bolster his standing with a domestic audience and with foreign leaders.

At home Brezhnev tried to improve the living standards of Soviet citizens. This was revealed in the attention he gave to agriculture and in extensions to social benefits. The positive effects this bestowed upon Brezhnev's reputation as leader have been pointed out, among others, by his doctor, E. Chazov:

> Today many people forget that at that time the introduction of the five-day working week made a strong impression on ordinary Soviet people. This was also the case with the lowering of the pension age to 55 for women and 60 for men, the payment of wages and pensions to kolkhoz workers, wage rises and price reductions on children's clothes, watches, motorbikes, cameras, and so on. This strengthened the authority of the leadership in general, and of Brezhnev in particular.[51]

Brezhnev's critics would argue that such improvements could be only temporary. In general, the economy was on a downward spiral, overburdened by Brezhnev's commitment to an excessive military budget and by the First Secretary's refusal to undertake a much-needed restructuring of the Soviet economy. It was Brezhnev's failings in this regard that rendered his leadership non-existent. It was precisely Brezhnev who let real opportunities for a successful reform slip by.[52] Such an analysis was very popular in the Gorbachev era by Gorbachevists, who claimed that at last *perestroika* offered a chance to move from 'the lowest [Brezhnev] stage of socialism to its higher, contemporary form'.[53] Such hopes were not justified by subsequent developments. In this context, one can understand Gorbachev's desire to lay the blame for the collapse of the USSR upon Brezhnev. According to Gorbachev, the Soviet system was to pay the ultimate price for Brezhnev's excessive caution.[54]

No doubt some may regret the overly optimistic predictions they made about the potential of the USSR under *perestroika*. However, with the benefit of hindsight, one can as little blame them for their mistaken views as one can blame Brezhnev for not taking action that may not have been obvious at the time. All evidence of root and branch reform pointed to the conclusion that it would lead to the destruction of the system, as indeed happened under Gorbachev. When economists mention the advantages of the old command-administrative system, the guaranteed employment and other social benefits, they write predominantly about the Brezhnev era.[55] Viewed in this perspective, perhaps Brezhnev was correct to resist reform after all. Furthermore, the view that if Brezhnev had been a more intelligent leader, the problems besetting the Soviet economy could have been corrected may rest upon an overestimation of what any leader could have achieved. After all, even arch-critic Medvedev admits that there are objective limits to political action, such as 'the development of science and technology, economic progress and the changes in the social structure it brings forth'.[56]

If Brezhnev's authority as leader was helped by improvements in the general standard of living, it has been argued that a traditional Soviet political tactic to highlight a First Secretary's leadership talent, that is, the cult of personality, actually made of Brezhnev a laughing-stock as leader. The cult of personality and its negative impact on Soviet political life had been an important element in Khrushchev's critique of Stalin's leadership. That Khrushchev and subsequent Soviet leaders encouraged their own cults suggests that the leadership cult was a necessary aspect of the Soviet political system. The case against the cult under Brezhnev, though, rests upon the claim that it reached previously unseen, ridiculous proportions. No other leader, for example, accepted so many awards. The gap between the medals Brezhnev loved to collect and his lack of real achievement and personality fatally undermined his position as leader. It would indeed be difficult to justify each of Brezhnev's awards. Textbooks on the Brezhnev era usually focus upon the conferment of the Lenin Prize for Literature in 1979.[57] Unsold in their millions, Brezhnev's writings clearly did not merit an award given for 'their popularity and their educative influence on the mass of readers'. It is for this reason that jokes about Brezhnev were part and parcel of everyday Soviet life.

However, such accounts omit the positive aspects of the cult, the way in which it cemented Brezhnev's relationship with East European communist leaderships, for example. It would be incorrect to claim that Brezhnev was unaware of the humorous side-effects of his impressive award collection. Shelest recounts how in response to Podgorny's warning that his thirst for awards was the butt of many jokes, Brezhnev stated: 'If they are poking fun at me, it means they like me.'[58] It is difficult to gauge the exact social impact of the Brezhnev cult, but it seems silly to discount Brezhnev's view. Negative comments and jokes about the leadership fit well into the 'Us' and 'Them' paradigm, in which positive and negative evaluations of the leader coexist.[59] Perhaps the tendency to satirise Brezhnev should also be seen as part of a general rise in political satire across Europe. That Soviet citizens could joke in safety about Brezhnev may have increased a sense of affection for him, or at least prevented the emergence of outright hostility, even if he was considered to be a fool.

If Brezhnev was perceived as a joke figure in part of the popular memory, this cannot be said of his standing among foreign leaders. An important function of any Soviet leader was to project an image of a strong Soviet Union abroad. In this Brezhnev could be said to have succeeded as a leader, an area in which Khrushchev failed. It is clear that Khrushchev's antics won him respect from few foreign leaders, including the American Presidents with whom he shared office.[60] In contrast, Richard Nixon has left the following, flattering evaluation of Brezhnev:

> There is no question about Brezhnev's overall strength . . . he has a strong, deep voice – a great deal of animal magnetism and drive which comes through whenever you meet him . . . he always comes through forcefully, and he has a very great shrewdness. He also has the ability to move off a point in the event that he is not winning it.[61]

Less appreciative are Kissinger's memoirs, particularly his description of Brezhnev in physical decline (of which more below). According to Kissinger, Brezhnev was not well-versed in the intricacies of international affairs, and only rarely displayed personal initiative to reach a desired outcome. For the most part Brezhnev had to be corrected by his advisers, for he made many mistakes.[62] In another context, Central Committee functionary Georgy Arbatov has written that a cowardly Brezhnev had to be pushed into decisive action in Czechoslovakia in 1968.[63] Medvedev has added that the most pleasurable aspect of Brezhnev's meetings with other heads of state was the gift of fine automobiles, which the General Secretary added to his private collection.[64] During 1968, it was only when the Czech press began to criticise and ridicule the Soviet leader that Brezhnev resolved that the Prague Spring had turned 'counter-revolutionary'.[65] The decisive factor in an important, and in Medvedev's view mistaken, foreign policy decision was therefore Brezhnev's vanity!

Against this view of a feeble leader, guided by vanity during crisis situations, one can place evidence of Brezhnev's leading role in negotiations with Dubček in 1968, in which the decision to intervene was taken out of clear security and political concerns.[66] Moreover, it was Brezhnev who remained firm, exerting a calming influence on worried comrades.[67] If Brezhnev was not a good negotiator during key summits with the West, his performances were never so bad as to bring his colleagues to rebellion.

Brezhnev's fulfillment of his leadership duties, at home and abroad, was more than sufficient to secure his position as leader. This emerges with clarity when one considers the fate of Brezhnev's opponents. Contradicting an earlier assertion that Brezhnev did not seek absolute power and that he had to be pushed into the leading position, Medvedev focuses upon several cases in which Brezhnev successfully resisted contenders for the leadership.[68] What is striking about all of these cases is the ease with which Brezhnev upheld his dominant position. A master of Kremlin intrigue, Brezhnev was able to guarantee a consensus for any personnel changes he wished to make. This is obvious from first-hand descriptions of how people experienced demotion. Shelepin, identified by Medvedev as a leading opponent of Brezhnev,[69] for example, states that he was unexpectedly told of his demotion from the Central Committee's Secretariat to head of the trades unions in Brezhnev's office, before being led to a full gathering of the Politburo which unanimously approved the decision.[70] Shelest has confirmed how Brezhnev increased his grip on the KGB by having Semichastny moved to the Ukraine in similar fashion.[71] An interesting aspect of Brezhnev's style of demotion was the care he took to ensure that the demoted received some reward for their service, normally by phoning to ask if he could render any particular assistance. Burlatsky has argued that in this way Brezhnev guaranteed that no-one would dislike him personally.[72] Whatever the reason, Brezhnev's generosity compares favourably to Stalin's mistreatment of his victims' families, and even to Yeltsin's downgrading of Gorbachev's state benefits.

Whatever merits Brezhnev may have possessed, a final critique of his leadership should be considered, namely that Brezhnev should have resigned. In the literature it is quite common to come across a periodisation of Brezhnev's leadership. Here there is a division between an 'early', 'good' Brezhnev and a 'bad', 'late' Brezhnev. The former tried hard to master state affairs, consulted with colleagues, and made progress in domestic and foreign policy. The latter avoided self-criticism, was increasingly incapable of giving his attention to state affairs, by-passed consultation with the Party, and led the country to a state of crisis both internally and internationally. The emergence of the 'bad' Brezhnev is normally linked to the onset of illness, which, depending upon the source, paralysed Brezhnev as leader from the last eight to the final two years of his rule.[73]

In a period of leadership spanning some eighteen years it would be unusual if the burdens of office and bouts of illness had no impact upon Brezhnev's effectiveness. If, though, he deteriorated to the extent that he could not follow the course of any discussion, that he found it increasingly difficult to read even the shortest of prepared texts, and that sessions of the Politburo descended into mere farce, it is legitimate, along with Shelepin,[74] to ask why Brezhnev lacked the courage to step down. In Brezhnev's defence one can say that few leaders possess the skill of knowing when to announce a timely resignation. Most have to be pushed or voted out of office. On the other hand, historians' evaluations would no doubt be more favourable if Brezhnev had entered the history books as the only Soviet leader to tender a voluntary resignation. But this leaves unanswered why Brezhnev's colleagues did not ask him to consider making way for a younger, more able comrade. Shelepin has put the blame upon himself and other comrades for not having the bravery to say to Brezhnev: 'we cannot go on working like this, it is time for you to resign!'[75] No doubt the fact that the party had no tradition of an honorable resignation influenced Brezhnev. Khrushchev's disappearance into obscurity may have encouraged him to maintain a hold on the reins of power. Finally, Gorbachev's evidence suggests that Brezhnev's colleagues thought that Brezhnev was still performing important, stabilising functions for the party and the state, whatever the condition of his health. After all, when Gorbachev confided his doubts about Brezhnev to Andropov, the latter stated: 'we must do everything possible to support Leonid Ilych, even in his present state. It is a matter of stability within the Party and the state as well as an issue of international stability'.[76]

Gorbachev's portrayal of the late Brezhnev is however contradictory. Alongside a picture of a clearly malfunctioning General Secretary, there are glimpses of Brezhnev continuing to make crucial decisions over appointments. If Brezhnev was incapable of retiring himself on grounds of ill-heath, he was sufficiently cognisant to arrange for Kirilenko's retirement on this basis.[77] Moreover, if Brezhnev was not to be the only Soviet leader to resign on his own initiative while in office, he may be unique in arranging a succession. Lenin's political testament criticised his colleagues, warned of the relations between Stalin and Trotsky, but made no firm recommendation for a new leader. Stalin preferred to remain silent on this issue. There was a power struggle of several years before Khrushchev emerged as undisputed leader. Brezhnev, in contrast, seems to have played a key role in ensuring that Gorbachev's favoured candidate Andropov would triumph over Chernenko, encouraging the former to take up the Chair at meetings of the Secretariat.[78] At the end, therefore, Brezhnev may have performed the key leadership function of arranging a smooth transfer of power.

Conclusion

Rather than deserving a reputation as the most vilified of all Soviet leaders, Brezhnev should be praised as one of the most successful exponents of the art of Soviet politics. Well versed in its rules, he promoted collegiality and a stable leadership. At the same time he was not afraid to take the initiative in decision-making, as for example during the Czechoslovak crisis of 1968. Of course, there are legitimate criticisms to be made of Brezhnev's leadership. In particular, one may wish to make a distinction between Brezhnev as manager of the Soviet political game and bureaucratic intrigue, at which he excelled, and Brezhnev as head of state, at which he was less successful.

The latter case will be at its strongest in the late Brezhnev era, in which policy undoubtedly went astray both internationally (most notably in Afghanistan) and domestically (for example, in the economy). However, this chapter has argued that Brezhnev's leadership certainly stands up against its harshest critics of the Gorbachev era and beyond. Indeed, viewed sympathetically, especially against the background of what came before and what occurred after, the period of Brezhnev's leadership can be considered as the golden age of the Soviet system.

Further reading

Brezhnev awaits a competent scholarly biography. The existing literature should be consulted with a certain level of caution. For an official Soviet view there is the Institute of Marxism–Leninism's *L. I. Brezhnev: A Short Biography* (Oxford: Pergamon, 1977).

D. Volkogonov, *The Rise and Fall of the Soviet Empire* (London: HarperCollins, 1998) contains a brief, but hostile, post-Soviet account.

G. W. Breslauer's *Khrushchev and Brezhnev as Leaders* (London: George Allen & Unwin, 1982) remains a useful study.

Khrushchev's biographer, W. Tompson, has now turned his attention to Brezhnev. We can look forward to his projected *The Soviet Union under Brezhnev, 1964–82* (Harlow: Longman, 2003).

Notes

1. K. Marx and F. Engels, *The Communist Manifesto*, in M. Cowling (ed.), *The Communist Manifesto: New Interpretations* (Edinburgh University Press, 1998), p. 23.
2. See, for example, Lenin's pamphlet of 1902, *What is to be Done*?
3. L. Trotsky, *History of the Russian Revolution* (London: Pluto Press, 1977), pp. 343–4; J. E. Marot, 'Class Conflict, Political Competition and Social Transformation: Critical Perspectives on the Social History of the Russian Revolution', *Revolutionary Russia*, 7/2, 1994, pp. 155–6.
4. R. Pipes, *The Russian Revolution 1899–1919* (London: Collins, 1990).
5. Stalin, as is well known, criticised opponents for their 'anti-Leninism', most notably in the campaign against Trotsky. The extent to which Gorbachev presented his perestroika within a Leninist tradition is clear from M. Gorbachev, *Perestroika i novoye myshleniye* (Moscow: IPL, 1988).
6. See, for example, Khrushchev's famous Secret Speech to the 20th Party Congress of February 1956.
7. Cited in R. Medvedev, *Khrushchev: politicheskaya biografiya* (Moscow: Kniga, 1990), p. 245.
8. See, for example, Gorbachev's defence of industrialisation and collectivisation in his speech commemorating the 70th anniversary of the October Revolution.
9. M. Gorbachev, *Memoirs* (London: Doubleday, 1995), p. 210.
10. Brezhnev has been criticised for not reading in general and for not reading the Marxists' classics in particular. (A. Aleksandrov-Agentov, *Ot Kollontai do Gorbacheva* (Moscow: Mezhdunarodnye otnosheniya, 1994), pp. 115–16). To this criticism, M. Sturua has issued the following interesting rebuttal: 'One should not confuse the intellectual mediocrity of a politician with his ability to become a leader.

The two attributes rarely go together (This should clear up our [Russian] amazement at the "mediocrities" that become US Presidents.) It is truly possible that Brezhnev, like Esenin, never read a single line from *Capital*. But this did not prevent the latter from becoming a great poet and the former number one in the state. Both possessed talent: one as a poet, the other as a leader' (M. Sturua, 'Dve fotografii k odnomu portretu', in Yu. Aksyutin (ed.), *L. I. Brezhnev: materialy k biografii* (Moscow: IPL, 1991), p. 170).

11. For works which point out the differences between Brezhnev's war-time record as stated in his official biographies and the actual record see, for example, N. Kirsanov, 'Ne osobenno tseremonyas s faktami', in Yu. Aksyutin (ed.), *L. I. Brezhnev: materialy k biografii* (Moscow: IPL, 1991), pp. 30–8 and D. Tabachnik, 'Zapyataya v biografii genseka', in Yu. Aksyutin (ed.), *L. I. Brezhnev: materialy k biografii* (Moscow: IPL, 1991), pp. 38–45.
12. R. Medvedev, *Lichnost i epokha. Politicheskii portret L. I. Brezhneva* Vol. 1 (Moscow: Novosti, 1991), p. 7.
13. G. Breslauer, *Khrushchev and Brezhnev as Leaders* (London: George Allen & Unwin, 1982); J. Dornburg, *Brezhnev. The Masks of Power* (London: Deutsch, 1974); P. J. Murphy, *Brezhnev. Soviet Politician* (Jefferson, NC: McFarland, 1981)
14. V. Bunce and J. M. Echols, III, 'Soviet Politics in the Brezhnev Era: "Pluralism" or "Corporatism?"', in D. R. Kelly (ed.), *Soviet Politics in the Brezhnev Era* (New York: Praeger, 1980), pp. 20–1.
15. See, for example, Yu. Aksyutin (ed.), *L. I. Brezhnev: materialy k biografii* (Moscow: IPL, 1991).
16. See, for example, V. V. Shelud'ko (ed.), *Leonid Brezhnev v vospominaniyakh, razmyshlenniyakh, suzhdeniyakh* (Rostov-on-Don: Feniks, 1998); V. V. Grishin, *Ot Khrushcheva do Gorbacheva. Politicheskie portrety pyati gensekov i A. N. Kosygina* (Moscow: ASPOL, 1996).
17. F. Burlatsky, *Khrushchev and the First Russian Spring* (London: Weidenfeld and Nicolson, 1991), esp. pp. 207–14.
18. A. Shelepin, '"Istoriya-Uchitel surovyi"', in Yu. Aksyutin (ed.), *L. I. Brezhnev: materialy k biografii* (Moscow: IPL, 1991), pp. 230–44, esp. pp. 232–3.
19. A. Shelepin, '"Istoriya-Uchitel surovyi"', in Yu. Aksyutin (ed.), *L. I. Brezhnev: materialy k biografii* (Moscow: IPL, 1991), p. 235.
20. G. Voronov, 'Oshibki s Brezhnevym my sebe ne proshchaem', in Yu. Aksyutin (ed.), *L. I. Brezhnev: materialy k biografii* (Moscow: IPL, 1991), pp. 181–2.
21. Cited in V. V. Shelud'ko (ed.), *Leonid Brezhnev v vospominaniyakh, razmyshlenniyakh, suzhdeniyakh* (Rostov-on-Don: Feniks, 1998), p. 194.
22. V. V. Grishin, *Ot Khrushcheva do Gorbacheva. Politicheskie portrety pyati gensekov i A. N. Kosygina* (Moscow: ASPOL, 1996), p. 27. Apart from himself Grishin claims that Brezhnev also personally recruited Central Committee Secretaries Demichev and Shelepin, Minister of Defence Malinovsky, Chairman of the KGB Semichastny, and Kosygin. Indeed, 'Brezhnev carried out the practical work for preparing Khrushchev's removal' (V. V. Grishin, *Ot Khrushcheva do Gorbacheva. Politicheskie portrety pyati gensekov i A. N. Kosygina* (Moscow: ASPOL, 1996)).
23. N. Egorychev, 'U nas byli raznye vzglyadi', in Yu. Aksyutin (ed.), *L. I. Brezhnev: materialy k biografii* (Moscow: IPL, 1991), pp. 192–3.
24. K. Mazurov, '"Glavnoi zabotoi Brezhneva byl lichnyi avtoritet"', in Yu. Aksyutin (ed.), *L. I. Brezhnev: materialy k biografii* (Moscow: IPL, 1991), p. 207.
25. V. Vrublevskii, *Vladimir Shcherbitskii: pravda i vymysly* (Kiev: Dovira, 1993), p. 32.

26. Voronov claims that Brezhnev had particular support from the Ukrainian, Moldavian and Kazakh sections of the party ('Oshibki s Brezhnevym my sebe ne proshchaem', in Yu. Aksyutin (ed.), *L. I. Brezhnev: materialy k biografii* (Moscow: IPL, 1991, p. 182).
27. N. Egorychev, 'U nas byli raznye vzglyady', in Yu. Aksyutin (ed.), *L. I. Brezhnev: materialy k biografii* (Moscow: IPL, 1991), p. 191.
28. Cited in V. V. Shelud'ko (ed.), *Leonid Brezhnev v vospominaniyakh, razmyshlenniyakh, suzhdeniyakh* (Rostov-on-Don: Feniks, 1998), p. 195.
29. Yu. Aksyutin, 'Oktyabr 1964 goda: "V Moskve khoroshaya pogoda"' in Yu. Aksyutin (ed.), *L. I. Brezhnev: materialy k biografii* (Moscow: IPL, 1991), p. 47.
30. For example, Aksyutin writes: 'Malinovsky . . . stated that it was not the army's business to become involved in such doubtful exercises as the arrest of the head of party and state' (Yu. Aksyutin (ed.), *L. I. Brezhnev: materialy k biografii* (Moscow: IPL, 1991), p. 48).
31. Cited in M. Dokuchaev, *Moskva. Kreml. Okhrana* (Moscow: Biznes-Press, 1995), p. 172.
32. G. Arbatov, 'Iz nedavnego proshlogo', in Yu. Aksyutin (ed.), *L. I. Brezhnev: materialy k biografii* (Moscow: IPL, 1991), pp. 64–7.
33. R. Medvedev, *Lichnost i epokha. Politicheskii portret L. I. Brezhneva*. Vol. 1 (Moscow: Novosti, 1991), p. 125.
34. See, for example, the trouble caused by the Secret Speech in Poland recounted by T. Kemp-Welch, 'Khrushchev's "Secret Speech" and Polish Politics: The Spring of 1956', *Europe–Asia Studies*, 48(2), 1996, pp. 181–206.
35. F. Burlatsky, *Khrushchev and the First Russian Spring* (London: Weidenfeld & Nicolson, 1991), pp. 217–18.
36. A. Gromyko, *Pamyatnoe*. Vol. 2 (Moscow: IPO, 1997), p. 529.
37. For this and other irrational aspects of this campaign see, A. Nove, *An Economic History of the USSR* (Harmondsworth: Penguin, 1992), pp. 372–7.
38. M. Gorbachev, *Memoirs* (London: Doubleday, 1995), p. 86.
39. M. Gorbachev, *Memoirs* (London: Doubleday, 1995), p. 112.
40. See, for example, N. Leonov, *Likholet'e* (Moscow: Mezhdunarodnye otnosheniya, 1995), p. 259.
41. It is interesting to note the similarities between Trotsky's critique of Stalin as leader and the case made by Brezhnev's critics. For example, the following evaluation of Stalin by Trotsky is similar to that of Volkogonov and Medvedev on Brezhnev: 'Stalin remains a mediocrity. His mind is not only devoid of range but is even incapable of logical thinking. Every phrase of his speech has some immediate practical aim. But his speech as a whole never rises to a logical structure' (L. Trotsky, *Stalin* (New York: Harper & Bros., 1941), p. 393).
42. M. Gorbachev, *Memoirs* (London: Doubleday, 1995), p. 87.
43. M. Gorbachev, *Memoirs* (London: Doubleday, 1995), pp. 115–16.
44. See, for example, the following authors, all of whom stress Brezhnev's close ties with regional colleagues: A. Aleksandrov-Agentov, in V. V. Shelud'ko (ed.), *Leonid Brezhnev v vospominaniyakh, razmyshlenniyakh, suzhdeniyakh* (Rostov-on-Don: Feniks, 1998), p. 140; and V. Boldin, *Krushenie p'edestala* (Moscow: Respublika, 1995), p. 37.
45. R. Medvedev, *Lichnost i epokha. Politicheskii portret L. I. Brezhneva*. Vol. 1 (Moscow: Novosti, 1991), p. 277.
46. A. Shelepin, 'Istoriya – uchitel surovyi', in Yu. Aksyutin (ed.), *L. I. Brezhnev: materialy k biografii* (Moscow: IPL, 1991), pp. 239–40.

47. For example, V. Pribytkov lists, alongside Brezhnev, Suslov, Gromyko, Ustinov, Andropov and Chernenko; Yu. Churbanov agrees but omits Suslov; V. Kryuchkov omits Suslov and Chernenko (V. V. Shelud'ko (ed.), *Leonid Brezhnev v vospominaniyakh, razmyshlenniyakh, suzhdeniyakh* (Rostov-on-Don: Feniks, 1998), pp. 247–8).
48. For this point see also V. Medvedev, in V. V. Shelud'ko (ed.), *Leonid Brezhnev v vospominaniyakh, razmyshlenniyakh, suzhdeniyakh* (Rostov-on-Don: Feniks, 1998), p. 247.
49. K. Mazurov, 'Glavnoi zabotoi Brezhneva byl lichnyi avtoritet', in Yu. Aksyutin (ed.), *L. I. Brezhnev: materialy k biografii* (Moscow: IPL, 1991), pp. 206–7.
50. See, for example, L. Trotsky, *My Life* (Harmondsworth: Penguin, 1975), p. 521.
51. E. Chazov, *Zdorov'e i vlast. Vospominaniya 'kremlevskogo vracha'* (Moscow: Novosti, 1992), pp. 14–15.
52. See, for example, G. Arbatov, 'Iz nedavnego proshlogo', in Yu. Aksyutin (ed.), *L. I. Brezhnev: materialy k biografii* (Moscow: IPL, 1991), p. 80.
53. A. Bovin, 'Kurs na stabilnost porodil zastoi', in Yu. Aksyutin (ed.), *L. I. Brezhnev: materialy k biografii* (Moscow: IPL, 1991), p. 100.
54. M. Gorbachev, *Memoirs* (London: Doubleday, 1995), p. 138.
55. See, for example, M. Harrison, 'Stalinism in Post-Communist Perspective', *Europe–Asia Studies*, 49/3, 1997, pp. 499–502.
56. R. Medvedev, *Lichnost i epokha. Politicheskii portret L. I. Brezhneva. Volume 1* (Moscow: Novosti, 1991), p. 153.
57. See, for example, P. Dukes, *A History of Russia c.882–1996* (Basingstoke: Macmillan, 1998), pp. 322–3; G. Hosking, *A History of the Soviet Union* (London: Fontana, 1990), p. 368.
58. P. Shelest, 'On umel vesti . . . ', in Yu. Aksyutin (ed.), *L. I. Brezhnev: materialy k biografii* (Moscow: IPL, 1991), p. 218.
59. For the 'Us' versus 'Them' paradigm, see A. Nove, 'Is There a Ruling Class in the USSR?', *Soviet Studies*, 27/4, 1975, p. 624. For the application of this conception in the Stalin era, see S. Davies, *Popular Opinion in Stalin's Russia* (Cambridge University Press, 1997).
60. Khrushchev's most recent biographer, for example, states that, 'Khrushchev's view of Eisenhower was far better than the President's view of him . . . Macmillan, who met with Kennedy after the summit [with Khrushchev], found the President "rather stunned . . . completely overwhelmed by the ruthlessness and the barbarity of the Russian premier"' (W. Tompson, *Khrushchev. A Political Life* (Basingstoke: Macmillan, 1997), pp. 211, 234).
61. R. Nixon, *Memoirs* (New York: Sidgewick & Jackson, 1978), p. 620. See also Nixon's description of Brezhnev as 'Leonid the Great' (R. Nixon, *Leaders* (London: Sidgewick & Jackson, 1982), p. 204).
62. See, for example, H. Kissinger, *Years of Renewal* (London: Weidenfeld & Nicolson, 1999), pp. 264, 265–6, 288, 658–60.
63. G. Arbatov, 'Iz nedavnego proshlogo', in Aksyutin (ed.), *L. I. Brezhnev: materialy k biografii* (Moscow: IPL, 1991), p. 72.
64. R. Medvedev, *Lichnost i epokha. Politicheskii portret L. I. Brezhneva*. Vol. 1 (Moscow: Novosti, 1991), pp. 306–9.
65. R. Medvedev, *Lichnost i epokha. Politicheskii portret L. I. Brezhneva*. Vol. 1 (Moscow: Novosti, 1991), pp. 290–1.
66. See, for example, K. Williams, 'New Sources on Soviet Decision Making during the 1968 Czechoslovak Crisis', *Europe–Asia Studies*, 48/3, 1996, pp. 457–70;

M. Kramer, 'New Sources on the 1968 Soviet Invasion of Czechoslovakia', *Cold War International History Project Bulletin*, 2, Fall 1992 and 3, Fall 1993.

67. A. Shelepin, 'Istoriya-uchitel surovyi', in Yu. Aksyutin (ed.), *L. I. Brezhnev: materialy k biografii* (Moscow: IPL, 1991), p. 234.
68. R. Medvedev, *Lichnost i epokha. Politicheskii portret L. I. Brezhneva.* Vol. 1 (Moscow: Novosti, 1991), pp. 101–48.
69. R. Medvedev, *Lichnost i epokha. Politicheskii portret L. I. Brezhneva.* Vol. 1 (Moscow: Novosti, 1991), pp. 121–5. Breslauer identifies Kosygin as Brezhnev's main rival: 'Brezhnev was able to seize the initiative from Kosygin, coopt, preempt, and redefine issues, and force through changes in direction' (Breslauer, *Khrushchev and Brezhnev as Leaders* (London: George Allen & Unwin, 1982), p. 265).
70. A. Shelepin, 'Istoriya-uchitel surovyi', in Yu. Aksyutin (ed.), *L. I. Brezhnev: materialy k biografii* (Moscow: IPL, 1991), p. 240.
71. P. Shelest, 'On umel vesti', in Yu. Aksyutin (ed.), *L. I. Brezhnev: materialy k biografii* (Moscow: IPL, 1991), p. 228.
72. F. Burlatsky, cited in V. V. Shelud'ko (ed.), *Leonid Brezhnev v vospominaniyakh, razmyshlenniyakh, suzhdeniyakh* (Rostov-on-Don: Feniks, 1998), p. 214.
73. Compare, for example, D. Volkogonov: 'from the middle of the 1970s Brezhnev took no active part in either Party or state activity' (D. Volkogonov, *The Rise and Fall of the Soviet Empire* (London, 1998), p. 324) and M. Gorbachev, 'The removal of Podgorny in 1977 and of Kosygin in 1980 finally sealed the personal power of Brezhnev. The irony was this happened when his capacity for work was already ebbing. His grip on power had by then become ephemeral' (M. Gorbachev, *Memoirs*, (London: Doubleday, 1995), p. 113).
74. A. Shelepin, 'Istoriya-uchitel surovyi', in Yu. Aksyutin (ed.), *L. I. Brezhnev: materialy k biografii* (Moscow: IPL, 1991), p. 244
75. A. Shelepin, 'Istoriya-uchitel surovyi', in Yu. Aksyutin (ed.), *L. I. Brezhnev: materialy k biografii* (Moscow: IPL, 1991).
76. M. Gorbachev, *Memoirs* (London: Doubleday, 1995), p. 114.
77. M. Gorbachev, *Memoirs* (London: Doubleday, 1995), p. 143.
78. M. Gorbachev, *Memoirs* (London: Doubleday, 1995), pp. 126, 132.

3
Economic Growth and Slowdown

Mark Harrison

Phases of economic development are rarely synchronised with the personal regimes of political leaders. At the beginning, the Soviet economy under Brezhnev was little different from the economy under his predecessor Khrushchev. At the end, the economy under Brezhnev shaded into the economy under Andropov, then Chernenko. If there was a significant break in the pattern of development it came half-way through the Brezhnev years in the early or middle 1970s. We can say with some confidence that the economy that Brezhnev bequeathed to his successors was less dynamic than that which he and his prime minister Kosygin had taken over in 1964. In this chapter I will review the pattern of economic slowdown, its possible causes, and the measures taken to try to overcome it. I will conclude that the Soviet economy at the end of the Brezhnev years faced serious problems but was not yet a hopeless case.

Benchmarks of economic performance (Figure 3.1)

To gauge the performance of the economy under Brezhnev we need figures. Which should we use? The Soviet economy was intrinsically difficult to measure. One problem was that statistics were subordinated to economic management. Soviet production statistics, used at all levels as control variables and success indicators, provided a strong illustration of Goodhart's law: when an indicator is used to control behaviour, behavioural responses will cause that indicator to become distorted. Another problem lay in the structural features of the command economy: excessive accumulation combined with pervasive limitations on the quality, variety and availability of commodities made the relationship between production possibilities and welfare outcomes everywhere uncertain.

One result was that the measurement of Soviet economic performance became an arena of East–West competition. What began as a private research initiative of Abram Bergson became a national project of the United States to reconstruct the Soviet national income and product accounts under the

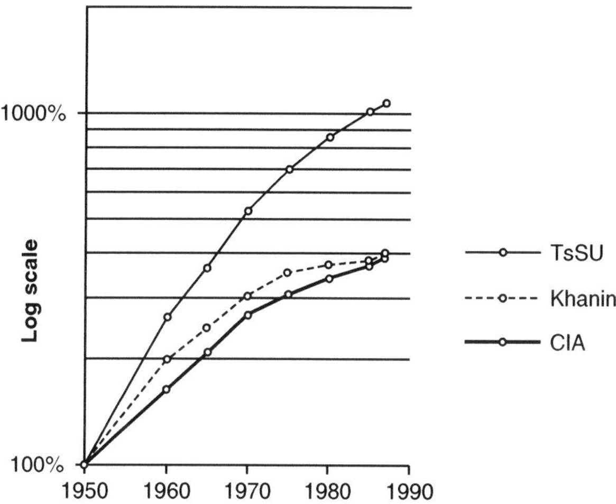

Figure 3.1 Soviet real national income, 1950–87: alternative estimates (per cent of 1950 on a logarithmic scale)
Sources: see Table 3.1.

auspices of the Central Intelligence Agency (CIA). As Figure 3.1 illustrates, the American figures for Soviet gross national product (GNP) per head showed Soviet performance in a much less favourable light than the official Soviet figures. The figures themselves are reported in Table 3.1. According to official estimates Soviet net material product in 1987 was 10.8 times the level of 1950, suggesting an annual average growth rate over the post-war period of 5.2 per cent, but the most recent estimates of the US Central Intelligence Agency showed the achieved level of the Soviet GNP in 1987 as only 5.8 times the 1950 level, based on growth of only 3.8 per cent annually.

The American figures commanded widespread respect, but never full acceptance. Eventually, in the years of Soviet *perestroika* and early Russian transition they were subjected to an intense assault. Critics charged Bergson and his successors on two counts; the charges were separate but related to the same offence. The first was that they relied on the measure of things, not utilities.[1] The second was that they failed even in the measure of things, being excessively reliant on the flawed record of Soviet statistics.[2] From a guilty verdict on both counts followed the judgement that, measuring things rather than utilities, and exaggerating the measure of things, the Americans had overvalued Soviet national income in terms of both level and growth. In short the American figures, although much less favourable than the official record, were still too high.

When it came to detail, it was noteworthy that growth rates evoked less real divergence than size comparisons. When impassioned critics computed

Table 3.1 Soviet national income, 1950–87: alternative annual average growth rates (per cent)

	Net material product based on moving weights:		*GNP at 1982 factor cost: US CIA*
	TsSU-Goskomstat USSR	*Grigorii Khanin*	
1950–87	5.8	3.8	3.8
1950–60	10.2	7.2	5.2
1960–5	6.5	4.4	4.8
1965–70	7.7	4.1	4.9
1970–5	5.7	3.2	3.0
1975–80	4.2	1.0	1.9
1980–5	3.5	0.6	1.8
1985–7	3.0	2.0	2.7

Note: National income can be measured in different ways. On the whole these differences are unimportant for the purposes of this chapter. This note is included to avoid confusion in the event that the figures provided are used for other purposes.

Western studies measure Soviet national income as GNP or GDP. The gross domestic product (GDP) is the value of all final goods and services produced by the factors of production in the economy, 'domestic' because at home and 'gross' because including replacement capital. The gross national product (GNP) is the same plus income from factor services abroad and remitted home, a distinction that was unimportant for the Soviet Union; in other words Soviet GDP and GNP are interchangeable. National income at 'factor cost' means that goods and services are valued as closely as possible to the incomes generated for the factors of production; this requires subtraction of indirect taxes from and addition of subsidies to the prices at which goods and services were officially exchanged.

The Soviet Union measured its own national income as the net material product, 'material' because it counted the value of all final goods produced, including intermediate but not final services, 'net' because excluding replacement capital. The net material product was measured at official or 'established' prices, not at factor cost.

Sources: Goskomstat SSSR, *Narodnoe khoziaistvo SSSR za 70 let* (Moscow: 1987); G. I. Khanin, 'Ekonomicheskii rost: al'ternativnaya otsenka', *Kommunist*, no. 17, 1988, pp. 83–90; Central Intelligence Agency, *Measures of Soviet gross national product in 1982 prices* (Washington, DC, 1990).

their own Soviet growth rates the figures that emerged were surprisingly similar to those under attack. One of their authors, for example, is Grigorii Khanin, one of the first of the domestic critics of Soviet official statistics to win a public hearing and probably the most original of them.[3] The most recent CIA estimate for annual average growth in Soviet real GNP from 1950 to 1987 and reported in Table 3.1 was 3.8 per cent. The alternative figure offered by Grigorii Khanin for net material product growth over the same period was also 3.8 per cent (on GNP and other national income measures please see the note to Table 3.1). All, including Soviet official statisticians, agreed that the post-war period had witnessed a remarkable deceleration, already noticeable when Brezhnev and Kosygin took over the reins of government, and still more pronounced when Brezhnev died.

The various estimates distributed Soviet growth differently through time, with significant implications for an evaluation of the Brezhnev years. Consider Table 3.1: did Soviet growth decline from a rapid 6–8 per cent in the 1960s to a more modest 4–6 per cent in the 1970s and a more sedate but still respectable 3.5 per cent in the early 1980s (the official figures)? Or was it a decline from nearly 5 per cent in the 1960s to a feeble less than 2 per cent in the late 1970s and early 1980s (the CIA)? Or from an already modest 4 per cent in the 1960s to a disastrous less than 1 per cent in the early 1980s (Khanin), indicating that by the end output per head was virtually stationary?

On size comparisons divergences were positively spectacular and somewhat discreditable to the profession of Sovietological economics. Contemporary estimates of Soviet real national income per head in the late 1980s, expressed as a percentage of United States incomes, are listed in Table 3.2. These ranged from 57 to no more than 12 per cent. Only a small part of the gap between higher and lower estimates could be explained by technical factors such as differences of date (Soviet incomes probably rose somewhat between the early and late 1980s), currency basis (valuations in ruble prices could be expected to give lower figures than US or international dollar valuations) or adjustment for purchasing power parity (again, lack of PPP adjustment could be expected to result in a lower figure). Nor was it even the case that Soviet official figures headed the ranking; among the dollar comparisons at purchasing power parity western estimates were both highest and lowest. Most of the differences among non-Soviet sources were due to factors that could not be resolved by debate. Different authorities discounted differently for quality, variety and availability, especially in consumer durables, machinery and services, and then buttressed their estimates by reference to the unanswerable authorities of personal experience, intuition and anecdote.

The lack of consensus among economists and their inability to come to a common view interacted disastrously with other tendencies which were strongly expressed at the time. These were the belief that in statistics there is one truth, a desire for statistics to encapsulate everything, an adherence to an absolute standard of statistical perfection, and preferences for intuition and experience over scholarship and transparency and for low figures over high ones.

The belief that in statistics there is one truth was important because, when one particular figure was identified as true, it imputed falsehood to all the others. This belief had its roots more perhaps in the East, where independent-minded social and economic observers found themselves engaged in a bitter struggle for the truth against official lies. In the West, statistical philosophies and institutions drew more upon traditions of pluralism and relativism which made of statistics no more than a prism through which the truth might be viewed, and which also allowed more than one angle on the truth.[4]

Table 3.2 Soviet national income per head: alternative size comparisons in the 1980s (per cent of the United States)

Source	*Year*	*Currency*	*Adjusted for purchasing power?*	*Nationa income per head*
CIA (A)	1989	$US	✓	57
Bolotin (IMEMO)	1986	$INT	✓	56
Goskomstat USSR	1988	$US	✓	55
Ehrlich (A)	1980	–	✓	51
Summers and Heston (PWT4)	1985	$INT	✓	50
Campbell (World Bank) (A)	1980	$US	✓	48
Marer (World Bank)	1980	$INT	✓	47
Martynov (Goskomstat) (A)	1985	$INT	✓	37
Martynov (Goskomstat) (B)	1985	$INT	✓	36
Campbell (World Bank) (B)	1980	$US	✗	35
Ehrlich (B)	1980	–	✗	34
CIA (B)	1989	rubles	✓	34
Åslund	1986	–	✓	33
Summers and Heston (PWT5.5)	1985	$INT	✓	30
Belkin (A)	1987	rubles	✓	24
Belkin (B)	1987	rubles	✓	12

Note: National income is measured as GNP or GDP unless otherwise stated below; for definitions see the note to Table 3.1. $US are US dollars valued at current prices or exchange rates. $INT are international dollars valued at purchasing power of 1980. In some cases aggregate figures are adjusted to a *per capita* basis from population figures for the appropriate year.

Sources: A. Åslund, 'How Small is Soviet National Income?', in H. S. Rowen, and C. Wolf, eds (1990), *The Impoverished Superpower: Perestroika and the Soviet Military Burden* (San Francisco: ICS Press, 1990) p. 43; Åslund does not specify a currency for his figure, but a PPP concept is implicit.

Belkin, cited by S. Rosefielde, 'The Illusion of Material Progress: the Analytics of Soviet Economic Growth Revisited', *Soviet Studies*, 43/4 (1991), p. 606; Rosefielde states that Belkin uses current ruble values, although he denominates Belkin's figures in dollars.

Bolotin, 'Sovetskii soiuz v mirovoi ekonomiki (1917–1987 gg.)', *Mirovaya ekonomika i mezhdunarodnye otnosheniya*, no. 11, 1987, p. 150 (net material product).

R. W. Campbell, 'The conversion of national income data of the USSR to concepts of the system of national accounts in dollars and estimation of growth rate', Staff Working Papers, no. 777, The World Bank, Washington, DC, 1985, p. iii(A), table 9 (B).

Central Intelligence Agency, *Handbook of Economic Statistics*, 1989, (Washington, DC, 1990), p. 38.

E. Ehrlich, 'Contest between countries: 1937–1986', *Soviet Studies*, 43, 1991, p. 880; the method of physical indicators used gives results in percentages of the base country, but not in currency units.

Goskomstat SSSR, *Narodnoe khoziaistvo SSSR v 1988 godu*, (Moscow, 1989) p. 680 (net material product).

P. Marer, *Dollar GNPs of the USSR and eastern Europe* (London: World Bank, 1985) p. 86.

V. Martynov, 'SSSR i SShA po materialam mezhdunarodnykh sopostavlenii OON i SEV', *Vestnik statistiki*, no. 9, 1990, p. 15; (A) involves bilateral comparisons through Poland, and (B) through Hungary.

R. Summers, and A. Heston, 'The Penn World Table (Mark 5): an expanded set of international comparisons, 1950–1988', *Quarterly Journal of Economics*, 1991, pp. 106, 327–68; data disks for the Penn World Table 4, and (1991) for the Penn World Table 5.5.

The desire for statistics to encapsulate everything was expressed when users of statistics demanded measures of national income that would take into account not only production possibilities and the potential to satisfy wants but also the actual welfare losses reflected in time spent standing in line, frustrated consumer purchases, the waste of resources in controversial national projects and so on. In retrospect we see that these were all important determinants of welfare, and ought to be measured, but it may not be desirable to collapse every aspect of welfare into one measure.[5] At best the change in national income can be regarded as measuring the change in economic welfare so long as trends in its context are held equal. When the context – including factors contributing to consumer frustration – is changing, it may be more realistic and more transparent to aim to measure separately national income on the basis of a given context, and trends in the context itself.

Adherence to an absolute standard of perfection was the traditional mark of Bergson's western critics. Undoubtedly, the adjusted factor cost standard (AFCS) which Bergson developed and the CIA inherited was a compromise. Soviet prevailing prices could not serve as a standard of opportunity cost because they were distorted by administered wage setting, the failure to price land and capital inputs and the unequal incidence of indirect taxes and subsidies. The question became whether an accounting exercise could lead to the marginal costs and prices that would have emerged from a competitive market solution. To this a first answer is probably no, neither in theory nor in practice.[6] AFCS was not a perfect solution. But if perfection was the standard to which statisticians must perform, there is probably not a figure in the world that would pass the test. Whether the gross national or domestic product approximates sufficiently to a theoretical ideal is a problem everywhere, even in highly developed market economies. Everywhere taxes distort, resources are inadequately valued, and price–quality ratios exploit consumer ignorance. These problems are usually worse in low-income countries with many economic rigidities and poor statistical coverage. The Soviet Union was just such a country.

Lastly, I mention the preference for intuition over transparent scholarship, allied to the powerful belief that, even if all figures are suspect in some degree, then lower figures are more likely to be true than higher ones. Credibility was attached to figures more because they were lower, not so much because of their scholarly foundations.[7] The result of this was a competition for credibility that could proceed in only one direction – downwards. Not only were there many different figures for the Soviet income level. There were also many different western estimates of Soviet aggregate or industrial growth rates, and Bergson's were not the lowest. It became the tendency to use lower figures to cast unfavourable light on the higher ones. If the higher ones were sometimes more elaborate, and took into account a wider base of knowledge and reference, then this became the evidence to support the charge that they were *too* elaborate, *too* scholarly, *too* detached from the experience and intuition that supported lower estimates.[8] Thus the discreditable disarray of professional opinion over income levels was also used to cast doubt on the best western estimates of growth rates, too.

Today a consensus is re-emerging. The Soviet period is becoming history, and the size of Soviet national income has become less charged with political controversy. The heat is being taken out of the measurement issue, but economists and now historians too still need national income figures. Maybe there can be more realism about what can be learned from national income and less perfectionism about how it may be measured. If the common problems of poor countries with many distortions and market rigidities were writ large in the Soviet Union's statistical system, that does not make it wrong to try to compensate for the distortions and approximate more nearly to the truth. Our understanding of how to measure welfare, real growth, and inflation is improving; when the methodologies used in western studies to account for substitution of consumer products or of new industrial products are disassembled and scrutinised by modern standards we find that higher growth rates may be more, not less reliable.[9] Here it is transparency, not intuition, that counts for credibility, and transparency was the outstanding virtue of the Bergson tradition. Finally, the merits of the Bergson–CIA tradition have been reasserted by adherents old and new (including at least one Russian).[10]

In conclusion, the CIA figures will form the basis of my discussion. These figures are not perfect and can and should be criticised in order to improve them. This is especially urgent with regard to investment and the capital stock. But improvement will be incremental. New archival documentation and new methodologies will be brought to bear, and Russian scholars will direct the work. Eventually our picture of Soviet economic development may bear little relation to what we once thought we knew. But I am convinced that there will be a genetic inheritance of principles and methodology.

Soviet economic growth in the Brezhnev years (see Figure 3.2)

The estimates we will use are illustrated in Figure 3.2 and reported in Table 3.3. These are gross domestic product (GDP) figures from Angus Maddison's dataset: CIA estimates calibrated in relation to the United States from Phase 6 of the International Comparisons Project with Soviet GDP per head at 31.4 per cent of the United States in 1990.[11] The Maddison dataset is therefore positioned at the lower end of the western estimates shown in Table 3.2.

Figure 3.2 shows the whole Brezhnev period both annually and in long-run comparison. Soviet figures are compared with those of western Europe and the United States. We could think of the United States as the ultimate comparator, and western Europe as the proximate comparator. The United States set a more demanding benchmark in its high productivity level; this was the frontier of technology and living standards to which the Soviet

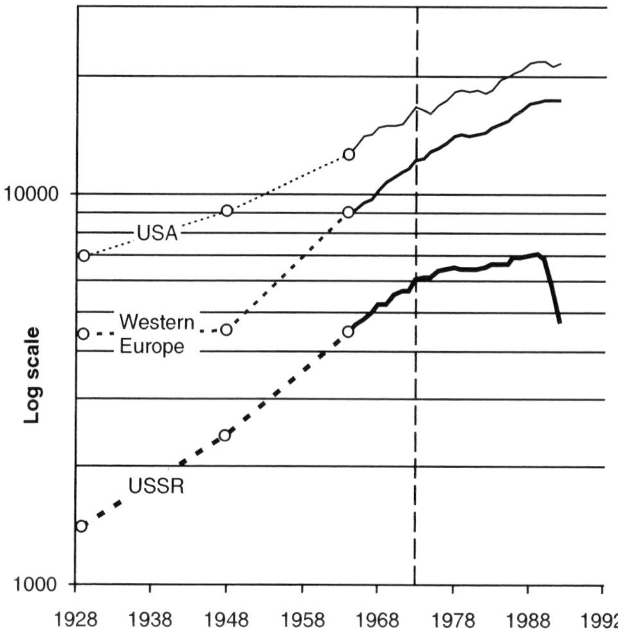

Figure 3.2 GDP per head of the United States, western Europe, and the USSR: 1928, 1948 and 1964–92 (US dollars and 1990 prices, on a logarithmic scale)
Source: as Table 3.3. On GDP see the note to Table 3.1. The vertical dotted line shows 1973.

economy aspired. Western Europe provided a competition which was less challenging in levels at each moment in time since western Europe was poorer than the United States, but more challenging in post-war growth rates since from 1948 onwards western Europe was also gradually catching up with the United States.

The long-run context shows that from 1928 until 1973 the Soviet economy was on a path that would catch up with the United States one day. This was in spite of a huge US advantage: it did not suffer the severe capital losses inflicted on the Soviet economy first by Stalin through his policy of farm collectivisation, then by Hitler's war of aggression. However, in 1973, half-way through the Brezhnev period, the process of catching up came to an abrupt end. This year is widely recognised as marking a downturn in the post-war growth of the whole global economy. But the growth rates of the Soviet Union and the Central and East European socialist states turned down much more severely than those of western Europe or the United States.

Table 3.3 reveals that over the eighteen years of Brezhnev's rule Soviet national income per head rose by roughly one-half; however, three-quarters of this improvement was won in the first half of the period, and only one-quarter in the second half.

Table 3.3 Soviet GDP per head, 1929–92, selected years (dollars at 1990 international prices and per cent)

	GDP per head, dollars	*Annual average change in GDP per head over previous period, per cent*	*GDP per head, per cent*	
			of USA	*of Euro-12*
1929	1,386	–	20	32
1948	2,402	2.9	26	54
1964	4,430	3.9	35	49
1973	6,058	3.5	36	49
1982	6,544	0.9	36	45
1989	7,078	1.1	32	41
1964	4,430	3.9	35	49
1965	4,626	4.4	35	50
1966	4,796	3.7	34	51
1967	4,955	3.3	35	51
1968	5,194	4.8	35	51
1969	5,218	0.5	35	49
1970	5,569	6.7	37	50
1971	5,663	1.7	37	50
1972	5,640	–0.4	36	48
1973	6,058	7.4	36	49
1974	6,175	1.9	38	50
1975	6,136	–0.6	38	48
1976	6,366	3.8	38	48
1977	6,459	1.5	37	48
1978	6,565	1.6	36	47
1979	6,480	–1.3	35	46
1980	6,437	–0.7	35	45
1981	6,442	0.1	35	45
1982	6,544	1.6	36	45
1983	6,692	2.2	36	45
1984	6,715	0.4	34	44
1985	6,715	0.0	33	43
1986	6,924	3.1	34	43
1987	6,943	0.3	33	42
1988	7,032	1.3	33	42
1989	7,078	0.7	32	41
1990	6,871	–2.9	31	40
1991	5,793	–15.7	27	33
1992	4,671	–19.4	22	27

Source: A. Maddison, *Monitoring the World Economy, 1820–1992* (Paris: OECD, 1995) pp. 196–7, 200–1, 212. On GDP see the note to Table 3.1. The Euro-12 are Austria, Belgium, Denmark, Finland, France, Germany, Italy, Netherlands, Norway, Sweden, Switzerland and the United Kingdom.

In the first half of the Brezhnev period income per head expanded at 3.5 per cent per annum, slightly less fast than over the previous fourteen years which were still dominated by post-war recovery and a return to the pre-war trend. In fact, all the slowdown of the early Brezhnev period could be explained simply by the gradual return to a slow underlying trend.[12] The Soviet economy expanded more rapidly than the United States economy, though only by a small margin, and kept pace with western Europe large parts of which were also still recovering from wartime devastation. Thus in both 1964 and 1973 the Soviet economy stood at roughly half the output per head of western Europe and a little more than one third that of the United States. These were substantial gains over the 1929 figures of one-third and one-fifth respectively.

The pattern of the late Brezhnev period was quite different. Output per head stagnated, rising by less than 1 per cent per annum. The Soviet economy continued to keep pace with the US economy, which also slowed down, but fell back sharply compared with western Europe. Absolute declines in output also became more frequent. This deceleration could no longer be explained by the exhaustion of post-war recovery possibilities: it was a new phenomenon with contemporaneous roots.

The growth rates of value added in industry and construction, agriculture, and the residue of the economy (transport, trade, and services) are shown separately in Table 3.4. Each of these sectors grew more slowly after the mid-1970s than before. However, deceleration was most marked in industrial production, which had driven aggregate economic growth in the 1950s and 1960s but was virtually marking time by the 1980s. Table 3.4 also shows the significant volatility of year-to-year agricultural production relative to a trend that was dismal and, by the end of the Brezhnev years, negative.

In this chapter I will not deal separately with agriculture. In the long sweep of Soviet history agriculture deserves much special attention.[13] However, the outstanding feature of the agricultural system under Brezhnev was the extent to which it became more and more like the rest of the economy. The heritage of Stalinist discrimination against agriculture and the peasant was largely overcome. Agriculture was no longer exploited to foster industrialisation; on the contrary, it became a net recipient of government subsidies paid for by the rest of the economy. The special features of the collective farm were blurred, and the terms and conditions of employment of farm labour became more and more like those of any state employee. Thus agriculture could be viewed simply as a large sector in relative decline which responded badly, but not differently, to the pressures and constraints of the system as a whole.

Finally, Table 3.5 reports trends in consumption. Over the Brezhnev years measured average consumption per head rose by some 70 per cent, but again three-quarters of the total advance was recorded in the first half of this period, and only one-quarter in the second half. As might be expected the growth of household durables consumption was particularly marked.

Table 3.4 Soviet output by sector of origin, 1950–87: annual average growth at 1982 factor cost (change over previous period, per cent)

	Industry and construction	*Agriculture*	*Trade, transport, communications, and services*
1950	–	–	–
1964	8.2	2.9	4.7
1973	5.7	2.9	5.0
1982	2.5	–1.1	2.9
1987	2.6	1.1	2.2
1964	–	–	–
1965	6.3	3.9	6.5
1966	5.0	4.2	5.2
1967	7.5	–0.7	5.9
1968	5.8	6.7	5.5
1969	5.0	–6.4	4.4
1970	6.3	14.3	4.9
1971	4.8	–2.3	4.6
1972	4.5	–8.9	3.8
1973	5.9	18.9	4.4
1974	6.0	–3.8	4.4
1975	5.2	–12.5	4.0
1976	2.7	11.5	3.1
1977	2.4	2.4	2.2
1978	1.8	3.5	2.9
1979	1.0	–8.3	2.8
1980	1.3	–6.9	3.3
1981	1.1	–2.4	2.5
1982	0.7	8.9	1.4
1983	2.6	5.9	2.3
1984	2.6	–2.1	2.2
1985	2.1	–3.8	2.1
1986	2.9	10.3	2.1
1987	3.0	–4.0	2.5

Source: Central Intelligence Agency, *Measures of Soviet Gross National Product in 1982 Prices*, (Washington, DC, 1990), pp. 54–7. On 'factor cost' see the note to Table 3.1.

The consumption of soft goods, and household services also rose rapidly, while food consumption rose more gradually. But outlays on 'communal services' such as health and education also rose relatively slowly, and more slowly in real terms than national income per head.

Paths of high accumulation

Observers of the Soviet economy were driven to cross–country comparisons by two quite different traditions. One is the tradition of Stalin, who more

Table 3.5 Soviet consumption per head, 1950–87: annual average growth at 1982 established prices (change over previous period, per cent)

	Food	*Soft goods*	*Durables*	*Household services*	*Communal services*	*Total*
1950	–	–	–	–	–	–
1964	2.7	5.3	10.5	4.6	2.9	3.6
1973	3.1	5.4	10.0	5.0	2.6	4.1
1982	1.1	2.3	5.1	3.0	1.3	1.9
1987	–1.8	1.7	5.5	2.6	1.0	0.6
1964	–	–	–	–	–	–
1965	3.0	5.7	10.0	6.3	4.1	4.3
1966	3.4	7.7	11.3	5.0	3.4	4.8
1967	4.9	7.8	9.2	6.1	2.5	5.5
1968	4.5	7.8	10.2	5.8	3.5	5.4
1969	5.0	6.5	6.1	4.9	2.9	5.1
1970	3.3	6.1	10.6	4.6	3.2	4.4
1971	2.3	3.5	11.9	4.2	1.9	3.3
1972	0.3	1.5	13.5	4.5	0.9	1.9
1973	1.3	2.1	7.1	3.9	1.2	2.2
1974	3.5	2.5	7.3	4.8	2.1	3.6
1975	3.1	3.8	8.5	4.3	1.5	3.6
1976	0.5	3.6	5.6	3.3	1.6	2.0
1977	0.9	2.5	7.9	0.8	1.0	1.9
1978	–0.2	1.8	3.3	3.1	1.6	1.1
1979	2.0	3.0	3.6	3.3	1.2	2.4
1980	1.6	2.9	6.3	3.3	0.6	2.4
1981	–0.1	2.0	6.2	2.6	0.1	1.3
1982	–1.4	–1.6	–2.6	1.7	1.9	–0.9
1983	1.4	0.6	1.7	2.2	0.3	1.2
1984	1.6	2.4	4.5	2.4	1.1	2.1
1985	–3.2	3.1	5.2	2.5	1.0	0.1
1986	–7.7	2.2	10.6	2.5	0.5	–1.4
1987	–0.9	0.4	5.5	3.5	2.0	1.1

Source: CIA (1990a), pp. 90–3. Household services are housing, utilities, transportation, communications, repair and personal care, and recreation. Communal services are education and health. On 'established prices' see the note to Table 3.1.

than eighty years ago launched the Soviet economy on a drive 'to catch up and overtake' the advanced capitalist powers. His strategy was one of convergence on western levels of technology and living standards through forced high accumulation. High accumulation was secured by pouring resources into the building sites of 'socialist construction': the new factories, furnaces, mines, power stations, railways, schools, hospitals and apartment blocks of each successive five-year plan. Stalin's instruments were planning and the compulsory mobilisation of resources: mass consumption was restricted and effort forced through a complex mixture of bribes, threats and exhortations. The strategy of forced high accumulation was diffused to the other countries in Central and Eastern Europe and East Asia which adopted state-socialist institutions after the Second World War, and was also continued by Stalin's heirs.

Another tradition that prompts us towards cross-country comparisons is that of western growth economics. In the traditional western story international convergence should come about without being forced, through an automatic market mechanism. Suppose that globalisation is making all countries more alike in both supply and demand characteristics. In supply, all firms have access to the same technology. In demand, all consumers increasingly prefer the same goods and services. With a lower ratio of capital to labour, poorer countries have a higher marginal product of capital; they should accumulate more and grow faster than richer, more capital-abundant countries. Eventually, all countries should converge on the same path of income per head. However, global experience suggests that convergence is at best conditional; even among market economies, if it happens at all, it depends on policies with regard to investment and trade, and tends to come about through a process of regionalisation.[14]

The state-socialist economies were not the only ones to attempt convergence on the west through high accumulation. Led by Japan, several Asian market economies took the route of convergence through high accumulation based on a market system. Table 3.6 shows comparative figures for three large economies (the state-socialist USSR and China, and market-based Japan,) and twelve small economies (five state-socialist economies in central and eastern Europe, and seven market economies in east Asia) over a period beginning just before and ending just after the Brezhnev years. The starting point of Japan and the smaller East Asian market economies in 1960 was behind that of the USSR and eastern Europe, although ahead of China, but they grew more rapidly, and their growth advantage over eastern Europe increased through time. After 1973 China began to catch up, but from a position even further behind than in 1960.

As Table 3.6 shows the East Asian market economies encouraged not only saving and investment, but also integration into the world economy through export promotion. A differentiating factor in the East Asian newcomers' strategy most easily captured with figures lay in their foreign trade ratios ('openness' in Table 3.6), which we can take as an indicator of openness to information and ideas as well as to commodities and competition. However, size mattered: a large economy like Japan's could gain more from internal trade, competition and specialisation than small ones, which needed to open up more to the international economy.

Allowing for the advantages of size, openness to international trade was still important even for large economies (if, say, we compare the openness of Japan with that of the USSR or China) because it accelerated the globalisation of technology and preferences and the convergence of income levels.

Table 3.6 Economic growth under state socialism and East Asian capitalism: a comparison, 1960–87 (per cent)

	Initial GDP per head, % of USA	*Real GDP per head growth, % per year*	*Investment, % of GDP*	*Openness (gross trade), % of GDP*
(A) 1960–73				
USSR	35	3.4	39	6
Japan	30	8.5	32	20
CEE-5	29	3.9	28	41
East Asia-7	13	5.8	17	93
China	8	2.3	16	7
(B) 1973–87				
Japan	61	2.7	34	25
USSR	36	1.0	39	14
CEE-5	31	1.4	30	56
East Asia-7	20	5.1	25	126
China	7	5.1	21	16

Notes and sources: Countries and country groups are ranked by GDP per head in the initial year of each period. GDPs (growth rates and US relatives) for USSR, China and CEE-5 are calculated from Maddison (1995), Appendix D; all other figures are calculated from the Penn World Table 5.6 <http://www.nber.org>. CEE-5 are the state-socialist economies of Czechoslovakia, Hungary, Poland, Romania and Yugoslavia; East Asia-7 are the market economies of Indonesia, Hong Kong, Korean Republic, Malaysia, Singapore, Taiwan and Thailand. Country figures are at current international prices or chain index numbers and international prices. Regional averages are computed as unweighted means of country figures. GDP shares are annual averages over the period shown. On GDP see the note to Table 3.1.

It allowed poorer countries to exploit their higher marginal product of capital and lower marginal product of labour to encourage inward foreign investment and the outward migration of labour. And it allowed poorer countries to exploit their comparative advantage in labour-intensive products, raising demand and labour incomes towards the level of the richer countries. Thus their policy of seclusion is one candidate for the factor that condemned the state-socialist economies to relative stagnation. Committed to an inward-looking development strategy, the Soviet Union and its post-war East European allies pinned everything on the advantages of high accumulation, but were unable to gain from the equalising influences of competitive trade and capital flows.

Paul Krugman was first to offer a comparison between state socialism and East Asia. His intention in doing so was to downgrade the East Asian 'miracle' by showing the similarities – two regions growing rapidly on the basis of high accumulation and the mobilisation of resources, with little overall factor productivity growth, their growth doomed by diminishing returns to end in exhaustion.[15] Whether or not this disparaged the East Asian achievement remains to be seen. Until recently the East Asian economies had probably been doing better relative to state socialism than Krugman suggested – or was it rather that state socialism had really been doing much worse? More recently Easterly and Fischer concluded from a wider cross-country comparison that between 1960 and 1989, after correcting for the tendency of small, poor countries' growth performance to show greater variance, 'the Soviet economic performance conditional upon investment and human capital accumulation was the worst in the world'.[16]

In short, the path of high accumulation did not lead to convergence on its own. When combined with an outward-looking orientation to the global economy it brought rapid growth, while returns diminished slowly. When combined with non-competitive institutions, barriers to information and seclusion from the world economy, the acceleration of growth bought by high accumulation was relatively short-lived. Diminishing returns placed an invisible 'glass ceiling' on the relative productivity of Soviet and CEE economies. On the other hand their role should not be overstated. The time series tell us that returns were diminishing – but there was no reason for them to become negative. In the Soviet case measured growth was slowing, the underlying 'natural' growth rate to which the Soviet path was converging was always slow, and trends worsened after 1973. However, post-1989 collapse cannot be read back into the statistical record of the past.[17]

A background to economic reform

In the Brezhnev years economic institutions were subject to continual reorganisation. But in a sense this was nothing new. We could think of it as one phase in a stream of reorganisations which had been going on since the first tumultuous years of the Stalin era. The underlying dynamic was that of trial-and-error: Soviet institutions were constantly being invented and reinvented in the light of experience. Individuals and organisations made mistakes, plans clashed with realities, incentives failed, and the resulting tensions drove leaders to search for institutional improvement.[18]

The leaders who followed Stalin shared a strong belief in the soundness of the basic Soviet institutions established under the late dictator: an entrenched governing party, state ownership of land and non-agricultural capital, collectivised farming, centralised planning of most production and intermediate consumption, state provision of housing and basic amenities. They believed that individual leaders had built bureaucratic empires and abused power; it was easier for them to portray the excesses of the Stalin regime as 'crimes' for which individuals, even Stalin, bore personal responsibility than as 'mistakes' that might be attributed to the system itself. Khrushchev's reforms were consistent with this analysis. He vilified Stalin for his use of terror to rule the party and state while defending his economic policies of forced high accumulation. He rooted out a minority of old-time

Stalinist conservatives formed in the tradition of personal dictatorship: first Beriya, then Malenkov, Molotov, Kaganovich and so on; he sought initially, at least, to collectivise political authority. He retained the services of the basic core of Stalin's military–industrial leaders, but attempted to break up their empires and disperse their powers from Moscow to the provinces by transforming the system of limited coordination of relatively self-sufficient production-branch ministries into a system of limited coordination of relatively self-sufficient territorial units, the 'councils of national economy' (*sovnarkhozy*) of 1957.

By 1964 the Soviet leadership's confidence in this diagnosis and prescription had been undermined. One important factor undermining confidence was the severe decline in Soviet national income growth (for the official figures on which they relied, see Table 3.1). Without criticising the Stalinist strategy, they came to believe that its effectiveness had reached natural limits. It was no longer possible for the economy to continue rapid growth by mobilising resources. In the past the economy had grown primarily through big new capital-widening projects of job creation in industry and construction and the movement of millions of workers from low-productivity rural labour to higher-productivity employment in the urban sector, a pattern that came to be known as 'extensive' growth. However, the economy was running short of reserves of rural and unskilled labour. Khruschchev's successors did not criticise Stalin for pursuing extensive growth in the 1930s, but they did criticise Khrushchev for trying to sustain extensive growth by periodic 'campaigning' to mobilise resources in the 1950s and early 1960s.

If the Soviet economy was to catch up with western Europe and the United States in the foreseeable future, its growth had to be maintained at the rates of the 1950s; it became accepted that this could be achieved only by shifting the economy to a new pattern of 'intensive' growth. This meant improving the efficiency of use of existing resources rather continually mobilising new resources; capital-deepening investment to raise the productivity of existing production and distribution facilities instead of capital-widening investment in new facilities; raising the growth rate of human capital relative to that of physical capital through education, training and skilling; reallocating scarce labour from lower- to higher-productivity employment but out of unskilled work in industry rather than out of agriculture.

In all this there proved to be a degree of illusion. One misperception was that the growth rates of the 1950s represented the natural growth rate of a state-socialist economy, provided that the right institutions could be devised, or that they were indefinitely sustainable by any means at all. In reality the high growth rates of the Soviet economy in the 1950s were largely a continuation of post-war recovery: although the Soviet economy had largely repaired its damaged production facilities and regained its pre-war output level by the end of the 1940s, it was not until the 1970s that it regained the path marked out by extrapolating its pre-war growth. This idea was originally proposed by the Hungarian economist Ferenc Jánossy, who argued that the great European post-war boom was largely a return to what he called the pre-war 'trendline'.[19] What was being perceived at the time as retardation was merely the end of a prolonged post-war recovery phase. The widespread failure to understand this point, he believed, had led policy-makers in both socialist and market economies into misperceptions and mistakes. Believing that the continuing recovery was a new permanent peace-time trend, their long-range plans became overambitious; they then treated the unexpected slowdown, when the trendline was finally approached, with an exaggerated sense of failure.

If this analysis is correct, it follows that the problem of the Soviet economy in the 1960s was not one of declining growth, or that the Soviet economy's growth rate was falling increasingly below its potential. The underlying problem was more intractable: the rapid growth rates of the 1950s were temporary and bound to fall regardless of policies. The underlying natural growth rate of the Soviet economy that would increasingly dominate actual growth was relatively slow, probably too slow to allow the Soviet economy to catch up with the United States within a lifetime.

However, this is mostly hindsight. At the time, there were convincing arguments to suggest that the Soviet economy of the late Khrushchev years was underperforming, and that institutional reforms could maintain and sustain higher growth rates than those being achieved at the time. Thus the early years of the Brezhnev–Kosygin leadership were a time of new hopes based on genuine institutional innovations. To give Khrushchev due credit it should be added that the reforms pursued in the Soviet Union by his successors were based on public discussions, local experiments and East European precedents dating from his last years in power. The task of national implementation, however, was undertaken by the new prime minister Kosygin.

Reform concepts

The reform of the Soviet economic mechanism under Brezhnev and Kosygin was driven by an attempt to alter the basic functioning of the Soviet production enterprise. Under the institutional arrangements inherited from Stalin, planners commanded firms to produce output, but had no automatic system for detecting inefficient production and so were unable to impose penalties for producing inefficiently unless the inefficiency was so flagrant as to be positively attention-seeking.

Planners' fundamental problem was their overloading with tasks: assigning plans to producers that would correspond with their true capacities, monitoring not only their fulfilment but also the efficiency with which they were fulfilled, and detecting violations. They set most ministries' and firms' production targets using the gross value of output in plan prices because industrial products were too numerous and variegated in quality and assortment to allow more than a handful of key basic products to be controlled from Moscow in physical units, but they could not prevent firms from bargaining plan prices upwards through the introduction of 'new' products so as to meet the plan more easily. In addition, since planners aimed to set production targets to as to use firms' production capacity fully, those firms that revealed surplus capacity by producing above planners' expectations were initially rewarded with praise and bonuses, then penalised by being set a more demanding target in all future plans. Thus high productivity was taxed and inefficiency was not penalised. Moreover, firms that hoarded resources in secret and established hidden reserves of machinery, materials and labour were positively rewarded because they could now fulfil planners' assignments with less effort.

In a similar vein, firms that made profits saw their profits taken by the state budget as tax revenue. Firms that made losses saw their losses automatically compensated by subsidies from the state budget. In a market economy, profits are a signal to invest, and persistent losses end in insolvency and closure of the firm. In the Soviet economy it was the other way around: if persistent losses attracted attention, they were most likely taken to signal the need to strengthen the firm through new investment, but this was just as likely to reward poor management.

Finally, planners could attempt to control firms' inefficient behaviour only by inventing ever more numerous performance indicators, ever closer monitoring of firms' decisions and auditing of their accounts, and threatening ever harsher punishment for violations. But as experience showed, the more numerous the controls, the harder it was to set them consistently, monitor them continuously, enforce them effectively and credibly threaten minor violators with severe punishment.

This was the pattern that conserved low productivity, inhibited resource-saving and rewarded firms' accumulation of excess reserves. The core of the reform process launched in 1965 was measures to realign firms' incentives so that planners and producers could coexist with greater harmony than under continual monitoring with traditional rewards and penalties. It was intended to delegate significant control rights to producers. If reforms were successful, planners could safely hand management over to managers without constant monitoring. Indeed, the trend of the Brezhnev period would be to reduce both the frequency of monitoring and the severity of punishments of plan violations for managers and workers alike. A parallel intention was to update and enlarge the concept of the Soviet 'firm' from a single-plant enterprise to an integrated multi-plant corporation that could internalise the coordination of the stages of production, distribution, research and development (R & D) and innovation, generate its own finance, borrow from state credit instititions on its own responsibility and become financially self-reliant, halting the drain of subsidies on the state budget.

Some proponents of economic reforms in eastern Europe in the early 1960s favoured a kind of 'market socialism' that would free prices partially or completely and eliminate most direct controls on output, establishing a quasi-market for state investment and leaving other regulation to conventional fiscal and monetary policy. However, Soviet orthodoxy was more conservative than this. Rather, official schemes favoured an arrangement in which some parts of the economy including allocations to investment and defence should continue to be administered directly, while others should be guided by an incentive system still controlled by government. Planners would continue to fix broad output targets and ministries would assign them to firms, but detailed supply planning of intermediate transactions from above was to be replaced by market subcontracting between producers; this was to start with materials, components and semi-manufactures, and extend eventually to capital goods. The main purpose was to encourage firms to fulfil plans efficiently, i.e. to use resources efficiently within firms and reach efficient decisions in new inter-firm markets.

Controls on firms' gross output and bonuses for gross-output plan fulfilment were therefore to give way to controls on sales value (so as not to reward the production of unsaleable output) and value added (so as not to reward excessive consumption of non-labour inputs). Plan assignments were to be guaraneed over longer periods with greater stability so as to protect firms from having the gains of higher performance instantly taxed away in higher targets; firms that volunteered for higher targets were to be rewarded not only with immediate bonuses but also with guarantees against inflated future targets. Firms were to be subject to fewer controls, with direct controls on the supply and use of inputs replaced by incentive funds based on the surplus of revenues over costs. To make revenues and costs representative of management performance, not just of accidents in the history of administrative price-fixing, wholesale prices were to be reformed. Finally, households were to be left free to allocate labour in the labour market and purchasing power in a retail market from which shortages were to be cleared by increased supplies, subject to prices and wages fixed from the centre and local efficiency-based incentives fixed by their immediate employers.

Effectively the enterprise would be handed over to insider stakeholders. What about the balance between the different insider interests, in particular the relationship between managers and workers? Across eastern Europe there was wide variation; in Poland, Czechoslovakia, and of course Yugoslavia, various schemes for managerial power-sharing with the workers were envisaged at various stages. In East Germany, Hungary and the USSR, on the other hand, reform proposals aimed to enhance managers' prerogatives over the workforce, and to redistribute previously shared costs of poor management so that profit-oriented managers would lose from poor decisions and be motivated to raise profitability by reallocating workers, rather than to raise output regardless of cost by hiring additional workers. Workers would be motivated to stop shirking and seek higher-income, higher-productivity jobs as living standards rose and the cost of shirking increased. But no provision was made to punish persistent loss-makers by firing redundant workers or liquidating the firm; the obligation laid on employers to reemploy redundant workers in other capacities was reaffirmed in 1967.

What kind of efficiency improvements could be expected? Efficiency could be thought of as two–dimensional. Greater *productive efficiency* could be achieved if firms were forced to share in the social costs and benefits of their own behaviour; this was expected to eliminate the tendencies to hoard resources and produce below capacity. Greater *allocative efficiency* could be achieved if firms used inputs and capacities more efficiently: planners could cut back on resources for heavy industry and accumulation and raise the status of consumers; increased supplies to the retail market could eliminate queues, shortages, and waiting time. Gains could also be thought of as static and dynamic. A *static* (that is, once-for-all) gain in total output would be registered if managers shifted resources from lower- to higher-productivity uses and if workers increased effort. A *dynamic* gain would be registered in higher output growth if inventions were stimulated and if managers sought out and adopted them at a higher rate.[20]

This concept of economic reform was conservative, not radical. Far from presaging a revival of the market economy or a return to capitalism, as some western observers mistakenly concluded, it was intended to strengthen public ownership and make centralised plans more effective. It departed substantially from Stalinist orthodoxy in recognising that incentive problems are inherent in hierarchical organisations. It was ready to draw radical conclusions from capitalist experience by studying large-scale, financially self-reliant western corporations and analysing how they allocated resources internally, raised productivity, delegated authority and achieved compatibility of the various incentives facing shareholders, managers and workers. But all this was designed to reinforce the basic institutions of the Soviet command economy: state ownership and control, the system of central planning and ministerial guidance and the dominant role of the communist party. Thus side by side with elements of decentralisation, the Kosygin reform restored traditional instruments of centralisation and created new ones. The production-branch ministries with their headquarters in Moscow were re-established, consigning to oblivion the regional *sovnarkhozy* created in 1957 by Khrushchev. New state committees were created to oversee the new inter-firm subcontracting system (*Gossnab*), the wholesale price reform (*Gostsen*), and the hoped-for acceleration of industrial innovation (*Gostekhnika*).

Initial outcomes and counter-reforms

The main lines of economic reform were announced by prime minister Kosygin in September 1965.[21] These reforms were pursued vigorously at first, with implementation of a wholesale price reform in 1966–7; subsequently they ran into increasing problems, and were tacitly shelved in the early 1970s. Measures to permit the formation of large-scale multi-plant socialist corporations (the 'state production associations' and 'science-production associations') were not enacted until 1973. There was one more attempt at a system overhaul in a major decree of July 1979 to 'improve planning and strengthen the economic mechanism'. Beneath the surface, what had begun as a serious if still conservative project of 'reform' degenerated into a stream of piecemeal 'reforms' that Gertrude Schroeder came to characterise as a 'treadmill' – a cycle that was at the same time exhausting, never-ending, self-perpetuating, and pointless.

Casual observation might suggest a link between the abandonment of economic reform and the slowdown of Soviet economic growth in the early 1970s. This would almost certainly be a mistake. There is no strong evidence that economic reform made growth rates in the late 1960s higher than they would otherwise have been (indeed Khanin's figures suggest a slowdown), or that cancellation of the reform contributed to slowdown. A case could just as easily be made for the opposite: that economic reform was damaging to economic growth, and that counterreforms were growth-promoting. But the truth is that there is no evidence either way.

The fundamental problem of the economic reform can be seen most easily in the issue of prices. In a market economy competitive self-interested producers will allocate resources efficiently when outputs and inputs are priced at their marginal social costs. If prices diverge arbitrarily then producers will allocate resources wrongly – they will use too much of resources that are scarce but undervalued and not enough of others that are abundant but overpriced, and they will underproduce commodities that are undervalued, or the inputs of which are overpriced, while overproducing others. In the Soviet economy wholesale prices were usually fixed by average variable production costs plus a markup to cover overheads early in the life of the product cycle. This did not just neglect many factors which might properly enter into the determination of marginal costs such as technological or locational disadvantages. In addition, the tens of thousands of centrally administered wholesale prices of commodities currently in production at a given moment actually reflected the production costs of previous years with a varying lag and a relationship to current costs which depended arbitrarily on the period when the product had been introduced and the history of input prices since that date.

The Soviet authorities of the 1960s did not want flexible prices that would actively equate supplies with demands and take resource allocation out of the hands of planners altogether. They wanted administered prices that would encourage producers to fulfil government objectives at least cost. The economy of 1965 had inherited a structure of administered wholesale prices last reformed in 1949, and that reform had been been largely reversed in the intervening years. If producers were to be encouraged to demand, produce, and supply efficiently the resources envisaged in government plans, a wholesale price reform was urgently needed, and such a reform was implemented in 1966–7. However, a government prices committee following an administrative formula was incapable of delivering a full set of the tens of thousands of marginal costs that would allocate resources to satisfy the plan efficiently, even for one year at a time.

Consequently the first result of relaxing direct controls on producers was that allocative efficiency was often worsened, since managers were temporarily freed to respond to a pattern of prices and costs that was still to a large extent accidental. Some products that Soviet society needed were not produced because they were underpriced relative to social marginal cost, and producing them would have reduced enterprises profits and incentive funds. Planners were forced to resume direct control of management decisions in order to correct such consequences. As a result, the old supply planning system continued to be kept in being, while the contracts that firms made among themselves proved ineffective and could not be enforced. New incentives had to be cancelled because the distribution of profits and losses continued to be uncorrelated with producer performance for several reasons: because the relationship between prices and costs continued to be arbitrary, because planners overrode profit-maximising inter-firm contracts and continued to prevent producers from maximising profits in the interests of maintaining production, and because firms, discovering that still the plan was more powerful than the market, continued to hoard resources and place the ease of fulfilment of output quotas before efficiency.

The result was a cycle of reforms and counter-reforms. In the reform phase new incentives were imposed to encourage efficient behaviour. Unforeseen producer responses meant that allocative efficiency was often worsened. In the counter-reform phase controls were reimposed to correct the consequences. Meanwhile the original problems had not been solved, so calls for reform were soon heard once more. Some consequences of the reform phase endured, for example rationalisation measures to popularise new management techniques and administrative methodologies such as systems analysis and linear programming, and these may have led to some static gains in particular branches of the economy. But some enduring consequences may have been negative, for example a growing loss of confidence in the basic institutions of centralised planning. There is evidence that increasingly planners sought to secure 100 per cent plan fulfilment by lowering plans rather than demanding increased effort; this became known as 'fulfilling the plan with the plan' (as opposed to with production). However, reductions in plans may have simply encouraged reductions in performance.[22]

Perhaps related to this loss of confidence was an increased toleration of sideline economic activity and the resort to unofficial markets to reallocate state products in ways not prescribed in government plans. The American economist James R. Millar called this the 'Little Deal'. The Big Deal had been Vera Dunham's term for Stalin's pact with the new Soviet labour aristocracy to give them access to a middle-class lifestyle through piece-rates, bonuses, and the supply of household durables in return for their production effort and political loyalty.[23] The Little Deal was Brezhnev's pact with the urban population to permit private trading and the private use of state-owned facilities as long as it was discreet and kept within limits set by the most important government priorities.[24] This shadow economy sometimes usefully reallocated resources from less to more efficient uses. Through the activities of thieves and private traders, households could secure the commodities they desired, and factories could also obtain the materials and supplies necessary to fulfil their plans. But it also tended to undermine work discipline, public morality and the legitimacy of state property. In particular, it tended to draw ministerial officials and enterprise managers into a web of bribery and corrupt relationships with a growing underworld of economic criminality.[25]

Labour and consumption

The reform dilemmas of the Soviet economy were particularly acute in the labour market. In a well-functioning market economy both productive and allocative efficiency are promoted by labour market slack. Profit-maximising firms are motivated to put workers in low-productivity jobs back in the pool of unemployment from which they may be re-employed at higher productivity to the advantage of both worker and employer. Workers in work are motivated to work hard both by the employer's incentive system and also by the fear of unemployment. The costs of this system are those of maintaining a permanent labour reserve at society's expense, the general insecurity associated with its existence, and the danger that macroeconomic coordination failures may cause unemployment to vary persistently either above or below its the natural rate.

In place of the sticks and carrots of the capitalist market economy, the instruments for control over labour in the Soviet economy were limited. For reasons already outlined there was a permanent state of labour shortage, with vacancies exceeding the number of workers available. Once hired, workers had job security, both in law and in practice. The law guaranteed them the right to work according to their skill, and gave them protection against forced redundancy without an offer of alternative employment within the firm. Legal rights are not always honoured, but in practice Soviet enterprises were never closed by their parent ministries on grounds of depreciation of assets or technological obsolescence, or because labour costs prevented the creation of surplus revenues. Production ministries needed all their enterprises to fulfil ministerial plans for output; the output plan was more important than the profit plan, so ministries did not gain from closing inefficient or overstaffed capacity.

Consequently, it was very difficult to displace workers who were in some sense surplus to requirements, for example unskilled workers whose jobs could be automated, craft workers whose skills were obsolete, or workers whose plant was depreciated or obsolete. Such workers tended to be retained by firms as a reserve to spread the labour of meeting output assignments and reduce the effort involved in doing so.

In the Stalin era productive efficiency was stimulated by both sticks and carrots. Positive inducements to effort took the form of material rewards and privileges. A negative stimulus was the threat to punish shirking by firing or forced labour. (Firing, although an ineffective threat against most workers under conditions of a general labour shortage, was a powerful threat against managers and officials who would also lose a privileged lifestyle and career chances.) However, such methods could do little to improve allocative efficiency, especially because firing and forced labour both usually transferred workers from higher- to lower-productivity employment.

If the Soviet economy was to make a successful transition to intensive growth it was essential to tackle the problem of redundant labour. By definition, intensive growth meant improving the efficiency of use of existing resources, including the labour already employed in existing facilities, rather than continually mobilising new labour into new facilities. The difficulty was that, while planners could guess at the extent of inefficient labour utilisation and true labour redundancy, they could not generally detect it without mounting a comprehensive watch on every factory, workshop and machine, which was beyond their means. Instead, they sought to establish new incentives to persuade firms to reveal their labour reserves and give them up for re-employment elsewhere.

The most famous of these began as an experiment at the Shchekino chemical works. From 1967 this factory was allowed to reduce its workforce by voluntary means while retaining its former wage funds, which would then be divided among the smaller workforce, as long as the factory continued to meet its output assignments; as a result, the remaining workers would gain substantial productivity-related wage increases. Within three years the workforce was reduced by roughly 15 per cent, output per worker had more than doubled, and average real incomes and profit norms had both increased substantially. The experiment was declared a success and officially redesignated the 'Shchekino system'. Propagated through Soviet industry, by the early 1980s it was said to be in operation to a greater or lesser extent in 11,000 enterprises with 21 million employees, and to have reduced job creation in industry under the tenth five-year plan by nearly 1 million, or 5 per cent of the industrial workforce.[26]

In practice, gains to both the firm and the macroeconomy were much less than this implies, and may have been no more than temporary. The problem lay in the planners' commitment to protect the wage fund of enterprises that went over to the Shchekino system as long as they fulfilled the output plan. This commitment was typically time-inconsistent: once enterprises had acted upon it, it became optimal for planners to break it. This is what appears to have happened at Shchekino: continual rule changes allowed ministers to withhold benefits and planners to confiscate savings. Once the firm had given up its labour reserve, it was expected to continue to perform indefinitely at its new peak of labour productivity. During the 1970s, plan fulfilment deteriorated, bonuses were cancelled, morale fell, effort slackened and employee turnover rose. In the early 1980s the plant was reported impoverished and failing.[27]

More generally, the best strategy for managers under pressure was to adopt the scheme partially, so the firm could show nominal compliance while workers displaced in one part of the firm could continue to be held in reserve elsewhere. Thus reports of success and the popularisation of the Shchekino system were not to be taken seriously: once the prestige of the authorities had been pinned to it, it was impossible to abandon but was bureaucratised; everyone signed up to it but nobody really practised it.

From the Brezhnev years there is evidence that positive rewards were generally failing to act as incentives to higher effort. Of nearly 3,000 Brezhnev-era emigrants surveyed by Gregory (1987), three-quarters reported the impression that average productivity was falling (although it was not); of these, three-fifths listed inadequate incentives as the most important reason for productivity problems, and also that their own real living standards had been in decline over the past five years.[28] From the same sample Millar and Clayton found 41 per cent very or somewhat dissatisfied with their former overall standard of living in the Soviet Union; this figure could be compared with 19 per cent reporting similar life dissatisfaction in the annual *Eurobarometer Survey*, which covered roughly 1,000 people per country per year in western Europe, between 1975 and 1991.[29] Of course the Soviet survey was of emigrants who might be expected to show relative dissatisfaction. However, more recent research by Blanchflower and Freeman confirms that achieved levels of job satisfaction and general happiness in central and eastern Europe remained low by west European standards.[30]

The Soviet economy after Brezhnev: a hopeless case?

When Gorbachev came to power in 1985 he claimed to have inherited a 'pre-crisis situation'. Hindsight proved him right. However the evidence available to him at the time was thoroughly ambiguous, raising the possibility that he was right by accident.

Had an overwhelming economic disaster become inevitable by the early 1980s? Almost certainly not. At the end of the Brezhnev years most Soviet citizens lived adequately and there was relatively full or overfull employment. The economy was still just growing, although its sluggishness was certainly alarming. Government spending and revenues were under control;

there was a small, well-concealed budget deficit which tended to be monetised in the absence of an organised market in government securities, but the inflationary impact remained small.[31] A domestic monetary overhang had been growing slowly over many years; a substantial proportion of personal saving deposits, now amounting to roughly two-thirds of the value of annual retail purchases, represented forced saving. Apart from this the Soviet Union's internal and external debts were not a worry. There was a growing gap between state prices and the higher unregulated prices in the collective-farm markets where private produce was legally traded, and this gap was steadily raising the profitability of illegally transferring resources from the state to the private sector. The spread of official corruption and a shadow economy were sources of acute concern.[32]

Alarm bells were already ringing in the Kremlin when Brezhnev died, and Andropov and Chernenko both took determined steps to correct the crisis by traditional means, intensifying centralisation, work discipline and the policing of state property.[33] Moreover, the statistical evidence (Tables 3.3–3.5) shows that these measures paid off: in 1983 the growth slowdown stopped. Thus the situation that Andropov and Chernenko passed on to Gorbachev was no worse than that which they had inherited from Brezhnev, and in some respects better. The Soviet economy was not already a lost cause; indeed Gorbachev's intention in declaring an emergency was not to predict a crisis but to galvanise the efforts necessary to avert one, and he clearly believed that this was still possible. That a crisis resulted, and proved terminal, does not mean that collapse was already inevitable.

Further reading

W. Easterly and S. Fischer, 'The Soviet Economic Decline', *World Bank Economic Review*, 9, 1995, pp. 341–71.

G. Grossman, 'The "Second Economy" of the USSR', *Problems of Communism*, 26, 1977, pp. 25–40.

V. Kontorovich, 'Lessons of the 1965 Soviet Economic Reform', *Soviet Studies*, 40/2, 1988, pp. 308–16.

J. R. Millar, 'The Little Deal: Brezhnev's Contribution to Acquisitive Socialism', *Slavic Review*, 44/4, 1985, pp. 694–706.

A. Nove, *An Economic History of the USSR, 1917–1991*, 4th edn (Harmondsworth: Penguin, 1992).

G. E. Schroeder, 'Reflections on Economic Sovietology', *Post-Soviet Affairs*, 11/3, 1995, pp. 197–234.

Notes

1. For a summary of the most recent charges, see A. C. Becker, 'Intelligence Fiasco or Reasoned Accounting? CIA Estimates of Soviet GNP', *Post-Soviet Affairs*, 10/4, 1994, pp. 291–5.

   Traditional critics of the Bergson methodology included Peter Wiles, whose many writings on the subject were synthesised in: P. J. D. Wiles, 'The Theory of

International Comparisons of Economic Volume', in J. Degras and A. Nove (eds), *Soviet Planning: Essays in Honour of Naum Jasny* (Oxford: Blackwell, 1964), pp. 77–115.

For a more recent critical survey by an independent Russian scholar see G. I. Khanin, *Sovetskii ekonomicheskii rost: analiz zapadnykh otsenok* (Novosibirsk: Ekor, 1993).

2. On investment and machinery, see P. Hanson, 'The CIA, the TsSU and the Real Growth of Soviet Investment', *Soviet Studies*, 36/4, 1984, pp. 571–81.

   On consumption, see I. Birman, *Personal Consumption in the USSR and the USA* (Basingstoke: Macmillan, 1989).

   For a more general framing of such criticisms, see A. Åslund, 'How Small is Soviet National Income?', in H. S. Rowen and C. Wolf (eds) (1990), *The Impoverished Superpower: Perestroika and the Soviet Military Burden* (San Francisco: ICS Press, 1990), pp. 13–62.
3. M. Harrison, 'Soviet Economic Growth Since 1928: The Alternative Statistics of G. I. Khanin', *Europe–Asia Studies*, 45/1, 1993, pp. 141–67.
4. Becker 1994, (p. 319) comments that critics of the CIA's size comparisons were bemused by the even-handed presentation of a higher figure based on dollar weights and a lower rouble-weighted figure for each year; they attacked the dollar-weighted ratios for understating 'the difficulty the Soviet Union would have had producing the American mix in that year', although the latter was best measured by rouble–weighted figures. A. C. Becker, 'Intelligence Fiasco or Reasoned Accounting?: CIA Estimates of Soviet GNP', *Post-Soviet Affairs*, 10/4, 1994, pp. 291–329.
5. CIA figures were criticised for being excessively aggregated (taking *too much* into account), as well as for not trying to measure every aspect of welfare (taking *too little* into account). See A. C. Becker, 'Intelligence Fiasco or Reasoned Accounting?: CIA Estimates of Soviet GNP', *Post-Soviet Affairs*, 10/4, 1994, pp. 317–18.
6. V. Kontorovich, 'Inflation in the Soviet Investment and Capital Stock Series', *Soviet Studies*, 41/2, 1989, pp. 18–30; S. Rosefielde, 'The Illusion of Material Progress: The Analytics of Soviet Economic Growth Revisited', *Soviet Studies*, 43/4, 1991, pp. 597–611; S. Rosefielde and R. W. Pfouts, 'Neoclassical Norms and the Valuation of National Income in the Soviet Union and its Post-Communist Successor States', *Journal of Comparative Economics*, 21/3, 1995, pp. 375–89.
7. For examples see A. C. Becker, 'Intelligence Fiasco or Reasoned Accounting?: CIA Estimates of Soviet GNP', *Post-Soviet Affairs*, 10/4, 1994, p. 321.
8. G. I. Khanin, *Sovetskii ekonomicheskii rost: analiz zapadnykh otsenok* (Novosibirsk: Ekor, 1993), p. 147.
9. For recent work on these lines see R. C. Allen, 'The Standard of Living in the Soviet Union, 1928–1940', *Journal of Economic History*, 58/4, 1998, pp. 1063–89; M. Harrison, 'Soviet Industrial Production, 1928 to 1950: Real Growth and Hidden Inflation', *Journal of Comparative Economics*, 28/1, 2000, pp. 134–55.
10. A. C. Becker, 'Intelligence Fiasco or Reasoned Accounting?: CIA Estimates of Soviet GNP', *Post-Soviet Affairs*, 10/4, 1994, pp. 291–329; R. W. Davies, M. Harrison and S. G. Wheatcroft (eds), *The Economic Transformation of the Soviet Union, 1913–1945* (Cambridge University Press, 1994); G. E. Schroeder, 'Reflections on Economic Sovietology', *Post-Soviet Affairs*, 11/3, 1995, pp. 197–234; A. Bergson, 'Neoclassical Norms and the Valuation of National Income in the Soviet Union: Comment', *Journal of Comparative Economics*, 21/3, 1995, pp. 390–3; V. M. Kudrov, 'Sovetskii ekonomicheskii rost: ofitsial'nye dannye i al'ternativnye otsenki', *Voprosy ekonomiki*, 1995, No. 10, pp. 1–13; M. Harrison, *Accounting for War: Soviet*

Production, Employment, and the Defence Burden, 1940–1945 (Cambridge University Press, 1996); V. M. Kudrov, *Sovetskaia ekonomika v retrospektive: Opyt pereosmysleniya* (Moscow, 1997); A. Maddison, 'Measuring the Performance of a Communist Command Economy: An Assessment of the CIA Estimates for the USSR', *Review of Income and Wealth*, 44/3, 1998, pp. 307–23; V. Kontorovich, 'Economists, Soviet Growth Slowdown, and the Collapse' (Haverford College, Department of Economics, 1999).

11. A. Maddison, *Monitoring the World Economy, 1820–1992* (Paris: OECD, 1995), p. 174, and 'Measuring the Performance of a Communist Command Economy: An Assessment of the CIA Estimates for the USSR', *Review of Income and Wealth*, 44/3, 1998.
12. M. Harrison, 'Trends in Soviet Labour Productivity, 1928–1985: War, Postwar Recovery, and Slowdown', *European Review of Economic History*, 2/2, 1998, pp. 171–200.
13. For a survey and further references see M. Harrison, *Accounting for War: Soviet Production, Employment, and the Defence Burden, 1940–1945* (Cambridge University Press, 1996).
14. R. Levine and D. Renelt, 'A Sensitivity Analysis of Cross-Country Growth Regressions', *American Economic Review*, 82, 1982, pp. 942–63.
15. P. Krugman, 'The Myth of Asia's Miracle', *Foreign Affairs*, 73, 1994, pp. 62–78. The diminishing-returns story is a familiar one, summarised by A. Bergson, *Planning and Performance in Socialist Economies: The USSR and Eastern Europe* (Boston, Mass.: Unwin Hyman, 1989), esp. Chapters 6 and 7. Other stories may also be told, such as that of a constraint on the elasticity of substitution of capital for labour; see most recently W. Easterly and S. Fischer, 'The Soviet Economic Decline', *World Bank Economic Review*, 9, 1995, p. 346.

    The latter fits the evidence of the growth series well superficially, but has implausible implications for the rate of return on Soviet capital before Brezhnev. For an attempted reconciliation with interesting data on a slowdown in Soviet inventiveness in the mid-1970s, see V. Kontorovich, 'Soviet Growth Slowdown: Econometric vs Direct Evidence', *American Economic Association Papers and Proceedings*, 1986, pp. 181–5.

    The whole field of Soviet growth economics was surveyed authoritatively before the collapse of the Soviet System by G. Ofer, 'Soviet Economic Growth: 1928–1985', *Journal of Economic Literature*, 25/4, 1987, pp. 1767–1833.
16. W. Easterly and S. Fischer, 'The Soviet Economic Decline', *World Bank Economic Review*, 9, 1995, p. 346.
17. For discussion of the relationship between decay under Brezhnev and collapse under Gorbachev see A. Dallin, 'Causes of the Collapse of the USSR', *Post-Soviet Affairs*, 8/4, 1992, pp. 279–302; M. Ellman and V. Kontorovich (eds), *The Disintegration of the Soviet Economic System* (London: Routledge, 1992); V. G. Treml and M. Ellman, 'Debate: Why Did the Soviet Economic System Collapse?', *Radio Free Europe/Radio Liberty Research Report*, 2/23, 1993, pp. 53–8; A. C. Becker, 'Intelligence Fiasco or Reasoned Accounting?: CIA Estimates of Soviet GNP', *Post-Soviet Affairs*, 10/4, 1994, pp. 291–329; G. E. Schroeder, 'Reflections on Economic Sovietology', *Post-Soviet Affairs*, 11/3, 1995, pp. 197–234; A. Brown, *The Gorbachev Factor* (Oxford University Press, 1997); M. Ellman and V. Kontorovich, *The Destruction of the Soviet Economic System: An Insider's History* (London: M. E. Sharpe, 1998); M. Harrison, 'Coercion, Compliance, and the Collapse of the Soviet Command Economy', University of Warwick, Department of Economics (2001).

18. R. W. Davies, *Soviet Economic Development from Lenin to Khrushchev* (Cambridge University Press, 1998).
19. F. Jánossy, *The End of the Economic Miracle: Appearance and Reality in Economic Development* (White Plains, M. E. Sharpe, 1971).

    For recent empirical investigation of this idea see: N. F. R. Crafts and T. C. Mills, 'Europe's Golden Age: An Econometric Investigation of Changing Trend Rates of Growth', in B. van Ark and N. F. R. Crafts (eds), *Quantitative Aspects of Europe's Postwar Growth* (Cambridge University Press, 1996), pp. 415–31; M. Harrison, 'Trends in Soviet Labour Productivity, 1928–1985: War, Postwar Recovery, and Slowdown', *European Review of Economic History*, 2/2, 1998, pp. 171–200; D. F. Good and T. Ma, 'The Economic Growth of Central and Eastern Europe: a Comparative Perspective, 1870–1989', *European Review of Economic History*, 3/2, 1999, pp. 103–38.
20. On Soviet institutional obstacles to innovation see: J. S. Berliner, *The Innovation Decision in Soviet Industry* (Cambridge, Mass.: MIT Press, 1976); J. Dearden, B. W. Ickes and L. Samuelson, 'To Innovate or Not To Innovate: Incentives and Innovation in Hierarchies', *American Economic Review*, 80/5, 1990, pp. 1105–24.
21. This account of the reform process relies heavily on: G. E. Schroeder, 'The 1966–67 Soviet Industrial Price Reform: A Study in Complications', *Soviet Studies*, 20/4, 1969, pp. 462–77; G. E. Schroeder, 'The 'Reform' of the Supply System in Soviet Industry', *Soviet Studies*, 24/1, 1972, pp. 97–119; G. E. Schroeder, 'The Soviet Economy on a Treadmill of "Reforms"', in US Congress, Joint Economic Committee, *Soviet Economy in a Time of Change*, Vol. 1 (Washington, DC, 1979), pp. 312–40; G. E. Schroeder, 'Soviet Economic 'Reform' Decrees: More Steps on the Treadmill', in US Congress, Joint Economic Committee, *Soviet Economy in the 1980s: Problems and Prospects*, Part 1 (Washington, DC, 1982), pp. 65–88; J. S. Berliner, 'Planning and Management', in A. Bergson and H. S. Levine (eds), *The Soviet Economy: Towards the Year 2000* (London, Allen and Unwin 1983), pp. 350–9; P. Hanson, 'Success Indicators Revisited: The July 1979 Decree on Planning and Management', *Soviet Studies*, 35/1, 1983, pp. 1–13; M. Bornstein, 'Improving the Soviet Economic Mechanism', *Soviet Studies*, 37/1, 1985, pp. 1–30; W. Brus, '1950 to 1953: The Peak of Stalinism', '1953 to 1956: The "Thaw" and the "New Course"', '1956 to 1965: In Search of Balanced Development', and '1966 to 1975: Normalization and Conflict', in M. Kaser (ed.), *The Economic History of Eastern Europe 1919–75*, Vol. 3, *Institutional Change within a Planned Economy* (Oxford University Press, 1986), pp. 3–249; J. Kornai, 'The Hungarian Reform Process: Visions, Hopes, and Reality', *Journal of Economic Literature*, 24/4, 1986, pp. 1687–1737; V. Kontorovich, 'Soviet Growth Slowdown: Econometric vs Direct Evidence', *American Economic Association Papers and Proceedings*, 1986, pp. 181–5; V. Kontorovich, 'Discipline and Growth in the Soviet Economy', *Problems of Communism*, 34/6, 1986, pp. 18–31.

    For an excellent summary see also P. R. Gregory and R. C. Stuart, *Soviet Economic Structure and Performance* (London: HarperCollins, 1990).
22. G. E. Schroeder, 'The Slowdown in Soviet Industry, 1976–1982', *Soviet Economy*, 1/1, 1985, pp. 42–74.
23. V. S. Dunham, *In Stalin's Time: Middle-Class Values in Soviet Fiction* (Cambridge University Press, 1976).
24. J. R. Millar, 'The Little Deal: Brezhnev's Contribution to Acquisitive Socialism', *Slavic Review*, 44/4, 1985, pp. 694–706.
25. G. Grossman, 'The 'Second Economy' of the USSR', *Problems of Communism*, 26, 1977, pp. 25–40; G. Grossman, 'Subverted Sovereignty: Historic Role of the

Soviet Underground', in S. S. Cohen, A. Schwartz and J. Zysman (eds), *The Tunnel at the End of the Light: Privatization, Business Networks, and Economic Transformation in Russia* (Berkeley, Cal.: University of California, International and Area Studies Research Series, No. 100, 1998), pp. 24–50.

26. P. Rutland, 'The Shchekino Method and the Struggle to Raise Labour Productivity in Soviet Industry', *Soviet Studies*, 36/3, 1984, pp. 345–65.
27. H. Knorr, 'Shchekino: Another Look', *Soviet Studies*, 38/2, 1986, pp. 141–69; R. Arnot, *Controlling Soviet Labour* (Basingstoke: Macmillan, 1988).
28. P. R. Gregory, 'Productivity, Slack, and Time Theft in the Soviet Economy', in J. R. Millar (ed.), *Politics, Work, and Daily Life in the USSR: A Survey of Former Soviet Citizens* (Cambridge University Press, 1987), pp. 241–75.
29. J. R. Millar and E. Clayton, 'Quality of Life: Subjective Measures of Relative Satisfaction', in J. R. Millar (ed.), *Politics, Work, and Daily Life in the USSR: A Survey of Former Soviet Citizens* (Cambridge University Press, 1987), pp. 31–60; R. Di Tella, R. J. MacCulloch and A. J. Oswald, 'The Macroeconomics of Happiness', University of Oxford, Institute of Economics and Statistics and London School of Economics, Centre for Economic Performance, *The Labour Market Consequences of Technical and Structural Change*, Discussion Paper Series, No. 19, 1997.
30. D. G. Blanchflower and R. B. Freeman, 'The Attitudinal Legacy of Communist Labor Relations', *Industrial and Labor Relations Review*, 50/3, 1997, pp. 438–59.
31. G. Ofer, 'Budget Deficit, Market Disequilibrium, and Soviet Economic Reforms', *Soviet Economy*, 5/2, 1989, p. 124.

    Until 1986 the financial deficit of the Soviet state budget was running at approximately 4 per cent of total budget spending according to the CIA, *USSR: Sharply Higher Budget Deficits Threaten Perestroyka* (SOV-88–10043) (Washington, DC, 1988).

    For a relatively sombre view of Brezhnev-era public finance, see I. Birman, 'The Financial Crisis in the USSR', *Soviet Studies*, 32/1, 1980, pp. 84–105.
32. Figures on personal saving, and on relative prices in official and collective-farm retail trade are to be found in Tsentral'noe Statisticheskoe Upravlenie SSSR (TsSU), *Narodnoe khoziaistvo SSSR v 1985 godu* (Moscow, 1986); Goskomstat SSSR, *Narodnoe khoziaistvo SSSR v 1988 godu* (Moscow, 1989).

    For new research on the monetary overhang, see B.-Y. Kim, 'Income, Savings, and Monetary Overhang of Soviet Households', *Journal of Comparative Economics*, 27/4, 1999, pp. 644–68.
33. V. Kontorovich, 'Discipline and Growth in the Soviet Economy', *Problems of Communism*, 34/6, 1986, pp. 18–31.

4
The National Question in the Soviet Union under Leonid Brezhnev: Policy and Response

Ben Fowkes

Observers have often remarked upon the contrast between the stability of the Soviet Union in the Brezhnev era of the 1960s and 1970s and the bubbling cauldron of discontent that confronted Gorbachev in the late 1980s. This is nowhere more apparent than in the case of the 'national question', a shorthand expression which is meant to cover relations between the Russians and the non-Russians, between the non-Russians and the central authorities, and finally between different groups of non-Russians.

The explosion of national discontents that took place after 1985 has been amply documented and analysed in many places. This chapter, in contrast, aims to give some explanation for the stability of the Brezhnev era in the national sphere. The short form of my explanation runs as follows: Leonid Brezhnev pursued a policy of corporatist compromise, ethnic equalisation, and masterly inactivity, and this was sufficient to allow the Soviet way of dealing with the national question a few more years of calm, unthreatened existence.

The concept of *corporatism* was first applied to the Soviet Union in 1980 by two US political scientists, Valerie Bunce and John M. Echols, III. They defined corporatism as a 'structure in which major fractional interest groups are incorporated into the policy process by the state and its leaders'.[1] Three traits of corporatism are apparent in the Brezhnev era: the avoidance of conflict between the state and the elites and its replacement by compromise; the role of major interest groups in policy-making; and the stability of elites. Corporatism, then, implied striking a compromise between the centre and the periphery of the empire. This involved handing over a considerable amount of power to local elites. In Russian areas these would be of Russian nationality, but in non-Russian areas (at least in the union republics) it was a deliberate policy to appoint members of the dominant local titular nationality to the top job – the job of First Secretary of the Central Committee of the Communist Party. Khrushchev had occasionally appointed outsiders (that is, those not of the titular nationality), but this changed when Brezhnev came into office. 'First Secretaries', wrote Dmitri Volkogonov in his recent comparative study of Soviet leaders since Lenin, 'acquired virtually unlimited power' under Brezhnev. Something like a 'feudal system' came into existence, he added.[2]

Brezhnev's policy of 'trust in cadres', though not exactly new, was far more consistent than Khrushchev's. His predecessor was constantly reorganising the administrative system, intervening at times to give more power to the regions, at other times to restore centralisation. Under Brezhnev, in contrast, there were far fewer direct interventions by the centre into the affairs of the union republics. The most high profile of these interventions were the removal of Shelest as party boss in Ukraine in 1972, and the three personnel changes in Transcaucasia at about the same time, which were intended to facilitate the centre's struggle against corruption and localism. In Azerbaijan Gaidar Aliev was transferred from the KGB to the Party leadership in 1969; three years later Eduard Shevardnadze made a similar move in Georgia; and the Caucasian anti-corruption triumvirate was completed in 1974 by the appointment of Karen Demirchian to head the Armenian Party.[3] Apart from this the period is one of extreme stability – during Brezhnev's eighteen years in office the average length of tenure for a First Secretary of a union republic was eleven years – and a move towards the permanent occupation of Party positions in each republic by a local. In Ukraine, for instance, 88 per cent of the Politburo members and 92 per cent of the provincial Party secretaries were ethnic Ukrainians in 1979, although a strictly ethnic criterion would have entitled them to rather less than this, as their population share stood at 74 per cent. The replacement of Petro Shelest by Volodymyr Shcherbytskii in 1972, which from one angle certainly represented a reassertion of control by the centre, since it led to the abandonment of Shelest's policy of promoting the Ukrainian language and Ukrainian culture and the arrest of hundreds of dissidents previously tolerated by the Ukrainian authorities,[4] did not put a stop to the process of indigenisation. In fact it continued unabated. The proportion of ethnically Ukrainian provincial secretaries rose from 84 per cent in 1966 to 96 per cent in 1980, while the proportion of Russians fell from 16 per cent to 4 per cent. Only after Brezhnev's death in 1982 did the Ukrainian proportion fall, to 83 per cent in 1985.[5] A Ukrainian political elite was constituted which was likely to consider Ukraine's (or at least its own) interests first and Moscow's interests second. The situation was similar in the rest of the country. In twelve out of the fourteen non-Russian union republics the titular nationality was over-represented in the republican elite in proportion to its population. The two exceptions were Belorussia (21 per cent less) and Moldavia (62 per cent less).[6]

Under the Soviet system one political party was permanently in power, and without the countervailing effect of personnel changes imposed from the centre this permanence tended to result in corruption. Despite the appointment of Eduard Shevardnadze, Gaidar Aliev and Karen Demirchian in Georgia, Azerbaijan and Armenia respectively, with a mandate to sweep away these practices, Brezhnev's general attitude was to let sleeping dogs lie. He regarded the 'shadow economy' as a perfectly normal phenomenon. Burlatsky reports his reply to a call for an improvement in the wages of the low-paid: 'You don't know life. Nobody lives just on his wages. I remember how we used to load wagons – three sacks inside and one on the side'.[7] In any case, corruption was so deeply entrenched in Georgia that Shevardnadze's purges made little difference. 'The great mass of the party was involved', says Suny, in a system which 'in fact benefited a large part of the population'.[8]

The second aspect of Brezhnev's policy towards his far-flung empire was *ethnic equalisation*, in other words the attempt to iron out the inequalities between the dominant nations of the union republics, in the economic, political and cultural spheres. Viktor Zaslavsky has summed this up succinctly as the 'consistent pursuit of proportional ethnic representation in education, administration, and government'.[9] Soviet statistics on educational progress and changes in social structure during the Brezhnev period bear out this claim in part. Western Sovietologists began in the 1970s to test the degree of equalisation between regions by using a statistical measure, the Coefficient of Variation (CV), which is derived by dividing the standard deviation of a set of data by the mean of the data and multiplying by 100. The lower the CV the more equal the distribution. A CV above 50 per cent would represent a considerable degree of inequality. There are other, more sophisticated, measures, but this is the simplest one to calculate.

For secondary and higher education the CV for the group of fifteen titular nations of the union republics declined very impressively, from 22 per cent in 1959 to 14 per cent in 1970, 9 per cent in 1979 and 7 per cent in 1985.[10] A similar picture is presented by the figures for specialists with higher education (the CV fell from 40 per cent in 1960 to 36 per cent in 1970 and 32 per cent in 1980). The coefficient for urbanisation changed more gradually: it fell from 42 per cent in 1959 to 39 per cent in 1970 and 36 per cent in 1979.[11] As a direct consequence, since an increase in city dwellers was seen by the authorities as a reason to recruit more Party members of the given nationality,[12] membership of the Communist Party also became more evenly distributed (the CV went down from 42 per cent in 1961 to 33 per cent in 1982).[13] Contemplating all this evidence, Jones and Grupp concluded in 1984: 'Statistical measures point unambiguously to convergence' between the nations.[14] Whether statistics were an adequate measure for this alleged phenomenon will be explored in more detail below.

It was much more difficult to overcome inherited differences in the economic sphere. Certain favoured republics possessed immense geographical and resource advantages. Brezhnev's initial policy was to try to address this problem. The early Brezhnev years saw considerable equalisation through inter-republican transfers of wealth and balanced investment. There were some indications in the first half of the 1970s that the objective of equalisation in regional development was being attained (though it must be added that a 'union republic' cannot always be used as a surrogate for a 'nation'). The proportion of industrial workers in the less proletarian union republics of Central Asia and Transcaucasia increased, so that the CV in this case fell from 46 per cent in 1965 to 44 per cent in 1974 (curiously, after 1974 the Soviet authorities stopped issuing statistics on this point).[15] Bond, Belkindas and Treyvish give a fall in CVs for the union republics' income per head from 27 per cent in 1970 to 25 per cent in 1980.[16] Alastair McAuley commented at the end of the Brezhnev era that 'inequality in personal consumption (between regions) is only two-thirds of that found in the USA'.[17] In the middle of his period of office (1972) Brezhnev declared that 'the problem of equalising the levels of economic development of the national republics has been in the main solved'.[18] This statement was evidently an exaggeration. The Soviet authorities tried to reduce inter-republican income differentials but they failed to do so. In any case, equalisation of investment was pursued only in the provision of social benefits. The CVs for education and health investment were low over the whole period, varying from 17 per cent to 11 per cent and thus indicating that this form of government spending was spread relatively evenly. The CVs for economic investment overall were far higher, ranging between 41 per cent and 39 per cent.[19] This was because the main criteria for investment were economic growth and military security. Investment tended to go towards already developed areas of the country. The economic difficulties and the apparent stagnation of the late 1970s strengthened this tendency. As Ericson has commented, 'overall economic growth' had 'a much greater priority than regional development, never mind equalisation'.[20] This was not conducive to lessening the differences between the regions. Hence while disparities between the union republics in national income per head fell slightly during the 1970s, they increased again in the 1980s.

The CV increased to a level of 31 per cent in 1988.[21] To make these figures more meaningful one should recall that one group of republics was in each case at the top of the scale – the three Baltic republics and Russia – and one at the bottom – the Central Asian republics. Tajikistan always brought up the rear in these statistics, Estonia and Latvia alternately occupied first or second place. There was always a hierarchy of union republics. Owing to the extremely high birth rate in Central Asia, a low proportion of the population participated in economic activity, and this made it impossible for the Central Asians to catch up.[22] The relative positions of the union republics were not affected either by the progress made in economic equalisation during the 1970s or the steep rise in inequality during the 1980s. Moreover, the gap in key health indicators (such as the level of infant mortality and the average expectation of life) increased substantially during the 1970s. Within a general context of increases in infant mortality and a reduction in life expectancy, the CV for the union republics rose, for infant mortality, from 38 per cent to 48 per cent, and for life expectancy from 21 per cent to 35 per cent.[23]

It should be added that equalisation in the economic sphere was not always regarded as an unmixed blessing. Many of the complaints brought forward under Gorbachev related to the results of policies of industrial investment that local elites had lobbied for under Brezhnev. Thus the Lithuanian party leadership successfully pressed for an oil refinery to be built at Mažikiai, but the resultant pollution was a target for attacks twenty years later; while further east the extensive industrial development of the Brezhnev era was later denounced for its destructive impact on the traditional way of life of the Peoples of the North who lived scattered over Siberia.[24]

The Soviet Union was made up of a number of separate nations, the continued existence of which was anchored in Leninist nationality policy[25] and in successive constitutions. In Stalin's later years this fact was rather lost from sight, with greater stress being laid on the Russian character of the USSR. On the face of it, Brezhnev's approach to the national question looked like a return to the original position of the 1920s. Khrushchev, his immediate predecessor, had favoured the idea of the 'merging' (*sliyanie*) of the nations, a process which it was hoped would eventually produce a 'Soviet nation' and thus solve the national problem once and for all. Brezhnev continued to view this objective as desirable, but postponed it to the remote future. References to 'merging' disappear from Soviet publications after 1964. The new buzz words of the Brezhnev era were the 'blossoming' (*rastsvet*) of nations and their 'rapprochement' (*sblizhenie*). At the time many western observers, as well as local non-Russian nationalist dissidents, regarded this claim, that the cultures of the separate nations were being encouraged to 'blossom', as sheer nonsense. The Soviet Union, they said, was a state where Russification was continuing and indeed getting worse. The title of one article published in 1984 by Radio Liberty was typical of this view: 'Non-Russian languages: only for poetry and memoirs?'[26]

Actually the situation was more complex than that. Both views contain an element of truth. One needs to distinguish between different regions of the country. There was little evidence of a systematic policy of Russification in the vast majority of the union republics. The exceptions to this statement are located in the Western part of the country – Ukraine, Belorussia and Moldavia. Let us look first at the press. If we compare the circulation of newspapers with the proportion of the population of Ukraine, Belorussia and Moldavia who belonged to the titular nation, we find that not only were fewer copies of newspapers issued in Ukrainian, Belorussian and Moldavian than strict proportionality would require (a gap of respectively 3 per cent, 41 per cent and 16 per cent in 1964) but also the situation worsened under Brezhnev (by 1982 the gap between the requirements of language equality and the actual circulation of newspapers was 9 per cent in Ukraine, and 47 per cent in Belorussia, though it must be remembered that many who identified themselves as members of the titular nationality had Russian as their first language).[27] The same was true of book circulation, in all three cases.

The most glaring example is Belorussia, where by 1982 17 per cent of books came out in Belorussian, 81 per cent in Russian, when the Belorussians constituted 79 per cent of the republic, 66 per cent of them native Belorussian speakers.[28]

In all other union republics the position was reversed – members of the titular nationality had either the appropriate proportion of newspapers and books, or, in the case of Latvia, Lithuania, Estonia, Georgia and all Central Asian republics except Kazakhstan, they had more than strict proportionality would have entitled them to. This was true throughout the Brezhnev period.

The picture for education was similar. While the majority of union republics provided instruction in their own titular language to an appropriate proportion of pupils, more attention was paid to the national language in Transcaucasia and the Central Asian republics (except Kazakhstan) and less in Ukraine and Belorussia. In Ukraine the percentage of children taught in Ukrainian fell from 72 per cent in 1955 to 60 per cent in 1974 and 51 per cent in 1985. A similar decline was registered in Belorussia. Solchanyk calculated that between 1965 and 1972 the proportion taught in Ukrainian fell by 6 per cent while the Ukrainian population increased by 9 per cent. Moreover, teaching in the universities of Ukraine was conducted almost exclusively in the Russian language.[29] In Belorussian schools the decline of the local language was even steeper – Belorussian language teaching fell by 14 per cent while the Belorussian population increased by 11 per cent.[30] The Belorussian language had already in practice disappeared from urban education by 1972: 98 per cent of children were taught in Russian in the cities, and in Minsk 100 per cent. This situation was mirrored in the Russian Republic (RSFSR). Minority-language education seems to have almost vanished there; the proportion of the RSFSR's school children taught in Russian rose from 94 per cent in 1955–6 to 96 per cent in 1974–5.[31]

The demographic by-products of the growth of the Soviet economy (particularly the increase in the size of ethnic Russian minorities in many union republics) have sometimes been analysed in terms of deliberate Russification. There is no evidence that this intention was foremost in the planning of the Soviet authorities, but the development of industry under Stalin did bring with it an immigration of Russian (and to a lesser degree Ukrainian and Belorussian) workers into other union republics, which naturally gave them a more Russian aspect. But the Brezhnev era saw the phenomenon in reverse. Russians began to move out of Central Asia and Transcaucasia. Even in the West, where there was a continued Russian influx, this was not sufficient to balance the progressive indigenization of the cities (except in Estonia and Latvia).[32] This was true even in the RSFSR. In every republic (ASSR) of the RSFSR except Karelia and Komi the percentage of Russians in the cities declined over the period 1959–89, with very substantial declines of over 25 per cent taking place in the cities of the North Caucasus.[33]

The impact of the policies and demographic trends outlined above on the ethnic groups within the Soviet Union were mixed. There was substantial linguistic Russification during the Brezhnev period in the RSFSR and in the two Slav union republics of Ukraine and Belorussia. Within the RSFSR the nations most likely to adopt Russian as their language shared the common characteristics of being Orthodox in religious background, located in the centre of the country rather than the periphery and being either non-titular or titular on a lower level than the union republics. The Mordvins, the Udmurts, the Komi and the Karelians came into this category. In 1989 each of them contained a minority over 25 per cent strong which had adopted Russian as its first language. The Caucasians, in contrast, stuck to their own languages very stubbornly, especially if they were of Muslim cultural background. The proportion of Caucasians who spoke Russian as their first language never exceeded 5 per cent, and hovered around 1 per cent in the case of the Chechens, the Ingush and most of the Dagestan national groups. It should be added that these peoples were less urbanised than the others – the Chechens were 75 per cent rural in 1979, the Dagestanis (Avars and Lezgins) 69 per cent rural. Only the Tuvins (78 per cent rural) and Yakuts (75 per cent rural) had lower rates of urbanisation in 1979.[34] (There was a positive correlation between urbanisation and the adoption of Russian as first language.)[35] For the two Slav republics the proportions of Russian speakers were high but not devastatingly so: 12 per cent of ethnic Ukrainians described themselves as Russian speakers, 20 per cent of Belorussians, in 1989. These figures all relate to the language spoken by people who had not left their homeland; when people moved outside their own republic they had a far greater tendency to adopt Russian as their first language.

A change of language did not necessarily mean a change in national identity, especially as Point Five on the internal passport questionnaire made it extremely difficult to alter one's official nationality after the age of sixteen. There is no definite information available on the extent to which Soviet citizens converted themselves into Russians, although an impression can be gleaned from the population statistics by demographic methods.[36] There are also scattered sociological surveys on the choice of nationality made by the children of mixed marriages in a number of republics. There was a tendency for the children of marriages between Russians and members of non-titular nations in the union republics to take on Russian nationality. There were sufficient of these marriages to counterbalance the opposite trend, for the children of Russians who married members of titular nations to take on the titular nationality. Here are the estimates arrived at by Soviet demographers: ethnic reidentification contributed 17 per cent of the Russian population increase between 1959 and 1970 and 16 per cent between 1970 and 1979. This fell to 11 per cent between 1979 and 1989.[37] This may seem a large proportion, but the phenomenon was limited to the western part of the Soviet Union. It rarely happened in Central Asia or the Caucasus, except among Slav immigrants. The Muslims of Central Asia and the Caucasus very rarely intermarried with Russians. If they did, the children of the union took on the local nationality rather than the Russian one.[38] In Uzbekistan, for instance, 76 per cent of children from mixed Uzbek–Russian families surveyed in 1989 chose the national identity of the father, who was an Uzbek in 85 per cent of the cases[39]

Did the mixture of policies characteristic of the Brezhnev era (Russification in some areas, indigenisation in others, equalisation wherever possible) strengthen the hold of the Soviet regime over the nations and nationalities of the periphery, or was this merely a result of efficient repressive measures? The relationship between the dissidence of minorities and the broader Soviet society has not so far been examined in sufficient detail by historians to allow a definitive answer, but an analysis has been made of the reports of the KGB of the USSR, covering mass movements where it needed to intervene during these years. If we look at the period 1961–81 we find that the proportion of large-scale disturbances which took place in the non-Russian areas is in line with their share of the population (10 cases out of 20). However, only two of these 10 cases was the actual content of the disturbance reported as 'national'. In 1964 there was a riot between Chechens and Laks in the city of Khasaviurt, in the Dagestan ASSR, arising out of the alleged rape of a Lak girl by a Chechen; 700 people took part, and there were nine deaths. In 1981, in Ordzhonikidze, North Ossetia, the funeral of a murdered taxi driver sparked off 'nationalist hysteria'. This time 4,500 people took part and there were twenty-six deaths.[40] The paucity of this evidence tends to suggest that inter-ethnic conflict was not in the forefront during the Brezhnev era. It was only after Gorbachev took over in 1985 that the KGB reports started to be dominated by ethnic issues.

These points apply to the question of spontaneous popular movements. If we now turn to more deliberate and thought-out actions, in other words dissidence, we also find that ethnic issues are of subordinate importance. A total of three people were condemned between 1956 and 1975 under Article 74 ('breach of national and ethnic harmony'), while 236 were condemned under Article 142 ('breach of the law of the separation of church and state') and 129 under Article 227 ('engaging in religious rituals'). So the religious dissenters were far more significant numerically. Even in the Baltic lands, where resentment against Russian incomers was considerable, 'protest activities were at first sporadic and focused on specific issues (religious rights, creative freedom and freedom of information)'.[41] It must of course be admitted that many national dissidents would have fallen under the catch-all Article 70 ('Anti-Soviet agitation'), which accounts for a further 233 people convicted,[42] and that often religious activities might themselves be manifestations of ethnic or nationalist discontent. Moreover, there was a tendency to play down the significance of dissent by convicting dissidents for ordinary non-political crimes. We have the testimony of Viktor Fedorchuk, head of the KGB in Ukraine from 1970 to 1982, on this point: 'In the course of 1980 we did a great job: we rendered harmless forty Ukrainian nationalists. In order to avoid needless international frictions, the majority of them were sentenced for ordinary criminal offences.'[43]

Actions inspired by a spirit of national dissent certainly took place. They ranged all the way from the quiet publication of *samizdat* periodicals to events of extreme violence such as the suicide by fire of Romas Kalanta in 1972 in Lithuania, which set off a massive two-day demonstration in the capital, or the explosion of 1977 in the Moscow metro allegedly set off by Armenian nationalists, an act for which three people were executed two years later. The issue is rather whether these events and actions were frequent or infrequent, significant or unrepresentative. In the Baltic lands, according to Shtromas, 'activist dissent, although firmly entrenched . . . was practised only by a tiny minority of the . . . people'[44] and in general during this period, as Anatoly Khazanov pointed out, 'organized nationalist oppositions were composed of small and usually short-lived underground groups' which were unable to make much impact on the situation.[45] Finally, A. J. Motyl has tentatively calculated that 'no more than 22 per cent, or 2,200' out of the total number of 10,000 dissidents claimed to have been active in the 1970s were nationalists.[46]

Nevertheless, within the Soviet apparatus the actions of dissidents were taken very seriously. Recent Russian studies have shown that party leaders and police officials were very worried. They also provide a certain amount of documentary evidence. For example, in 1972 a functionary in the Communist Party of the Soviet Union Central Committee (CPSU CC), L. Onikov, wrote to Brezhnev about the growth of anti-Russian feeling in the union republics, and he warned the leadership that 'it is impossible to exclude the possibility that non-Russian nationalists will join together on an anti-Russian basis and this will call forth a reaction from the Russian population'. Brezhnev apparently rejected this warning and rebuked its author for calling the internationalism of the Soviet people into question on the fiftieth anniversary of the founding of the USSR.[47] Professor Pikhoia refers to 'an uninterrupted stream of communications from the KGB about conflicts in the national sphere'.[48] He instances letters from Kazakh intellectuals complaining that Russians have many top positions in the government and the party; leaflets distributed in Western Ukraine calling on the people to 'take arms and start smashing the red dragon'; appeals from Uzbeks in Tashkent calling on their fellow-countrymen to 'fight for the liberation of their nation and drive the Russian invaders from their land'. It is hard to know how representative these cases are. The head of the KGB, Yuri Andropov, used them in 1968 to argue in favour of 'taking measures to nip in the bud attempts to set up nationalist organisations' in various named parts of the country. His list was quite long. It included Ukraine, the Baltic lands, Azerbaijan, Moldavia, Armenia and four largely Muslim ASSRs.[49] It is clear that the agencies of repression were well aware of the threats to Soviet power; but it is equally clear that they were able to deal with them under Brezhnev without having to resort to armed force. The Ukrainian dissident movement, which was relatively active in the early Brezhnev years, was decimated by repression after 1977, and by 1981 it had been driven underground, according to Ludmila Alekseyeva.[50] The Baltic movement, which drew in many members of the literary elite of all three nations in the 1970s, was reduced to the protests of a few brave individuals after 1980.[51]

A final point in relation to national movements under Brezhnev relates to claims and appeals made to the centre, in other words not dissidence or revolt but pressure from within the elites. There were, at least according to the available documents, only two areas where this took place: Abkhazia, which was part of Georgia, and the Nagorno-Karabakh Autonomous Region, which was part of Azerbaijan. In Abkhazia a Committee of 20 was set up in 1967 by local demonstrators. The KGB reported that this committee consisted of 'respectable people including a professor of Abkhaz literature and the Assistant Town Prosecutor'. They went to Moscow to hand in a memorandum 'full of slanderous attacks on the Georgians' which enumerated a list of national demands very familiar to observers of the situation twenty years later: they called for the renaming of towns, the compulsory teaching of the Abkhaz language in the schools, the appointment of ethnic Abkhaz to positions of authority locally, the use of Abkhazian as the language of court proceedings and the separation of the Abkhaz ASSR from Georgia and its promotion to the status of union republic (SSR) as the sole way of achieving these demands. The Soviet leaders gave the Abkhazians short shrift. The demands were rejected and condemned as nationalistic.[52] Ten years later the Abkhazians returned to the charge. Once again there were demonstrations, letters of protest and telegrams demanding secession. Ivan Kapitonov, a Central Committee secretary, was sent from Moscow to investigate. He rejected the idea of secession from Georgia and had the local party leader dismissed for his failure to suppress the protests, although he also recommended some cultural and economic concessions, which were subsequently implemented.[53] Brezhnev's unvarying policy, unlike that of his predecessors Khrushchev and Stalin, was to keep the existing administrative structure of the Soviet Union. This meant retaining the union republics in their inherited shape. Thus repeated demands by Armenians during the 1960s for the unification of the Nagorno-Karabakh Autonomous Region with Armenia (sometimes even the ASSR of Nakhichevan as well, although by then there were few Armenians there) were also ruled out of court despite being supported in 1969 (it is said) by the Armenian party leadership[54] and in 1977 by Sero Khanzatian, a prominent Armenian writer and member of the Communist Party.[55]

I have so far presented a picture of the Brezhnev era as one of compromise with centrifugal forces at the periphery of the USSR, and of attempts to implement policies of indigenisation and equalisation. There are however three reservations to be made. First, the Brezhnev period needs to be divided into two parts. The later section, after roughly 1977, saw more stress being laid on the promotion of the Russian-language, less on the non-Russian languages. In October 1978 a secret decree was issued by the Central Committee introducing Russian-language teaching into the first three classes of all elementary schools and making it the sole language for teaching in the armed forces.[56] Moreover, hints began to be dropped that indigenisation might have gone too far. In 1981 Brezhnev urged republican communist parties to consider the needs of non-titular immigrants to non-Russian republics, who would obviously be largely Russian in nationality.[57] In 1982 Boris Ponomarev, a Candidate Member of the Politburo and an influential ideologist, asserted that every republic should 'serve the interests of all the working people whether or not they belong to the titular nationality'.[58] In the economic sphere, too, the later Brezhnev period brought a change of emphasis. There was a greater concern with efficiency and the fight against inherited geographical and resource advantages possessed by more favoured republics was abandoned. The year 1975 marks a turning-point after which the criteria of efficiency and appropriateness of investment were predominantly applied at the expense of equalisation.[59]

The second major reservation is that equalisation did not affect the practical Russian monopoly over the central institutions of the Soviet Union, as opposed to the periphery. The proportion of Russians in the Politburo of the CPSU rose from 62 per cent in 1961 to 73 per cent in 1983. This was at a time when the Russians made up slightly more than half of the population (53 per cent). In the Central Committee similarly the Russian proportion rose from 55 per cent in 1966 to 68 per cent in 1981. The balance was made up predominantly of Ukrainians and Belorussians.[60] Given the considerable degree of centralisation, this meant that for instance economic policies carried out by central ministries, which could be influenced only with difficulty by local party organs, were in effect Russian policies. With 61 per cent of industrial production under central control, 33 per cent under mixed central and local control and only 6 per cent under exclusive union republic control (1987 figures) the following Lithuanian outburst in 1988 is not surprising: 'How much longer will some Ivan Ivanovich in some Office 421 in Moscow be able to decide whether or not to build a toilet in some Lithuanian town the name of which he can't even pronounce?'[61] This was not just a question of toilets. The nuclear power station at Ignalina in Lithuania, which came on stream in 1984, was built on Moscow's orders without any consultation with the Lithuanian party leadership.[62]

The third reservation to be made relates to local variations in policy. Policy varied between the different union republics, and between the fifteen union republics (SSRs) and the thirty-eight lower-status bodies with less power and less autonomy (ASSRs, Autonomous Oblasts and Autonomous Okrugs).

In the union republics of Central Asia the tendency was to appoint a member of the indigenous elite as First Secretary of the Party, and to staff the Politburo with locals, but to put a Russian or Ukrainian in the background in the important positions of Second Secretary of the Party, and head of the local KGB. This policy even extended down to the regional level. In Uzbekistan in 1980 all but one of the regional Party Second Secretaries were Russians.[63] The same situation prevailed in Moldavia and Belorussia. Elsewhere, and particularly in the Baltic lands and Transcaucasia, a policy of indigenisation at the top level was consistently carried out. The head of the KGB in Ukraine, Lithuania, Georgia and Estonia was always a member of the titular nation during the Brezhnev era. In Armenia (83 per cent of the time) Azerbaijan (22 per cent) and Latvia (11 per cent) the local elite had at least a foothold in that institution.[64] It almost went without saying that the First Secretary of the Party would be a local (under Brezhnev, unlike Khrushchev, the proportion of locals was 100 per cent). Second Secretaries, with their watching brief as representatives of the centre, were more likely to be Russian, but not always. In Armenia and Estonia a representative of the titular nation sat in the Second Secretary's office for much of the Brezhnev period (for 50 per cent and 33 per cent of the time, respectively).[65]

There are several reasons for these differences of approach. One is the perceived danger of a rise of Islam in the Muslim Central Asian republics: it was felt that they could not entirely be trusted, so a Russian was needed in the background. The most dangerous, and most unassimilated, group of Muslims, the Chechens, present the most extreme case: the First Secretaries of their ASSR (shared with the Ingush) were always ethnic Russians brought from outside the area.[66] Differing historical traditions also played a part in determining which nation was allowed to rule locally. The three Transcaucasian republics had always had a more independent position within the USSR since the very beginning. The special character of the Baltic lands derived from their very recent integration into the country. In both cases the fact that the countries in question had enjoyed a period of independence after their separation from the Russian Empire also played a part, as did their possession of a highly developed national culture, which meant for instance that no attempt was ever made to Russianise their literature by adopting the Cyrillic alphabet (Azerbaijan is an exception here).

If we look now at the situation in the ASSRs, almost all of them situated in the Russian Republic (RSFSR), we find that it was far less favourable to the titular nation (or 'nationality') than it was in the union republics because the late Brezhnev era shift towards promotion of the Russian language was carried out with much greater determination in the RSFSR. First, the Russians dominated the press and publishing in all cases. There was little change in this respect during the Brezhnev era. In 1964 98 per cent of the newspapers and 99 per cent of the books were published in Russian; the figures for 1982 are 99 per cent and 95 per cent, respectively. This meant that the Russians had 16 per cent more newspapers and 16 per cent more books than they were 'entitled' to in 1964 and 16 per cent and 12 per cent more, respectively, in 1982 – a decline, not an increase, in the proportion of Russian-language books (as opposed to newspapers) over the Brezhnev period was thus registered, but within the general context of vast over-representation of the Russian language.[67] Specific information on individual ASSRs is hard to find, but in Dagestan in 1975, for instance, 61 per cent of the journal circulation was in Russian, although the Russians made up only 12 per cent of the population,[68] while in the Mordvinian ASSR the proportion of books published in Mordvinian languages was a mere 25 per cent in 1965 (35 per cent of the people were Mordvinians).[69]

In education, too, the Russian language was promoted. There was a continuous decline in the use of non-Russian languages as medium of instruction in schools, and a corresponding increase in Russian, from 1956 onwards, in both the sixteen ASSRs and the sixteen Autonomous Regions and Districts, which were stilll lower in status than the ASSRs. By 1980 Russian was used from the first grade onwards in all Autonomous Regions and Districts and from the third grade in ASSRs. This contrasts with the situation in the SSRs where all ten grades were taught in the titular nation's language.[70] Rasma Karklins, who interviewed a sample of Jewish and German immigrants on their arrival in the United States between 1979 and 1982, concluded that while the titular nations were treated better than the Russians in the union republics (except Belorussia and Latvia where equal treatment was the rule), the Russians were treated better in the autonomous republics of the RSFSR.[71] Generally speaking, it was the smaller and less influential nations, overwhelmingly located in the RSFSR, which suffered from the post-1977 turn towards Russian. There was a clear hierarchy: the titular nations of union republics did best; titular nations of autonomous republics did less well; nations without any formal institutional place in the Soviet structure did worst. The point was demonstrated statistically for education by Anderson and Silver in 1984.[72]

In this context, Georgia was at the top of the pile. The demonstrations that took place there in 1978 are significant less because of the centre's attempt to abolish the position of Georgian as state language (the rationale behind this was probably the desire to achieve consistency across the USSR rather than to downgrade the position of the Georgian language, since the republics of Transcaucasia were unique in having their languages anchored in the constitution as state languages) than because of the rapid abandonment of the attempt as a result. This reversal of policy was no doubt due in part to a fear that Georgia would become ungovernable, but much more to the strong lobby in Moscow in favour of keeping the status quo. On 23 December 1977 four leading members of the Central Committee of the CPSU, B.N. Ponomarev, I.V. Kapitonov, M.V. Zimianin and no less a personage than K.U. Chernenko advised that 'it cannot be ruled out that the removal from the constitution of the Transcaucasian republics of the articles on the state language which have been part of their constitution since the earliest days of Soviet power may call forth a negative reaction on the part of definite sections of the population and also in the international arena. The leaders of the said republics have also recommended caution on this issue in discussions with the Central Committee.'[73] Accordingly, Article 75 of the Georgian constitution of 1978 guaranteed that 'the state language of the Georgian SSR is the Georgian language'.[74] Similar provisions were inserted into the Armenian and Azerbaijani constitutions. The failure of the centre to impose its will in Transcaucasia only confirms the point that the SSRs had priority over ASSRs. It was the Abkhazians, who had an ASSR within Georgia, who would have benefited from the abandonment of Georgian as state language, rather than the small number of local Russians.

Brezhnev's national policy seemed at the time to be both rational and successful. But it contained the seeds of its own destruction. There were essentially four reasons for this. First, the policy was implemented in a very hesitant and ambiguous way. Second, Brezhnev pursued contradictory objectives alongside it, such as the attempt to strengthen the unity of the Soviet Union and to promote economic efficiency. Third, local national elites tended to take advantage of the compromise offered by Moscow by rooting themselves so deeply in their environment that they could evade or at least modify the instructions of the centre.[75] They also occasionally had an impact on central policy-making. Examples of this are the Ukrainian pressure on the centre to develop the Donbas coal region[76] and the Central Asian republics' proposal to divert the course of the river Irtysh in Siberia from north to south to provide water for irrigation, in a desperate attempt to halt the desiccation of the Aral Sea.[77] Only after Gorbachev came to power was it possible for the Russian ecological movement to force the cancellation of this project, thus incidentally alienating most of the Central Asian leaders.

The danger inherent in Brezhnev's policy of trust in cadres, concluded Mark Beissinger after examining political recruitment in Ukraine, was that 'native elites in the republics ... might eventually lose touch with the centre and come to identify their personal interests with those of their regions'.[78] In Central Asia Muslim cadres, already well entrenched, tended to appoint members of their own national group, or even their own clan, to positions of authority. They were gradually pushing the Russians out. The proportion of Russians fell everywhere in Central Asia during the 1970s, partly because of their lower birth rate but also because they were moving back to the Russian heartland. The decline was generally of the order of 10 per cent to 15 per cent over the decade.[79] Soviet demographers of the Brezhnev era were well aware of this, and some of them pressed for a differential use of family allowances 'to encourage an evening out of the indices of birth rate and natural popular growth in the various regions of the country',[80] or, in plain language, to raise the Slav birth rate in Central Asia, which had fallen far behind that of the local Muslim population. The child allowance programme of the 1970s was not in fact targeted in this way, and had the result of encouraging more births in areas where natality was already high. The Party Programme of February 1981 called for the 'phased introduction of birth incentives in different regions', but this was never put into effect.[81]

Moreover, life was getting less pleasant for Russians in Central Asia. Rasma Karklins found that 67 per cent of the German emigrants from the Soviet Union she questioned thought the Kazakhs were becoming more powerful in their own republic, and only 2 per cent thought the Russians were.[82] Her informants told her that 'for the Russians it is getting difficult to live in Kazakhstan . . . formerly it was the Russians who were putting the screw on the Kazakhs, now it is the other way round'.[83] Thus a creeping decolonisation was taking place in the eastern part of the USSR. This process was pushed forward by the non-Russian elites, despite the fact that as the local representatives of Soviet power they were also obliged to expand the use of the Russian language as the international language of communication.[84]

The fourth reason for Brezhnev's ultimate failure in the national sphere was the pervasive hidden opposition to Soviet nationality policy practised by almost every non-Russian national group, involving refusal to speak Russian in public places, refusal to admit a knowledge of Russian to Soviet census-takers,[85] disapproval of mixed marriages, attempts to preserve traditional cultures and gestures of sympathy towards foreign nations that were the objects of Soviet hostility (particularly Israel in 1967 and Czechoslovakia in 1968). Many national grievances were quietly nursed until in the late 1980s they were able to come to the surface. Resentment about the influx of Russians into the cities of Estonia has been identified as the leading factor in the growth of the movement for Estonian independence.[86] The same can surely be said of Latvia. Ultimately the Brezhnev compromise was very fragile.[87]

But was Brezhnev responsible for the disintegration of the USSR? Did he 'prepare the way for the demise of the Soviet state'.[88] This claim, which is often made, is as absurd as the claim that the Emperor Francis Joseph was responsible for the fall of the Austrian Empire in 1918. In both cases the measures they were asked to undertake by radical nationalists would have led to piecemeal disintegration in any case. Moreover, at the relevant time (for Austria the 1900s, for the Soviet Union the 1970s) the radical nationalists did not represent more than a tiny minority of their fellow citizens. Other, less extreme, demands could have been granted without destroying the state – such as the removal of Nagorny Karabakh from Azerbaijan or of Abkhazia from Georgia – but thereby weak friends would be gained and powerful enemies created. Where Brezhnev was faced with insistent demands that could be granted, especially when these were backed up strongly from abroad, he made concessions. These were not damaging. On the contrary, if the emigration of 249,000 Jews and 64,000 Germans between 1971 and

1980 weakened the USSR culturally and economically it strengthened it politically by removing many potential dissidents. It also removed rivals to the Russians in the Soviet job market. The number of Jewish postgraduates in the USSR fell by 40 per cent between 1970 and 1975.[89]

I would prefer to say instead that, by taking the line of least resistance in most cases, Brezhnev preserved the USSR in aspic for a couple of decades. This is not to deny the existence of underlying forces of integration into the world economy and the information revolution, which worked against the continued existence of the Soviet Union in the long run.[90] But these forces lay dormant under Brezhnev and his immediate successors. When Gorbachev came to power he brought all the problems back to the surface, with policies pursued less from a sense that they were inescapable than from a deep psychological need, felt by himself and by his closest colleagues, to bring movement into a situation everyone recognised as stagnant. The decision to allow open discussion then made an authoritarian solution impracticable. The way was now open for the nations to claim complete independence. But this was a situation Brezhnev had neither created nor foreseen.

Further reading

L. Hajda and M. Beissinger, *The Nationalities Factor in Soviet Politics and Society* (Boulder, Col: Westview Press, 1990).

H. R. Huttenbach (ed.), *Soviet Nationality Policies. Ruling Ethnic Groups in the USSR* (London: Mansell, 1990).

E. Jones and F. W. Grupp, *Modernization, Value Change and Fertility in the Soviet Union* (Cambridge University Press, 1987).

R. J. Kaiser, *The Geography of Nationalism in Russia and the USSR* (Princeton University Press, 1994).

R. Karklins, *Ethnic Relations in the USSR. The Perspective from Below* (London: Allen & Unwin, 1985).

I. T. Kreindler (ed.), *Sociolinguistic Perspectives on Soviet National Languages* (Berlin: Mouton de Gruyter, 1985).

G. Simon, *Nationalism and Policy Toward the Nationalities in the Soviet Union* (Boulder, Col.: Westview Press, 1991).

Notes

1. V. Bunce and J. Echolls, III, 'Soviet Politics in the Brezhnev Era: Pluralism or Corporatism', in D. R. Kelley (ed.), *Soviet Politics in the Brezhnev Era* (New York: Praeger, 1980), pp. 3, 7, 8.
2. D. Volkogonov, *The Rise and Fall of the Soviet Empire. Political Leaders from Lenin to Gorbachev* (London: HarperCollins, 1998), p. 278.
3. The replacement of Babysh Ovezov by Mukhamednazar Gapurov in 1969 in Turkmenistan may be a fifth case, but it was not followed by any change in local policy or personnel.
4. O. Subtelny, *Ukraine. A History*, 2nd edn (Toronto: University of Toronto Press, 1994), pp. 512–517.

5. M. Beissinger, 'Ethnicity, the Personnel Weapon, and Neo-Imperial Integration: Ukrainian and RSFSR Provincial Party Officials Compared', *Studies in Comparative Communism*, 21/1, Spring 1988, pp. 71–85 (here p. 75).
6. The other figures are Armenia+9 per cent, Azerbaijan+50 per cent, Estonia +23 per cent, Georgia+47 per cent, Kazakhstan+100 per cent, Kyrgyzstan +79 per cent, Latvia+51 per cent, Lithuania+8 per cent, Tajikistan+41 per cent, Turkmenistan+5 per cent, Ukraine+15 per cent and Uzbekistan+41 per cent. They are calculated from G. Hodnett and V. Ogareff, *Leaders of the Soviet Republics 1955 to 1972. A Guide to Posts and Occupants* (Canberra: Australian National University, 1973). See E. Jones and F. W. Grupp, 'Modernisation and Ethnic Equalisation in the USSR', *Soviet Studies*, 36/2 (April 1984), p. 175.
7. F. Burlatskii, *Russkie Gosudari Epokha Reformatsii* (Moscow: Firma 'Shark', 1996), p. 155.
8. R. G. Suny, *The Making of the Georgian Nation*, 2nd edn (Bloomington, Ind.: Indiana University Press, 1994) p. 308.
9. V. Zaslavsky, 'Ethnic Groups Divided: Social Stratification and Nationality Policy in the Soviet Union', in P. Potichnyj (ed.), *Soviet Union. Party and Society* (Cambridge University Press, 1988), pp. 208–28 (here p. 226).
10. Calculated from the figures in Table 5.8. 'Higher and Secondary Education Complete or Incomplete per 1,000 population over the age of 10', in R. J. Kaiser, *The Geography of Nationalism in Russia and the USSR* (Princeton University Press, 1994), p. 227.
11. Calculated from Table 5.2 'Urban Population of the USSR, by Nation and Home Republic, 1959–1989 (percent)', in R. J. Kaiser, *The Geography of Nationalism in Russia and the USSR* (Princeton University Press, 1994), p. 203.
12. This point was demonstrated by Mary McAuley, in 'Party Recruitment and the Nationalities in the USSR', *British Journal of Political Science*, 10, 1980, pp. 461–87 (here p. 486).
13. Tables 5.13 (Specialists with a Higher or Specialized Secondary Education by nation per 1,000) and 5.12 (Class Composition of Soviet Nations, 1959–1979), in R. J. Kaiser, *The Geography of Nationalism in Russia and the USSR* (Princeton University Press, 1994), pp. 237 and 239, and Table A 15, in G. Simon, *Nationalism and Policy Toward the Nationalities in the Soviet Union* (Boulder, Col.: Westview Press, 1991), p. 415. The calculations are based on the figures for the fifteen union republic titular nations. I have not included lower-level titular and non-titular nations as the statistical evidence for them is patchy (no statistics were issued for their class composition, for instance). The inclusion of the other nations in the calculation would lead to much higher CVs (for example, in the case of specialists with higher education the CVs for 1960, 1970, and 1980 would be, respectively, 86 per cent, 67 per cent and 46 per cent).
14. E. Jones and F. W. Grupp, 'Modernisation and Ethnic Equalisation in the USSR', *Soviet Studies*, 36/2, April 1984, p. 178.
15. CVs have been calculated from issues of *Narodnoe Khozyaistvo SSSR* for 1965 and 1974. It should be added that figures for nations rather than union republics would give a different picture, but they are available only for industrial and agricultural workers taken together, which is not helpful.
16. Calculated from A. R. Bond, M. V. Belkindas and A. I. Treyvish, 'Economic Development Trends. Part I', *Soviet Geography*, 31, 1990, pp. 705–31 (here Table 4, p. 713).
17. A. McAuley, *Economic Welfare in the Soviet Union. Poverty, Living Standards and Inequality* (London: Allen & Unwin, 1979), pp. 114–15.

18. Quoted by V. Holubychny, in 'Spatial Efficiency in the Soviet Economy', in V. N. Bandera and Z. L. Melnik (eds), *The Soviet Economy in Regional Perspective* (New York: Praeger, 1973), pp. 1–43 (here p. 25).
19. J. Bielasiak, 'Policy Choices and Regional Equality', *American Political Science Review*, 74, 1980, pp. 394–405 (here Table 1, p. 398).
20. R. E. Ericson, 'Soviet Economic Structure and the National Question', in A. J. Motyl (ed.), *The Post-Soviet Nations. Perspectives on the Demise of the USSR* (New York: Columbia University Press, 1992), p. 249.
21. A. R. Bond, M. V. Belkindas and A. I. Treyvish, 'Economic Development Trends in the USSR, 1970–1988. Part I', *Soviet Geography*, 31, 1990, p. 713.
22. A. McAuley, *Economic Welfare in the Soviet Union. Poverty, Living Standards and Inequality* (London: Allen & Unwin, 1979), p. 172.
23. Calculated from data in *Narkhoz SSSR v 1987 g.* (Moscow, 1988), p. 357. After 1980 divergence was followed by convergence, though not sufficiently to restore the pre-1970 position. See also A. R. Bond, M. V. Belkindas and A. I. Treyvish, 'Economic Development Trends. Part II', *Soviet Geography*, 32, 1991, pp. 23–7.
24. G. Fondahl, 'Native Peoples and Newcomers', in I. Bremmer and R. Taras (eds), *Nations and Politics in the Soviet Successor States* (Cambridge University Press, 1993), p. 487.
25. In Central Asia the Bolsheviks did more than just recognise the existence of nations; they created many of them.
26. R. Solchanyk, 'The Non-Russian Languages in the USSR–Only for Poetry and Memoirs?', *Radio Liberty Research Bulletin*, 376/84, 3 October 1984.
27. In Moldavia the gap narrowed, to 6 per cent.
28. The figures for book circulation for Ukraine are 72 per cent in 1964 and 65 per cent in 1982, for Moldavia 51 per cent and 48 per cent.
29. Y. Bilinsky, 'The Communist Party of Ukraine after 1966', in P. Potychnyj (ed.), *Ukraine in the 1970s* (Cambridge University Press, 1988), p. 246.
30. R. Solchanyk, 'Russian Language and Soviet Politics', *Soviet Studies*, 34, 1982, pp. 23–42 (here p. 26). Solchanyk's figure for the number of Belorussians in Belorussia recorded in the 1970 census is wrong and has been corrected.
31. G. Simon, *Nationalism and Policy Toward the Nationalities in the Soviet Union* (Boulder, Col.: Westview Press, 1991), pp. 327–8, quoting K. Ts. Khanazarov, *Reshenie natsional'no-yazykovoi problemy v SSSR*, 2nd edn (Moscow, 1982), pp. 173–8 and Yu. V. Bromlei (ed.), *Sovremennye etnicheskie protsessy v SSSR* (Moscow, 1977), pp. 268–70.
32. The following table for Russian minorities in the Western union republics makes this clear:

Republic	*Total % 1959*	*Total % 1989*	*% change*	*Urban % 1959*	*Urban % 1989*	*% change*
Ukraine	17	22	+5	30	29	−1
Belorussia	8	13	+5	19	18	−1
Moldavia	10	13	+3	30	24	−6
Lithuania	9	9	0	17	12	−5
Latvia	27	34	+7	34	41	+7
Estonia	20	30	+10	31	39	+8

33. R. J. Kaiser, *The Geography of Nationalism in Russia and the USSR* (Princeton University Press, 1994), Table 5.6, pp. 220–1.
34. Figures taken from R. J. Kaiser, *The Geography of Nationalism in Russia and the USSR* (Princeton University Press, 1994), Table 5.2, p. 203.
35. This correlation is clear from Table 6.6, pp. 276–8 of R. J. Kaiser, *The Geography of Nationalism in Russia and the USSR* (Princeton University Press, 1994).
36. See for example the comparison between expected and actual cohort survival ratios by B. A. Anderson, 'Some Factors in Ethnic Reidentification in the Russian Republic', in J. R. Azrael (ed.), *Soviet Nationality Policies and Practices* (New York: Praeger, 1979), pp. 309–33.
37. The first two figures are from S. Bruk and V. Kabuzan, 'Dinamika chislennosti i rasseleniya Russkikh posle velikoi oktyabr'skoi sotsialisticheskoi revolyutsii', *Sovetskaya Etnografiya* 5, 1982, pp. 3–21 (here p. 13); the third is from A. Topilin, 'Vliyanie migratsii na etnonatsional'nuiu striukturu', *Sotsiologicheskie Issledovaniya*, 7, 1992, pp. 31–42 (here p. 32).
38. J. F. Besemeres, *Socialist Population Politics. The Political Implications of Demographic Trends in the USSR and Eastern Europe* (White Plains: M. E. Sharpe, 1980), pp. 81–2. See also R. J. Kaiser, *The Geography of Nationalism in Russia and the USSR* (Princeton University Press, 1994), pp. 317–20.
39. A. Volkov, 'Etnicheski smeshannye sem'i v SSSR: dinamika i sostav (natsional'nost' detei v etnicheski smeshennykh sem'yakh)', *Vestnik Statistiki*, 8, 1989 pp. 2–24.
40. *Istochnik*, 6, 1995, 'O massovykh besporyadkakh s 1957 goda. Zapiska V. Chebrikova 1988 g.', pp. 147, 151.
41. A. Shtromas, 'The Baltic States as Soviet Republics Tensions and Contradictions', in G. Smith, *The Baltic States. The National Self-Determination of Estonia, Latvia, and Lithuania* (Basingstoke: Macmillan, 1994), p. 103.
42. A. V. Savelev, 'Politicheskoe svoeobrazie dissidentskogo dvizheniya v SSSR 1950-kh–1970-kh godov', *Voprosy Istorii*, 4, 1998, pp. 109–21 (here p. 110).
43. As quoted in Y. Bilinsky, 'Shcherbytskyi, Ukraine and Kremlin Politics', *Problems of Communism*, 32/4, July–August 1983, p. 10.
44. A. Shtromas, 'The Baltic States as Soviet Republics: Tensions and Contradictions', in G. Smith, *The Baltic States. The National Self-Determination of Estonia, Latvia, and Lithuania* (Basingstoke: Macmillan, 1994), p. 108.
45. A. Khazanov, *After the USSR. Ethnicity, Nationalism and Politics in the Commonwealth of Independent States* (Madison, W.S.: University of Wisconsin Press, 1995), p. 19.
46. A. J. Motyl, *Sovietology, Rationality, Nationality. Coming to Grips with Nationalism in the USSR* (New York: Columbia University Press, 1990), p. 156.
47. N. Mesheriakova (ed.), *Natsional'naya Politika Rossii: Istoriya i Sovremennost'* (Moscow, 1997), p. 343, quoting TsKhSD, fond 5, opis' 68, d. 453, l. 48.
48. R. G. Pikhoya, *Sovetskii Soyuz: Istoriya Vlasti, 1945–1991* (Moscow: Rossiiskaya Akademiya, 1998), p. 292.
49. R. G. Pikhoya, *Sovetskii Soyuz: Istoriya Vlasti, 1945–1991* (Moscow: Rossiiskaya Akademiya, 1998), p. 294.
50. L. Alexeyeva, *Soviet Dissent* (Middletown, Conn: Wesleyan University Press, 1985), p. 55.
51. R. Misiunas and R. Taagepera, *The Baltic States: The Years of Dependence 1940–1990*, revised edn (London: Hurst & Co., 1993), p. 300.
52. TsKhSD, Moscow, fond 5, opis' 59, dok. 967-b, S. Barmikov to V. E. Semichastny, (KGB Moscow, 22 April 1967).

53. R. G. Suny, 'Transcaucasia: Cultural Cohesion and Ethnic Revival in a Multinational Society', in L. Hajda and M. Beissinger, *The Nationalities Factor in Soviet Politics and Society* (Boulder, Col: Westview Press, 1990), pp. 244–5. The centre's response to the Abkhaz demands of 1978 is examined in detail in D. Slider, 'Crisis and Response in Soviet Nationality Policy: The Case of Abkhazia', *Central Asian Survey* 4/4, 1985, pp. 51–68.
54. G. J. Libaridian, 'Armenia and the Armenians: A Divided Homeland and a Dispersed Nation', in W. O. McCagg, Jr. and B. D. Silver (eds), *Soviet Asian Ethnic Frontiers* (New York: Pergamon Press, 1979), pp. 27–60 (here p. 41).
55. R. G. Suny, *Looking Toward Ararat. Armenia in Modern History* (Bloomington, Ind.: Indiana University Press, 1993), p. 195.
56. TsKhSD, f. 89, p. 23, d. 13, CC CPSU Decree of 29 August 1978.
57. *XXVI s''ezd kommunisticheskoi partii Sovetskogo Soyuza. Stenograficheskii otchet* (Moscow, 1988), Part I, pp. 70–5.
58. G. Smith, 'Nationalities Policy from Lenin to Gorbachev', in G. Smith (ed.), *The Nationalities Question in the Soviet Union* (London: Longman, 1990), p. 11.
59. G. van Selm and E. Dölle, 'Soviet Inter-Republican Capital Transfers and the Republican Level of Development 1966–1991', *Most-Most*, 1, 1993, pp. 133–49.
60. G. Simon, *Nationalism and Policy Toward the Nationalities in the Soviet Union*, (Boulder, Col.: Westview Press, 1991), Table A16, p. 418.
61. J. P. Kubilius, rector of Vilnius State University, speaking in 1988 at the *Pravda* round table on the national question, *Current Digest of the Soviet Press*, 40/45, p. 6.
62. R. Misiunas and R. Taagepera, *The Baltic States: The Years of Dependence 1940– 1990*, revised edn (London: Hurst & Co., 1993), p. 290.
63. M. Rywkin, *Moscow's Muslim Challenge. Soviet Central Asia* (London: C. Hurst & Co., 1982), Table 22, p. 126. Rywkin does admittedly add (p. 127) that these people increasingly identified themselves with 'their non-Russian colleagues and local interests'. (p. 127).
64. A. Knight, *The KGB. Police and Politics in the Soviet Union* (London: Unwin Hyman, 1988), p. 168.
65. J. H. Miller, 'Cadres Policy in Nationality Areas: Recruitment of CPSU First and Second Secretaries in Non-Russian Republics of the USSR', *Soviet Studies*, 29/1, January 1977, p. 10.
66. J. H. Miller, 'Cadres Policy in Nationality Areas: Recruitment of CPSU First and Second Secretaries in Non-Russian Republics of the USSR', *Soviet Studies*, 29/1, January 1977, p. 15, gives a list of Russian First Secretaries of the Chechen–Ingush ASSR, showing that they were experienced administrators brought from outside the region.
67. Calculated for 1964 from the 1959 census figures and *Pechat' SSSR v 1964 Godu. Statisticheskie Materialy* (Moscow: Izdatel'stvo 'Kniga', 1965), pp. 83–292 and for 1982 from 1979 census figures and *Pechat' SSSR v 1982 Godu. Statisticheskii Sbornik* (Moscow: Izdatel'stvo 'Finansy i Statistika', 1983), pp. 138–141, 237–8.
68. C. Lemercier-Quelquejay, 'Problèmes ethno-linguistiques et politique soviétique au Daghestan', *Cahiers du monde russe et soviétique*, 31/2–3, 1990, pp. 363–4.
69. I. T. Kreindler, 'The Mordvinian Languages: A Survival Saga', in I. T. Kreindler (ed.), *Sociolinguistic Perspectives on Soviet National Languages* (Berlin: Mouton de Gruyter, 1985), p. 252.
70. B. A. Anderson and B. D. Silver, 'Some Factors in the Linguistic and Ethnic Russification of Soviet Nationalities: Is Everyone Becoming Russian?', Table 4,

p. 105, in L. Hajda and M. Beissinger, *The Nationalities Factor in Soviet Politics and Society* (Boulder, Col.: Westview Press, 1990).
71. R. Karklins, 'Nationality Policy and Ethnic Relations in the USSR', in J. R. Millar, (ed.), *Politics, Work and Daily Life in the USSR: A Survey* (New York: Columbia University Press, 1987), pp. 301–31.
72. B. A. Anderson and B. D. Silver, 'Equality, Efficiency and Politics in Soviet Bilingual Policy 1934–80', *American Political Science Review*, 78, December 1984, Table 5, p. 1073.
73. R. G. Pikhoya, *Sovetskii Soyuz: Istoriya Vlasti, 1945–1991* (Moscow: Rossiiskaya Akademiya, 1998), p. 369.
74. G. Hewitt, 'Georgia: A Noble Past, A Secure Future', in I. T. Kreindler, *Sociolinguistic Perspectives on Soviet National Languages* (Berlin: Mouton or Gruyter, 1985), p. 175.
75. S. Bialer, *Stalin's Successors. Leadership, Stability and Change in the Soviet Union* (Cambridge University Press, 1980), p. 219. He adds, however, that intra-republican competition for funds placed the centre in the position of arbiter and thus lessened the force of local resistance.
76. G. E. Schroeder, 'Nationalities and the Soviet Economy', in L. Hajda and M. Beissinger, *The Nationalities Factor in Soviet Politics and Society* (Boulder, Col.: Westview Press, 1990), p. 61, and for the politics of regional budgetary allocations in general, see D. Bahry, *Outside Moscow: Power Politics and Budgetary Policy in the Soviet Republics* (New York: Columbia University Press, 1987).
77. P. P. Micklin, 'The Fate of *Sibaral*: Soviet Water Politics in the Gorbachev Era', *Central Asian Survey*, 6/2, 1987, pp. 67–88.
78. M. Beissinger, 'Ethnicity, the Personnel Weapon and Neo-Imperial Integration: Ukrainian and RSFSR Provincial Party Officials Compared', in R. Denber (ed.), *The Soviet Nationality Reader. The Disintegration in Context* (Boulder, Col.: Westview Press, 1992), pp. 211–25 (here p. 223).
79. The precise figures for the decline in Russian residents between 1970 and 1979 are: Azerbaijan 21 per cent, Kazakhstan 4 per cent, Kirgizia 11 per cent, Tajikistan 13 per cent, Turkmenistan 13 per cent and Uzbekistan 14 per cent.
80. G. I. Litvinova, 'Demograficheskoe zakonodatel'stvo sotsialisticheskikh stran', *Sovetskoe Gosudarstvo i Pravo*, 7 September 1980, pp. 67–75.
81. E. Jones and F. W. Grupp, *Modernization, Value Change and Fertility in the Soviet Union* (Cambridge University Press, 1987), p. 280.
82. M. Rywkin, *Moscow's Muslim Challenge* (London: C. Hurst and Co., 1982), p. 116.
83. R. Karklins, *Ethnic Relations in the USSR. The Perspective from Below* (London: Allen & Unwin, 1985), pp. 80–4.
84. A. Khazanov, *After the USSR. Ethnicity, Nationalism and Politics in the Commonwealth of Independent States* (Madison, Wis.: University of Wisconsin Press, 1995), pp. 59–60.
85. R. Misiunas and R. Taagepera, *The Baltic States: The Years of Dependence 1940–1990*, revised edn (London: Hurst & Co., 1993), p. 213. The fall in the proportion of Estonians who could speak Russian as a second language from 29 per cent in 1970 to 24 per cent in 1979 can hardly be explained otherwise.
86. A. Kirkh *et al.*, 'Etnosotsial'naya differentsiatsiya gorodskogo naseleniya Estonii', *Sotsiologicheskie Issledovaniya*, 3, 1988, pp. 30–5.
87. D. Zisserman-Brodsky, 'Sources of Ethnic Politics in the Soviet Polity: the Pre-Perestroika Dimension', *Nationalities Papers*, 1994, 22(2), pp. 337–45.
88. R. Brubaker, *Nationalism Reframed* (Cambridge University Press, 1996), p. 23.

89. Z. Irwin, 'Soviet–Jewish Emigration Policy', in H. R. Huttenbach (ed.), *Soviet Nationality Policies. Ruling Ethnic Groups in the USSR* (London: Mansell, 1990), p. 276. It should be added that V. Zaslavsky and R. J. Brym, *Soviet–Jewish Emigration and Soviet Nationality Policy* (London: Macmillan, 1983) regard job competition, rather than Western pressure or the agitation of the *refuseniks*, as the main factor in the Soviet decision to permit large-scale Jewish emigration in the 1970s.
90. The role of increased access to information in destroying the Soviet system is well described by Scott Shane, in *Dismantling Utopia: How Information Ended the Soviet Union* (Chicago: Ivan R. Dee, 1994).

5
Brezhnev and Superpower Relations

Mike Bowker

Introduction

During his eighteen years as General Secretary, Leonid Brezhnev's one major policy innovation was détente, the relaxation of tensions with the West (*razryadka napryazhennosti*). In some respects, détente was simply a continuation of Khrushchev's thaw. For despite times of high tension, under Khrushchev East–West relations had generally improved, as evidenced by the Partial Test Ban Treaty and the installation of the Hotline between the Kremlin and the White House in 1963. Brezhnev's détente, however, differed in two fundamental ways from the earlier thaw. First, détente was more comprehensive and wide-ranging in its aims. Over two dozen treaties were signed by the two superpowers in the 1970s, including agreements on arms control, crisis prevention, crisis management, East–West trade, European security and even human rights. Second, Brezhnev's détente was based on essential military equivalence between the two superpowers. When Khrushchev was removed from office by his colleagues in October 1964, he was accused of bluff and bluster involving, amongst other things, 'imprudent and indiscreet conduct of foreign affairs'.[1] Embarrassing climbdowns over Berlin in 1961 and Cuba in 1962 clearly indicated that Khrushchev's rhetoric had run far ahead of Soviet capability. Therefore, Brezhnev's main aim was to add greater substance to Moscow's claims to being a superpower, and to do this he believed it was necessary to build up Soviet military power.

Even official statistics accept that defence spending in the USSR rose 40 per cent between 1965 and 1970, and annual increases continued thereafter at rates which never fell below 2 per cent in real terms.[2] As a percentage of GDP, military spending rose by approximately 3 per cent over the period rising to at least 15 per cent of GDP by the time of Brezhnev's death in 1982.[3] Despite the constraints such levels of spending placed on the civilian economy, it appeared to be a price the Soviet leadership felt was worth paying. In strategic terms, it certainly achieved its aims. At the time of the Cuban Missile

Crisis, Washington enjoyed a superiority in strategic nuclear missiles over the Soviet Union of more than 17:1; but just a decade later when SALT I was signed in May 1972, Moscow had caught up with Washington, achieving rough strategic parity.[4] Moreover, Brezhnev's military build-up was not confined to nuclear missiles. During Brezhnev's time in office, the number of troops under arms rose to 5 million, while Moscow also greatly enhanced its air and naval capabilities. Although the United States always retained a significant advantage in these latter two areas, Moscow's much improved lift-capability provided better opportunities for Moscow from the mid-1970s to support allies abroad and to challenge American dominance in the Third World. As Foreign Minister Andrei Gromyko declared at the 24th CPSU Congress in 1971: 'There is no question of any significance which can be decided without the Soviet Union, or in opposition to her.'[5] It appeared that Brezhnev had achieved his aim of turning the Soviet Union into a truly global power. Why then did the Soviet Union seek détente at a time when its power and influence around the world appeared to be inexorably on the rise?

Why détente?

There was a debate in the Kremlin from 1966 to 1971 over the future of East–West relations. It was part of a general debate over policy which saw Brezhnev emerge as the dominant figure in the Politburo.[6] Although Brezhnev initially appeared sceptical of the value of détente, by the late 1960s he had come round to the view that it could be highly advantageous to Moscow. There were a number of reasons for this. First, as indicated above, Brezhnev saw détente as a means of formalising the Soviet Union's status as a superpower. The acceptance of the Soviet Union as the equal of the United States was important, not only in political but also in ideological terms. For it suggested that Marxist–Leninist ideology had been right in predicting that history was on Moscow's side. There was a danger, however, that as the correlation of forces shifted in Moscow's favour, it could cause instability in the international system. International relations theory teaches that the risk of a major war increases when the dominant state comes under challenge from another rising power. Moscow hoped that this risk could be reduced through superpower détente and international agreements on arms control, Europe, and crisis management.[7]

The mounting economic problems in the Soviet Union represented another factor in persuading Brezhnev to accept the logic of détente. Growth rates and productivity levels were slipping from the high rates of the 1950s. The gap in living standards between the Soviet Union and the United States was widening, and this both undermined Marxist–Leninist ideology and ultimately endangered Moscow's position as a superpower. Yet Brezhnev refused to cut defence spending and he was fearful of the potentially destabilising effects of domestic reform – a fear that seemed vindicated by events in Czechoslovakia in spring 1968. In the absence of any obvious alternative, Brezhnev began to see international trade as a possible way out of the impasse.[8] Trade with the West could help plug gaps in the Soviet economy and begin to satisfy consumer demand, whilst allowing the state to maintain its existing priorities on spending. In this sense, East–West trade was perceived in Moscow as a means of avoiding reform and difficult policy choices over investment.[9]

The third major issue for Moscow was European security. Since the erection of the Berlin Wall in 1961, the possibility of East–West conflict in Europe had diminished. However, Moscow had been unable to gain popular legitimacy for its dominance of the Soviet bloc. This was most clearly apparent in a series of major uprisings which took place across Eastern Europe during the post-war period. Brezhnev's response was not to revert back to Stalinist-style imposed conformity, but nevertheless to reserve the right to use force in Eastern Europe when it was deemed necessary. This became known as the Brezhnev Doctrine. The clear intention of this strategy was to impress upon the peoples of the Soviet bloc the utter futility of rebellion. On the one occasion when Brezhnev used force in eastern Europe – to suppress the Prague Spring in 1968 – the generally passive response from the Czechoslovakian people when confronted with the overwhelming military power of the Warsaw Pact indicated reluctant acceptance of their nation's limited sovereignty. The suppression of the Prague Spring was important in allowing Brezhnev to proceed with détente. He had to show his colleagues in the Politburo, and the leaders of the Soviet bloc countries in Eastern Europe, that détente implied no weakening of Soviet alliance structures. Indeed, a primary aim of détente in Europe was to reinforce Moscow's position through gaining formal recognition from the West of its claims over the region. At the same time, it was hoped that détente, through increased trade and easier communications across the political divide, would make life more tolerable for the vast majority of people in the Soviet bloc, thereby reducing the risk of rebellion in the future.

The final factor propelling Moscow towards détente was a deterioration in relations with the People's Republic of China (PRC). Moscow had been wary of China ever since the communist revolution in 1949, but by the late 1960s Beijing was perceived by the Soviet leadership to be the country's primary security threat. China's army was second in size only to the Soviet army itself and backed up by a huge population. When Mao made claims to vast tracts of Soviet Siberia in 1964 – the same year that Beijing tested its atomic bomb – Moscow began its concerted military build-up on the Sino-Soviet border. The twelve understrength divisions on the Chinese border in 1961 rose to 25 full-strength divisions in 1969 and to 45 divisions by 1973 (as much as a quarter of Moscow's total forces).[10] There were many skirmishes on the border in the 1960s but they climaxed in all-out war along the Ussuri River in 1969. At the time, the Politburo seriously discussed the possibility of punitive strikes against the Chinese, and even floated the idea of a nuclear strike.[11] However, calmer minds prevailed and the conflict was rapidly 'de-escalated'. Fears in Moscow were revived, however, after Kissinger's secret diplomacy in China and President Nixon's official visit to Beijing in February 1972. In a desperate effort to avoid the possibility of a Sino-American alliance directed against the USSR, Moscow accelerated negotiations with Washington on a whole series of issues, including the Vietnam war and arms control.

Richard Nixon, who became President in 1969, manipulated Moscow's fear of Beijing with considerable skill, but he had good reasons of his own to pursue a policy of détente. For Nixon recognised that the United States had neither the economic nor the military power to continue its post-war policy of containment. Détente was formulated as a means of curbing Soviet ambition and defending America's global position. Most immediately, Nixon wanted 'peace with honour' in Vietnam, and hoped to extricate the United States from the war with Moscow's support. For if the United States could offer sufficient inducements to the USSR, in the form of trade, credit and arms control, Moscow might act with greater restraint around the world and become more of a status quo power. As the American political analyst, Stanley Hoffman put it, in this scenario containment would be replaced by Soviet 'self-containment'.[12]

The problem with the American concept of détente, however, was that it ran directly counter to Moscow's. This was made clear in a series of speeches by Brezhnev and other party officials. Brezhnev declared in 1972 that détente could not halt 'historical progress'; the international class struggle will continue, he said, 'it cannot be otherwise, for the world outlook and the class aims of socialism and capitalism are opposite and irreconcilable'.[13] This is not to imply that the Soviet Union was unilaterally undermining the 'spirit of détente'. For détente did not signify an end to superpower rivalry. Moscow was not giving up on communism any more than the United States was abandoning liberal democracy and the market. On the contrary, both saw détente as an opportunity to further their own interests in the Cold War world. This competitive element in détente, as will be seen, pervaded every aspect of policy – from arms control to human rights – and always made it likely that tensions between the two superpowers would re-emerge. Indeed, many commentators have argued that détente was bound to fail right from the start because of different expectations for the process in the two capitals.[14] Such an argument cannot lightly be dismissed, but it is still true that the term proved flexible enough for some significant advances to be made in a number of areas. This chapter will now consider the substance of détente and look at four important policy areas in turn.

Arms control

The centre-piece of superpower détente was arms control and most progress was made in relation to nuclear weapons. The key treaties were: the multilateral

Nuclear Non-Proliferation Treaty (NPT); the Strategic Arms Limitation Treaties (SALT I and SALT II); and the Anti-Ballistic Missile Treaty (ABM). The first treaty to be signed was the multilateral Non-Proliferation Treaty in 1968. It was an important treaty for Moscow since it formalised the Soviet Union's status as an official nuclear power. The primary aim of the treaty was to reduce the risk of nuclear proliferation. Most states, including the USSR, viewed the prospect of uncontrolled nuclear proliferation with genuine foreboding. In deference to a commitment in the treaty by the official nuclear powers to disarmament, the United States and USSR began negotiations on strategic arms a year later and signed SALT I in May 1972.

SALT I was the first major arms treaty to limit long-range nuclear missiles. It was based on the concept of rough strategic parity and froze the total number of ballistic missile launchers over a five-year period. The treaty allowed the Soviet Union to have an advantage (2,347 to 1,710) in the number of intercontinental ballistic missiles and submarine-launched ballistic missiles (ICBMs and SLBMs), but this disparity in missile launchers was balanced on the US side by its lead in missile warheads, strategic bombers, total warheads and Forward-Based Systems, and by the fact that British and French forces remained unconstrained by the treaty. The United States also retained a significant lead in most fields of weapons technology, but Moscow hoped the treaty would at least reduce the risk of the United States leaping ahead in the arms race as a result of some future breakthrough in weapons research.

Expectations of a quick follow-up treaty were disappointed, but SALT II was finally signed in Vienna in June 1979. SALT II was far more comprehensive than its predecessor. It sought to compensate Moscow's advantage in throw-weight with American advantages in number of warheads and Submarine-Launched Ballistic Missiles (SLBMs), and Forward-Based Systems which still remained outside the SALT process. The treaty limited each side to 2,250 launchers for the period 1981–5, of which no more than 1,320 could be equipped with more than one warhead. Bombers were included in the treaty and definitions on the modernisation of strategic missiles were tightened up. Although SALT II represented a significant achievement, by the time it was signed the climate in the USA had shifted decisively against détente and President Carter chose not to present the treaty for ratification to the Senate after the Soviet invasion of Afghanistan in December 1979.

Why was there such criticism of the SALT process? The left was critical because SALT scarcely slowed the nuclear arms race. SALT limited the number of missile launchers, albeit at very high levels, but due to the latest MIRV (multiple independently-targetable re-entry vehicles) technology the total number of strategic warheads continued to rise on both sides (see Table 5.1). Arms controllers protested that the primary aim of arms control was not disarmament but the enhancement of nuclear deterrence. They argued that the acceptance of rough strategic parity in the SALT agreements reinforced this concept, since neither side could seriously contemplate ever winning a nuclear

Table 5.1 Strategic nuclear missiles, warheads and throw-weights of United States and USSR, 1964–82

Year	*Launchers*		*Warheads*		*Megatonnage*	
	USA	*USSR*	*USA*	*USSR*	*USA*	*USSR*
1964	2,416	375	6,800	500	7,500	1,000
1966	2,396	435	5,000	550	5,600	1,200
1968	2,360	1,045	4,500	850	5,100	2,300
1970	2,230	1,680	3,900	1,800	4,300	3,100
1972	2,230	2,090	5,800	2,100	4,100	4,000
1974	2,180	2,380	8,400	2,400	3,800	4,200
1976	2,100	2,390	9,400	3,200	3,700	4,500
1978	2,058	2,350	9,800	5,200	3,800	5,400
1980	2,042	2,490	10,000	6,000	4,000	5,700
1982	2,032	2,490	11,000	8,000	4,100	7,100

Source: Gerald Segal, *The Simon & Schuster Guide to the World Today* (Simon & Schuster, 1987), p. 82.

war. The agreed restrictions on new missile deployment and modernisation also reduced the risk of either side stealing a march and gaining a significant military advantage over the other. SALT also aided transparency by allowing the monitoring of arms control treaties by satellite reconnaissance. Therefore, the arms controllers argued that SALT stabilised the strategic balance even if it failed to stop the arms race.

However, by the late 1970s a growing number of critics in the West argued that SALT had failed even according to the arms controllers' minimalist criteria. The American right, for example, argued that Moscow never accepted the concept of 'mutually assured destruction' (MAD) and was building up its forces to be in a position to fight and win a nuclear war.[15] Statements from some leading military officials only added to Western concern. For example, Defence Minister Marshal Grechko stressed the importance of military preparedness and implied that the class war could be won through nuclear war.[16] Soviet deployment patterns also appeared to support the concept of a war-fighting strategy. Thus, Moscow concentrated deployment on highly destructive missiles, such as the SS18, which were perceived to have first-strike potential, while modernising its ballistic missile defence (BMD) around Moscow and extending its civil defence preparations, thereby suggesting a belief in the survivability of the USSR in a nuclear war.

On the other hand, Moscow's rejection of MAD did not necessarily mean that the Soviet Union was preparing for a nuclear war. In fact, liberal writers, such as David Holloway and Michael MccGwire, argued that Moscow was equally anxious to avoid nuclear war and had simply adopted a deterrence strategy that was more robust than MAD.[17] Moreover, those hardliners who did appear to favour a war-fighting strategy were not representative of the

Soviet leadership as a whole. Indeed, when Grechko died in 1976 and Ustinov was appointed as Defence Minister, there were some signs of a moderation in military policy.[18] Shortly after Ustinov's appointment, Brezhnev made a key-note speech at Tula in January 1977 when he formally renounced superiority as a concept and argued publicly for the first time in favour of nuclear deterrence and military sufficiency.[19] Brezhnev took this argument further at the 26th CPSU Congress in 1981 when he stated unequivocally that nuclear war was unwinnable.[20]

Despite such policy statements, the Soviet military build-up never slowed and the debate between the politicians and certain members of the Soviet military elite continued unabated well into the 1980s.[21] Adding considerably to the confusion were doubts over Brezhnev's exact meaning of the term 'parity'. A number of Soviet writers later argued that Brezhnev was referring to parity with all of the Soviet Union's potential enemies – the United States, western Europe, Japan and China – *in coalition*.[22] It was highly unlikely that the Soviet Union would ever reach such a position of safety, but the attempt would only deepen suspicions of Soviet motives and further fuel the arms race.

Overall, the results of SALT were disappointing, but the ABM Treaty, signed at the same time as SALT I, was viewed far more positively by politicians and commentators alike. The treaty restricted the deployment of defensive weapons to two BMD sites each (with a maximum of 100 interceptors at each site), reduced in 1974 to just one site. It also prohibited the development and testing of BMDs in space, at sea, in the air, or mobile on land. Initially, Moscow thought it was ahead in defensive systems and was reluctant to discuss their prohibition. However, as the United States developed its multi-warhead (MIRV) technology, it became increasingly apparent that the Soviet BMDs would be unable to defend effectively against any significant US attack. As a result, a treaty to limit defensive systems began to look far more attractive. It also offered the added advantage of ensuring America's vulnerability to nuclear attack and therefore the continued value of Moscow's strategic forces. The United States abandoned any attempt to deploy a defensive system, but Moscow (in accord with the treaty) maintained and modernised its *Galosh* system around its capital city in the 1970s.

European security

It could be argued that détente had little impact on geopolitics in Europe. There was no arms agreement to parallel that of SALT and no change to the continent's bipolar division. Indeed, the main aim of détente appeared to be the ratification of the existing status quo in Europe through Willy Brandt's *Ostpolitik* and the Helsinki Final Act of 1975. This was certainly how Brezhnev viewed those agreements. In a speech welcoming the Helsinki Final Act, Brezhnev argued that the accord was the 'summing up of the political results of the Second World War'.[23] However, western critics argued that European détente represented the worst kind of appeasement. For it seemed to demand that the people of eastern Europe accept continued Soviet oppression for the greater good of peace and stability in Europe.[24] Supporters of European détente, on the other hand, argued that there was never any realistic alternative strategy. In the nuclear age, there was no way the West could *force* the Soviet Union out of eastern Europe. Far better, then, to seek accommodation and reduce the risk of East–West tensions escalating into direct superpower conflict. This, undoubtedly, was the underlying rationale in the West for both *Ostpolitik* and Helsinki.

Yet European détente also contained a more subversive subtext. Brandt always claimed that the *de facto* recognition of East Germany did not signify an abandonment of the Federal Republic's long-term goal of reunification. On the contrary, he hoped that détente would bring the two German states closer together through aid, increased trade, travel and cultural exchanges. Brandt seemed to envisage a form of convergence between the two states which would ultimately result in the two Germanies merging into one.[25] Walter Ulbricht, the East German leader, recognised the long-term dangers of *Ostpolitik* and visited Moscow in 1970 to express his concerns. However, his arguments failed to convince the Politburo. He was ousted from office in May 1971 and détente in Europe was allowed to proceed. Although Brandt's vision of convergence never happened – East Germany simply collapsed as a state – détente did succeed in opening up East Germany. So when the revolution started in 1989, at least the East Germans knew what was happening, largely because West German TV was broadcast to every corner of the country.

The subversive element of the Helsinki Final Act was rather different. While Helsinki acknowledged the political and ideological division in Europe, it also made reference in Basket Three to universal human rights and the right of emigration. This was a highly sensitive matter for the Politburo at the time. There was considerable resistance to signing the accord until Foreign Minister Gromyko persuaded his colleagues that the security benefits far outweighed the possible political ramifications of Basket Three. Furthermore, Gromyko claimed that the continued primacy of sovereignty, emphasised by all signatories in the agreement, would mean the articles would have little practical effect on domestic Soviet politics.[26] Many commentators have since argued that this was a grave miscalculation on Gromyko's part. For example, Martin Walker, a British journalist, described Basket Three of the Helsinki Final Act as a ticking 'time-bomb' placed under the Soviet bloc.[27] Without wishing to underestimate the importance of the Helsinki Final Act, this is almost certainly something of an exaggeration. All the rights enshrined in the Helsinki Final Act were already guaranteed to Soviet citizens in international treaties or in the 1977 Soviet Constitution. Helsinki simply gave the dissidents another opportunity to highlight to the outside world the cavalier attitude of their leaders towards the law.

Arms control never progressed very far in Europe. There was no agreement at all concerning conventional forces as the Mutual and Balanced Force Reduction (MBFR) talks meandered on from 1973 to 1988 without any sign of an agreement. Tensions also rose over the Soviet deployment of multi-warheaded SS20s in 1977. Although Moscow claimed they were merely modernising their existing SS4 and SS5 missiles, Western Europe had no land-based equivalent and became concerned over the implications for security. At the initiative of Helmut Schmidt, the West German Chancellor, NATO agreed in December 1979 to counter the SS20s with the deployment of Cruise and Pershing. It was a controversial decision which led to the rise of the peace movement in the West. Moscow attempted to exploit the mounting concern over Reagan's policies in Western Europe by depicting the deployment of Cruise and Pershing erroneously as an American initiative. This blatant attempt at wedge-driving ultimately failed but when Cruise and Pershing were deployed from 1983, Moscow carried out its threat and walked out of the arms control talks in Geneva. The Soviet Union, now that Brezhnev had died, had finally abandoned détente. It needed Gorbachev to get the process back on track.

East–West trade

As stated earlier, Brezhnev wanted East–West trade to modernise the economy without the need for potentially destabilising domestic reform. The value of trade with the capitalist world rose dramatically through the 1970s. However, it should be noted that much of this increase was due to a ten-fold rise over the decade in the international price of the two main Soviet exports – oil and gold.[28] Despite this growth, however, the Soviet share of world trade actually dropped from 1.8 per cent in 1970 to 1.6 per cent in 1982.[29] Trade with the United States remained disappointing, with the USSR accounting for only 2 per cent of all US exports and 0.3 per cent of imports.[30] There were two main reasons for such low levels of trade between the superpowers. First, the United States wanted to use trade as a bargaining counter, thereby politicising the process; and second, the United States feared that the export of certain high-technology goods could be exploited by Moscow for military purposes.

Nevertheless, in the more relaxed climate of détente, an ambitious trade agreement was signed in Washington in October 1972 which provided for the American export of machinery, plant and equipment, agricultural and industrial products and consumer goods. The agreement committed Washington to granting the USSR Most Favoured Nation (MFN) status, thereby lifting certain tariffs on Soviet exports. Separate from the trade agreement but of equal importance were arrangements for large-scale credit to the Soviet Union. As a result of these agreements, US–Soviet trade and American investment increased dramatically in the period 1972–3, and at the June 1973 summit, the two superpowers set a target of $3 billion over the next three years.

However, the trade agreement proved controversial in the United States. The central question was whether the United States should trade with an enemy. Would trade make the Soviet Union a more formidable enemy, or would it modify Soviet behaviour? Two significant amendments were proposed as the legislation proceeded through Congress. The first was the Jackson–Vanik amendment which demanded higher annual rates of emigration for Soviet Jews; the second, the Stevenson amendment, limiting credit to the Soviet Union to $300 million. Although the Kremlin remained sensitive to the idea of American intervention in its own internal affairs, Moscow was willing to be more flexible on emigration for minority groups in the Soviet Union. Rates of Jewish emigration peaked at 35,000 in 1973 and Moscow even signed up for the UN Covenant on Human Rights in September 1973, which included articles on the rights of emigration. However, the Stevenson amendment limiting credit meant that the trade agreement was not as valuable to Moscow as originally expected. So, when it became clear that both amendments would be passed by Congress, the Soviet leadership decided to abrogate the agreement at the Central Committee plenum of December 1974. Abrogation represented a major setback for Brezhnev's plan to modernise the Soviet economy. It also revealed the extent of the opposition to aspects of détente within the Politburo.

The Third World

Alongside arms control, Soviet policy in the Third World was the most controversial during the détente period. Such policy is dealt with in detail by Mark Webber in Chapter 6 in this volume, and this chapter will therefore concern itself only with Soviet policy in the Third World in terms of its influence on détente and East–West relations.

In the Brezhnev era, Moscow was quite open about its continued support for national liberation movements across the globe. Thus, Brezhnev said on announcing his peace programme at the 24th CPSU Congress: 'We declare that, consistently pursuing a policy of peace and friendship among the peoples, the Soviet Union will continue to wage a resolute struggle against imperialism and will administer a firm rebuff to the intrigues and sabotage of aggressors. We will continue, as in the past, steadfastly to support the struggle of the peoples for democracy, national liberation and socialism.'[31] Yet at the same time the Soviet Union also acknowledged the need for restraint. Thus, in 1977, Brezhnev said: 'Détente is a readiness to resolve differences and conflicts not by force, not by threats and sabre-rattling, but by peaceful means, at the negotiating table.'[32] It was the latter sentiment which set the tone of the two key agreements on crisis management and crisis prevention: the Basic Principles Agreement (BPA) of 1972 and the Agreement on the Prevention of Nuclear War (APNW) of 1973. Together, these two agreements committed both superpowers to act with restraint and to seek to settle any differences by peaceful means. They also acknowledged that efforts by either side to obtain unilateral advantage at the expense of the other, directly or indirectly, were incompatible with the notion of restraint.[33]

In the light of these agreements, Moscow was heavily criticised for its subsequent interventionism in the Third World, particularly from the mid-1970s. As a result, Angola, Mozambique, Ethiopia, Afghanistan, South Yemen, Nicaragua and Grenada all shifted into the Soviet camp over a brief four-year period up to 1979. How can this shift towards greater activism be explained? A number of possible reasons were put forward. First, critics argued that the Soviet leadership, who had never abandoned the international class struggle, were intervening more actively overseas simply because they now had the military capability to do so. Détente was not constraining Soviet behaviour, it was making the world safe for Soviet expansionism. A Soviet writer seemed to accept this when he wrote: 'Détente not only did not slow down the revolution and national liberation movement, but actually prompted the victory of revolutions in a number of countries.'[34]

A second view downplays Soviet expansionist tendencies and argues its greater activism from the mid-1970s was the result of international events independent of Moscow. Thus, a series of leftist revolutions from the mid-1970s in Portugal, Ethiopia and elsewhere presented Moscow with opportunities to extend its influence in the Third World. In these circumstances, Moscow gave aid and support to defend governments and rebels against counter-revolutionary forces but, according to this interpretation, such actions scarcely represented a concerted drive for international communism. The regions where the Soviet Union was most active were generally those where the United States had few interests. Moscow, therefore, did not view itself as acting unilaterally or risking the possibility of escalation.[35] A third and related view argues that Moscow was not more active in the Third World in the late 1970s, simply more effective, due to the relative passivity of the United States in the wake of Watergate and Vietnam.[36] Thus the Soviet-backed MPLA in Angola was successful only after the US Congress had voted to abandon its military support for UNITA. American paralysis had little to do with the faults of détente, according to this view, and rather more with the domestic crisis confronting President Nixon. In all the above explanations, the emphasis is on continuity – Moscow was simply acting according to its 'revolutionary conscience'.[37]

The final explanation for Moscow's activism, however, is rather different from the others. According to this view, the Soviet Union became disillusioned with détente and the Politburo adopted a more activist policy after the December 1974 Central Committee plenum.[38] Certainly, there were reasons for disillusionment. Trade with the United States had become highly politicised, leading to the abrogation of the trade agreement at that meeting. The USSR had also been disappointed by US support for the Pinochet *coup* in Chile in September 1973 against the freely elected socialist government of Allende. The *coup* weakened the hand of those in the Kremlin who had argued in favour of a peaceful road to socialism. It may have also strengthened the resolve of the Politburo to act forcibly during the Middle East in October 1973.[39] If so, it was the source of another diplomatic failure. After the war, Kissinger successfully marginalised the Soviet Union from the Middle East peace process. Subsequently Egypt, the most powerful state in the region, abrogated the Treaty of Friendship and Cooperation with the USSR in 1976 and signed up for a separate peace with Israel in 1978 under the auspices of the United States. The loss was a great one for Moscow for it was an area of strategic importance. In sum, from the Soviet perspective, there was mounting pressure on détente. However, there was little evidence of a concerted attack on détente as a policy. At most, there was a readjustment, with a greater willingness to exploit American weakness in the Third World and a gentle tilt towards Europe.[40] Moscow learnt the lesson of Chile and argued that revolutionary governments required the military means to defend themselves,[41] but the rhetoric was largely defensive in nature and the 'export of revolution' remained off-limits.[42] In that sense at least, détente remained on track in the Third World.

Moscow was certainly more active in the Third World from the 1970s, but Soviet adventurism should not be exaggerated. The West remained dominant, and the more activist and interventionist force in the Third World.[43] Indeed, an official American report published in the early 1980s found that Moscow's international position was rather weaker than it had been in Khrushchev's time.[44] By then, only about thirteen Third World states were still on the non-capitalist path advocated by Moscow and many of these proclaimed themselves to be Marxist–Leninist only to obtain military aid from the Soviet Union. Yet the Kremlin soon discovered that this in itself was rarely enough to ensure continued support as Egypt, Somalia and Sudan all abandoned the Soviet camp in the 1970s. Even more disappointingly, from Moscow's perspective, the majority of Moscow's remaining Third World allies, such as Vietnam, Afghanistan, Angola and Ethiopia, faced impoverishment and civil war. Moscow's closest allies in the Third World had become a significant drain on the Soviet economy and in return offered little advantage in strategic terms. Thus the invasion of Afghanistan, which had been characterised in December 1979 as the height of Soviet arrogance and power, soon came to be seen as the last desperate act of a critically wounded giant. Afghanistan could not be controlled and the Soviet Union became bogged down in an interminable civil war. The USSR soon faced the same dilemma as the United States in Vietnam – how to contrive some kind of dignified withdrawal which would not undermine its status in the world.

The decline of détente

Why did détente decline from the mid-1970s? There were a number of different explanations. The first, the orthodox view, argued that détente failed because the Soviet Union did not adjust its foreign policy behaviour in line with the 'spirit of détente'. In arms control, Moscow rejected the concept of MAD and pursued a war-fighting strategy. In eastern Europe, there was no sign of liberalisation and the Brezhnev Doctrine remained firmly in place, as martial law in Poland showed in December 1981. In the Third World, Moscow adopted a more expansionist policy from the mid-1970s and sought to extend international communism by force. In sum, the Soviet Union took advantage of US restraint to relentlessly pursue the international class struggle. According to this theory, Washington could not accept détente on these terms and finally abandoned any hope of it after the Soviet invasion of Afghanistan in 1979.

A second view argued that détente failed because of the different concepts of détente in the two superpower capitals. Moscow sought to be recognised as a global power the equal of the United States whilst Washington sought to contain Moscow's rising ambition. The two concepts were incompatible and led to growing disillusionment on both sides. Brezhnev maintained a rather rickety consensus on the subject throughout the 1970s, but there were growing signs of dissension. In May 1972, Shelest opposed the upcoming superpower summit in Moscow after the American bombing of Haiphong harbour. It was a controversial issue, but Brezhnev prevailed. Shelest was promptly demoted and removed from the Politburo the following year. As stated earlier, the plenum of 1974 was also a tense period and, on this occasion, détente survived only after a certain readjustment of policy. However, there is little evidence that détente was abandoned in Moscow as a strategy even when the Soviet army invaded Afghanistan. Brezhnev was too closely linked personally to the policy to abandon it altogether. Indeed, Brezhnev continued up to his death to call for a return to détente, a policy he had deemed irreversible in 1973.[45] Moscow expected the invasion of Afghanistan to create problems for its relations with Washington, but the Politburo clearly believed that the international situation was retrievable. After all, the Soviet leadership hoped its intervention would be short and swift.[46]

The third and final view, the revisionist view, argues that US behaviour scuppered détente. It was not so much the differing concepts of détente that caused the problem, it was Soviet success in the competition which soured the relationship and led to questions being asked in American domestic politics. The United States was willing to compete with the Soviet Union until domestic problems constrained this ability. As it became increasingly obvious that détente was not having the effect Nixon and Kissinger had originally envisaged, the United States pulled the plug on the whole enterprise. This is a view which, in general terms, fits in with the Soviet interpretation too. Soviet commentators principally blamed the rise of the New Right in the United States and the power of the military–industrial complex for the collapse of détente in the 1970s. Washington was deemed to be hypocritical in its reaction to Soviet defence and Third World policy. The United States was considered not only a participant in but the instigator of the arms race; and not only a highly interventionist power but a reactionary power dedicated to preserving imperialism in the Third World.[47]

There may be some truth in all these theories. It was always going to be difficult to maintain détente over a longer period when it involved a complex mix of cooperation and competition. Détente was about the management of superpower rivalry, not its abandonment. For the United States, this might have been particularly difficult, since, as Kissinger himself has written, the United States has an antipathy towards *Realpolitik*, preferring a more moralistic kind of foreign policy.[48] But any kind of détente policy would have been difficult for Washington to manage. The 1970s was a particularly difficult decade for the United States and détente became inextricably linked in the minds of most Americans with decline. In the 1970s, the United States had to get used both to losing strategic superiority to Moscow and to increasing economic competition from western Europe and Japan. It was the decade when the dollar came off the gold standard and the United States, along with the rest of the western world, faced recession and economic restructuring in the wake of the 1973 oil crisis. It was also the time of Vietnam and Watergate and the subsequent collapse of presidential authority. It would always have been difficult for Washington to coordinate its détente policy and manage its relationship with the Soviet Union. In the aftermath of Watergate, it became virtually impossible.

The Soviet Union, for its part, publicly backed détente throughout the period. In contrast to the United States, it associated détente with a period of unprecedented strength and optimism. As indicated above, there were clearly periods when Brezhnev's policy was challenged. However, these difficulties were never fully thrashed out. Debates were conducted in small cabals at the top of the political hierarchy behind firmly bolted doors. As a result, decisions often went uncontested and official statements unchallenged. There was minimal discussion of such momentous decisions as the intervention in Afghanistan and the deployment of the SS20s.[49] Inconsistencies in policy went unexplored and the ramifications of decisions were rarely discussed.[50] An unwillingness to confront difficult choices in Moscow contributed to the decline of détente and ultimately to the fall of the Soviet Union. Hard decisions on expenditure were postponed and, as a result, defence spending rose inexorably. The Soviet military build-up was counter-productive in at least two ways – it bankrupted the country and fuelled the arms race. Owing to the massive Soviet military build-up throughout the 1970s, other nations became highly suspicious of the Soviet Union's intentions and Moscow was left remarkably isolated for a state with global pretensions.

Undoubtedly, détente declined in the 1980s, but how far is it true to say it collapsed altogether? Certainly, both superpowers abandoned détente – Washington after the Soviet invasion of Afghanistan in 1979, Moscow after the deployment of Cruise missiles in 1983. There was a standoff between the two superpowers with no US–Soviet summit meetings taking place between 1979 and 1985. The arms race quickened and the rhetoric of the Cold War returned. Relations cooled appreciably, but there was no return to the Cold War of the 1950s. There was no progress on arms control in the early 1980s, but existing arms control treaties were respected. The only exception was SALT II when Washington committed a technical breach in 1986. Nor was there any attempt to reverse the Helsinki process. On the contrary, the Reagan administration sought to improve the implementation of its articles on universal human rights. There were problems over East–West trade, but Reagan signed a new grain deal in 1982 and western Europe lobbied vigorously at the same time for the construction of a gas pipe-line from the Soviet Union. There was no desire for the appeasement of the USSR, but both the people and the leaders in Europe favoured a rapid return to the policies of détente. Reagan had enormous popular support at home, but even he felt it wise to moderate his Cold War rhetoric in 1984 as the presidential election campaign approached.

In Moscow, the walk-out from the arms control talks in 1983 was generally perceived to have been a mistake. A growing paranoia took hold in the Kremlin which also had its effects among the Soviet people.[51] Moscow also found itself under increasing pressure from its East European allies to return to the negotiating table. The Soviet bloc had become dependent on Western aid and trade, and feared the consequences of a return to Cold War posturing.

Conclusion

In conclusion, what, if any, were the longer-term ramifications of détente? One important question here is whether détente aided or obstructed the process which led to the end of the Cold War. There is insufficient space here to discuss this in any detail, but two points deserve mentioning. First, détente was about managing the Cold War, it was not about dismantling it. Therefore, there are limits to how far it is possible to attribute the end of the Cold War to détente. It required Reagan and Gorbachev in their different ways to challenge the political structures of the Cold War before there was any realistic chance of bringing it to an end. Furthermore, the actual achievements of détente were fairly limited. In many respects, the process has to be deemed a failure. Yet, more positively, détente could also be seen as a learning process. It set precedents and offered lessons for the future. SALT had failed to stop the arms race, so Reagan insisted that its successor, START, would put arms reductions at its heart. Moscow's concept of parity had held the Soviet Union in a straight-jacket in arms control negotiations, so Gorbachev replaced the concept of parity with reasonable sufficiency. This allowed him to make asymmetrical cuts and unilateral concessions which were vital to facilitate agreement in negotiations on intermediate nuclear forces (INF) and conventional forces in Europe (CFE). SALT was a first step; it needed a more radical approach to turn control into actual arms cuts.

Second, security in Europe was based on the political division of the continent. This structure remained in place under détente, but, as Brandt had predicted, the social barriers were lowered. The Soviet Union remained a very isolated state, but slowly Western consumer products, youth culture and Western ideas infiltrated parts of the country. It became easier for Soviet citizens to travel to the West. Although this privilege was generally confined to the Soviet elite, it was no less important for that. Gorbachev was just one of many such people who travelled extensively in the West as a young man and was deeply affected by it. Not only was Gorbachev permitted to visit countries in western Europe from 1972, but he was given a considerable degree of freedom to travel with his wife around France and Italy.[52] This would scarcely have been possible before détente.

The Cold War might well have ended without détente. For it had long been clear that Moscow had to cut back on its defence spending; its economy needed radical reform to stimulate growth and innovation, the political system had to accommodate a more pluralistic society and a better-educated population. It was also increasingly clear that the Soviet Union in the 1980s was unable to compete effectively with the West, although this was a reality Brezhnev seemed reluctant to face. The West may have had little to do with the collapse of the Soviet Union – to a large extent, it was a domestic crisis. Nevertheless, détente may have provided the context underlying its demise to the extent that it opened up Soviet society and made the political elite less hostile to the West.

The final question is whether détente has any relevance for the post-Cold War world. There are reasons to think it may have. Russia has declined as a great power, but we still live in a nuclear age. Arms control, it appears, still has a role to play in US–Russian relations. The ratification of START II and the Comprehensive Test Ban Treaty after Vladimir Putin's election as president in spring 2000 remains important for future peace and stability. Moreover, Europe remains an insecure continent in many respects. Its security in the post-Cold War era is based on NATO and the European Union, but the Organisation for Security and Cooperation in Europe (OSCE) (born out of Helsinki) remains an institution of some importance. It has played a role in mediating peace agreements and overseeing democratic elections in the former communist states. Despite its lack of military muscle, the OSCE remains uniquely well suited to such duties because it is the only truly pan-European institution which has escaped the taint of the Cold War.[53]

The ideological division of the Cold War period has gone, but national, cultural and economic divisions remain. The US–Russian partnership which blossomed amidst the euphoria of the Berlin Wall coming down faded into a cold peace, as Yeltsin referred to it, in the second half of the 1990s.[54] However, what seems to have emerged in the early years of the twenty-first century is a form of 'new détente', which after the terrorist attacks on New York and Washington on 11 September 2001 moved close to a full-blown alliance.

Like its predecessor though, the current US–Russian relationship is a complex one, based on a mixture of competition and cooperation. Russia, however, can no longer claim to be the equal of the United States. It is no longer a global power. Russia is a humbled, but still a proud nation. It will almost certainly rise again. It has a huge territory, an educated population and rich natural resources. It is important for the West to manage Russia's temporary decline with sensitivity to avoid the fruits of antagonism in future years. Russia and the West have many different interests in the post-Cold War world, but it should be possible to manage them better now that the ideological division has gone. If this can be achieved, there is no reason to believe that the 'new détente' cannot last rather longer than its predecessor of the 1970s.

Further reading

For a good general overview of Soviet foreign policy, see Caroline Kennedy-Pipe, *Russia and the World, 1917–1991* (London: Arnold, 1998). On the rise and fall of détente, see Raymond L. Garthoff, *Détente and Confrontation: Soviet–American Relations From Nixon to Reagan* (revised edn, Washington, DC: Brookings Institution, 1994); Mike Bowker and Phil Williams, *Superpower Détente: A Reappraisal* (London: Sage, 1988); and Harry Gelman, *The Brezhnev Politburo and the Decline of Détente* (Ithaca, London: Cornell University Press, 1984). For the Soviet perspective, see Georgi Arbatov, *Cold War or Detente? The Soviet Viewpoint* (London: Zed Books, 1983). There are also two useful internet sites, the Cold War International History Project which can be found at <cwihp.si.edu>; and <www.cnn.com/SPECIALS/cold.war>.

Notes

1. G. Hosking, *A History of the Soviet Union* (London: Fontana, 1985), p. 361.
2. *Soviet Imperatives for the 1990s*, Hearing Before the Subcommittee on European Affairs of the Committee on Foreign Relations US Senate, 99th Congress, 1st Session, 12 September 1985, Part 1 (Washington, DC: US Government Printing Office, 1986), pp. 22, 26.
3. M. Walker, *The Waking Giant: The Soviet Union Under Gorbachev* (London: Abacus, 1987), p. 38.
4. G. Segal, *Guide to the World Today* (London: Simon & Schuster, 1987), p. 82.
5. M. Bowker and P. Williams, *Superpower Détente: A Reappraisal* (London: Sage, 1988), p. 38.
6. For more detail than can be included in this short account, see H. Gelman, *The Brezhnev Politburo and the Decline of Détente* (Ithaca, London: Cornell University Press, 1984); and R. L. Garthoff, *Détente and Confrontation: American–Soviet Relations From Nixon to Reagan* (Washington, DC: Brookings Institution, 1985).

7. R. L. Garthoff, *Détente and Confrontation: American–Soviet Relations From Nixon to Reagan* (Washington, DC: Brookings Institution, 1985), pp. 38–9.
8. See B. Parrot, 'Soviet Foreign Policy, Internal Politics and Trade With the West', in B. Parrot, *Trade, Technology and Soviet–American Relations* (Bloomington, Ind.: Indiana University Press, 1985), p. 36.
9. A. Shevchenko, *Breaking With Moscow* (New York: Knopf, 1985), p. 213.
10. R. L. Garthoff, *Détente and Confrontation: American–Soviet Relations From Nixon to Reagan* (Washington, DC: Brookings Institution, 1985), p. 208.
11. A. Shevchenko, *Breaking With Moscow* (New York: Knopf, 1985), pp. 165–6.
12. Stanley Hoffman, *Dead Ends* (Cambridge, Mass: Ballinger, 1983), p. 90.
13. *Pravda*, 22 December 1972.
14. H. Gelman, *The Brezhnev Politburo and the Decline of Détente* (Ithaca, London: Cornell University Press, 1984).
15. See, for example, Richard Pipes, 'Why the Soviet Union Thinks it Can Fight and Win a Nuclear War', *Commentary*, July 1977.
16. A. Grechko, *The Armed Forces of the Soviet Union* (Moscow: Progress, 1977), pp. 92, 210.
17. David Holloway, *The Soviet Union and Arms Control* (New Haven, London: Yale University Press, 1984), pp. 33–5; and Michael MccGwire, *Military Objectives in Soviet Foreign Policy* (Washington, DC: Brookings Institution, 1987).
18. Certainly, the two men had rather different views on defence policy. Compare and contrast the two books, A. Grechko, *The Armed Forces of the Soviet Union* (Moscow: Progress, 1977) and D. Ustinov, *Serving the Country and the Communist Cause* (London: Pergamon, 1983).
19. *Pravda*, 19 January 1977.
20. *Pravda*, 24 February 1981.
21. See, for example, N. Ogarkov, *Istoriya uchit bditel'nosti* (Moscow: Voenizdat, 1985).
22. N. Spassky 'National Security: Real or Illusory', *International Affairs* (Moscow), July 1989, p. 6; and S. Plekhanov, 'A Long Look at America: A Discussion', *Moscow News*, 2 October 1988, p. 7.
23. L. Brezhnev, *Peace, Détente and Soviet-American Relations* (New York, London: Harcourt Brace Jovanovich, 1979), p. 95.
24. See, for example, T. Garton Ash, *In Europe's Name: Germany and the Divided Continent* (London: Vintage, 1990).
25. W. Griffith, *The Ostpolitik of the Federal Republic of Germany* (Cambridge, Mass.: MIT, 1978).
26. This issue was also discussed by the then Soviet Ambassador to Washington, Anatoli Dobrynin, in the video, 'Détente', from the Jeremy Isaacs and Taylor Downing series, *The Cold War* (London: BBC, 1998).
27. M. Walker, *The Cold War and the Making of the Modern World* (London: 4th Estate), p. 237.
28. J. Hough, *Opening Up the Soviet Economy* (Washington, DC: Brookings Institution, 1988), p. 55.
29. L. Geron, *Soviet Foreign Policy under Perestroika* (London: RIIA/Pinter, 1990), p. 28.
30. S. Rogov, *Is A New Model of Soviet–American Relations Possible?* (Moscow: Novosti Press, 1989), p. 48.
31. *Current Digest of the Soviet Press*, Vol. 23, No. 12, 1971, p. 13.
32. *Pravda*, 19 January 1977.
33. For agreements, see: Appendixes I and II, in Leonid I. Brezhnev, *Peace, Détente and Soviet–American Relations* (New York: Harcourt Bruce Jovanovich, 1979), pp. 225–30.

34. V. Kuznetsov, *Détente and the World Today* (Moscow: Progress, 1981), p. 37.
35. This is at least one aspect of the argument used by Fred Halliday in his book, *The Making of the Second Cold War* (London: Verso, 1989).
36. R. L. Garthoff, *Détente and Confrontation: American–Soviet Relations From Nixon to Reagan* (Washington, DC: Brookings Institution, 1985) puts much emphasis on the role of US domestic politics in undermining superpower détente.
37. Leonid Brezhnev at the 25th CPSU Congress, *Soviet News*, 2 March 1976, pp. 71–2.
38. P. Volten, *Brezhnev's Peace Programme* (Boulder, Col.: Westview Press, 1982), pp. 129–32; and H. Gelman, *The Brezhnev Politburo and the Decline of Détente* (Ithaca, London: Cornell University Press, 1984).
39. See for example: F. F. Sergeyev, *Chile: CIA Big Business* (Moscow: Progress Press, 1981), *Voprosy istorii KPSS*, No. 5, May 1974, pp. 48–50; and M. Bowker and P. Williams, *Superpower Détente: A Reappraisal* (London: Sage, 1988), p. 100.
40. R. L. Garthoff, *Détente and Confrontation: American–Soviet Relations From Nixon to Reagan* (Washington, DC: Brookings Institution, 1985), p. 466
41. L. Brezhnev, speech to the 25th CPSU Congress, February 1976, *Soviet News*, 2 March 1976, p. 76.
42. L. Brezhnev speech to the 25th CPSU Congress, February 1976, *Soviet News*, 2 March 1976, p. 77.
43. See, for example, A. P. Schmid, *Soviet Military Interventions Since 1945* (London: Transaction Books, 1985); and B. D. Porter, *The USSR in Third World Conflicts: Soviet Arms and Diplomacy in Local Wars, 1945–1980* (Cambridge University Press, 1984).
44. Center for Defense Information, 'Soviet Geopolitical Momentum: Myth and Menace', in Robbin F. Laird and Erik P. Hoffmann (eds), *Soviet Foreign Policy in a Changing World* (New York: Aldine, 1986), p. 706.
45. R. L. Garthoff, *Détente and Confrontation: American–Soviet Relations From Nixon to Reagan* (Washington: Brookings Institution, 1985), p. 346.
46. Minutes from selected Politburo meetings relating to the invasion in Afghanistan have been published in B. Gromov, *Ogranichennyi kontingent* (Moscow: Progress, 1994), pp. 22–5.
47. For examples of Soviet writing on this, see: Yu. Zhukov, *CCCP-SShA: Doroga dlinoyu v 70 let ili razkaz o tom, kak razvivalis' sovetsko-amerikanskoie otnosheniia* (Moscow: Izdatel'stvo politicheskoi literatury, 1988), pp. 237–40; and S. M. Plekhanov, 'Obostrenie politicheskoi bor'by v SShA po voprosam otnoshenii s SSSR vo vtoroi polovine 70-x godov', in G. A. Trofimenko and P. T. Podlesnyi (eds), *Sovetsko-Amerikanskie otnosheniya v sovremennom mire* (Moscow: Nauka, 1987), pp. 108–30.
48. This is a view which permeates much of his writing. See, for example, H. Kissinger, *Diplomacy* (London, New York: Simon & Schuster, 1995).
49. This is the argument of an anonymous editorial in the house journal of the Soviet Ministry of Foreign Affairs; see 'Foreign Policy: Lessons of the Past', *International Affairs* (Moscow), June 1989, pp. 81–3.
50. A. Shevchenko, *Breaking With Moscow* (New York: Knopf, 1985), pp. 214–16.
51. There were fears that the West was planning a nuclear attack against the Soviet Union in 1983, see C. Andrew and O. Gordievsky (eds), *Instructions from the KGB: Top Secret Files on KGB Foreign Operations, 1975–1985* (London: Hodder & Stoughton, 1991), pp. 67–90.
52. A. Brown, *The Gorbachev Factor* (Oxford University Press, 1996), pp. 42–3.

53. D. Lynch, 'Russia and the Organization for Security and Cooperation in Europe', in M. Webber (ed.), *Russia and Europe: Conflict or Cooperation* (Basingstoke: Macmillan, 2000), pp. 99–124
54. *International Herald Tribune*, 6 December 1994.

6
'Out of Area' Operations: The Third World

Mark Webber

Introduction

The Third World was, in many respects, a creation of the Cold War – a third world, literally, that was distinct from the first world of capitalist industrial states and the second world of the Soviet-led socialist bloc.[1] The Cold War's various antagonisms pitted the first two worlds one against the other yet much of its competitive energies were ventilated in the Third World. This was a consequence of the strategic and political stalemate in Europe (the territorial core of the Cold War) and the global implications of the nuclear balance of power. It also reflected the fact that the Cold War was a statement of ideology as much as of strategy. Its juxtaposition of two alternative systems of socio-economic and political organisation inevitably meant that the myriad of states which sat in between would be affected. This was all the more likely given that the Cold War followed upon and, in some cases, coincided with the end of colonialism and thus the coming to independence of dozens of new states throughout Africa, Asia and the Middle East.

The high-point of bipolar competition in the Third World corresponds roughly to the Brezhnev years in the Soviet Union – the late 1960s through to the early 1980s. As such, this also marked the high-point of Soviet global involvement. In retrospect, this now seems remarkable, so used are we to the Brezhnev period being characterised as lacklustre and bereft of innovation. The record is, in fact, mixed. Soviet expansion under Brezhnev certainly accorded with the inflated sense of status held in Moscow and the perception that socialism was on the march as a global force. This expansion brought with it, however, increasing costs measured in terms of economic overcommitment and political and military entanglements. It also contributed to a deterioration of relations with the United States and China. These costs of Third World involvement eventually came to be viewed as outweighing the benefits, thereby triggering a major reorientation of policy under Mikhail Gorbachev. The trend of disengagement he inaugurated came to be irreversible. It is, however, a trend now lamented somewhat in Moscow as it has left open the field to the United States and is a yet further reminder of Russia's diminished place in the world.

The Soviet Union and the Third World: a measure of greatness

The 1970s marked a seeming high-point in Soviet global influence. Throughout most of its history a continental power, the Soviet Union during this period extended its presence and influence throughout the Third World.

Although the Khrushchev period had been decisive in marking the concerted entry of the Soviet Union into this region it was not until the mid-years of Brezhnev's tenure as leader that the Soviet Union was able to demonstrate its credentials as a major actor there. In so doing, Moscow established itself as a serious contender for influence with the western states led by the United States and, of somewhat lesser significance, with China.

Among the most significant trends benefiting the Soviet Union was the assumption to power during the 1970s of left-leaning and, in some cases, openly pro-Soviet regimes. In South East Asia this involved the final victory of communist forces in Vietnam in 1975, an event which in turn facilitated the assumption to power of the Pathet Lao in Laos that same year and a pro-Vietnamese regime in Cambodia following an invasion by Vietnamese forces in late 1978. Elsewhere, during 1978 *coups* in Afghanistan and South Yemen brought to power communist leaderships keen to cultivate (or in the case of the latter deepen) relations with Moscow. Further afield in Africa, a civil war in Angola during 1975 saw the coming to power of the most radical and pro-Soviet faction, the MPLA. In Ethiopia some two years later, an internal coup within the ruling military council resulted in a victory for a Marxist–Leninist inspired faction under the leadership of Lieutenant Colonel Mengistu Haile Miriam. The seizure of power by the New Jewel Movement in Grenada and the Sandinista National Liberation Front (FSLN) in Nicaragua in 1979 (in turn, paralleled by an upsurge of guerrilla activities in El Salvador) finally, marked a re-animation of Cuban-inspired revolutionary change in central America.[2] Once established, the common pattern for these regimes was the consolidation of close relations with the Soviet Union, symbolically capped by treaties of friendship. The depth of these relationships varied. However, in Vietnam and Afghanistan (after the Soviet invasion of 1979) the relationship was particularly close as measured in terms of levels of military assistance (arms transfers and advisers), Soviet access to local military facilities, and the emulation of Soviet-inspired forms of political organisation (principally the entrenchment of vanguard parties). To lesser degrees, similar patterns were also evident in Angola, Ethiopia and South Yemen.

The Soviet Union during this period also continued to maintain longer-established relations. Of crucial significance in this respect was Cuba. Relations with Havana had, in fact, deteriorated during the 1960s owing, in part, to an alleged lack of support on the Soviet Union's part for national liberation struggles in Vietnam, Latin America and Africa.[3] During the 1970s, however, a major accommodation occurred. This was a consequence, to some degree, of Cuba's increasing reliance on Soviet military and economic assistance (Cuba joined the Council for Mutual Economic Assistance (COMECON) in 1972), but it reflected also an appreciation by the leadership of Fidel Castro of the Soviet Union's increasing involvement in the Third World. Indeed, the convergence of interests was such that by 1979, Castro found himself one of the few leaders outside of the Warsaw Pact who did not openly criticise the Soviet invasion of Afghanistan. Of only slightly less import for Moscow was India. Having enjoyed a central focus of attention in Moscow during the Khrushchev period, this state retained a privileged place in Soviet foreign policy under Brezhnev. A friendship treaty was concluded in 1971 and during the 1970s India was the largest non-Arab recipient of Soviet arms transfers (these arms accounted for over 90 per cent of India's inventory) and the largest taker outside of Vietnam and Cuba of Soviet economic aid. In the strategically significant Middle East, meanwhile, Syria, Iraq and Libya – countries which had cultivated ties to Moscow following the coming to power of anti-Zionist and anti-American leaderships in the late 1960s – established themselves as by far the largest customers of Soviet arms (outstripping even Cuba and Vietnam). In addition, all three of these states became the site of significant numbers of Soviet military advisers – 7,000, 1,200 and 1,800, respectively, by 1982.[4]

As well as the development of ties with individual states, the Brezhnev period was also significant for the manner in which the Soviet Union engaged with the Third World. During the Khrushchev period, Soviet policy had been based on a judicious mix of diplomatic gestures, political posturing, relatively generous economic assistance to a select few countries (Afghanistan, Algeria, Ghana, Egypt, India, Indonesia, Iraq and Syria) and the tentative cultivation of anti-colonial movements.[5] Under Brezhnev, by contrast, Soviet policy was marked by a far more obvious emphasis on military instruments. This has already been implicit in the levels of military assistance noted above and it is also worth noting that from the late 1960s a trend became established whereby overall economic assistance began to lag behind levels of military aid.[6] The real departure, however, came in the shape of a greater Soviet readiness to intervene in Third World conflict situations. In the Nigerian war of 1967–70, the Soviet Union was one of only two states (the other was the United Kingdom) willing to provide arms to the central government. During the Vietnam War, massive arms transfers proved decisive in facilitating the victory of the communist side over US forces and their south Vietnamese allies. In the Arab–Israeli war of 1973, the Soviet-backed Egyptian and Syrian forces did not emerge victorious; however, a number of significant precedents for Soviet policy were set. As well as the scale of the operation and the new tasks undertaken by Soviet military advisers *in situ*, the 1973 war marked the first time Moscow had engaged in the continuous re-supply of a non-communist combatant during ongoing hostilities. Two years later during the Angolan civil war, the Soviet Union undertook the first large-scale airlift of Cuban troops. Alongside a parallel air- and sea-lift of Soviet weaponry and the dispatch of a limited number of Soviet military advisers this proved decisive in the defeat of a South African intervention force and the pro-American and pro-Chinese guerrilla movements ranged against the MPLA. A similar operation was mounted in Ethiopia's favour during the 1977 Ogaden war with Somalia in the Horn of Africa. On this occasion, and in another unprecedented move, two ranking Soviet generals were dispatched to help oversee the Ethiopian campaign. Even more dramatically, the Soviet invasion of Afghanistan of 1979 marked the first occasion that the Soviet Union had deployed ground troops in a non-Warsaw Pact state since the Second World War. And within a year some 85,000 such personnel has crossed into that country.[7]

As well as these dramatic cases of intervention, the Brezhnev period, in addition, also witnessed numerous, less overt, examples of a Soviet 'diplomacy of force'.[8] This approach was manifest in shows of strength on the part of the Soviet navy (the deployment of warships in the eastern Mediterranean during the 1973 Arab–Israeli war and in the central and eastern Atlantic during the Angolan civil war) and in diplomatic warnings directed on the one hand at the United States and its clients (the threat to take unspecified 'unilateral' steps in the Middle East in response to Israeli gains against Egypt in the 1973 war), and on the other hand against China (the statement that Moscow would honour commitments under the Soviet–Vietnamese friendship treaty in response to the 1979 Chinese invasion of Vietnam). Throughout the 1970s Moscow also continued to back national liberation movements which had yet to achieve power. After the Angolan civil war, for instance, the Soviet Union took advantage of greater opportunities for contacts with SWAPO of Namibia, the Zimbabwean movement ZAPU and the ANC fighting apartheid in South Africa.[9]

As we shall see below, the pace and direction of events in the Third World was not always to the benefit of the Soviet Union. However, in light of this, a common view in the 1970s and early 1980s – held both in the Soviet Union and outside – was that developments in the region reflected a general and qualitative shift in the geopolitical balance of forces in Moscow's favour, a seeming march of Soviet influence and a commensurate retreat of American and Chinese positions.

Among the Soviet leadership the most authoritative statement of this view was Brezhnev's report to the 1976 Congress of the Communist Party of the Soviet Union (CPSU).[10] Held just weeks after the Soviet–Cuban intervention in Angola, this painted a sanguine picture of the consolidation of socialism in Cuba and Vietnam, the victories of national liberation and the readiness of the Soviet Union to strengthen cooperation with developing countries and 'peoples who are fighting for their freedom'. Developments of this sort,

Brezhnev added, were of epoch-making significance both because they indicated a positive trend in 'the development of the worldwide revolutionary process' and because they affirmed the growing international stature of Soviet-style socialism and of the Soviet state. Indeed, on this latter point, Brezhnev was particularly emphatic, suggesting that there was 'probably no spot on earth' beyond consideration in the formation of Soviet foreign policy. Interwoven with these themes, Brezhnev also alluded to two significant ideological formulations. The first concerned states of 'socialist orientation' in the Third World.[11] This seemingly bland label was, in fact, meant to signify a stage of revolutionary development more progressive than that of 'national democracy' popular in Soviet discourse in the 1960s. As such, it reflected an apparent reversal of a period of Soviet disillusionment in the late 1960s occasioned by the overthrow of radical regimes in states such as Indonesia, Ghana and Mali and was to come to signify an important tactical position – an emphasis on Marxist–Leninist vanguard parties – which was to become pronounced in Soviet policy from the mid-1970s to the mid-1980s.[12] The second was 'peaceful coexistence', a term of longer pedigree but of added significance in the mid-1970s given the context of détente. Its principal application was to Soviet relations with the capitalist states (and the United States in particularly); however, this relationship was viewed in broad terms and thus impinged upon the Third World. Here, the key Soviet formulation was that peaceful coexistence did not preclude support for national liberation. Such a position did, of course, carry with it a certain logical tension, even contradiction: the desire, on the one hand to preserve workable relations with the United States and western Europe (important in areas of nuclear arms control and external economic relations), yet the assumption, on the other, that this could occur while the Soviet Union simultaneously followed a course in the Third World likely to provoke tension with the West.[13] The willingness of the Brezhnev leadership to court such tension was justified by the fact that the United States itself was seen as actively involved in the Third World. Washington, rather than Moscow, therefore, could be painted as the true culprit of any deterioration in relations that might occur.[14]

The growing perception in the United States, however, was rather different. Increasingly, during the course of the 1970s it was felt that Moscow was willing to sacrifice cooperation for the sake of its Third World interventions. The American understanding of détente under Presidents Nixon, Ford, and Carter did not preclude the projection of America's own national interests and ideological preferences, and neither did it deny the basically adversarial nature of the Soviet–American relationship.[15] However, it did assume that this relationship could be managed in such a way as to promote greater opportunities for East–West cooperation, a view, in turn, premised upon notions of mutual restraint and a code of conduct for managing competition in the Third World.[16] The interventions in Angola and the Horn of Africa were seen, however, as running counter to these principles and, moreover, according to President Gerald Ford, as brute examples of 'Soviet expansionism by military means'.[17] Under the Carter Administration (1977–80), similarly, concern was increasingly expressed that the Third World was the site of an adventurous, militarily robust Soviet policy.[18] This was to culminate in American reactions to the invasion of Afghanistan, an event which spelled the final end of détente and which, for Carter, amounted to 'the greatest threat to [world] peace since the Second World War'.[19] Alexander Haig, Secretary of State in the first Reagan Administration (1981–4) was to subsequently declare that the Soviet Union during the 1970s had been able and willing 'to extend itself far beyond the natural limits of its own apparent interests and influence'. No longer simply of continental weight, it had assumed a global importance as a 'buoyant imperial power'.[20]

As for China, official assessment of Soviet Third World policy was equally condemning. Beijing had, in fact, suffered a number of reversals during the 1970s. The victory of the Vietnamese communists (a struggle which it had supported) saw, as noted above, the consolidation of a pro-Soviet direction in Hanoi and the subsequent ouster of the Chinese-backed Khmer Rouge in Cambodia. The Soviet–Cuban intervention in Angola, meanwhile, had resulted in a consolidation of Moscow's ties with Mozambique, Tanzania and Zambia, states which had previously enjoyed close links with Beijing. The condemnation of Soviet policy which these developments provoked among the Chinese was of significance both because it illustrated the depths of the Sino-Soviet rift and also because it revealed an assessment of Soviet ambition even more alarmist than that then current in Washington. Moscow, for instance, was castigated for pursuing a global strategy aimed not at national liberation but rather at competing with the United States for world hegemony. As such, the Soviets were just as colonial and exploitative as the West. Such a view did, of course, have a certain propaganda value, yet it cannot be entirely dismissed; it reflected a genuinely held concern at the demonstrative material advantage of the Soviet Union in championing the world revolutionary movement.[21]

Soviet interests in the Third World

Analyses of Soviet interests and motivation in the Third World were commonplace during and shortly after the Brezhnev period. Such studies were overwhelmingly based on conjecture and inference, as reliable documentation and memoirs on the process of Soviet decision-making and the calculations that informed it were almost entirely lacking. This did not rule out relatively sophisticated approaches to explanation. Indeed, the lack of reliable empirical material actually encouraged hypotheses and theorising in this vein.[22] However, at the same time – and given the increasingly charged atmosphere of East–West relations occasioned by the deterioration of détente and the Soviet leadership's own boasts about heading a wave of revolutionary change – it was relatively easy for analysts and, as we have seen above, policy-makers to form a somewhat blunter view that Soviet Third World policy was guided by some crude 'master-plan', the execution of which was orchestrated by a rational and calculating communist leadership in Moscow. In this scheme of things the Soviet Union provided political direction and military capabilities while allied 'proxy' forces from Cuba, East Germany, and even North Korea furnished military and special forces on the ground. The end purpose of these activities was, in the words of one analyst, the subversion of the Third World toward 'a global socialist system of totalitarianism'.[23]

Evidence concerning the mechanics and well-springs of Soviet foreign policy which has come to light since the late 1980s offers little credence for this viewpoint. Certain agencies of the Soviet state (principally the KGB) did seemingly plan activities in a strategic fashion aimed at exploiting opportunities for influence in the Third World.[24] It can also be argued that the Soviet leadership under Brezhnev increasingly thought in global terms and that Soviet foreign policy exhibited a generally expansionist predisposition toward obtaining a position of global advantage over the capitalist West.[25] Whether or not this amounted to a carefully conceived grand design is, however, a quite different matter. As Soviet insiders have subsequently admitted, successive Soviet leaderships, including that of Brezhnev, possessed neither the intellectual depth nor the organisational capabilities to conceive and execute any such scheme.[26]

The absence of a master plan did not preclude, however, the existence of certain objective Soviet interests in the Third World. First, in political terms, states in relatively proximity to the Soviet Union (India, Pakistan, the two Koreas, Vietnam) had long been a source of close attention (under Stalin and Khrushchev as well as Brezhnev), both to block American and Chinese influence and, if necessary (as in the case of Afghanistan), to staunch possible destabilisation in the Soviet Union's southern union republics. Under Brezhnev this political competition was taken further afield, both in response to Chinese encroachments into Africa and as part of a more assertive challenge to the United States and its regional allies (Israel in particular). It should also be noted that the Soviet Union's pretensions to global status had long been confounded by a very weak position on the Western Hemisphere. Moscow's support of Cuba and, latterly, Nicaragua can thus be seen as offering the political benefit of breaking a seeming American monopoly of influence there.[27] Second, strategically speaking, the Soviet military had since the early 1960s been alert to the need to obtain increasingly far-flung clients to provide basing, intelligence, and other facilities. This shift to forward deployment was related, in large part, to the contingencies of nuclear war planning and the need to counter US sea-based nuclear weapons and, of a lesser order of importance, to deal with contingencies relating to war with China.[28] With regard to the former, while détente and the Soviet Union's achievement of strategic nuclear parity were perceived as having made a general war less likely (a position marked symbolically by Brezhnev's 'Peace Programme' presented to the 1971 CPSU Party Congress), these developments had not eliminated the possibility of such an occurrence.[29] Hence, the keen attention to actual and potential support facilities in states such as Angola, Cuba, Egypt, Ethiopia and Vietnam.[30] Third, the Soviet Union during the Brezhnev years became much more economically minded in its dealings with the Third World. A political dimension was still apparent (hence, the lavish aid extended to Cuba and Vietnam and the generally soft terms of assistance to certain states of socialist orientation), however, Soviet policy became more attuned (in principle if not always in practice) to the needs of the Soviet economy. Hence, a tightening of terms in economic assistance, an appreciation of the comparative commercial advantages of arms sales, and an attention to regional economic powers (Brazil and Morocco) many of whom were clearly embarked upon a capitalist rather than a socialist path of development.[31]

Outlining these objectives may still, however, overstate the degree of long-term coherence and dynamism in Soviet policy. Moscow's approach toward the Third World was, in fact, often characterised by caution, short-term opportunism and pragmatic adjustment as well as at times cross-cutting considerations of a more ideological bent. To understand these qualities three central influences on policy during the Brezhnev period are important.

The first concerns the status of the central relationship with the United States. For the Brezhnev leadership détente was perceived as a considerable achievement. As well as the obvious benefits (a stabilisation of the arms race, a recognition of the post-war order in Europe, a climate for economic interchange with the West and a neutralisation of Sino-US collusion),[32] détente was perceived as reflecting two circumstances of political significance. Domestically, it was a policy course personally associated with the political ascendancy of Brezhnev, while in international terms (as noted above) it was regarded as confirmation of the Soviet Union's credentials as a global power and as an equal of the United States. These political circumstances had a paradoxical effect. On the one hand, it permitted the Soviet leadership the belief that it had a right to involve itself in any and all issues of international concern but, on the other, an awareness that the United States could not be disregarded willy-nilly owing to its own global interests and reach. Hence, notwithstanding the appearances of assertiveness noted above, Soviet policy often displayed a marked caution based on a desire to minimise damage to relations with the United States.

The second influence of note concerns the relatively bountiful policy opportunities the Soviet Union was presented with during the Brezhnev years. As a whole this period witnessed a marked turbulence in the Third World, the origins of which were quite separate from the effects of Soviet or American intervention. In the Middle East, the Arab–Israeli dispute reached new heights as a consequence of radicalised Arab governments in Egypt and

Syria; Africa witnessed the last great wave of decolonisation (the independence of the former Portuguese territories of, *inter alia*, Angola, Mozambique, Guinea–Bissau), the collapse of the monarchy in Ethiopia, the end of white-minority rule in Rhodesia/Zimbabwe and an upsurge of anti-apartheid agitation in South Africa; in South East Asia meanwhile the war in Vietnam provided a ready conduit for Soviet arms and influence. This war, in turn, had a longer-term impact, deterring US military involvement in the Third World in the latter half of the 1970s.[33]

Third, some consideration of the role of ideology needs to be made. The role of ideology as a framing influence on Soviet foreign policy has, in fact, long been downplayed. There are several reasons why this has been the case. There is much about Soviet foreign policy – its driving preoccupations of national security, status and economic gain – that would lead one to assume that is was driven by a fairly clear *raison d'être*. Further, it often exhibited trends at cross-purposes with ideological prescriptions. As already noted above, in the Third World, for instance, Moscow sought and maintained close relations with regimes of a clear capitalist orientation. In addition, it also developed ties with regimes with no clear ideological platform at all. In Africa during the 1970s this included personalist dictatorships in the Central African Republic, Equatorial Guinea, and Uganda. Finally, a large body of work exists which suggests that Soviet foreign policy can be understood as reflecting the domestic balance of political forces within the top Soviet leadership and the consequent bargaining between individuals within the Politburo and the institutional constituencies (the Ministries of Defence and Foreign Affairs, the CPSU International Department, the KGB and so on) which they favoured. Particular trends in policy (the pursuit of détente, activism in the Third World) may consequently be seen as the outcome of these processes and, in particular during the Brezhnev period, the efforts of the Soviet leader to foster a consensus within the party's top echelons while simultaneously attempting to stamp his personal authority and preferences on policy.[34] Brezhnev's consensual approach did not eliminate factional and personal differences, and specific decision-making events (the four cases of intervention described below, for instance) can be regarded as determined by the manoeuvrings of instituonal and personal interests and preferences; rather, that is, than the consequence of a shared ideological position.

These disclaimers aside, ideology did nonetheless affect Soviet foreign policy. The memoirs of Brezhnev-era officials bear this out[35] as do some of the criticisms levelled against the Brezhnev leadership in the Gorbachev period (see below). Exactly what effect ideology had on foreign policy-making, however, depends on how the concept is understood. It is too simplistic to suggest that foreign policy prescriptions could de deduced straight from the texts of Marx and Lenin. Rather, as George Breslauer has suggested, a Soviet 'foreign policy ideology' comprised a complex belief system that reflected an accumulation of philosophical and political assumptions based on the building of socialism within the Soviet state and the international environment in which that process occurred. This, in turn, was affected by the personal experiences of the Soviet leadership (exposure to war, the excesses of the Stalin period, and so on.) and learning from events (the impact of key foreign policy episodes such as the Nazi–Soviet Pact, the invasion of Czechoslovakia and the Sino-Soviet rift). The general assumptions fostered as a consequence of these processes are well known: the equation of the interests of international socialism with the maintenance of Soviet power in the Soviet Union; the antagonism between socialism and capitalism/imperialism; the unfolding of historical change in an anti-imperialist direction.[36]

These assumptions were, of course, all reformulated under Gorbachev. However, they remained valid during the Brezhnev period and informed the way in which the Third World was perceived and the nature of Soviet policy toward the region. In very general terms they allowed the Soviet leadership to frame its foreign policy in specific regions in relation to global trends (sometimes dubbed 'correlation of forces' analysis) relating to the state of Soviet relations with the United States (the socialist/imperialist dichotomy and modifications to it such as peaceful coexistence or détente) and the unfolding of national liberation processes and social and political change.[37] They also coloured the manner in which more specific circumstances were perceived. Hence, for instance, while it was assumed that revolutionary change in the Third World was internally generated, this did not preclude the permissive support of progressive (that is Soviet and allied) forces from outside.[38] Similarly, insofar as it was held that socialism was a secular historical trend, Soviet intervention could be justified on the grounds of preserving established socialist regimes.

The influences on Soviet foreign policy toward the Third World meant that while the Brezhnev leadership was presented with ample occasion to demonstrate its prowess as a global actor and to facilitate and further advantageous trends in the correlation of forces, it at the same time remained, for the most part, mindful of minimising damage to relations with the United States and of averting any escalation of Third World conflicts to the point of direct Soviet–US confrontation. Policy was, consequently, characterised by an odd mix of pragmatism and caution on the one hand, and ambition informed by ideology and *realpolitik* on the other.

By way of illustration, let us take the four obvious cases of Soviet interventionism during the Brezhnev period. First, the 1973 war in the Middle East. Here, for all its military backing of the Arab cause, the Soviet involvement displayed, in fact, a marked caution. Viktor Israelyan, a Soviet career diplomat and member of a Middle East task force assigned to the Politburo during the 1973 crisis, points out that Moscow had initially opposed the Egyptian–Syrian decision to attack Israel, tried on a number of occasions to persuade Egyptian leader Anwar Sadat of the wisdom of an early cease-fire, and provided weapons to the Arab side sufficient to avoid defeat but insufficient to wrest a victory over Israel.[39] In addition, Moscow tried anxiously to find a joint Soviet–US diplomatic solution and was prevented from doing so less by a lack of will on its side than by the determination of the United States to exclude Moscow from the Middle East.[40] When American resolve became clear with the issuing of a DEFCON III military alert and pressure against Israel to accept a cease-fire, Moscow was forced to concede leadership in the conflict to Washington, which then took upon itself the key role of mediator between the Arab and Israeli sides.[41]

In the Angolan civil war, secondly, caution was also in evidence. The Soviet leadership was mindful in the African context of the political challenge posed by American and Chinese involvement but saw in the south of the continent little intrinsic strategic or economic benefits. The International Department of the CPSU and the Politburo's main ideologue Mikhail Suslov did see some significance in the revolutionary potential of black Africa but it should also be noted that the political leadership in Moscow was largely ignorant of the continent and, in the case of Foreign Minister Andrei Gromyko, openly disdainful of its affairs. Interest in Angola seems to have been sparked first by the power vacuum left behind by the departure of the Portuguese and second by a perception that the war had become a test of Soviet–American (and, to a lesser degree, Soviet–Chinese) competition once Washington and Beijing had declared in favour of the FNLA and UNITA.[42] Even then, the Soviet Union wanted only a limited involvement. Its eventually decisive intervention was the consequence of a reluctant, ratchet-like escalation prompted by a need to support a deepening Cuban involvement on the side of the MPLA.[43]

The involvement in the Horn of Africa, thirdly, much more so than Angola was a consequence of strategic considerations. The Horn itself (abutting the Red Sea and the Arabian peninsular) was considered of greater strategic consequence than southern Africa. However, the war between Ethiopia and Somalia when it erupted confronted the Soviet leadership with some unwelcome choices. Moscow already enjoyed a close relationship with, and port facilities in, Somalia but was at the same time confronted with a regime in Ethiopia openly courting Soviet (and Cuban) assistance. Moscow's initial response to Somali attacks on Ethiopia in early 1977 was a diplomatic one – joint Soviet–Cuban diplomacy tried to persuade Ethiopia and Somalia to unite in a socialist federation. When this proved fruitless, Moscow threw in its lot with Ethiopia, partly because it had greater strategic promise and partly because Mengistu appeared a more reliable client than the Somali leader Said Barre. The military support operation which materialised in the former's favour in 1977–8 was born of these considerations and was a consequence also of a calculation that the United States was not inclined to back Somalia militarily.[44] It was, however, informed by limited battlefield objectives. Thus, once the Somali forces had been defeated, Moscow dissuaded the Ethiopian side from invading Somali territory.

Afghanistan, finally, seemingly presents a case of outright Soviet assertiveness. However, the intervention was not a favoured option among the Soviet leadership and was undertaken only after the exhaustion of other alternatives. The immediate context of the Soviet invasion of 1979 was a grave deterioration of civil order within Afghanistan following violent faction fighting within the ruling Afghan communist party – the People's Democratic Party of Afghanistan (PDPA) – and mounting resistance throughout the country to communist rule. Combined with the unfolding of the Islamic revolution in neighbouring Iran, it was feared that these events augured the possible fall of the PDPA regime.[45] This instability had already resulted in increased military assistance (both arms and advisers) to the ruling Khalq faction of the PDPA during 1978–9. There was no initial desire, however, to send in Soviet combat troops. Indeed, Moscow (and Defence Minister Ustinov specifically) repeatedly turned down requests to this end.[46] Moscow also made persistent efforts to persuade the Khalq leadership to moderate unpopular domestic reform and to broaden the regime by appointing to government members of the rival Parcham faction. The assassination of the Afghan President Mohammed Taraki by his deputy Hafizullah Amin in October, followed shortly after by Amin's efforts to open relations with the United States, heightened Soviet concerns of a wholesale slide into civil war and the possibility of American (as well as the still latent threat of Iranian) encroachment into the country. This fear of a loss of Afghanistan (an ideological as well as a strategic setback), coupled with an assumption that East–West relations were already so poor that any American response could be tolerated, prompted Defence Minister Ustinov, KGB Chairman Andropov, and Foreign Minister Gromyko to reverse their previous position to an infusion of Soviet troops. They then persuaded Brezhnev of the wisdom of the invasion and the Soviet operation was subsequently launched in December 1979, its ostensible purpose the removal of Amin, the consolidation of PDPA rule and the stabilisation of the Soviet Union's southern borders.[47]

The Soviet Union and the Third World – a house built on sand

Whatever caution the Soviet leadership may have displayed in the Third World, during the Brezhnev period it seemed clear that Soviet influence in the region was on the march and, consequently, that it had obtained an international position of global significance. Yet the seeming 'gains' of the Soviet Union often hid far less favourable developments; developments which meant that Moscow increasingly found itself to be an embattled and frustrated power.

One source of its problems was precisely the string of new socialist-oriented regimes that had emerged during the 1970s. Far from being an asset to the Soviet Union or a positive example of socialist development, these regimes were, from the outset, plagued by intractable problems. Few could be said to have enjoyed broad domestic support and consequently used the Soviet-endorsed vehicle of rule, the vanguard party, less as a device for mass participation and national, popular advancement and more as a means to maintain an unrepresentative and often unpopular elite in power. The inability of these regimes to forge national unity coupled with the fact that their initial ascent to power was based on violence meant that a number – Angola, Afghanistan, Cambodia, Ethiopia and Mozambique – soon became mired in civil wars, the seriousness of which was apparent even before the death of Brezhnev in 1982. The willingness of the Brezhnev regime to support these embattled regimes with arms and advisers meanwhile ensured their survival but did little to consolidate their rule. Indeed, copious amounts of Soviet arms had the effect of prolonging conflicts by deterring ruling parties from seeking political accommodation and negotiated political settlements.

These states (plus others such as South Yemen) were also the scene of often disastrous experiments in economic transformation, inspired, at least in part, by Marxist–Leninist ideology and the experience of the Soviet Union. Combined with ongoing economic problems in the more fully fledged socialist regimes of Cuba and Vietnam this imposed a growing economic cost on the Soviet Union in the form of direct subsidies, unpaid loans and trade credits. Even though its assistance programme more broadly had become better tailored to Soviet economic needs, this meant that Moscow was facing an increasingly unsustainable drain on its resources by the late Brezhnev period. A 1987 study sponsored by the US Congress suggested that the Soviet economic assistance programme having been 'self-sustaining' (that is, without cost to the Soviet Union) since the mid-1960s had entered into deficit in the early 1980s.[48] Statistics released in 1990 outlined the scale of the problem, showing as they did 85,000 million roubles worth of accumulated debts to Moscow (25,000 million from Cuba and Vietnam alone), built up, in large part, during the Brezhnev years.[49] Even in the light of such figures, however, many Third World states had long been disillusioned with the limitations of Soviet assistance and trade. Whereas Cuba and Vietnam had little alternative but to rely on the Soviet Union, some states of socialist orientation were adroit in their pursuit of economic diversification. Angola, for instance, even during the most radical early phase of its post-1975 development, sought the involvement of western oil concerns in its offshore reserves, courted western investment, and maintained the trade ties with Europe, Brazil and North America built up during the period of Portuguese colonialism. Finally, these states were of limited value strategically. The Soviet Union did gain landing rights and access to port facilies in Angola, Ethiopia, Mozambique and South Yemen, but not formal basing rights. Ethiopia rejected Soviet overtures to this end in 1980, while Angola's declared status as a non-aligned nation prohibited the extension of such rights.[50]

Looking beyond simply the socialist-oriented states which assumed power in the 1970s, in other cases where Moscow enjoyed apparently close relations it also experienced difficulties. With states such as Egypt, India, Iraq, Libya, and Syria, ties had been built on the basis of copious amounts of economic assistance, large-scale transfers of arms and military advice, and a certain political convergence based on anti-Zionism, an intuitive anti-Americanism (in the case of the Arab states), or non-alignment. Such ties, did provide some material benefits to the Soviet Union, notably in the form of transfers of petro-dollars for Soviet arms. However, they never fully translated into the establishment of reliable Soviet partners. The reasons for this are complex but relate to the peculiarities of nationalism, the caprice of personalist rule,[51] and the failure of the Soviet bloc to offer an alternative to American and European oil markets, technology and investment. Iraq, for instance, despite large-scale arms purchases from Moscow (noted above) and a Treaty of Friendship with the Soviet Union dating from 1972, defied Soviet policy in important areas. It was a critic of the Soviet–Cuban intervention in the Horn and of the Soviet invasion of Afghanistan, and paid little heed to Soviet sensibilities when, in 1978, it clamped down on the Iraqi communist party. In 1980 Iraq attacked Iran with weapons largely supplied by the Soviet Union, even though this precipitate step was opposed in Moscow.[52] Syria was a comparable case. Following the 1973 Middle East war relations were strained despite the substantial military relationship. Moscow opposed the Syrian intervention in Lebanon in 1976 and the same year found its requests for basing rights rejected. Relations improved in 1980 with the signing of a Friendship Treaty but deteriorated once more in 1982 following a further Syrian intervention in Lebanon in a limit war against Israel. On this occasion a lack of Soviet support was met by Syrian dissatisfaction at the poor performance of Soviet-supplied advisers and weaponry.[53] As for India, relations here were fostered by a joint antipathy toward China and a shared suspicion of Pakistani influence in southern and central Asia. This helped overcome some clear political divergences (the Soviet Union was the world's largest communist state, India the world's most populous democracy).[54] It did not, however, eliminate differences stemming from India's non-aligned stance and its reluctance to follow Soviet foreign policy prescriptions. New Delhi, for instance, would not endorse Brezhnev's proposals for an Asian collective security zone; neither did it support the invasion of Afghanistan. India's own initiatives – the apparent acquisition of a nuclear weapon following a test explosion in 1974 and proposals in the early 1970s to demilitarise the Indian Ocean – furthermore, ran counter to Soviet preferences.[55]

Egypt, finally, offers perhaps the most profound case of disappointment to the Soviet Union. Ties to the regime of Gamal Abdel Nasser had formed a cornerstone of Soviet Third World policy under Khrushchev and constituted an early success in spreading Soviet influence into the Middle East.

As we have seen above, the Soviet Union was a large-scale supplier of military aid to Egypt during the Middle East War of 1973 and it had mounted a major re-supply of Egyptian forces following their losses at the hands of Israel in the Six-Day War of 1967. Relations with Nasser's successor Anwar al-Sadat were never as close. Even prior to the 1973 war, Sadat had curtailed Soviet basing access and had reduced the number of Soviet military advisers. The war itself was the occasion for further frictions as Sadat accused the Soviets of being laggardly in their deliveries of military hardware (Moscow, for its part, accused Sadat of ignoring Soviet military advice).[56] Following the war, Sadat concluded that territorial losses at the hands of Israel could best be won back through diplomatic means. This increased his interest in American mediation and led to a commensurate shift away from Moscow. In 1976 Cairo unilaterally abrogated the 1971 Soviet–Egyptian Treaty of Friendship and terminated Soviet naval access. Soviet marginalisation was completed in 1979 when Egypt signed, along with Israel, the US-brokered Camp David Accords.[57]

This event also signified a wider trend that was to rebound to the Soviet Union's disadvantage, namely, a reawakened American engagement in the Third World. The passivity the United States had displayed over the wars in Angola and Ethiopia can be regarded as anomalous and owing to a rare coincidence of external and domestic conditions favouring non-intervention (post-Vietnam *ennui* and, in the case of Angola, the Watergate crisis). In this connection it should not be forgotten that the United States had traditionally been militarily active in the Third World. Unlike the Soviet Union it had been prepared to commit ground troops to favoured causes (as in the Korean and Vietnam wars) and had not been averse to threatening either Moscow (as in the case of the DEFCON III alert over Egypt noted above) or certain Third World states (as with the blockade of Cuba and the bombing of Cambodia/Kampuchea in 1970 and 1975).[58] The United States had covertly destabilised certain radical Third World regimes with connections to Moscow or Havana (it played a role in the overthrow of President Sukarno in Indonesia in 1965 and of Salvador Allende in Chile in 1973).[59] Further, it had a power projection capability far in excess of the Soviet Union's, a reliable network of allies and friendly states spread throughout South and South East Asia (South Korea and Pakistan), Africa (Zaire, Kenya and South Africa), Latin America (Brazil following the 1964 military coup), and the Middle East/Gulf region (Israel, Saudi Arabia and, until 1979, Iran). It was also the beneficiary of Egypt's and Somalia's break with the Soviet Union during the 1970s. For all these reasons, whatever the perception US Administrations may have held of Soviet advantage in the Third World, the perception of the Brezhnev leadership (for all its hubs about the upsurge of the world revolutionary process) was of an ongoing American activism and presence.[60]

Following the hiatus of the mid-1970s, US policy sought in the last years of the Carter administration to deliberately counter the Soviet Union in the

Third World, particularly in the area of the Horn of Africa and the Persian Gulf. This involved an increase in military assistance to Somalia, Egypt and Saudi Arabia, a show of military force in the Gulf of Aden in 1979 to bolster North Yemen against the pro-Soviet South Yemen regime and agreements on the use of military facilities in Kenya and Oman. The Soviet invasion of Afghanistan crystallised these trends in the 'Carter Doctrine' of containment.[61] The succeeding Administration Reagan was even more robust and took a number of steps shortly prior to Brezhnev's demise. These included the beginning of covert support for anti-Marxist insurgents in Nicaragua, Angola and Afghanistan.

As well as the obstacles that Moscow faced in the field, certain deep-seated problems were inherent in Soviet Third World policy owing to the manner of its genesis and formulation. Here the issue of ideology is again important. The Soviet leadership was aware that the ideological credentials of its favoured Third World leaders were often shallow. Indeed, the very notion of socialist orientation was a compromise meant to compensate for the absence of rule by formal communist parties in the Third World.[62] A number of Third World leaders who proclaimed fealty to socialism were consequently often mistrusted by Moscow because of various ideological deviations. That said, the Brezhnev leadership was also taken in by false professions of ideology. Its support of Mengistu in Ethiopia, for instance, was based on the latter's public commitment to Marxism–Leninism even though this was largely a political camouflage that hid nationalist and militarist tendencies.[63] At a broader level, the ideological framework of the Soviet approach led it to overestimate the possibilities of socialist advance in the Third World. Its initial backing for new regimes in Angola, Ethiopia and Afghanistan and subsequent material commitment to their consolidation was based on the misplaced assumption that the difficulties of socialist transformation could be overcome.[64] By the time of Brezhnev's death this assumption had been qualified but not abandoned. Perhaps most destructively of all, ideological constructs led to perceptions of the world in Manichean terms. The old 'two-camp' thesis of Zhdanov had long been replaced by peaceful coexistence and the centrepiece of Brezhnev's foreign policy was, as already noted, détente. However, this did not prevent a reading of the international system as a sphere of competition between social systems. The Third World, moreover, was the main site of this competition owing to the pitical rigidity of the state system in Europe. The upshot was a Soviet leadership unwilling to countenance the status quo in the Third World and an automatic and ultimately self-defeating hostility to American (and the West more broadly) and Chinese policies.

Other miscalculations, less the consequence of ideology, also occurred. Of no small importance was the closed and very narrow decision-making process in Moscow. Key foreign policy decisions under Brezhnev were the preserve of an inner Politburo group comprising Brezhnev himself plus Gromyko,

Andropov and Ustinov (in regard to the Third World, Suslov also had some influence); Brezhnev's ill-health from the mid-1970s meant that even he often took a back seat.[65] The upshot was a decision-making process that lacked exposure to debate and the full airing of alternatives. Thus not even the full Politburo, let alone the Central Committee, was party to the deliberations that led to the invasion of Afghanistan.[66] Further, Soviet policy toward individual Third World countries, for instance, was often made on the basis of very little knowledge of local circumstances. This occurred either because Moscow had had no prior presence in a country (as was the case in formerly Portuguese Africa) and had to rely on information provided indirectly (in the Angolan case, intelligence on the MPLA prior to 1975 often came via the Portuguese Communist Party), or because the complexities of local politics were simply so peculiar (as was the case in Afghanistan and South Yemen).[67] There are also numerous cases, particularly in Africa, where Soviet personnel (advisers and embassy staff) on the ground, seemingly blind to local sensibilities and guilty of condescension and arrogance, offended their host regime and harmed the broader relationship.

Brezhnev, Gorbachev and beyond

Concern at the mounting predicaments facing the Soviet position in the Third World were, in fact, voiced in the late Brezhnev period. These pronouncements were of a largely subtle nature. Among the Soviet scholarly community and within the CPSU International Department, for instance, there was a good deal of commentary which suggested increasing reservations about the political and economic development of the states of socialist orientation and, by extension, the problems these states faced in constructing socialist societies in conditions that were unpropitious domestically and hostile internationally.[68] At the political level, some disquiet was also apparent. Brezhnev's report to the 26th CPSU Congress in February 1981 contained far less of the hubris which characterised the comparable report five years earlier and was replete with references to the variety of obstacles facing revolutionary change in the Third World.[69]

These reservations aside, however, there was no fundamental reassessment of policy at this juncture. The years immediately after the Soviet invasion of Afghanistan did, it is true, witness a certain circumspection in Soviet behaviour in the Third World under first Brezhnev and then Andropov. There was certainly no desire to seek out additional clients during this period and Moscow became increasingly cognisant of the resurgence of American will under President Reagan – hence, Moscow's response to punitive American actions against Grenada in 1983 was only verbal, and the Soviet Union refused to supply the Sandinista regime in Nicaragua with weapons such as the Mig-21 fighter jet that would have provoked American countermeasures. However, Moscow remained committed to those states with which it had already established close relations. Embattled governments in Afghanistan, Angola and Iraq enjoyed rising levels of Soviet military assistance in the first half of the 1980s, Cuba was the recipient of a second squadron of Mig-23 fighter jets in 1982, and that same year (following the Israeli invasion of Lebanon) Syria took delivery of SA-5 surface-to-air missiles (SAMs), a weapon not previously deployed outside of the Soviet Union. Throughout this period, Moscow also took the position that the Third World remained a zone of competition with the United States and China. Indeed, with regard to the former, the superpower antagonism acquired an increasingly dangerous dynamic as the Reagan administration increased its covert destabilisation of Afghanistan, Angola and Nicaragua.

A much more decisive alteration in Soviet Third World policy occurred, of course, during the Gorbachev period. The variety of shifts after 1985 are well known. Most importantly there was a decisive break with the Brezhnevian strategy of competitive interventionism and military support for Third World clients. During 1988–9 this permitted negotiated settlements to long-running civil conflicts in Afghanistan and Angola along with the removal of Soviet troops from the former and Cuban troops from the latter.[70] Cooperative Soviet–US engagement in these two cases proved decisive, as indeed it did in the 1990 Gulf War. This latter case was arguably even more significant insofar as Soviet policy, for the first time, effectively condoned a major US intervention against a state (Iraq) with a long history of ties to Moscow. A second shift of note concerned a reshuffling of the hierarchy of states in the Third World worthy of Soviet courtship. Relations with once privileged states such as Cuba and Vietnam experienced a wholesale revision, involving during 1990–1 an overhaul of the Soviet economic and military aid programmes and a curtailment of Soviet access to local military facilities.[71]

A similar shift also occurred with regard to the states of socialist orientation which had come to prominence in the 1970s. These were the object of increasing criticism in Soviet policy circles and some – notably Ethiopia, Mozambique, South Yemen and Nicaragua – were effectively abandoned by Moscow as ongoing concerns in the late 1980s. In parallel, Soviet analysis began to openly discount the prospects of socialist development in the Third World and placed an increased emphasis on regional powers regardless of their domestic socio-economic orientation. Some, such as India, had long been important to Moscow, but others – Mexico, South Korea, Saudi Arabia, Jordan – had previously been neglected. This more pragmatic trend was capped by concerted efforts to repair relations with Egypt and to re-open formal relations with Israel broken since 1967.[72]

Several reasons account for the shift of policy under Gorbachev. Some relate to the domestic and international dynamics generated during the Gorbachev period itself. The pace and urgency of change in the Soviet Union and Eastern Europe between 1989 and 1991 meant that the Gorbachev leadership simply lacked the political inclination and policy-making resources to engage in the Third World. Disengagement was, in this sense, a trend by default. That said, retreat from the Third World cannot merely be seen as the consequence of preoccupations elsewhere. Key trends (notably the decision to withdraw from Afghanistan) had been evident since shortly after Gorbachev assumed power in 1985. Part of the explanation for this can be found in Gorbachev's own political and intellectual character – his receptivity to new ideas and an ability to undertake pragmatic analysis of policy challenges.[73]

That this approach yielded such dramatic shifts in Soviet policy suggests that Gorbachev's perception of Brezhnev's foreign policy was particularly censorious. In this respect, Gorbachev, and perhaps more so his Foreign Minister Eduard Shevardnadze, were critical of at least three trends. These included, in the first place, the economic cost of supporting states of socialist orientation. Second, and more far-reaching, ideology was seen as an iniquitous influence during the Brezhnev period. It had led the Soviet leadership to make overly inflated claims concerning progressive change in the Third World and had led it to support of far-flung regimes which offered Moscow little material benefit. Furthermore, ideology had compounded the Cold War, transforming, in the words of Shevardnadze, 'entire continents into arenas of East–West struggle under the banners of ideological implacability'.[74] This was not only harmful to the peoples of those continents but contributed to a pervasive level of tension between Moscow and Washington. The 'de-ideologisation' of foreign policy under Gorbachev thus had far-reaching consequences, removing as it did a principal rationale for Soviet involvement not just with the states of socialist orientation but even with Cuba, Vietnam and Afghanistan.

Third, the deterioration of relations with the West occasioned by competition in the Third World was seen as harmful to core Soviet security interests. Rather than exploiting the acquisition of strategic parity with the United States in the service of promoting a cooperative great power condominium in the Third World (paralleling, for instance, the settlement of the status quo in Europe during the 1970s), the Brezhnev leadership rather engaged in a harmful competition. This not only occasioned the strengthening of a Sino-American coalition of interests against Moscow but increased the threat of regional military escalation and even the risk of nuclear war.[75]

The disengagement from the Third World begun under Gorbachev accelerated markedly in the post-Soviet period. This reflects, in part, the termination of the Cold War and the end of the ideological imperative of Soviet (now Russian) foreign policy. It reflects also, however, the truncation of Russian power generally. Certainly, in much of the Third World, Russia is of only marginal consequence. It retains some influence in contiguous areas (for instance in the Persian Gulf, the Caspian basin and the 'new' Third World of post-Soviet Central Asia) and further afield as a commercial supplier of arms and through its permanent seat on the UN Security Council. However,

Russia lacks the economic resources, military reach and diplomatic clout necessary for presence and influence on a global scale. Thus, while there is constant reference to Russia's status as a 'great power' in official foreign policy discourse, this is in many respects an aspiration rather than a reality.

The mirror image of this state of affairs is the post-Cold War position of the United States. While the end of the Cold War has removed Washington's keen interest in certain regions (Africa notably), it remains the case that the United States continues to regard its foreign policy in globalist terms and has been able to act largely unencumbered by the threat of Russian opposition. It has thus continued its lead role in mediating the Arab–Israeli dispute but, more tellingly, has been able to employ coercive measures against states (Iraq, for instance) which during the Brezhnev period would have been deterred, or met by Soviet counter-measures. The final burial of the Soviet model of development has also meant that neo-liberal strategies of economic development championed by the United States and backed by bodies such as the International Monetary Fund (IMF), the World Bank, and the World Trade Organisation (WTO) have assumed an even greater international pre-eminence.[76]

Such developments have led to mounting criticism in Moscow and have provided part justification for one of the conceptual cornerstones of Russian foreign policy since the late 1990s – the positing of a 'multipolar' world in juxtaposition to a 'one-dimensional model' centred around American power.[77] It has led also to an implicit revisionism in Russia concerning Brezhnev's foreign policy, focusing in particular on the global interests and equivalence with the United States that Moscow once enjoyed, and contrasting this with the retreat and concessions of the Gorbachev period.[78] This type of analysis is not merely about post-imperial nostalgia. The all too easy criticisms of the Brezhnev period can easily lead one to ignore the equally culpable role of the United States. Claims made by the Brezhnev leadership of unwarranted American interference in the Third World were not without substance. Indeed, in the post-War period the United States increasingly enjoyed the economic whip hand in the region and – along with its French and British allies – was more militarily interventionist than the Soviet Union.[79] In this light, the Brezhnev period can be regarded as something of an anomaly – the one brief period in the twentieth century in which Moscow enjoyed a global significance as a diplomatic actor, a military power, and a superpower patron, and in which the ascendancy of the West in the colonial and then the Third World was truly challenged.

Further reading

R. D. Anderson, Jr, *Public Politics in an Authoritarian State: Making Foreign Policy During the Brezhnev Years* (Ithaca, London: Cornell University Press, 1993).

A. Bennett, *Condemned to Repetition: The Rise, Fall, and Reprise of Soviet–Russian Military Interventionism, 1973–1996* (Cambridge, Mass.: MIT Press, 1999).

R. L. Garthoff, *Détente and Confrontation. American–Soviet Relations from Nixon to Reagan* (Washington, DC: Brookings Institution, 1985).
V. Israelyan, *Inside the Kremlin During the Yom Kippur War* (Pennsylvania State University Press, 1995).
J. Steele, *The Limits of Soviet Power. The Kremlin's Foreign Policy – Brezhnev to Chernenko* (Harmondsworth: Pelican Books, 1984).
See also the *Bulletin and Working Papers* series of the Cold War International History Project <http://cwihp.si.edu/publications.htm>, which cover Soviet policies in the Brezhnev era toward Vietnam, Angola and Afghanistan.

Notes

1. The second world or socialist camp also included China, but as its inclusion suggests this was a 'world' that was economically, politically and ideologically heterogeneous.
2. D. Zagoria, 'Into the Breach: New Soviet Alliances in the Third World', in E. P. Hoffmann and F. J. Fleron (eds), *The Conduct of Soviet Foreign Policy* (New York: Aldine, 1980), pp. 495–6.
3. W. R. Duncan, *The Soviet Union and Cuba: Interests and Influence* (New York: Praeger, 1985), pp. 59–75.
4. M. N. Kramer, 'Soviet Arms Transfers to the Third World', *Problems of Communism*, 36/5, 1987, pp. 58–61.
5. E. K. Valkenier, *The Soviet Union and the Third World: An Economic Bind* (New York, etc.: Praeger, 1983), pp. 3–11; C. R. Saivetz and S. Woodby, *Soviet–Third World Relations* (Boulder, Col., London: Westview Press, 1985), pp. 30–44.
6. M. N. Kramer, 'Soviet Arms Transfers to the Third World', *Problems of Communism*, 36/5, 1987, p. 54.
7. Z. Khalilzad, 'Soviet-Occupied Afghanistan', *Problems of Communism*, 29/6, 1980, p. 23. The other interventions noted in this paragraph are covered in detail in B. D. Porter, *The USSR in Third World Conflicts: Soviet Arms and Diplomacy in Local Wars, 1945–1980* (Cambridge University Press, 1984).
8. J. M. McConnell and B. Dismukes, 'Soviet Diplomacy of Force in the Third World', *Problems of Communism*, 28/1, 1979.
9. G. Golan, *The Soviet Union and National Liberation Movements in the Third World* (Boston: Unwin Hyman, 1988), pp. 271–4, 286–8.
10. *Izvestiya* and *Pravda*, 24 February 1976, as translated in *The Current Digest of the Soviet Press*, 28/8, 1976, pp. 3–15. This speech was a summation of a general rising of expectations regarding the Third World in professional party and military thought in the Soviet Union during the 1970s. See G. W. Breslauer, 'Ideology and Learning in Soviet Third World Policy', *World Politics*, 34/3, 1987, pp. 435–8.
11. In Soviet pronouncements this formulation came to apply to, *inter alia*, Afghanistan, Angola, Ethiopia, Cambodia–Kampuchea, Mozambique, Nicaragua and South Yemen. Regimes of somewhat longer duration in Algeria, Guinea, India, Iraq, Syria and Tanzania were also accorded this distinction and referred to as 'first-generation' states of socialist orientation. As for Cuba and Vietnam these enjoyed the more elevated status of fully fledged socialist states ruled by properly constituted communist parties and on a par with the states of eastern Europe (who like Cuba and Vietnam were full members of COMECON). On these distinctions see F. Fukuyama, *Moscow's Post-Brezhnev Reassessment of the Third World* (Santa Monica: Rand Corporation, 1986), pp. 83–4.

12. F. Fukuyama, 'The Rise and Fall of the Marxist–Leninist Vanguard Party', *Survey*, Summer 1985.
13. For a discussion of this strand of Soviet thinking and how the seeming contradiction was resolved theoretically see D. S. Papp, 'National Liberation during Détente: The Soviet Outlook', *International Journal*, 32/1, 1976–7. For consideration of how the peaceful coexistence/national liberation nexus was perceived by Brezhnev and his leadership contemporaries, see V. Israelyan, *Inside the Kremlin During the Yom Kippur War* (Pennsylvania State University Press, 1995), pp. 17–19, 33–40, 160–1, 208–9, 215, and R. L. Garthoff, *Détente and Confrontation. American–Soviet Relations from Nixon to Reagan* (Washington, DC: Brookings Institution, 1985), pp. 36–53.
14. A. Dobrynin, *In Confidence* (New York: Times Books, 1995), p. 410.
15. H. Kissinger, *Years of Renewal* (London: Weidenfeld & Nicolson, 1999), pp. 98–103, 249.
16. Z. Brzezinski, *Power and Principle: Memoirs of the National Security Adviser, 1977–1981* (New York: Farrar, Straus, Giroux, 1985), pp. 147–50; R. L. Garthoff, *Détente and Confrontation. American–Soviet Relations from Nixon to Reagan* Washington, DC: Brookings Institution, 1985), pp. 25–36.
17. President Gerald Ford, January 1976, as cited in G. R. Ford, *A Time to Heal* (London: W. H. Allen, 1979), p. 358.
18. R. Legvold, 'The Super Rivals: Conflict in the Third World', *Foreign Affairs*, 57/4, 1979, pp. 755–7.
19. President Carter, cited in R. L. Garthoff, *Détente and Confrontation. American–Soviet Relations from Nixon to Reagan*, (Washington, DC: Brookings Institution, 1985), p. 972.
20. A. M. Haig, *Caveat: Realism, Reagan and Foreign Policy* (London: Weidenfeld & Nicolson, 1984), pp. 26–7.
21. G. T. Yu, 'Sino-Soviet Rivalry in Africa', in D. E. Albright (ed.), *Africa and International Communism* (London: Macmillan, 1980), pp. 180–7.
22. E. K. Valkenier, *The Soviet Union and the Third World: An Economic Bind* (New York, etc.: Praeger, 1983); H. Gelman, *The Brezhnev Politburo and the Decline of Détente* (Ithaca, London: Cornell University Press, 1984); A. Z. Rubinstein (ed.), *Soviet and Chinese Influence in the Third World* (New York: Praeger, 1975); J. Valenta and W. Potter (eds.), *Soviet Decisionmaking for National Security* (Hemel Hempstead: George Allen & Unwin, 1984).
23. F. M. Casey, 'The Theory and Tactics of Soviet Third World Strategy', *Journal of Social, Political and Economic Studies*, 12/3, 1987, p. 258.
24. C. Andrew and O. Gordievsky, *KGB: The Inside Story of its Foreign Operations from Lenin to Gorbachev* (London: Sceptre, 1991), pp. 545–6; C. Andrew and V. Mitrokhin, *The Mitrokhin Archive: The KGB in Europe and the West* (London: Penguin Press, 1999), pp. 265, 472.
25. V. V. Aspaturian, 'Soviet Global Power and the Correlation of Forces', *Problems of Communism*, 29/3, 1980, pp. 16–17; A. N. Shevchenko, *Breaking with Moscow* (London: Jonathan Cape, 1985), pp. 285–6; W. C. Wohlforth, 'New Evidence on Moscow's Cold War. Ambiguity in Search of Theory', *Diplomatic History*, 21/2, 1997, pp. 229–42.
26. A. Dobrynin, *In Confidence* (New York: Times Books, 1995), pp. 161–2, 198; interview with K. Brutents conducted for *Cold War: Episode 17*, 'Good Guys, Bad Guys' at <http://cnn.com/SPECIALS/cold.war/episodes/17/interviews/brutents/>. Brutents was a deputy head of the International Department of the CPSU Central Committee.

27. R. Garthoff, *The Great Transition. American–Soviet Relations and the End of the Cold War* (Washington, DC: Brookings Institution, 1994), p. 718.
28. M. MccGwire, 'Naval Power and Soviet Global Strategy', *International Security*, 3/4, 1979, pp. 135–89.
29. On the subtleties of this position see M. MccGwire, *Perestroika and Soviet National Security* (Washington, DC: Brookings Institution, 1991), pp. 24–32.
30. F. Fukuyama, *The Military Dimension of Soviet Policy in the Third World* (Santa Monica: Rand Paper Series, P-6965, February 1984).
31. E. K. Valkenier, *The Soviet Union and the Third World: An Economic Bind* (New York, etc.: Praeger, 1983), pp. 11–33.
32. R. C. Nation, *Black Earth, Red Star. A History of Soviet Security Policy, 1917–1991* (Ithaca, London: Cornell University Press, 1992), pp. 256–8.
33. Hence, in the case of the Angolan civil war of 1975, the US Congress rejected appeals by President Ford to increase funding for covert support of the US-favoured FNLA and UNITA movements.
34. R. D. Anderson Jr, *Public Politics in an Authoritarian State: Making Foreign Policy During the Brezhnev Years* (Ithaca, London: Cornell University Press, 1993).
35. V. Israelyan, *Inside the Kremlin During the Yom Kippur War* (Pennsylvania State University Press, 1995), pp. 215–16.
36. G. W. Breslauer, 'Ideology and Learning in Soviet Third World Policy', *World Politics*, 34/3, 1987, pp. 430–2. See also A. Bennett, *Condemned to Repetition: The Rise, Fall, and Reprise of Soviet-Russian Military Interventionism, 1973–1996* (Cambridge, Mass.: MIT Press, 1999), pp. 1–38, 75–126.
37. This generalisation holds even though there was considerable debate within the Soviet scholarly and policy-making communities on the theoretical subtleties of applying Soviet ideological categories to the Third World. See the discussion in M. Light, *The Soviet Theory of International Relations* (Brighton: Wheatsheaf, 1988), pp: 1–24, 111–44.
38. S. N. MacFarlane, 'The Soviet Conception of Regional Security', *World Politics*, 37/3, 1985, pp. 299–307.
39. V. Israelyan, *Inside the Kremlin During the Yom Kippur War* (Pennsylvania State University Press, 1995), pp. 2, 17, 32–3, 41, 46, 57–61, 78, 107, 116–19, 148, 153–61, 186–8. See also, J. M. Goldgeier, *Leadership Style and Soviet Foreign Policy: Stalin, Khrushchev, Brezhnev, Gorbachev* (Baltimore Md., London: Johns Hopkins University Press, 1994), Chapter 5.
40. H. Kissinger, *Years of Upheaval* (Boston, Toronto: Little, Brown & Co., 1982), p. 594.
41. R. L. Garthoff, *Détente and Confrontation. American–Soviet Relations from Nixon to Reagan* (Washington, DC: Brookings Institution, 1985), pp. 379–85.
42. A. Dobrynin, *In Confidence* (New York: Times Books, 1995), pp. 366–7.
43. Interview with K. Brutents conducted for *Cold War: Episode 17*, 'Good Guys, Bad Guys', at <http://cnn.com/SPECIALS/cold.war/episodes/17/interviews/brutents/>; and O. A. Westad, 'Moscow and the Angolan Crisis, 1974–1976: A New Pattern of Intervention', *Bulletin* (Cold War International History Project), Issues 8–9, Winter 1996–7, p. 24.
44. E. Abebe, 'The Horn, the Cold War, and Documents from the former East-Bloc: An Ethiopian View', and P. B. Henze, 'Moscow, Mengistu, and the Horn: Difficult Choices for the Kremlin', both in *Bulletin* (Cold War International History Project), Issues 8–9, Winter 1996–7, pp. 40–9.
45. This was the conclusion of a report presented by Foreign Minister Andrei Gromyko, Defence Minister Dmitri Ustinov, head of the KGB Yuri Andropov

and the head of the CPSU International Department Boris Ponomarev to the Politburo in April 1979 and of a KGB report on the situation in Iran presented in October. See O. A. Westad, 'Prelude to Invasion: The Soviet Union and the Afghan Communists, 1978–1979', *The International History Review*, 16/1, 1994, pp. 59, 67.

46. O. A. Westad, 'Prelude to Invasion: The Soviet Union and the Afghan Communists, 1978–1979', *The International History Review*, 16/1, 1994, p. 60; F. Halliday, 'Soviet Foreign Policymaking and the Afghanistan War: From "Second Mongolia" to "Bleeding Wound"', Review of International Studies, 25/4, 1999, p. 678.
47. A. Dobrynin, *In Confidence* (New York: Times Books, 1995), p. 446; O. A. Westad, 'Concerning the Situation in "A": New Russian Evidence on the Soviet Intervention in Afghanistan', *Bulletin* (Cold War International History Project), Issues 8–9, Winter 1996–7, pp. 128–32.
48. C. Fogarty and K. Tritle, 'Moscow's Economic Aid Programs in Less Developed Countries: A Perspective on the 1980s', in *Gorbachev's Economic Plans: Volume 2*, Study Papers Submitted to the Joint Economic Committee, Congress of the United States, November 1987 (Washington, DC: US Government Printing Office, 1987), p. 534.
49. M. Light, 'Soviet Policy in the Third World', *International Affairs*, 67/2, 1991, p. 273. (These debts were, in part, the consequence of arms sales as well as of trade and economic assistance programmes.)
50. R. Menon, *Soviet Power and the Third World* (New Haven, London: Yale University Press, 1986), pp. 230–2.
51. Throughout most of the Brezhnev period Iraq, Libya and Syria were ruled by Saddam Hussein, Mu'ammar al-Qadhdhafi and Hafiz al-Hassad, respectively
52. K. Dawisha, 'Soviet Decision-Making in the Middle East: The 1973 October War and the 1980 Gulf War', *International Affairs*, 57/1, 1980–1, pp. 54–7.
53. P. Ramet, 'The Soviet–Syrian Relationship', *Problems of Communism*, 35/5, 1986, pp. 35–46.
54. S. K. Gupta, 'Indo-Soviet Relations', *Problems of Communism*, 22/3, 1974, p. 65.
55. P. J. S. Duncan, *The Soviet Union and India* (London: Royal Institute of International Affairs, 1989), pp. 40–68.
56. V. Israelyan, *Inside the Kremlin During the Yom Kippur War* (Pennsylvania State University Press, 1995), pp. 47–55, 72, 82, 107, 167–8.
57. The extent of Soviet disillusionment with Sadat is apparent in the memoirs of Andrei Gromyko. Brezhnev's foreign minister accuses the Egyptian leader of political bankruptcy, an astounding ignorance of Arab interests and 'pathological megalomania'. Andrei Gromyko (trans. Harold Shukman), *Memories* (London: Hutchinson, 1989), pp. 270–3.
58. R. L. Garthoff, *Détente and Confrontation. American–Soviet Relations from Nixon to Reagan* (Washington, DC: Brookings Institution, 1985), p. 678.
59. D. S. Painter, 'Explaining US Relations with the Third World', *Diplomatic History*, 19/3, 1995, p. 545.
60. Soviet accounts were also alert to the continuing influence of the British and French in the Third World and periodically of the Chinese. See R. L. Garthoff, *Détente and Confrontation. American–Soviet Relations from Nixon to Reagan* (Washington, DC: Brookings Institution, 1985), pp. 666–72.
61. R. L. Garthoff, *Détente and Confrontation. American–Soviet Relations from Nixon to Reagan* (Washington, DC: Brookings Institution, 1985), pp. 972–3.
62. As suggested in no. 11 above, Cuba and Vietnam were rare exceptions.

63. E. Abebe, 'The Horn, the Cold War, and Documents from the former East-Bloc: An Ethiopian View', *Bulletin* (Cold War International History Project), Issues 8–9, Winter 1996–7, p. 42.
64. O. A. Westad, 'Moscow and the Angolan Crisis, 1974–1976: A New Pattern of Intervention', *Bulletin* (Cold War International History Project), Issues 8–9, Winter 1996–7, p. 29.
65. A. Dobrynin, *In Confidence* (New York: Times Books, 1995), pp. 408–10; J. Haslam, 'Russian Archival Revelations and Our Understanding of the Cold War', *Diplomatic History*, 21/2, 1997, p. 226.
66. O. A. Westad, 'Prelude to Invasion: The Soviet Union and the Afghan Communists, 1978–1979', *The International History Review*, 16/1, 1994. For the nature of a slightly more broad, but similarly faulty, decision-making process during the 1973 Middle East crisis, see V. Israelyan, *Inside the Kremlin During the Yom Kippur War* (Pennsylvania State University Press, 1995).
67. O. A. Westad, 'Prelude to Invasion: The Soviet Union and the Afghan Communists, 1978–1979', *The International History Review*, 16/1, 1994, p. 66 has argued that the Soviet Union's frustration at factionalism within the People's Democratic Party of Afghanistan during 1978–9 stemmed from an ignorance of the cultural premises of the Khalq factions political outlook.
68. This literature is summarised in E. K. Valkenier, 'Revolutionary Change in the Third World: Recent Soviet Assessments', *World Politics*, 38/3, 1986.
69. *Izvestiya* and *Pravda*, 24 February 1981, as translated in *The Current Digest of the Soviet Press*, 33/8, esp. pp.7–8.
70. Soviet pressure on Vietnam also facilitated a political settlement in Cambodia in 1991.
71. M. Webber, 'The Third World and the Dissolution of the USSR', *Third World Quarterly*, 13/4, 1993, pp. 693–4, 697–8.
72. M. Light, 'Soviet Policy in the Third World', *International Affairs*, 67/2, 1991, p. 272.
73. J. G. Stein, 'Political Learning by Doing. Gorbachev as Uncommitted Thinker and Motivated Learner', in R. N. Lebow and T. Risse-Kappen (eds), *International Relations Theory and the End of the Cold War* (New York: Columbia University Press, 1995).
74. *Izvestiya*, 27 March 1990.
75. M. Gorbachev, *Perestroika: New Thinking for Our Country and the World* (London: Fontana, 1987), p. 143. See also C. A. Wallander, 'Third World Conflict in Soviet Military Thought: Does the "New Thinking" Grow Prematurely Grey?', *World Politics*, 42/1, 1989.
76. C. Thomas, 'Where is the Third World Now?', *Review of International Studies*, 25 (Special Issue), 1999, p. 225.
77. I. Ivanov (Russian Foreign Minister), 'Russia and Today's World', *Nezavisimaya gazeta*, 20 January 2000, as translated in *The Current Digest of the Post-Soviet Press*, 52/3, 2000, p. 9.
78. See, for instance, I. Ivanov (Russian Minister of Foreign Affairs), 'An Architect of the Post-War World Order', *International Affairs* (Moscow), 5, 1999; B. Piadyshev, 'The Iron Man of Soviet Diplomacy', *International Affairs* (Moscow), 5, 1999.
79. J. Steele, *The Limits of Soviet Power. The Kremlin's Foreign Policy – Brezhnev to Chernenko* (Harmondsworth: Pelican Books, 1984), p. 31.

7

A Triumph of Ideological Hairdressing? Intellectual Life in the Brezhnev Era Reconsidered

Mark Sandle

> It is true that the Brezhnev years were lost years for many of our people. But people in the West are mistaken in thinking that life in Soviet Union was so suppressed during the two decades before Gorbachev that nobody with good brains, a strong spirit and a good conscience could exist. It's just not true. In very reserved and disguised ways, you could express almost everything, if you were skilful enough. There may have been peace and quiet in the press, but some intellectuals and even ordinary people found useful ways to say what had to be said. Even a few leaders raised the real questions that faced the country in their speeches and memoranda.[1]

Introduction

On the surface, the contrast appears stark. *Perestroika*: an era of vibrant change, startling revelations and stalled revolutions, popular protest and dethroned rulers. The Brezhnev era: grey suits, stasis, decay and crushing, stifling conformity. But what lies beneath? During the 1970s and early 1980s the intellectual life of the Brezhnev years tended to be viewed as an era dominated by the orthodox platitudes of the official ideology, of paeans of praise to the achievements of the Soviet state, of the heroism of its milk-maids and miners. The only ripples on this stagnant pond appeared to come from the dissident movement, lone voices critical of the regime, its values and practices. *Perestroika* (and after) has begun to change these perceptions. Scholars searching for the roots of the ideas and thinking that inspired *perestroika* are increasingly turning their attention to the Brezhnev years, an approach exemplified by John Gooding's contribution to this volume. The publication of memoirs and interviews with the leading protagonists has thrown new light on intellectual life under Brezhnev.

This chapter will highlight some of this 'new light', and piece together a picture of intellectual life under Brezhnev which is one of heterogeneity, struggle, conflict and creativity. The recollections and memoirs of some of the key figures in the intellectual establishment under Gorbachev will provide the basis for the analysis that follows. This material provides more than a reconsideration of intellectual life, though. First, in recreating the narrative of their life-histories from the fall of Khrushchev, it provides a portrait of the *evolution* of the Brezhnev regime, its oscillations in policy, its political struggles and the overall rhythms of reform, retrenchment, reaction and stability. This reveals a complex picture of cross-currents and conflicting perspectives.

Second, as the 'architects' of *perestroika*, this group of intellectuals, journalists and party figures were instrumental in constructing the conceptualisations of Brezhnev and his era in the period after 1985. Unveiling their 'story' allows us to understand how these experiences contributed to the construction of an interpretation of the Brezhnev era as one of stagnation and neo-Stalinist reaction. While John Gooding's Chapter 9 in this volume deals with the ideas and debates of the 'Alternative tradition' and the origins of *perestroika*, this chapter examines their recollections of how they lived and worked under Brezhnev, before coming to prominence under Gorbachev. This provides wider contextual information in understanding the intellectual origins of *perestroika*. At the moment, the voices and ideas of the reformist intellectuals are somehow disembodied from their own history.

The nature and structure of the post-Stalin intelligentsia

Mainstream intellectual life in the post-Stalin era has been relatively poorly-studied in the West. There are a number of good reasons for this. First, the party's control of intellectual life through the various forms of domination it exercised – ideology (via Marxism–Leninism), censorship and personnel (controlling employment, promotion, etc.) – gave the impression of a sector with little autonomy or life of its own. It appeared to be dull, grey, and conformist on the whole. Secondly, attention was focused upon the visible signs of life that emerged in the mid-1960s: the dissidents. Given that there seemed to be little signs of life or creative thinking in the official intellectual sector, this was understandable, but it reinforced even further the perceptions of the 'official' intellectual sector. But did this focus on the dissident phenomenon obscure the shifts and developments within the main body of the Soviet intelligentsia?[2] Has the scholarly community in general overestimated the impact of the dissidents and consequently neglected to study the way in which within-system opposition was expressed? As John Gooding has pointed out, the whole *perestroika* project began with a rapprochement between the reformist leadership and the 'best of the intelligentsia'. The role played by the creative intelligentsia – artists, poets, musicians, writers, playwrights, filmmakers, satirists – is being examined anew. The search for the origins of *perestroika* has led scholars away from the high-profile dissidents, attending instead to the members of the intellectual establishment appointed by Gorbachev. What has emerged from a number of detailed case studies is a heterogeneous picture of intellectual life in the period since 1953.

The roots of this heterogeneity lie in the dynamics of the post-Stalinist system. The increasing levels of education among the population created a large pool of intellectual labour to meet this demand. As Lloyd Churchward, Vladimir Shlapentokh and others have shown, the Soviet intelligentsia expanded numerically throughout the 1950s and 1960s. Churchward notes that the 'Soviet intelligentsia during the 1960s represented the most rapidly growing sector of Soviet society, expanding by over 70 per cent between January 1959 and December 1967'.[3] The significance of the intelligentsia began to increase along with its numerical strength. The challenge to the Communist Party of the Soviet Union (CPSU) to find a *modus operandi* without the use of mass, random terror resulted in an intellectual and cultural 'thaw' in the immediate years following Stalin's death. Gradually restrictions on writing and publishing were selectively lifted, allowing the creative intelligentsia a little room for manoeuvre. A group of liberal artists, writers and sculptors – including Vasili Aksionov, Viktor Nekrasov, Andrei Voznesenski, Yuri Kazakov, Vladimir Tendriakov, Ernst Neizvestny and others – explored many new and controversial topics, themes and styles. This 'thaw' was not a consistent one though. 'Freezes' punctuated the period between 1957 and 1964, as more conservative figures sought to re-establish control over the creative arts, and when the party felt that the extent of the experimentation or the content of the literature might pose a threat to the ideological 'purity' of Soviet Marxism–Leninism. Gradually a spectrum began to emerge among the creative intelligentsia, ranging from liberals and experimentalists at one end, to conservatives and party conformists at the other.

The increasing complexity of governing a maturing industrial society required a greater reliance on specialists and experts in a variety of fields. In the process of discussing policy alternatives after the death of Stalin in areas such as economic policy, foreign affairs, welfare, housing and legal reform, it became possible for scientific and technical institutes outside of the party–state hierarchy to develop a degree of autonomy. The Academy of Sciences (consisting of around 200 research institutes) began to be used (highly selectively) by the party under Khrushchev as a policy resource. The participation of 'consultants' in the policy-making process inaugurated the process of opening up the politico-ideological complex to influence from outside. This created a hitherto non-existent 'space' in Soviet intellectual life for (a limited) expression of unorthodox ideas. However, the overwhelming majority of the Soviet intelligentsia remained content to work within the parameters set by the CPSU.

After Khrushchev, these trends – numerical growth, greater pluralism and heterogeneity, oscillating party policy – continued. This created a complex spectrum of intellectual expression. At one end of this spectrum lay the dissidents, a complex group typified according to Ostellino by 'their opposition to the constituted power and their refusal to keep it to themselves, their readiness to broadcast it'.[4] At the other end lay the obedient functionaries: those who chose to restrict themselves to passive obedience to party *diktat*. Little has been written about them. The temptation has always been to paint a picture of this group as careerists who took the party's money, status and security and wrote what they were told without qualm. Their 'real' views were either deliberately suppressed in order to maintain their positions, or the alternative (rather uncharitable) view was that they had no original or interesting views of their own. Churchward subdivides these careerist professionals into two: party-minded loyalists (who genuinely believed in the doctrines of Leninism), and pure careerists. Until members of this group begin to tell their story, this picture will remain in place.[5]

But what of those in between? Little is known about the *non-party* intellectuals who shared the critical attitudes of the dissidents but remained quiet, refusing to publicise or broadcast their opposition. This group was termed the 'lost' intelligentsia by Churchward, individuals who opted out of the system and retreated into their own private world, a group of 'internal émigrés'.[6] One exception to this was a personal piece by George Fiefer. He outlined the reasons why many intellectuals, contemptuous of the party and its ideology, remained passive and did not move into the 'dissenting' camp. Some of the comments are quite revealing. Inactivity was explained partly in terms of despair about the potential for real, meaningful change in the foreseeable future. Protest was thus seen as futile; it could not possibly change anything. Most were unwilling to give up the relatively privileged lifestyle they enjoyed in pursuit of an unattainable ideal. Members of this passive 'minority' were also quite critical of the motivations of many of the dissenters, failing to view them in the heroic terms used by some western commentators. While some dissidents were viewed positively, others were considered to be self-righteous, arrogant and responding primarily to their own psychological requirements:

> These good people have a need to do something about our condition...To express their own moral outrage, to purify their own souls. Fine. But this is hardly a plan of action. Why don't they join the party and burrow from the inside? Perhaps because although possibly more effective, that would be less personally satisfying than unfurling a banner for two seconds on Pushkin Square.[7]

It is interesting to note that these criticisms of the dissidents reflected the views of many of the reformist party intellectuals set out below. Fiefer himself posed the question (in 1975) of whether it might not have been more effective to 'settle for millimetres of progress instead of risking everything on stirring but, to the large majority, quixotic gestures?'[8]

But what of those between the 'dissenters' and the 'obedient functionaries' who opted for the millimetres rather than the grand gestures? Churchward calls them 'loyal oppositionists'.[9] The stories of those who occupied this 'space' between conformity and dissent illustrates the shifting, complex nature of intellectual life under Brezhnev and provides a social context for understanding many of those who constructed the thinking behind *perestroika*. The analysis which follows attempts to map the contours of this 'space' by examining how the frontiers between dissident, conformist and non-dissident thought shifted and evolved in line with the attitudes of the state towards intellectual autonomy. The chapter has three main sections. A brief opening section highlights the main figures involved, and how they came to prominence after 1956. The following section examines their experiences under Brezhnev. The final section assesses the significance of their experiences and reflects on the way in which these have shaped perceptions of the Brezhnev era.

A note on sources and selection

Any study based primarily on memoir literature is inherently fraught with problems. But this should not prevent us from using such sources, as long as the requisite care is taken. This is compounded by the problems of selection. The focus on some of the key figures of the *perestroika* era intellectual establishment necessarily narrows the field. The memoirs of reformist politicians have been utilised elsewhere, and will be touched on only briefly here. This leaves us fishing in a fairly small pool, which makes one cautious in making substantive judgements based purely on these sources. But it is not just the quantity of sources which needs to be borne in mind. All memoir literature lives under the shadow of the fallibility of human memory. In the case of these memoirs it is also important to acknowledge their 'present-mindedness'. The majority of these works were written during, or just after, the *perestroika* period, by authors who were instrumental in designing and/or implementing the reforms. This creates a two-fold problem. One, the memoirists need to defend the *perestroika* present (which will inevitably colour their judgement of the Brezhnev era, whose problems *perestroika* was ostensibly designed to address). Two, the memoirists need to defend their own past, which casts a shadow over their descriptions of their lives and activities. These points will be in the foreground of the analysis that follows.

Architects of *perestroika*: the '*shestidesyatniki*' and the Khrushchevite thaw

Who were these intellectuals, and where did they come from? 1956 is widely perceived as the key moment in the birth of the stream of intellectual renewal that was to burst forth under *perestroika*. The Secret Speech, the process of de-Stalinisation, and the cultural and intellectual thaw that followed the revelations at the 20th Congress were an important catalyst for the creation of a 'liberal', reformist group of intellectuals. The atmosphere, both in academia and within the party, was far more conducive (albeit within selected areas) for the fostering of more innovative thinking and ideas. This atmosphere was institutionalised under Khrushchev, who began to draw groups of consultants from outside the party hierarchy into the policy-making process. This opened up the politico-ideological complex to 'influence' from the academic hierarchy.[10] Khrushchev set up a number of initiatives, both within the CPSU and in the academic sector, which were to be the sources for much of the reformist thinking which occurred prior to 1985, but which was never absorbed into the official discourse. Moreover, these initiatives constituted a network or web by which like-minded thinkers were able to meet, discuss and debate significant issues in a (reasonably) secure environment. The contacts, relationships and solidarity that this generated persisted throughout the Brezhnev years. The academics, journalists and political figures who rose to staff the ideological hierarchy under Gorbachev were almost all members of this group, the self-styled 'lost generation'.

The ideological consequences of de-Stalinisation became known by 1957–8, when the vacuity and inappropriateness of Stalinist ideological formulae became apparent. The consequent ideological renewal opened the way for young intellectuals to be drawn into the politico-ideological hierarchy. This was an incredibly fertile time in the field of ideology, as they sought to move away from the simplistic dogmas of the Short Course. A new Soviet philosophy textbook, *Osnovy Marksizma–leninizma*, was drawn up. A new History of the CPSU was written. A new Party Programme was commissioned and put together, and finally an international conference of communist parties met in 1960, and a series of discussions ensued on the nature of relationships within the socialist bloc.[11]

It was the study of the International Socialist bloc that had probably the greatest impact on the creation of havens for the reformist, liberal intellectuals. In 1958, in Prague, the journal *Problemy mira i sotsializma* was founded, under the editorship of Aleksandr Rumyantsev. For Georgi Arbatov, the significance of this journal lay not in the ideas and concepts elaborated, but in the theoretical and political preparation it provided for the journal's cadres. Many of these individuals played a crucial role, providing an 'intellectual bridge' between the 20th Congress and *perestroika*, and a 'barricade' preventing the re-Stalinisation of the system. The list of figures recruited by Rumyantsev included: Arbatov, Georgi Shakhnazarov, Yuri Krasin, V. V. Zagladin, Gennadi Gerasimov.[12] All were to play significant roles in *perestroika*. Rumyantsev was, in Shlapentokh's words 'the leader of the liberal wing of the Party' protecting a group of young liberal *apparatchiki*, and helping to foster their intellectual development.[13]

Perhaps the most important grouping was the consultant group set up by Yuri Andropov in 1961 as part of the Central Committee Department for Relations with Communist and Workers' Parties of the Socialist Countries.[14] This Department had been created when the International Department was split in 1957. They were drawn into the ideological apparatus proper, having input into the discussions and policy formation and making contacts with party officials at all levels. Fedor Burlatskii describes how he played a formative role in the elaboration of the concept of the 'All-People's State', a central part of the Third Party Programme of 1961. He also relates how he drew up a proposal for inner-party democratisation (including limiting party officials to a two-term tenure), a proposal which was defeated by the Politburo.[15] This direct relationship with a Central Committee Secretary (and one who was to go on to become General Secretary) gave this group access and influence within the politico-ideological complex. The experience gained, and the contacts made, were to survive the years of stagnation, re-emerging after 1982. Burlatskii, Arbatov, Aleksandr Bovin, Shakhnazarov, Oleg Bogomolov, Nikolai Shishlin and Gerasimov all worked in this consultant group at various times between 1961 and 1967 (led by Burlatskii).

In what ways did these institutes seek to influence the policy process? In terms of direct contact, the institutes that were 'outside' the bureaucratic apparatus in general responded to the initiatives of the bureaucracy, usually in the form of research reports, proposals or analytical studies. Consultants had a more central role, as they were formally attached to the party bureaucracy, without being full 'insiders'. Their brief was to write documents, memoranda and speeches and to draft Central Committee decisions, all of which were subject to subsequent revision and redrafting by *apparatchiki* or political leaders.[16]

The institutes and *institutteniki* also contributed to the wider political and intellectual climate by publishing ideas and proposals via a number of different outlets. Many institutes generated their own 'in-house' journals. Newspapers with editors sympathetic to the publication of more unorthodox ideas, or with contacts among members of the institutes, were another potential outlet. However, the continued existence of prior censorship set clear limits to the ability of institutes to extend the bounds of discussion and thereby contribute to the shaping of policy through shifting the parameters of the debate, developing new concepts and so on.

The extent and character of the influence exerted were also heavily constrained. The policy process was dominated by the party–state apparatus. Yet it became evident by the 1950s that the analytical capacity of this apparatus had dwindled substantially. The bureaucracy was dominated by careerists who avoided responsibility, were intellectually conformist, highly resistant to change and ill-equipped for the challenges of de-Stalinisation.[17] The imperatives of economic modernisation, the challenge of post-Stalinist social policy and the new international commitments in Eastern Europe required levels of analysis that the apparatus could not meet. The party elite initiated the process of soliciting expert contributions in these areas, but without shifting control of policy outside of the apparatus itself.

The Brezhnev years – from thaw to the big freeze?

By the time of Khrushchev's removal in October 1964 a network of young academics and apparatchiks was firmly entrenched within the system. Individuals such as Arbatov, Burlatskii, Shakhnazarov, Ivan Frolov, Gerasimov, Bovin, Abel Aganbegyan, Tatyana Zaslavskaya and Oleg Bogomolov formed a core of liberal, reformist opinion within the Soviet politico-intellectual hierarchy. A succession of conferences, discussions, seminars and publications in the late 1950s and early 1960s had breathed life into parts of the Soviet intellectual community, and opened the way for a more critical approach to some of the key ideas of the official ideology. What is remarkable about this is how a significant degree of pluralism had been restored to Soviet intellectual life within four years of Stalin's death. The contrast with the stultifying orthodoxy of Zhdanovism, and the hegemony of intellectual charlatanism in the last years of Stalin's life is a stark one. The Khrushchevite thaw had created a 'space' between conformity and dissent for Soviet party intellectuals and reformers. But what would happen to this group, and to the climate of intellectual life with the removal of Khrushchev?

1965–8 – reform and reaction?

Expectations about the new leadership were mixed. Interestingly, some believed that the removal of Khrushchev would actually enhance the prospects for reform. Karpinsky reasoned that Khrushchev's increasingly erratic and authoritarian behaviour after 1961 made him an unreliable proponent of reform:

> Yegor Yakovlev, my oldest and dearest friend, and I drank some Cognac to celebrate Khrushchev's removal... We believed that Khrushchev had become an obstacle to the programme he had initiated himself at the 20th Congress. We thought he could no longer lead the process of de-Stalinisation and democratisation and the new Brezhnev leadership would be better. We didn't realise that Brezhnev and the others got rid of him to stop those reforms.[18]

Smirnov also recognised that Khrushchev's weaknesses – impulsiveness, erratic behaviour, constant experimentation – were undermining further de-Stalinisation. He saw the potential for further change under the new leadership, 'during his first years as leader, Brezhnev had a lot of energy and a desire to improve things'.[19] Arbatov also welcomed the removal of

Khrushchev. Others were a little more apprehensive, recognising the strength of the Stalinist faction in the Central Committee, and the likely consequences if they were to gain the upper hand. But this was probably based more on an apprehension about the unknown, rather than any informed views on the likely orientation of Brezhnev, Kosygin, Podgorny, *et al.* As it turned out, the first few years of the Brezhnev era were complex and contradictory, with little discernible pattern to events. At one and the same time, moves were afoot to deepen the process of economic reform and de-Stalinisation, and also – from figures such as Trapeznikov and Pospelov – to rehabilitate Stalin, ban public discussions of Stalinism and increase censorship. The spectre of Stalin continued to cast a long shadow over intellectual life under Brezhnev.

It was in the first year after Khrushchev's fall that the dissident movement came to public prominence. The catalyst for this was the arrest of the writers Sinyavsky and Daniel in Moscow in September 1965, and the concurrent arrest of twenty Ukrainian intellectuals. Sinyavsky and Daniel had sent their work – a satire on the myths and realities of contemporary Soviet life – abroad to be published under a pseudonym (Sinyavsky published under the name Abram Tertz, Daniel as Nikolai Arzhak).[20] This sparked a public demonstration in December 1965 that gave rise to a petition campaign, and to the first issue of the *Chronicle of Current Events* in April 1968. Yevtushenko's memoirs concerning these arrests shed some interesting light on the institutional factors at play in the control of intellectual life. Yevtushenko claims that Brezhnev knew nothing of the decision to arrest the two writers. On hearing of the arrest, Brezhnev approached the First Secretary of the Writer's Union (Konstantin Fedin), and asked whether Sinyavsky and Daniel should be tried in a criminal court, or through the internal procedures of the Writer's Union. Fedin argued vehemently for the former, and Brezhnev acquiesced. Increasingly strident criticisms of the writers came from other writers; Mikhail Sholokhov denounced them at the 23rd CPSU Congress in March 1966.

The two writers were sentenced to seven years (Sinyavsky) and five years (Daniel). The trial in early 1966 marked the start of the end of the 'thaw' in cultural policy and appeared to set the tone for a much more conservative and increasingly controlled intellectual sector. Yet the party was also rather uneasy at the trial and the publicity it aroused, and so began to seek new, less overtly repressive means of control. Medvedev relates how in the aftermath of the demonstrations and protests against the arrest and trial, the head of the KGB (Semichastny) asked the Politburo for permission to arrest 5,000 people. The request was denied, and Andropov was soon to replace Semichastny in 1967. Andropov's brief was to eradicate the *samizdat*[21] and human rights movement that had grown out of the protest movements against restrictions on cultural autonomy, the first indication of which was the trial in January 1968 of Yuri Galanskov, Aleksandr Ginzburg, Vera

Lashkova and Aleksei Dobrovolsky. But the broad thrust of party cultural policy was towards greater bureaucratic control, and a more explicit set of crime and punishment statutes to prevent the emergence of critical voices. What then was intellectual life like for those in this 'space' between dissent and passive obedience?

At first it appeared that the removal of Khrushchev would not disturb the growing influence of the currents of reformist thought, or threaten the position of the *shestidesyatniki* (the 'generation of the 1960s') and their protectors. Rumyantsev was appointed as editor-in-chief of *Pravda* in 1964. The Central Committee was continuing to recruit more independent-minded consultants to the ideological apparatus. It became possible to publish works attacking Lysenko and Lysenkoism, signifying an atmosphere hostile to the old Stalinist dogmas and increasingly open to new approaches and thinking. Innovative new institutes were created: the Central Economic and Mathematical Institute, and the Institute for Concrete Social Research, in response to pressure from this group of liberal intellectuals.[22] The formation of these institutes was highly significant. In the economic sphere, the mid-1960s was a period of innovative thought as the leadership explored avenues of economic development. These centres – along with the Institute of Economics at Novosibirsk – began to formulate ideas and proposals that called into question many of the economic principles and values that underpinned the official ideology. The debate over priority – heavy industry or consumer goods – in industrial development (which had broken out into the open at the 22nd Congress in 1961) raged on. Numerous debates and positions were adopted on issues such as pricing, value, the plan and the market. Increasingly critical appraisals of the problems of the Soviet economy began to appear. More favourable examinations of the performance of the economies of capitalist countries were floated. The broad conclusions which slowly filtered out of this discussion – need for greater autonomy for lower levels of the system, emphases on efficiency, intensification and productivity, more scope for initiative and incentives – formed the core of the Kosygin economic reforms of 1965, what Kagarlitsky has termed a 'second liberalisation'.[23] Interestingly, this flowering of thought in the field of economics evoked a demand for further intellectual renewal, particularly in the other social sciences.

Even in the field of history, traditionally kept under close control by party ideologists, there were moves to loosen the constraints on intellectual activity. Markwick has recently written of the pioneering work done in the Sector of Methodology at the Institute of History between 1964 and 1968. A group of revisionist historians began to question the conceptual schema contained within the Short Course, and sought to eliminate dogmatism in the study of history.[24] According to Vladimir Shlapentokh, this period (from 1964–7) marked the high watermark of participation by the intelligentsia in the work of the party. He argues that in this period, up until the invasion of

Czechoslovakia in 1968, the Brezhnev leadership 'sought to present itself as the true supporter of scholarship'.[25]

Others are less enthusiastic. Churchward, writing in 1973, noted that from the end of 1965, the controls on the work of the intelligentsia were gradually reimposed. Lewis Feuer noted a distinct cooling in the attitude of the Soviet authorities towards Soviet scientists at Obninsk. Press reports remarked critically on the unwillingness of some of the scientists at Obninsk to carry out party political duties, and on their propensity to conduct their scientific work without reference to their ideology.[26] Arbatov identifies a process of 'creeping re-Stalinisation' after October 1964. His account of these years is an interesting one. He rejects the notion of a simple periodisation of post-revolutionary Soviet history: Stalin (cult of personality); Khrushchev (voluntarism and subjectivism); Brezhnev (stagnation). He believes that the Brezhnev era should be divided into two: an early Brezhnev and a later Brezhnev, the dividing-point coming in 1973–4 when Brezhnev became seriously ill. In the 'early' phase there was an intense struggle over Brezhnev's 'soul', as the Stalinists and the anti-Stalinists each sought to swing the leader to their line. But, according to Arbatov, 'positive' developments could still be discerned up until the mid-1970s. He identifies the period 1965–7 as essentially a progressive era, citing the Kosygin economic reforms of September 1965 and the resolutions and decisions of the 23rd CPSU Congress in 1966 which made no moves to overturn the positions adopted at the 20th and 22nd Congresses.

Simultaneously, though, the forces of reaction were gaining ground. The first inkling of this came in May 1965, when Brezhnev made his speech commemorating the 20th anniversary of the defeat of fascism. Arbatov identifies how the conservatives began their 'creeping' offensive. The objective was to secure access to and influence over Brezhnev. His working style – cautious, indecisive and apparently without a clear ideological or political platform of his own – was to invite a range of opinions and views. His self-confessed weakness on matters of theory led him to broaden his circle of advisers in order to elicit a wide range of opinions. This inevitably placed great significance on the personnel involved in the drafting of speeches, articles and policies. The key to establishing hegemony for a particular world-view was to control the flow of ideas and information to the General Secretary. The struggle for Brezhnev's soul became a personnel struggle, as each group sought to exclude the other from the process of policy discussion and formation. This was manifest as the insertion of clauses, phrases and sentences into key speeches and party documents, and the excision of Khrushchevite ideas and notions (All-People's State, for example).

Gradually, Arbatov notes, the key sectors for the control of theory and ideology – the Central Committee departments of science and education, culture and propaganda – were captured by the forces of conservatism and re-Stalinisation. A central figure in this manoeuvre was Sergei Trapeznikov, the head of the Department of Science, described by Arbatov as a reactionary, aggressive and spiteful figure. He was to become the 'high priest' of re-Stalinisation and the scourge of the *shestidesyatniki*. Other key players in seeking influence over Brezhnev were Golikov, Tsukhanov and Aleksandrov-Agentov. They formed, according to Arbatov, a Stalinist fifth column in the operation of the Politburo and Secretariat. There were countervailing forces though, most notably Yuri Andropov and Boris Ponomarev, but also rather surprisingly Mikhail Suslov (according to Arbatov). Suslov, in this narrative appears as a cautious centrist figure who wished to avoid sharp lurches in policy and was disinclined to see a sharp turn back towards re-Stalinisation after the upheavals of de-Stalinisation between 1956 and 1961. Elsewhere, Suslov is seen as Trapeznikov's main ally and the driving force behind the removal of Andropov and the architect of the re-Stalinisation after 1968. In general, Arbatov describes a situation of great fluidity, as the struggle for Brezhnev's soul ebbed and flowed after 1965.[27]

Burlatskii paints a slightly different picture. He concurs with Arbatov in his evaluation of Brezhnev: a cautious, centrist, figure, a typical *apparatchik*. But he argues that the general orientation of the Brezhnev leadership – towards stability and conservatism, and away from the 20th Congress position – was noticeable almost immediately:

> When Brezhnev became General Secretary in 1964 many things began to change. By early 1965 you could see that they were breaking with the XX Congress and taking a new approach to Stalin's role in our history...very soon I started getting orders to write speeches contrary to what I had been writing.[28]

The reforms of Kosygin, explains Burlatskii, were a hangover from the Khrushchev era: 'the final burst' of change. He denies that it is possible to detect a distinct 'break' within Brezhnev's leadership, between an 'early' pro-reform period, and a 'later' conservative orientation. Brezhnev's opposition to the continuation of the changes introduced by Khrushchev was evident right from the start. Gradually and inexorably the ethos of the regime shifted. How? Again personnel issues were crucial. Burlatskii notes that

> People connected with the 20th party congress, or simply people with a bold innovative frame of mind, were not shot as they had been in the thirties. They were quietly pushed aside, barred, restricted, suppressed. Everywhere mediocrity triumphed. These cadres were neither stupid nor totally incompetent, but they were clearly without talent, devoid of principles or fighting spirit. Gradually they filled posts in the party and state apparatus, in the economy, in science and in culture. Everything turned grey and went into decline.[29]

The heart of this struggle Burlatskii believed to be the growing antipathy among the apparatchiki to the influence exerted by the scholarly intelligentsia. This became evident across a whole range of activities.

In particular, new departures or innovations were stifled. Developments in sociology were looked upon with great suspicion by the guardians of orthodoxy. Within the intelligentsia, the new centres of economic thought were vehemently opposed by those institutions that devoted themselves to churning out the old formulae and defending the old methods. Defending the old dogmas was an intrinsic means by which the old guard defended their economic and social status. These economists were located, according to Arbatov, in the Economics Department of Moscow State University, the I. I. Kuzminov Chair at the Academy of Social Sciences of the Central Committee and to a lesser extent at the Economics Institute of the Academy of Sciences. In history, the shadow of Stalin still loomed large. Aleksandr Nekrich published a book in Moscow in 1966 (with official approval) which outlined Stalin's shortcomings prior to the Nazi invasion in 1941. A discussion of the work ensued at the Institute of Marxism–Leninism in 1967, after which he was expelled from the party and the book withdrawn.

The backlash had links higher up in the politico-intellectual hierarchy, though. The notorious guardians of ideological orthodoxy, Mikhail Suslov and Sergei Trapeznikov, began to intervene more frequently, vetoing Andropov's attempts to draw more liberal opinions into the Politburo, radically altering speeches to give them a more conservative gloss, and conducting a conservative counter-offensive against critical and innovative sectors in the Academy of Sciences.[30] Burlatskii highlights the influence that these conservative ideological and theoretical figures had. These 'ideological hairdressers' as he terms them, were able to style and shape a potentially fruitful idea, and turn it into empty rhetoric. A good example of this was the idea of 'Developed Socialism'. Burlatskii had first written about this in *Pravda* in 1966, seeing it as a concept to promote reform in the USSR. Then, he relates, how these 'hairdressers' subtly shifted the interpretation of Developed Socialism, arguing that a Developed Socialist society *had already been built in the USSR*, thus reducing all subsequent pronouncements to propaganda, window-dressing, and a celebration of things accomplished. As the apparatchiks gained the upper hand from 1965 onwards, intellectual life was dominated by 'terrible phrase-mongering'.[31]

The interesting aspect of this process is the importance of the individual figures within the hierarchy in establishing the intellectual climate within a particular department or sector. The most compelling example of this was in the ideology department of the Central Committee. This was divided into three: the Science and Education department (headed by Trapeznikov), a bastion of neo-Stalinism; the Cultural department (headed by V. F. Shauro), a section which conformed to the prevailing political winds; and the Propaganda department, officially without a head until 1972, but with one

Alexandr Nikolaevich Yakovlev – later to be known as 'the father of *perestroika*' – as its acting chief. Yakovlev's section became a haven for unorthodox and critical thinkers. The other two sections were bastions of orthodoxy.

Gradually, through a variety of means, increasing pressure was put upon these intellectuals to curb their output, restrain their thinking and conform to official ideological standpoints. The tightening of ideological control took many forms. Rumyantsev was removed in 1965. Burlatskii was sacked from his job at *Pravda* in 1967 for some contentious articles about theatre censorship, and about the authoritarian regime in Spain under Franco (although the real topic was the USSR itself).[32] Andropov was shipped off to run the KGB[33] and his circle of consultants was dispersed. The Institute of Methodology was closed down in 1968. Censorship was increased and the activities of the KGB were gradually stepped up in their surveillance of intellectual activity.

But Burlatskii's recollections about the struggle to maintain intellectual innovation and creativity need to be questioned. Although there was high-level hostility to the establishment of new disciplines and approaches, the party's need for analytical work and empirical research continued. Interestingly, the size of the bureaucratic apparatus, and the wide variety of bureaucratic agencies involved (divided according to geography as well as functional specialism) actually helped to foster the work of policy research centres at this time. A good example of this is the Institute of Sociological Studies (ISS). It was set up solely to undertake field research for the party in order to facilitate policy-making. The multiple access points within the apparatus afforded by the extent and reach of the bureaucracy meant that the Institute was able to create a Union-wide network of centres, commissioned by the party to do fieldwork on a variety of issues. The endorsement and funding by the party ensured that, in spite of the overarching ideological constraints, conditions were conducive to specific field research. The best example was a study on 'Socialism and Youth' conducted in 1968 for the Central Committee of the Komsomol (the Communist Youth League). The outcome of this research was questioned by the party, as it revealed a disparity between ideology and attitudes among the youth, yet at this point the party was willing to accept this type of information.[34]

The turning point – the invasion of Prague?

While it is difficult to disentangle the threads of simultaneous liberalisation and re-Stalinisation, all commentators are agreed on the importance of events in Prague in 1968 in determining intellectual developments in the Soviet Union during the rest of the Brezhnev era. But was this a watershed in both the intellectual life of the Brezhnev era, and of the regime in general?

The crushing of the Prague Spring, and the end of Dubček's 'humanist socialism' dealt a massive blow to the 'progressive forces' struggling with the forces of conservatism and re-Stalinisation. The period of relative intellectual autonomy which had opened up between 1956–67 began to narrow once more. Unorthodox thinking risked being labelled as 'dissident', with a consequent loss of position, status, income and possibly liberty. But the events of August 1968 cannot be seen as marking either a sharp turn towards reaction, or even of dealing a fatal blow to the reformist cause. As we have seen, many developments pre-date the invasion of Czechoslovakia. What did change was the correlation of forces: a great impetus was given to those who were opposed to the extension of economic reforms and to the continuation of the 20th Congress line. Events in Czechoslovakia threatened to extinguish the liberal intelligentsia's hopes for an extension and deepening of the 1965 economic reforms. This was manifest in a change of atmosphere and approach. Intellectual life was affected in a number of ways.

Although there was no formal rehabilitation of Stalin, it was a close-run thing. There were four very high-profile anniversaries between 1967 and 1970 (50th anniversary of 1917; 100 years since Gorky's birth in 1868; 90 years since the birth of Stalin in 1879; and 100 years since Lenin's birth in 1870) that provided the opportunity to herald the triumph of orthodoxy and the demise of the 'thaw'. 1969 was the most interesting year. In February–March moves were initiated to rehabilitate Stalin, including plans to sell portraits and busts.[35] One of the victims of this campaign was Roi Medvedev, who was working on his *Let History Judge*. The Moscow party committee summoned Medvedev to appear before them, and accused him of a host of charges of an anti-party/anti-Soviet nature, even though the manuscript had already been examined by the authorities in 1967. Medvedev was expelled from the party. His manuscript was published abroad in 1971. Interestingly, though, Stalin was never formally rehabilitated. It appears that the Politburo backed down when the leaders of the Polish, Hungarian, and Italian communist parties refused to agree to any rehabilitation.[36]

The fate of Roi Medvedev was indicative of the change of atmosphere. The authorities increased the pressure on the whole spectrum of intellectual activity. The suppression of dissent took a more virulent form, with a marked increase in political arrests. The state deployed a whole variety of sanctions – sackings, harassment, public humiliations and coercing people into psychiatric hospitals – in their quest to eradicate dissident voices. The arrest and subsequent incarceration of Pyotr Grigorenko – a defender of the rights of the Crimean Tartars – is a good illustration of the regime's willingness to quell troublesome voices.[37] But there were other weapons in the armoury that they used to wage war. Control of personnel was strengthened. In the press, the artistic unions and the ideology department, individuals were appointed who would faithfully root out and eradicate any signs of anti-Stalinism. The Brezhnev leadership also sought to change the criteria by which intellectuals were selected and/or promoted. Notions of professional competence and outstanding scholarship were replaced by political loyalty, as the party elite began to look to create a tame, acquiescent intelligentsia.[38] At Obninsk, scientists were publicly criticised for a failure to take political work seriously and for an uncritical attitude to bourgeois societies during trips abroad. For instance the people appointed to head the Institute of Sociological Studies in the 1970s were invariably drawn from other areas – philosophy or economics – due to their political leanings rather than their professional background.

Many scholars were fired for publishing 'unorthodox' opinions. In February 1970, Tvardovsky was removed as editor-in-chief of *Novyi mir*, the literary journal that had been the flagship of the 'thaw', by Mikhail Suslov. In the Soviet Writers' Union, financial inducements were offered to those willing to write on state-approved topics, or produce panegyrics to Soviet achievements. Ostracism, exile and loss of earnings were the fates of those who refused.[39] The most notable section that bucked this trend was Alexandr Yakovlev's Department of Propaganda. However, his appointment as Ambassador to Canada meant that this section became another stronghold of neo-Stalinism after 1973.

But it was not just in the arena of personnel that pressure on the intelligentsia was increased. History (as usual) began to be re-rewritten, particularly with regard to Stalin and the Great Patriotic War. The chief victim of this was the 20th Party Congress, which was virtually written out of the annual CPSU histories produced in the 1970s. Massive amounts of energy and paper were devoted to re-falsifying the role of Stalin in the victory over Hitler. This had been the most flagrant of the attacks on Stalin at the 20th Congress, and was the quickest and easiest way to signal to the people that Stalin was being rehabilitated. History was the first. But soon the other areas of academic activity – most notably the social sciences, but also literature – also came under the same pressure to conform. Dogmatism, conformism, ideological hairdressing, and intellectual mediocrity seem to have held sway from 1968 onwards.

What was the response of the unorthodox thinkers to this change in the intellectual climate? Dissident activity and output continued, in spite of the increased pressure. The period from the late 1960s until 1973–4 was marked by a prolonged campaign of petitions and letter-writing to the party leadership from prominent dissidents, including Sakharov, Turchin and Aleksandr Solzhenitsyn. Gradually there was a fragmentation of dissident activity, as the broad movement opposed to the growing repression and control of intellectual life evolved into a plethora of different concerns: religious rights, national and ethnic rights, ecological concerns, greater openness, democratisation. Solzhenitsyn outlined the need for a moral rebirth for

Russia, based around a rejection of both western and Soviet practices and the creation of a society reflecting Russia's spiritual heritage and her native cultural patterns. A broad Russian nationalist dissident movement grew up, centred on the *samizdat* journal *Veche*, and the Komsomol publication *Molodaya gvardiya*.

Sakharov preferred to extol the virtues of pluralism and liberal democracy. Many in the republics – Ukrainians, Lithuanians – and minority nationalist groups – Jews, Germans, Crimean Tartars – began to give expression to their grievances. While this fragmentation was inevitable as general grievances became specific programmes, this tended to weaken the dissident movement which at the same time came under renewed pressure from the KGB between 1972 and 1974, as the party sought to silence dissenting voices in order to facilitate the progress of *détente*. A renewed interest among western media led to something of a mini-thaw in the spring of 1974, as the KGB reduced its pressure.[40]

What was the experience of the *shestidesyatniki* in this period? The nature and extent of the post-Prague Spring reaction differs dependent upon the source consulted. Burlatskii paints a very negative picture, arising out of his own circumstances. Having been removed from a position at *Pravda*, he moved into academic life. Having a position at IMEMO (Institute of World Economy and International Relations), he attempted – in tandem with Alexandr Rumyantsev – to create an Institute of Sociological Studies, but was thwarted by his *bête noire*, Sergei Trapeznikov. Moving on to the Institute of State and Law, he tried without success to create a Department of Political Sociology. He finally found a niche in the philosophy department of the Institute of Social Sciences, and was also appointed vice-president of the Soviet Political Sciences Association. His experiences led him to view the Brezhnev years as a total package: developments after 1968 merely extended and deepened what had been apparent from 1965 onwards. The 1970s merely witnessed the apogee of phrase-mongering and empty propaganda. Right from the time of Khrushchev's removal, the evidence of *zastoi*, of mediocrity and of pressure to conform to a grey, lifeless conservative ideology, were apparent.

Arbatov has a more positive appraisal of the years after 1968, seeing progressive moves up until 1973–4, and marking the slide into stagnation only from 1975 until 1982. As the head of the Institute of USA and Canada (ISKAN), he was able to participate in debates on economic and foreign policy issues, and also to propose new initiatives. For example he cites how, in the period after the 24th Party Congress,

> the Politburo decided to hold a special Central Committee plenum on the technological revolution. As usual the preparations for this meeting were entrusted to a commission consisting of several secretaries of the Central Committee; it was headed by Andrei Kirilenko... Some prominent

> economists worked with us, including Fedorenko, Aganbegyan and Ivanov. Upon request, the working group was given 'extraordinary privileges' – the right to invite government ministers, directors of enterprises and prominent scientists in a wide range of fields, and 'interrogate' them. Many months of intensive work produced a thick – 130 page – comprehensive economic reform programme that for those days was quite progressive. We had reached the conclusion that quicker progress in science and technology was simply unthinkable without radical changes in the economy. The document was delivered . . . And there it died a quiet death. Nobody criticised it; some even praised it. But the whole idea of the plenum sank like a stone . . . The authorities wanted something smoother, something more propagandistic that envisioned administrative measures for scientific and technological development, but in no way did they want fundamental economic reform.[41]

Arbatov is clear about who were the villains in this set-up: the *apparatchiki* and officials in the Central Committee and Council of Ministers. The political leadership – at national and even occasionally at regional levels – continued to search for answers to the problems which confronted the USSR. Reports were commissioned, and proposals passed upwards. The quality of the work commissioned from the 'official' centres of economic, social and political thinking proved to be highly unsatisfactory, little more than paeans of praise to Soviet economic achievements. The leadership then turned to the more innovative institutes – USA and Canada, IMEMO, IEMSS (Institute of the Economy of the World Socialist System) – to develop more creative responses. Their approach (to focus on problems and not to sing hymns of praise) meant they became saddled with the nickname of 'the slanderers'. But the practical outcome was nil. In Arbatov's words, 'the attempts to breach the stout walls of the administrative–bureaucratic fortress were fruitless'.[42] This paradox – searching for answers without resorting to solutions – appears to have been mirrored at local and regional levels. In an interview conducted with a figure from the Institute of Sociological Studies, the situation during the 1970s was described:

> It was a very strange situation at that time. We were very popular as sociologists. Every seminar, every meeting of lecturers or political leaders of regional Central Committee of ideological workers we were invited to . . . and they were very interested in the results of our research. But it was closed information, only for them. It was prohibited to publish this information in the press.[43]

There appears to be a peculiar paradox here, between the drab conformism and dogmatism of official ideological life, and yet a continued search and prompting for intellectual creativity and dynamism.

For Arbatov, the situation deteriorated rapidly after 1972, moving into a time of genuine stagnation from the mid-1970s onwards. This was caused by a number of issues. Brezhnev was seriously ill in late 1974. His incapacity and his tendency to promote mediocre, talentless individuals seriously hindered the governing process. The OPEC oil crisis of 1973 – which earned the USSR massive revenues – merely allowed the leadership to postpone the modernisation of the economy. Setting their faces against radical change, the leadership became set upon defending their own positions. The tasks facing the media, apparatchiks and scholars was to preserve the illusion of stability, progress and success in order that the leadership could maintain the status quo unquestioningly. More and more topics became taboo to discuss. More and more sanctions were applied against dissenting voices. How would the intelligentsia who did not move into open opposition react to this?

Blossoms in the desert – the *'shestidesyatniki'* continue the struggle

By the early 1970s, most of the *shestidesyatniki* had found niches within the system. What would their attitude to the new political climate be? The problem was how to express their ideas, while safeguarding their positions. Some sought to explore new ideas in ideologically desensitised areas. Others paid lip-service to the official dogmas, while within the confines of their institute they analysed new approaches and developed new concepts.[44] Their survival was due to the creation of havens within select institutes inside the academic sector, or within certain sectors within the apparatus of the Central Committee, where more innovative and critical research could be undertaken because of the protective role played by prominent individuals. The research centres struggled on, adopting diverse strategies to survive during the period until 1982. The institutes at Akademgorodok benefited by their distance from Moscow, and were somewhat insulated from the creeping re-Stalinisation. The attitudes of those in charge of the centres were crucial: often they would 'shelter' critical-minded scholars, and would promote the dissemination of ideas and proposals through specialist departmental journals with a restricted readership. The links between the creative intelligentsia and party reformers remained. The network was maintained through informal contacts. 'Closed' seminars, and 'salon discussions' helped to maintain an exchange of ideas, without lapsing into outspoken dissidence. Perhaps the greatest sustaining factor was the deeply held conviction expressed by Aganbegyan 'we shall outlive them': the period of re-Stalinisation and retrenchment would not snuff out the spark of change and liberalisation that began in 1956.[45]

While the surface of the intellectual pond in the Brezhnev years barely registered any noticeable changes, the same cannot be said of the currents swirling deep beneath. The vitality and creativity of intellectual life continued in spite of the growing political retrenchment. The nature and expression of this intellectual output changed to reflect the triumph of Burlatskii's 'ideological hairdressers'.

Many of the *shestidesyatniki* continued to occupy key positions in the intellectual hierarchy, although they were dependent on senior figures to shelter them. Many continued to write and discuss, but were forced to change the way they wrote and debated. The problem that confronted these individuals and institutes was the fact that they were attempting to occupy a politico-ideological 'space' between the dissidents on the one hand, and the official ideological establishment on the other that did not publicly exist. This twilight zone, between conformity and dissent, was almost completely submerged in the Brezhnev years by the stultifying domination of the ideological apparatus (orchestrated by Suslov and Trapeznikov). The slight 'space' that had opened up under Khrushchev between the official ideological establishment and anti-Soviet elements had by now disappeared, and so there was little prospect of tolerance for intellectual non-conformity.

Finding a means of public expression proved difficult. They were forced to search for ingenious ways to write and to air their views. As Arbatov has noted:

> The pressure of censorship and the restrictions on the freedom of speech had one benefit. They forced you to become finely tuned, to write cleverly, to express important thought between the lines – through innuendo, through omissions and through irony. To a certain extent I tried to do this, as did the majority of my colleagues at the institute.[46]

Many of the aforementioned institutes created their own departmental journals. This created a discrete arena in which ideas, research proposals, studies, data, etc. could be published, albeit in very specialised journals with a restricted readership. Journals such as *Sotsialisticheskiye issledovaniya, EKO, Voprosy filosofii, MEMO* and *Rabochii klass i sovremennyi mir* emerged to create just such a setting. Indeed, Lewin has argued that the mushrooming of the various branches of the social sciences during the 1970s and 1980s formed the basis for an alternative to the official ideology: the (informal) growth of sociology, the struggle of political science to gain acceptance and recognition for itself, systems analysis, globalism, futurology and others.[47]

These latter three are, with hindsight, particularly interesting. As relatively new (at least in Soviet official discourse) 'disciplines', they were unencumbered by the concepts, language, and doctrinal framework of Soviet Marxism–Leninism. Lewin noted that this allowed room for the exploration of concepts such as spontaneity, complexity, the role of the human factor, spirituality, the importance of information and public opinion in decision-making.[48] The idea of globalism was also an interesting field, as many of its underlying themes (world economic interdependence, the threat of nuclear and/or ecological catastrophe) prefigured many of the ideas of Gorbachev's 'New Political Thinking'.

The streams of reformist thought continued to flow beneath the surface of the official ideological discourse. Hardly any ideas penetrated the surface until the beginning of the 1980s. There was some elite-sponsored ideological renewal in the 1970s (with the emergence and elaboration of the concept of the Socialist Way of Life – *Sotsialisticheskii obraz zhizni*).[49] Occasionally, an individual would float a (previously approved) idea in one of the main party journals. M. P. Mchedlov attempted to introduce the idea of a 'communist civilisation' into the official discourse through *Kommunist*.[50] However, it was in the many technical and specialist journals that there were more and more discussions of innovative ideas and research, as social scientists became increasingly aware of the growing problems in Soviet society. Questions of material stimulation of labour, social justice, social innovations, managerial relations, planning techniques and many more began to appear.[51] IMEMO in particular, and ISKAN (Institute of USA and Canada) to a lesser extent, tried to push a radically new vision of the international order in the early 1980s, which was more empirical and based on a non-class approach to the world.[52]

Towards the end of the Brezhnev era, the streams of reformist thought and the intensity of conservative dogmatism were both on the increase. The clash between these streams and the official discourse was brought about by the concurrence of two events: the deaths of Brezhnev and Suslov, and the birth of Solidarity in Poland. The two worlds collided in what seemed at first to be a fairly obtuse and obscure debate about the nature of contradictions under socialism, provoked by the events in Poland. The debate, carried out almost exclusively within the pages of academic journals (especially *Voprosy filosofii*) between 1982 and 1984 was ostensibly about Poland. The heat generated by this argument revealed the existence of a different agenda: an evaluation of the problems and prospects of Soviet society under Brezhnev.[53] The latter years of the Brezhnev era cannot be seen as the onset of the intellectual revival and renewal of the Gorbachev years. In fact there was something of a conservative onslaught unleashed in the early 1980s. Most notably, IMEMO was investigated, in order to discredit it and to destroy its prestige and its position. Conservatives disliked the institute because it refused to spew out the rhetoric of success and progress. IMEMO was spared when Brezhnev died in November 1982 and was replaced by Andropov. One of his first moves was to bring back Yakovlev from Canada. His new post? Head of IMEMO.

By 1984, the contradictions debate had begun to peter out, and new issues were coming on to the scholarly agenda. This debate was crucial in providing a public forum for a clash between representatives of the reformist sector and the official ideological establishment. Many of the themes that were expressed reflected the persistence of reformist ideas in the Soviet social science sector, and can be seen in hindsight as a turning point in the erosion of the official orthodox interpretation of Soviet Marxism–Leninism from within. In five years, the ideas and values that the *shestidesyatniki* had clung to had become the new orthodoxy.

Assessing intellectual life in the Brezhnev era

A reconsideration of Soviet intellectual life under Brezhnev highlights its persistent vitality and diversity after 1964. Although on the surface the non-dissident sector appeared to be overwhelmingly stagnant, grey, and empty, the quest for new ideas, new solutions and alternatives continued. Soviet intellectual life prior to *perestroika* was both *diverse* and *conflictual*. There was a vast spectrum of intellectual activity between 'dissent' and 'orthodoxy' (and also within these rather generalised labels themselves). This diversity encompassed a growing specialisation of knowledge within existing fields and the development of 'new' disciplines. This was primarily a function of the numerical growth of the Soviet intelligentsia and the increasing dependence of the regime on its 'experts' in its attempts to manage, administer and govern a modern industrial society. Non-dissident thought entailed a form of incipient intellectual pluralism located within the monolithic fortress of Soviet Marxism–Leninism, and was an essential part of the destruction of the 'citadel of dogmatism' after 1985. This diversity also extended to different trends and currents of thought existing within the party itself, prefiguring the fragmentation of the CPSU under *perestroika*.

Arising out of this diversity was an intellectual sector that was increasingly conflict-ridden. 'Struggle' is perhaps the unifying theme of all those who refused to take the road of passive obedience to party diktat. At times it was a life-or-death one. For some the struggle was a high-profile public one; for others it took place behind closed doors. On occasions the struggle saw lone individuals lined up against the state; on others it was one individual wrestling with his/her own conscience. Individuals struggled to break free of the constraints of the official belief system and sought various ways to publicise their views. Individuals struggled to meet together informally to discuss their views. Institutes struggled to maintain their autonomy.

On the other side, the state struggled to silence dissenting voices and unorthodox thinkers, and also struggled to understand and govern the society over which it ruled. The entire post-Stalinist period demonstrates that any analysis of ideas, ideology, and intellectual life in the USSR needs to start with the politico-ideological complex – the array of agencies, institutes, and departments engaged in the production, dissemination, and control of ideas – and its internal workings, conflicts and personal rivalries. The linkages between intellectual debates and the power struggles within the party (particularly concerned with the 'Stalin question') demonstrates the intense politicisation of all intellectual life in Brezhnev's USSR, irrespective of the discipline concerned.

Aside from these general perceptions, a wider question presents itself.

Have we overestimated the importance of the dissidents?

Until recently, the dissidents were seen as the only worthwhile intellectual phenomenon to emerge after 1966–7, and as the spiritual and intellectual forebears of *perestroika* and *glasnost'*. The alternative view, which identifies the within-system or 'loyal' opposition of the *shestidesyatniki* as playing a pivotal role in the events after 1985, has been stressed by a variety of people:

> *Perestroika* was prepared by people within the system who continued to speak out for revolutionary structural reforms... These were people who did not allow themselves to be pushed outside the political system, who did not retreat into dissidence.[54]

In similar vein, Markwick has also argued that

> The focus on the outstanding dissidents has been at the cost of observing movement within the mainstream intelligentsia, which has remained hidden within the penumbra of the dissident phenomenon... the relationship between intellectual non-conformism and dissidence has been obscured... the legal dissidents posed potentially at least a far more serious challenge to the regime than the illegal dissidents.[55]

Roi Medvedev also questioned the effectiveness and significance of dissent. He argued that a distinction should be drawn between compromise (which all those who remain within the system must do) and unprincipled behaviour (which is of a very different quality). Those who became within-system oppositionists did not lapse into the 'unprincipled behaviour' of those who wrote the official songs of praise. Although forced to compromise at times, overall their contribution was much more effective than the open dissenters.[56] Arbatov outlined the respective roles of dissident and within-system reformer. While paying tribute to the bravery and selflessness of the dissidents, without whom he argues the process of change would not have progressed so quickly, he also asserts that it was the activities of the 'many hundreds and thousands' within the system that made *perestroika* possible.[57]

Not all share this view. Karpinsky asserts that 'Of course they played a role, more so the full dissidents than the half-dissidents who mainly sat at home and didn't try to distribute what they wrote or to organise anything. We half-dissidents were timid.'[58] Vladimir Bukovsky, a long-standing dissident and critic of the Soviet system, was rather more scathing, arguing that those 'ants' within the system needed 'elaborate theories to justify their submission'. He outlines a long list of reasons/excuses that people deployed to justify their compliance with the regime, including 'you have to get on quietly with your career, get to the top and try to change things from there; you won't achieve anything from the bottom', and also 'you have to gain the trust of the leaders' advisers and teach and educate them on the quiet, there's no other way of influencing the government's course'.[59] Were the loyal opposition being disingenuous in their defence of their tactics and their critique of the dissidents? How important were the *institutniki* and the liberal party *apparatchiki* in events after 1985?

The question of intellectual non-conformity and its impact is difficult to quantify in any meaningful sense. However, the existence of a broad network of scholars, intellectuals and *apparatchiki* with a critical anti-Stalinist outlook meant the persistence of an alternative world view that was essentially subversive. Anti-orthodoxy appears to have been widespread, although constrained by the dominance of conformists and careerists. It also highlights the importance of avoiding dichotomous generalisations of the Soviet intelligentsia. There was a substantial body of individuals who fell between the two stools of unprincipled conformity on the one hand, and dissent on the other. In this sense, the ideological basis of the system was eroded from within as well as from without. The loyal, or legal dissidence of the *perestroishchiki* existed within the main body of the Soviet intelligentsia, and was not confined to a few prominent individuals.

The forms this half-dissidence or non-conformity took – empirical criticisms of Soviet shibboleths, exploration of new disciplines and approaches, writing about the Soviet system by proxy – cut away the basis of ideological dogmatism long before Gorbachev came to power. A couple of examples. Markwick documents how the Sector of Methodology's concern with empirical historical research led it into conflict with the dogmatic framework contained within the Short Course paradigm. The ideological challenge posed to the Short Course paradigm was at the same time a challenge to the ideological authority of the Soviet historical scholar–bureaucrats, and the Sector faced severe criticism from the party ideologues such as I. I. Mints (who had formed part of the collective working on the new History of the CPSU in 1959).[60] The closure of the sector under pressure from the guardians of orthodoxy halted the emergence of a more critical reflective outlook in history, but did not eradicate it. For Markwick, 'it proved to be not only a powerful catalyst for Soviet historiography [and] hastened the demise of Marxism–Leninism as a dogmatic ideology . . . the 20th Congressers played a crucial role not only in igniting the debates which erupted in history under *perestroika*, but also in conceptually clearing the way for them'.[61]

In similar vein, researchers and scholars at IMEMO developed a number of ideas and new concepts from the 1960s onwards which when they reached the official discourse under Gorbachev, radically revised the tenets of Marxism–Leninism. In particular, the issues of all-human values/class approach to the world, the growing interdependence of the world economy and a new more benign view of capitalism, all grew out of the specific research undertaken within the Institute.

In this sense these intellectuals and party reformers were crucial in paving the way for *perestroika*. Their conceptual critiques of various tenets of official Marxism–Leninism meant that much of the preparatory theoretical work – at least in the fields of international relations and in part in the economic field – had been accomplished prior to 1985. Moreover, the particular form and content which *perestroika* took between 1985 and 1990 was profoundly determined by the outlook and values of the *shestidesyatniki*. A focus on the dissident phenomenon does tend to overlook, downplay or ignore the role played by the mainstream intelligentsia in preparing the way for, and shaping *perestroika*. The half-dissidents were crucial in undermining the internal coherence of orthodox Soviet Marxism–Leninism, and so fostered a recognition among the political elite of the necessity of ideological and intellectual renewal. In this sense, communities of experts within the system played an important role in loosening the grip on power of the political elite, and in undermining those who argued for the continuation of the status quo.

But events after 1985 encompassed far more than the political programme of the Gorbachevian elite. The rise of civil society after 1985 had little direct link with the activities of the 'loyal' opposition. The sacrificial suffering of the high-profile dissidents was far more important in inspiring popular revolt and protest than the life and works of the *shestidesyatniki*. The importance of the dissidents has not been overestimated. But the significance of the loyal oppositionists has. Their respective roles need to be acknowledged.

To the victors the spoils?

One final point. The experiences of the dissidents and the *shestidesyatniki* cannot be assumed to be representative of Soviet society as a whole, nor even of large swathes of the intelligentsia itself. It is important to bear this in mind. It was this latter group which formed the intellectual elite at the heart of *perestroika*, and so they were in the main responsible for the construction of the narrative of Soviet history which came to predominate after 1985. Most notably, they identified the main periods of reform and progression (NEP, de-Stalinisation under Khrushchev, and *perestroika*), and the main periods of repression and reaction (War Communism, Stalinism, *zastoi* under Brezhnev). Their appraisal of the Brezhnev years as ones of *zastoi* was directly linked to their own experiences and arose out of a need to provide a justification for the radicalism of *perestroika*. By creating an image of the Brezhnev years as ones of intellectual mediocrity and stagnation (apart from their own heroic struggle to keep the fires of intellectual vitality burning), it was then possible to argue more plausibly for a radical restructuring of the system. An awareness of the problems in reading history as written by its 'winners' should perhaps make us wary of extending notions of 'stagnation' as applied to the intellectual life of the Brezhnev era to the rest of Soviet system. As Kagarlitsky has shown, at the time the Brezhnev era was seen as one of 'stability': stable prices, gradually rising living standards for the masses and so on. It was only under *glasnost'* that it became known as an era of stagnation.[62] Has our thinking on Brezhnev been shaped by an overdependence on the accounts of intellectuals?

Further reading

G. Arbatov, *Zatnayuvsheyesya vyzdorovlenie (1953–85gg.): svidetel'stvo sovremennika* (Moscow: Mezhdunarodnye otnosheniya, 1991).

F. Burlatskii, *Vozhdi i sovetniki: o Khrushcheve, Andropove i ne tol'ko o nikh* (Moscow: Politizdat, 1990). This was translated as *Khrushchev and the First Russian Spring* (London: Weidenfeld & Nicolson, 1991).

L. Churchward, *The Soviet Intelligentsia* (London: Routledge, 1973).

S. F. Cohen and K. van den Heuvel (eds), *Voices of Glasnost: Interviews with Gorbachev's Reformers* (New York: Norton, 1989).

B. Kagarlitsky, *The Thinking Reed* (London: Verso, 1988).

R. Markwick, 'Catalyst of Historiography, Marxism and Dissidence: The Sector of Methodology of the Institute of History, Soviet Academy of Sciences 1964–68', *Europe–Asia Studies*, 46/4, 1994.

R. Medvedev, *On Soviet Dissent* (New York: Columbia University Press, 1980).

V. Shlapentokh, *Soviet Intellectuals and Political Power* (London: Tauris 1990).

R. L. Tokes (ed.), *Dissent in the USSR* (Baltimore, Md.: Johns Hopkins University Press, 1975).

Notes

1. N. Shmelyov, 'The Rebirth of Common Sense', in S. F. Cohen and K. van den Heuvel (eds), *Voices of Glasnost: Interviews with Gorbachev's Reformers* (New York: Norton, 1989), p. 145.
2. R. Markwick, 'Catalyst of Historiography, Marxism and Dissidence: The Sector of Methodology of the Institute of History, Soviet Academy of Sciences 1964–68', *Europe–Asia Studies*, 46/4, 1994, p. 579.
3. L. Churchward, *The Soviet Intelligentsia* (London: Routledge, 1973), p. 9.
4. R. Medvedev, *On Soviet Dissent* (New York: Columbia University Press, 1980), p. 1.
5. L. Churchward, *The Soviet Intelligentsia* (London: Routledge, 1973), p. 136.
6. L. Churchward, *The Soviet Intelligentsia* (London: Routledge, 1973), p. 137.
7. G. Feifer, 'No Protest: The Case of the Passive Minority', in R. L. Tokes (ed.), *Dissent in the USSR* (Baltimore, Md.: Johns Hopkins University Press, 1975), p. 427.
8. G. Feifer, 'No Protest: The Case of the Passive Minority', in R. L. Tokes (ed.), *Dissent in the USSR* (Baltimore, Md.: Johns Hopkins University Press, 1975), p. 431.
9. L. Churchward, *The Soviet Intelligentsia* (London: Routledge, 1973), p. 136.
10. See J. Hough and M. Fainsod, *How the Soviet Union is Governed* (Cambridge, Mass.: Harvard University Press, 1979), pp. 422–4 for details on the role of consultants in the Central Committee apparatus.

11. Some new insights into the process of drafting the 1961 Party Programme can be found in N. Barsukov, 'Kommunisticheskie illyuzii Khrushcheva', *Dialog*, 5, 1991, pp. 75–83.
12. N. Barsukov, 'Kommunisticheskie illyuzii Khrushcheva', *Dialog*, 5, 1991, pp. 75–9.
13. V. Shlapentokh, *Soviet Intellectuals and Political Power* (London: Tauris, 1990), Chapter 5.
14. The work of this department has been mentioned in several sources. See for example, G. Arbatov, *Zatnayuvsheyesya vyzdorovlenie (1953–85gg.): svidetel'stvo sovremennika* (Moscow: Mezhdunarodnye otnosheniya, 1991), pp. 79–85 (translated as *The System: An Insider's Life in Soviet Politics* (New York: Times Books, 1992)); and in S. F. Cohen and K. van den Heuvel (eds), *Voices of Glasnost: Interviews with Gorbachev's Reformers* (New York: Norton, 1989), p. 309. Other detailed accounts can be found in F. Burlatskii, 'Posle stalina', *Novyi Mir*, 10 1988, pp. 18–80; and by the same author *Vozhdi i sovetniki: o Khrushcheve, Andropove i ne tol'ko o nikh* (Moscow: Politizdat, 1990). This was translated as *Khrushchev and the First Russian Spring* (London: Weidenfeld & Nicolson, 1991).
15. F. Burlatskii, 'Democratisation is a Long March' in S. F. Cohen and K. van den Heuvel (eds), *Voices of Glasnost: Interviews with Gorbachev's Reformers* (New York: Norton, 1989), p. 177.
16. J. Hough and M. Fainsod, *How the Soviet Union is Governed* (Cambridge, Mass.: Harvard University Press, 1979), p. 422; G. Arbatov, *The System: An Insider's Life in Soviet Politics* (New York: Times Books, 1992), pp. 82–90.
17. G. Arbatov, *The System: An Insider's Life in Soviet Politics* (New York: Times Books, 1992), pp. 142–8.
18. L. Karpinsky, 'The Autobiography of a "Half-Dissident"', in S. F. Cohen and K. van den Heuvel (eds), *Voices of Glasnost: Interviews with Gorbachev's Reformers* (New York: Norton, 1989), p. 289.
19. G. Smirnov, 'Restructuring the "Citadel of Dogmatism"', in S. F. Cohen and K. van den Heuvel (eds), *Voices of Glasnost: Interviews with Gorbachev's Reformers* (New York: Norton, 1989), p. 79.
20. Yevtushenko claims in his memoirs that it was the CIA that revealed the identity of Sinyavsky and Daniel to the KGB. Robert Kennedy apparently informed him that United States wanted to create a scandal to deflect attention from US involvement in Vietnam, see J. Garrard and C. Garrard, *Inside the Soviet Writers Union* (New York: Tauris, 1990), p. 275.
21. *Samizdat* (self-publishing) was a movement that sought to transmit illegal publications around an informal network.
22. V. Shlapentokh, *Soviet Intellectuals and Political Power* (London: Tauris, 1990), Chapter 5. See also the excellent M. Lewin, *Political Undercurrents in Soviet Economic Debates* (London: Pluto Press, 1975), esp. Part II, 'Economics and the State'.
23. B. Kagarlitsky, *The Thinking Reed* (London: Verso, 1988), p. 189.
24. R. Markwick, 'Catalyst of Historiography, Marxism and Dissidence: The Sector of Methodology of the Institute of History, Soviet Academy of Sciences 1964–68', *Europe–Asia Studies*, 46/4, 1994.
25. V. Shlapentokh, *Soviet Intellectuals and Political Power* (London: Tauris, 1990), Chapter 7.
26. L. S. Feuer, 'The Intelligentsia in Opposition', *Problems of Communism*, 3, 1971, pp. 1–16.
27. G. Arbatov, *Zatnayuvsheyesya vyzdorovlenie (1953–85 gg.): svidetel'stvo sovremennika* (Moscow: Mezhdunarodnye otnosheniya, 1991), Chapter 5.

28. F. Burlatskii, 'Democratisation is a Long March', in S. F. Cohen and K. van den Heuvel (eds), *Voices of Glasnost: Interviews with Gorbachev's Reformers* (New York: Norton, 1989), p. 177
29. F. Burlatskii, *Khrushchev and the First Russian Spring* (London: Weidenfeld & Nicolson, 1991), p. 218.
30. F. Burlatskii provides a somewhat unsympathetic portrait of Suslov in F. Burlatskii, 'Posle stalina', *Novyi Mir*, 10, 1988, pp. 18–80.
31. F. Burlatskii, *Khrushchev and the First Russian Spring* (London: Weidenfeld & Nicolson, 1991), p. 221.
32. Both Burlatskii and Karpinsky were sacked in 1967. However, they suffered very different fates in the 1970s. Burlatskii remained an important journalistic figure, whereas Karpinsky retreated into semi-dissidence. It has been rumoured that Burlatskii attempted to displace the 'blame' for the controversial articles onto Karpinsky. See L. Karpinsky: 'The Autobiography of a "Half-Dissident"', in S. F. Cohen and K. van den Heuvel (eds), *Voices of Glasnost: Interviews with Gorbachev's Reformers* (New York: Norton, 1989), pp. 280–306. Also D. Remnick: *Lenin's Tomb* (Harmondsworth: Penguin 1994), pp. 162–79.
33. Burlatskii argues that the decision to move Andropov to the KGB was a scheme of Suslov's to prevent the liberal group within the party gaining hegemony by installing Andropov as General Secretary: F. Burlatskii, 'Democratisation is a Long March' in S. F. Cohen and K. van den Heuvel (eds), *Voices of Glasnost: Interviews with Gorbachev's Reformers* (New York: Norton, 1989), p. 183.
34. The information on the ISS came from an interview conducted with Valeri Mansourov, Deputy Director of the Institute, in Moscow, 9 July 1996.
35. R. Medvedev, *On Soviet Dissent* (New York: Columbia University Press, 1980), p. 26.
36. R. Medvedev, *On Soviet Dissent* (New York: Columbia University Press, 1980), pp. 26–8.
37. P. Reddaway, 'The Development of Dissent and Opposition', in A. Brown and M. Kaser (eds), *The Soviet Union since the Fall of Khrushchev* (New York: Free Press, 1975), pp. 142–8
38. V. Shlapentokh, *Soviet Intellectuals and Political Power* (London: Tauris, 1990), Chapter 7, gives a detailed evaluation of the implications of political reaction for the Soviet intelligentsia.
39. J. Garrard and C. Garrard, *Inside the Soviet Writers Union* (New York: Tauris, 1990), Chapter 5.
40. P. Reddaway, 'The Development of Dissent and Opposition', in A. Brown and M. Kaser (eds), *The Soviet Union since the Fall of Khrushchev* (New York: Free Press, 1975), p. 134.
41. G. Arbatov, *The System: An Insider's Life in Soviet Politics* (New York: Times Books, 1992), pp. 160–1.
42. G. Arbatov, *The System: An Insider's Life in Soviet Politics* (New York: Times Books, 1992), p. 160.
43. Interview conducted with Valeri Mansourov, Moscow, 9 July 1996.
44. This was a matter of some contention after 1985. Many of the Gorbachev *institutеniki* (after 1988 in particular) were accused of having colluded with the Brezhnev leadership, and participated in the ideological retrenchment and clampdown a little too willingly. This accusation was, in particular, thrown at Georgii Arbatov, who as head of ISKAN, was said to have participated a little too zealously in the propagation of Brezhnevite orthodoxy.

45. T. Zaslavskaya, 'Socialism with a Human Face', in S. F. Cohen and K. van den Heuvel (eds), *Voices of Glasnost: Interviews with Gorbachev's Reformers* (New York: Norton, 1989), p.122.
46. G. Arbatov, *The System: An Insider's Life in Soviet Politics* (New York: Times Books, 1992), p. 145.
47. M. Lewin, *The Gorbachev Phenomenon* (London: Hutchinson 1988), Chapter 7, 'The Social Sciences: A New Ideology?', pp. 85–100.
48. M. Lewin, *The Gorbachev Phenomenon* (London: Hutchinson, 1988), Chapter 7, 'The Social Sciences: A New Ideology?', pp. 85–99.
49. For a fine analysis of this, see A. B. Evans Jr, *Soviet Marxism–Leninism: The Decline of an Ideology* (Westport, Conn.: Praeger 1993), Chapter 9.
50. See M. Mchedlov, 'K voprosu o stanovlenii kommunisticheskoi tsivilizatsii', *Kommunist*, 14, 1976, pp. 32–43. I am grateful to Julian Cooper for bringing this to my attention.
51. See for example M. Yanowitch, *Controversies in Soviet Social Thought: Democratisation, Social Justice, and the Erosion of Official Ideology* (Armonk, NY: ME Sharpe, 1991), esp. Chapter 1, 'Reformist Undercurrents in the Pre-Gorbachev Period'.
52. See T. W. Cobb, 'National Security Perspectives of Soviet Think-Tanks', *Problems of Communism*, 31, November–December 1981, pp. 51–9. Also J. Checkel, 'Ideas, Institutions and the Gorbachev Foreign Policy Revolution', *World Politics*, 45, 1993, pp. 271–300. The best-known development in this era and probably the most famous example of the growth of reformist thinking which existed in the 'twilight zone' between official public ideological pronouncement and dissidence was the so-called 'Novosibirsk Report'. This was a (confidential) seminar paper organised by economic departments of the Central Committee of the Communist Party of the Soviet Union, the USSR Academy of Sciences and USSR Gosplan at the Institute of the Economics and Organisation of Industrial Production (headed by Aganbegyan). It was compiled by Zaslavskaya, who has stated that the Novosibirsk report was the culmination of a number of initiatives that had been generated by Aganbegyan's institute after the late 1970s. Prepared throughout the course of 1982, the paper was sent out to other institutes at the end of the year, and the seminar took place in April 1983. The radical nature of the document is significant when considered alongside the apparent official sanction given to the discussion.
53. For an excellent summary of this whole debate see E. Kux, 'Contradictions in Soviet Socialism' *Problems of Communism*, 34, November–December 1984, pp. 1–27. On the Soviet side, see: V. S. Semenov, 'Problemy protivorechii na sotsializma', *Voprosy filosofii*, 7, 1982, pp. 17–32, and 9, 1982, pp. 3–21; A. Butenko: 'Protivorechiya razvitiya sotsializma kak obshchestvennogo stroia', *Voprosy filosofii*, 10, 1982, pp. 16–29, and 'Eshche raz o protivorechii sotsializma', *Voprosy filosofii*, 2, 1984, pp. 124–9.
54. F. Burlatskii, 'Democratisation is a Long March', in S. F. Cohen and K. van den Heuvel (eds), *Voices of Glasnost: Interviews with Gorbachev's Reformers* (New York: Norton, 1989), p. 180. Arbatov is more balanced in his assessment. He argues that, 'both those who sought to reform the system and those who fought against it played a role in subsequent events. Each in his own way was preparing for radical changes that started a few years later.' See G. Arbatov, *The System: An Insider's Life in Soviet Politics* (New York: Times Books, 1992), p. 279.

55. R. Markwick, 'Catalyst of Historiography, Marxism and Dissidence: The Sector of Methodology of the Institute of History, Soviet Academy of Sciences 1964–68', *Europe–Asia Studies*, 46/4, 1994, p. 579.
56. R. Medvedev, *On Soviet Dissent* (New York: Columbia University Press, 1980), pp. 126–8.
57. G. Arbatov, *The System: An Insider's Life in Soviet Politics* (New York: Times Books, 1992), p. 243.
58. L. Karpinsky, 'The Autobiography of a "Half-Dissident"', in S. F. Cohen and K. van den Heuvel (eds), *Voices of Glasnost: Interviews with Gorbachev's Reformers* (New York: Norton, 1989), p. 300.
59. V. Bukovsky, *To Build A Castle* (London: Andre Deutsch, 1978), pp. 62–5.
60. R. Markwick, 'Catalyst of Historiography, Marxism and Dissidence: The Sector of Methodology of the Institute of History, Soviet Academy of Sciences 1964–68', *Europe-Asia Studies*, 46/4, 1994, pp. 582–5.
61. R. Markwick, 'Catalyst of Historiography, Marxism and Dissidence: The Sector of Methodology of the Institute of History, Soviet Academy of Sciences 1964–68', *Europe–Asia Studies*, 46/4, 1994, pp. 590–1.
62. B. Kagarlitsky, *The Thinking Reed* (London: Verso, 1988), pp. 317–40.

8
Brezhnev and Developed Socialism: The Ideology of *Zastoi*?

Mark Sandle

Introduction

The official ideological centrepiece of the Brezhnev years was the concept of Developed Socialism. In the period since Brezhnev's death, it has become the archetypal symbol of the era of stagnation. Under Gorbachev (and after), Developed Socialism was subject to extensive criticism for a number of reasons. In marked contrast with the optimism, dynamism and utopianism of Khrushchev's ideological pronouncements – proclaiming the advent of the first phase of communism by 1980 in the Third Party Programme – Developed Socialism appeared to be pessimistic, conservative and pragmatic. It was 'credited' with covering Soviet intellectual life in a suffocating grey blanket, stifling creativity, breeding dogmatism and undermining the vitality of Soviet Marxism–Leninism. A huge gap was said to have emerged between the reality of Soviet life and the picture of Soviet life painted by Developed Socialism. In this sense, Developed Socialism was central in the massive loss of faith which Soviet citizens underwent in the 1970s and 1980s. Increasingly, Developed Socialism was said to have been not just a *symbol* of the era of stagnation, but one of the *causes* of stagnation.

This chapter will explore the accuracy of the above description. It will argue that the extent of the 'break' between Developed Socialism and the ideological outlook of Khrushchev has been substantially overstated. A reconsideration of Khrushchev's Third Party Programme, and the fate of many of the ideas central to Khrushchev's ideological renewal demonstrates that there are many lines of continuity running between the two eras, and the concept of a radical break or repudiation of Khrushchev's ideas may be difficult to sustain. Secondly, it will argue that Developed Socialism was a highly complex and at times contradictory concept and will question the validity of describing Developed Socialism as the ideology of stagnation. Revisiting the origins, content and influence of the concept reveals a far more progressive, reformist and radical face of Developed Socialism than currently in circulation. Let us begin by defining the constituent parts of the concept of Developed Socialism.

What was Developed Socialism?

The official inauguration of this new concept occurred at the 24th Congress of the Communist Party of the Soviet Union (CPSU) in March 1971, when Leonid Brezhnev talked about the notion of a developed socialist society having been built in the USSR.[1] Mention had been made earlier in the 1960s of a 'developed' or 'mature' socialist society, both within the USSR and eastern Europe (most notably in the 1960 joint communiqué of communist and workers' parties), but the speech in 1971 was the first public unveiling of a new interpretation of Soviet Marxism–Leninism. In 1967, Brezhnev had affirmed in a speech to mark the 50th anniversary of the October Revolution that the USSR was still in the process of 'the full-scale construction of communism', continuing the main ideological thrust of Khrushchev, as outlined in the Third Party Programme of 1961.[2] Four years later, the references to this Khrushchevian ideal of catching up with the West by 1970 (in terms of economic output) and of having constructed communism in the USSR by 1980 had all but disappeared. In its stead stood Developed Socialism. Why?

Aside from Brezhnev's personal quest for prestige and credibility as a Marxist–Leninist theorist, there was a growing unease with the grandiose promises of Khrushchev's timetable within the post-Khrushchev leadership. Yet they could not abandon the idea of making the transition to communism, as this was the entire *raison d'être* of the rule of the CPSU. A new interpretation was required. In addition the CPSU had to maintain its pre-eminent position within the socialist bloc. If the USSR was no longer engaged in the construction of communism, on what basis could it claim to be the dominant state in the socialist bloc? All the countries were 'socialist'. Developed Socialism became a means of differentiating the USSR from the other socialist countries, while asserting its leading role: it was the first state to complete the construction of a 'developed socialist' society.

At first it represented a further and fuller delineation of the nature of the post-revolutionary development of Soviet society towards communism. For Brezhnev and others socialism ceased to be a brief transitional period between capitalism and communism. It was a long historical phase, marked by its own laws of social development, not all of which had been revealed by the unfolding of the historical process. This argument maintained that the difference in the degree of the development of socialism had become so great as to require a qualitative distinction. Fedoseev noted that

> Developed Socialist society is not considered by us as something midway between socialism and communism ... It is a socialist society attaining a developed condition, characterised by the all-round disclosure of the advantages of socialism.[3]

In time, however, it was to become a full-blown doctrine that touched upon almost all aspects of Soviet society. Economic, political, social, cultural and international themes were assessed from the standpoint of this new stage in the evolution of the Soviet state. From 1971 onwards a large number of articles appeared in many journals (for example *Kommunist* and *Voprosy Istorii KPSS*) dealing with the form and content of Developed Socialism, and indeed the period 1971–81 has been characterised by one Soviet theorist as the era of Developed Socialism.[4] It occupied a central position in the party documents of the 25th Congress of the CPSU in 1976, and was codified in the 1977 Constitution.[5] At the 26th Party Congress in 1981, Brezhnev announced his intention to prepare a new Party Programme – the main ideological statement of the CPSU – which would reflect the changes since the 1961 Programme and which would contain Developed Socialism at its heart.

Evaluating Developed Socialism – contemporary views (Soviet and western)

The literature which Developed Socialism spawned was extensive (both in the USSR and among western Kremlin-watchers). Perusing this literature is an interesting exercise. It is clear (with, of course, the glorious benefit of hindsight) that attitudes towards the *concept* of Developed Socialism have been profoundly shaped by the prevailing attitudes towards the Brezhnev regime in general. In particular, the predominant perspectives of Brezhnev after 1985 have at best obscured and in many ways virtually erased other interpretations and views of Developed Socialism.

Within the USSR, the body of literature exponentially grew from general assessments of Developed Socialism to more detailed appraisals of the role of the party under Developed Socialism, or economic developments. The critical year for Soviet appraisals of Developed Socialism was 1971. It was here, during Brezhnev's speech to the 24th Congress of the CPSU, that it became the official ideological concept of the Brezhnev leadership. Looking back over the history of the economic development of the USSR, Brezhnev stated that,

> In our country, it will be recalled, socialism triumphed back in the latter half of the thirties. This was followed by more than three decades of the Soviet people's heroic struggle and labour... The developed socialist society to which Lenin referred in 1918 as the future of our country has been built by the selfless labour of the Soviet people.[6]

From this point, the Soviet ideological machine cranked into operation, dissecting the meanings of this concept in exhaustive detail. However, the first public discussion of the concept in the USSR had emerged five years earlier in 1966, when Fedor Burlatskii wrote an article in Pravda, '*O stroitel'stve razvitogo sotsialisticheskogo obshchestva'* which highlighted discussions in East European communist parties about future paths of development for socialist states.[7] This set in train four–five years of discussions in the national press and in specialist journals (most notably *Problemi mira i sotsializma* and *Kommunist*). These discussions embraced a number of Soviet scholars: Fedor Burlatskii, Anatolii Butenko, Richard Kosolapov, Petr Demichev, Petr Fedoseev, Viktor Kas'yanenko and Evgenii Chekharin, as well as occasional incursions from Brezhnev and his chief ideologist Mikhail Suslov. These early writings, in the absence of any official line, were marked by disagreements and debates about the meaning and significance of Developed Socialism. It was only after the 24th Congress that an orthodox interpretation emerged, although this did not put an end to the debates.

The most commonly used definition was provided by Brezhnev himself, who stated that Developed Socialism was 'a stage in the maturing of the new society when the restructuring of all social relations on the collectivist principles inherent in socialism is completed'.[8] This implied two things. First, a new way of periodising the transition from capitalism to communism. Second, a reappraisal of the nature of socialism itself. The impetus to elaborate the meaning and significance of Developed Socialism was given by Suslov in a speech to the All-Union Conference of heads of Social Sciences Departments of Higher Education. He outlined that

> The main guideline the 24th CPSU Congress set for our social scientists is the theoretical elaboration of the fundamental problems of a developed socialist society and the scientific substantiation of the ways and means of its gradual development into communism.[9]

All concurred with the view that the transition to communism would now be a prolonged, gradual process. Communism by 1980 had been quietly abandoned. Socialism was becoming less of a transitional stage between capitalism and communism, and more of an historical stage in its own right. But the details and nature of the gradual development of socialism into communism evoked different responses from Soviet theorists, dependent upon their general outlook and attitude to change. For Butenko (a progressive and unorthodox thinker within the Soviet intelligentsia), socialism would develop on the basis of its own laws and tendencies. It was not merely a synthesis of the negation of capitalism and the emergence of communism. Socialism had to be 'perfected'. The essential socio-political, economic and cultural aspects had to be fully developed before the construction of communism could commence. Butenko did not spell out a specific periodisation, but he seemed to imply that the era between capitalism and communism would involve: the creation of a Developed Socialist society; the perfection of Developed Socialism; and the transition from Developed Socialism to communism.[10]

Richard Kosolapov (a key establishment figure in the intellectual elite) was more explicit about the new timetable for the attainment of communism. He argued that there were three distinct post-revolutionary stages before communism. First, there was the transition from capitalism to socialism. Second, there was the construction of the foundations of socialism, followed by the preparation for the building of Developed Socialism. Finally, there was Developed Socialism proper. However, Kosolapov identified two distinct substages within Developed Socialism itself. In the first, the two forms of socialist ownership – state and collective – merge. In the second, socialist ownership by the people becomes predominant, and society becomes classless. This is the essential precondition for the transition to communism.[11] But it is important to stress here that Soviet ideology still made constant, explicit references to the construction of communism. This was no abandonment of utopia *pace* Gorbachev. Brezhnev continued to talk at length about 'building the material-technical basis of communism'. Indeed, it is probably correct to assert that too much has been made of the break with Khrushchev. The 1961 party programme was reprinted in 1976. The main shift was over questions of tempo and specificity. Socialism would 'gradually' evolve into communism. No timetable for this was spelled out.

As Developed Socialism was now a prolonged historical stage in its own right, analysts turned to a series of discussions of the processes occurring within this era. Although space precludes a detailed elaboration, the key idea that linked many writings was the imperative to 'perfect' the Soviet system. This was the central task of Developed Socialism. But what did this mean? Answers often depended upon the outlook of the particular theorist in question. One of the first theorists to discuss Developed Socialism was Fedor Burlatskii. In his writings, he emphasised its reformist potential. In the socio-political sphere Developed Socialism contained the potential to enhance the democratic nature of the Soviet state. In the economic sphere, the greater scope for rational planning and rapid increases in productivity inherent in the Scientific–Technological Revolution (hereafter STR) imparted a sense of optimism to ideological pronouncements of the late 1960s and early 1970s.[12] Butenko and other progressive figures, particularly in the early 1970s, highlighted how the application of rapid advances in technological innovation to the productive process opened the way for a more efficient, dynamic economy which in turn would lay the foundations for the material abundance of communist society. Developed Socialism embodied a great deal of optimism about the opportunities which now existed to overcome scarcity, and to replace Stalinist extensive, heavy-industrial based economic growth with intensive, balanced economic growth.

But Developed Socialism also offered solace to scholars of a more conservative bent. The emphasis upon 'enhancing' the party's leading role, the increased reliance upon expertise in policy-making and the continuation of economic management via hierarchical central planning all pointed to the preservation of the existing distribution of power and privilege. Although the Soviet leadership became increasingly critical of the inability to implement far-reaching technological advances, and also increasingly pessimistic as economic growth slowed, this should not obscure the optimism and reformism which accompanied much of the writing on Developed Socialism in the period 1971–7. The immediate attainment of communism may have disappeared, and socialism was to undergo a gradual process of transformation and perfection, but many Soviet theorists continued to emphasise the potential within Developed Socialism to bring about sustained, progressive change to the Soviet system.

Overall, Soviet writings, although encased within an official definition of Developed Socialism established from on high, and reinforced with a number of key precepts covering all aspects of Soviet life, displayed a surprising degree of heterogeneity. Beneath the general proposition (for example, enhance the leading role of the party) there existed distinct interpretations of what this might mean in practice. It was also seen as a progressive doctrine, which fostered a process of rational, scientifically planned, and efficient evolution towards communism. However, this heterogeneity existed only within a framework which was set by the politico-ideological hierarchy, and which was designed to legitimate and bolster the central institutions and operating values of Soviet socialism: the leading role of the communist party, central planning, the international hegemony of the USSR.

Broadly speaking, western writings on Developed Socialism can be subdivided into three particular contexts: ideology, domestic politics and the Soviet bloc. Let us begin with ideology. Probably the foremost theorist in this regard has been Alfred B. Evans. In a series of articles and pieces between 1977 and 1993, Evans set out the meaning and significance of Developed Socialism within the perspective of post-revolutionary Soviet Marxism–Leninism.[13] His analyses highlighted how Developed Socialism was both innovative in terms of the periodisation of the evolution of the post-revolutionary state, but also deeply conservative in consolidating the prevailing distribution of power within Soviet society and defending the core values of Soviet socialism. The emergence of this gradualist concept, which was a clear revocation of Khrushchev's timetable and a postponement of the communist utopia was central to his approach. This, he argued, amounted to the erosion of utopianism in Soviet thinking and reflected the conservative and cautious nature of the regime under Brezhnev. He identified that at the heart of Developed Socialism was a commitment to 'centralised political direction', and to the primacy of technological and economic development. In addition it acted to bolster the pre-eminence of the USSR within the socialist bloc. He concluded that

> The concept of developed socialism is new. Yet the central values embodied in Soviet ideological innovations represent a strong link with past experience.

> The principal goals expressed in the defence of mature socialism are the maintenance of authoritative political institutions and the continuation of industrial growth... It adapts communist ideology to defend existing Soviet social structures. Developed socialism expresses the outlook of a consolidative regime deeply convinced of the benefits of industrial advancement.[14]

For Evans, then, the gradualism and developmentalism inherent in Developed Socialism was evidence of a pronounced move away from utopianism and represented the advent of an era of conservatism and consolidation.

In terms of Soviet domestic politics the notion of Developed Socialism became, in Donald Kelley's words, 'the political formula of the Brezhnev era'.[15] He argues that Developed Socialism was more than just a theoretical construct and a reinterpretation of the periodisation of the post-revolutionary evolution of the Soviet state. He noted that

> the concept of Developed Socialism is also quintessentially about political leadership and authority-building. It must be regarded as a political formula, whose myriad purposes include not only the specification of the nature of the present society and the tasks confronting Soviet leaders, but also the embodiment of a particular style of leadership characteristic of the Brezhnev era.[16]

Kelley highlighted the political implications of Developed Socialism. It embodied the complex contradictory pressures for both stability and progressive, measured change during the Brezhnev era. The Brezhnev regime after 1964 required a period of stability and routine after the upheavals and staccato leadership style of Khrushchev. This was encapsulated in the phrase 'trust-in-cadres' by which the political leadership agreed not to disrupt the patterns of work and privilege of the key officials within the bureaucracy. Developed Socialism had to promote conservatism and caution. Yet the imperatives for change, to continue the appearance of progress towards higher and higher social and economic forms, required the introduction of new measures. Developed Socialism had to promote innovation as well. This complex amalgam of reformist and conservative pressures within Developed Socialism reflected, for Kelley, the political climate of the Brezhnev era. As an ideological construct, its main features – promotion of stability and measured, gradual, systematic change – were born out of the political requirements of the Brezhnev leadership.

The internationalist dimension of Developed Socialism reveals a substantially different picture, though. Sarah Terry has dissected the place of Developed Socialism in the evolution of Soviet–East European relations.[17] Her analysis is interesting in detailing the pre-1971 discussions and debates, and in demonstrating that the concept arrived in Moscow from eastern Europe, and was replete with fairly radical, transformatory implications in its initial stages. It was only after 1971, when it became the official doctrinal centrepiece of the Brezhnev years, that it was largely stripped of any radicalism. Terry notes that the term originated in the Czech Communist Party in June 1960, and became the theoretical basis for all the reform movements in Eastern Europe in the 1960s, particularly in Czechoslovakia, Hungary, Bulgaria and the GDR. The combined impact of an ideological recognition that the foundations of socialism had been built in these countries, and that economic problems were beginning to accumulate, led to a search for ways of developing and improving the nature of socialism.

Across a range of issues – economic planning and management, changes to the functioning of political institutions, more critical appraisals of Marxism–Leninism, and the nature of the social structure of Soviet-type societies – increasingly radical ideas and policies were discussed as part of the process of constructing a Developed Socialist society. These ideas were not explicitly rejected or criticised by the new post-Khrushchev leadership, which in turn gave further encouragement to innovative thinkers. Quite the reverse, in fact. Many thinkers in the Soviet system took up some of these themes, and began to discuss them in the Soviet context. This reflected the ambiguous, fluid nature of the Soviet regime between 1964 and 1968, in which reformist, de-Stalinising groups were struggling against more conservative, re-Stalinising elements. The crushing of the Prague Spring wrought a change in the correlation of forces. The hegemony of the USSR had to be restored. Reformist thinking was seen to be potentially destabilising and had to be countered. In this period (1968–71) the Soviet leadership used this opportunity to maintain the concept of developed socialism (as this allowed them to quietly abandon Khrushchev's timetable to construct communism, and to assert that the USSR was the most advanced socialist nation having already constructed this type of society), but to invest it with a much more conservative content, stripping away its earlier reformist themes. The positions were now reversed. The CPSU established the orthodox interpretation of Developed Socialism. Their East European clients fell into line.[18]

Terry Thompson echoed these themes.[19] His analysis portrayed Developed Socialism as the means of establishing the international hegemony of the USSR within the socialist bloc, and in particular in its rivalry with China. Thompson argues that the crucial aspect of Developed Socialism was its reassertion of the international primacy of the USSR. The implications of Khrushchev's polycentrism in Eastern Europe, and of Mao's attempt to 'leap' into communism through a Chinese model of development, were to erode the political and ideological authority of the USSR. Developed Socialism was the CPSU's response. Developed Socialism outlined a universal view of development for all socialist societies (undermining Khrushchev's polycentrism), and highlighted industrial progress as the basis for the transition to communism (in opposition to China's emphasis upon the People's Commune).

Thompson also identified a secondary domestic issue in the emergence of Developed Socialism: the Stalin question. Anti-Stalinists saw in Developed Socialism the chance to highlight the break in Soviet evolution which occurred in 1956. The Khrushchev and Brezhnev eras were both distinct from the Stalin era. Stalinists attempted to maintain a continuity of evolution from Lenin through Stalin to Brezhnev, and so denied the notion of a 'break' in 1956. Interestingly Thompson argued that the emphasis within Soviet writings shifted over the period 1966–71. In the early period (1966–8) the twin themes were apparent. From 1969 onwards, the Stalin question disappeared. The new focus, post-Prague Spring, was on maintaining the unity of the socialist bloc.[20]

Overall, western interpretations stressed the primacy of the political requirements of the Soviet state – both domestically and internationally – in shaping the content of Developed Socialism. Developed Socialism was much more than an ideological construct. It was a central pillar in the apparatus of power, and also it both shaped and embodied the political aspirations and frustrations of the Brezhnev regime. It was more than just a simplistic reflection of the ethos of the Brezhnev era. Its ideas, values, concepts and language all played a part in shaping the nature of the Soviet system under Brezhnev. But the specifics of western analyses vary substantially depending upon the particular analytical framework of the scholar.

Developed Socialism after Brezhnev–from critique to demolition

When Andropov succeeded Brezhnev in 1982, he was prepared to be more critical about the problems in the Soviet system. He argued that there were clearly problems within the Soviet system which could not be rationalised as 'vestiges' of capitalism, but which were attributable to shortcomings within the socialist system itself. This more critical slant gradually spilled over into an appraisal of Developed Socialism. According to Andropov, the Soviet Union had reached only the beginning of 'the long historical phase' of mature or Developed Socialism. The task now was to 'perfect' Developed Socialism: this necessarily meant revealing some of the problems and difficulties ('subjective' and 'objective') which had to be overcome in the process of 'perfection'.[21] Andropov also questioned the ability of the existing theoretical concepts, embodied in Developed Socialism, to comprehend the nature of Soviet society in the 1980s, or to come up with a remedy relevant to its assorted ills. In a speech to the Party veterans, he asserted that, 'Frankly speaking, we have not yet properly studied the society in which we live and work and have not fully disclosed its inherent laws.'[22]

It was clear from Andropov's own analysis of Soviet society that theoretical developments were necessary to take account of the new problems and conditions. As the dominant ideological and theoretical concept of a mature socialist society, Developed Socialism was clearly inadequate (or was being inadequately interpreted by Soviet scholars) and would have to be included in any theoretical rejuvenation which occurred. Konstantin Chernenko shared many of Andropov's perceptions of Developed Socialism. The USSR had entered the stage of Developed Socialism, although they were only at the beginning of this prolonged period. The attainment of Developed Socialism, while being an implicit recognition of the mature and developed nature of the Soviet system, should not, according to Chernenko, be interpreted either as signifying its total perfection, or lead to the idealising of what had been achieved. By the time of Chernenko's death significant strides in the theoretical and practical de-Brezhnevisation of Soviet society had already been made. However, the arrival of Gorbachev as General Secretary was to bring a qualitatively different treatment of Developed Socialism.

Initially it appeared that Gorbachev was reverting to the pattern adopted by both Khrushchev and Brezhnev in their treatment of their predecessor. The *Pravda* editorial of 10 November 1985 entitled, 'Flattery and Obsequiousness' was an attack upon the idolatry which had become apparent under Brezhnev. In addition to the previous characterisations of the Stalin era (the Cult of Personality) and the Khrushchev era (as one of subjectivism and voluntarism), the Brezhnev era was deemed to be one of 'flattery, obsequiousness, sycophancy and fawning'.[23] Hence it seemed that the Gorbachev leadership was reverting to type in blaming the systemic problems and failures on the former leadership.

As the process of de-Brezhnevisation got under way, Developed Socialism, as the theoretical centrepiece of the Brezhnev years, was emptied of its content, abandoned and replaced (initially) by the concept of the 'acceleration of socio-economic development'. Thus, in tandem with the start of a process aimed at renovating Soviet society, there emerged a conscious attempt to remove the theoretical underpinning of the Brezhnev era. This was elaborated most fully by Gorbachev in his Congress speech:

> It is proper to recall that the thesis on Developed Socialism has gained currency in our country as a reaction to the simplistic ideas about the ways and period of time for carrying out the tasks of communist construction. Subsequently, however, the accents in the interpretation of Developed Socialism were gradually shifted. Things were not infrequently reduced to just registering successes. It became a peculiar vindication of sluggishness in solving outstanding problems. Today, when the Party has proclaimed and is pursuing the policy of accelerating socio-economic development, this approach has become unacceptable. The prevailing conditions compel us to focus theoretical and political thought not on recording what has been achieved, but on substantiating the ways and methods of accelerating socio-economic progress.[24]

This analysis of Developed Socialism contains three interesting strands. First, its initial emergence is seen overwhelmingly in terms of a mere reaction to

Khrushchev's timetable for the direct transition to communism, and can at first be explained in terms of an addition to the post-revolutionary periodisation of Soviet society. Second, it is perceived as an inherently conservative doctrine. Its emphasis is seen not just as a positive accent in favour of consolidation and stability, but rather as a doctrine which fostered complacency and operated by extolling the positive aspects of Soviet society. The other side of this coin is that Developed Socialism was thus seen as a doctrine which glossed over any problems which existed, and so hindered the resolution of contradictions. In this way it made an active contribution to the growth of negative phenomena and crises in Soviet society, and also helped to block the emergence and implementation of policies and ideas to address these problems. Finally, it is viewed as having played a major role in communicating to, and inculcating in, the population and the officials a mentality of stagnation and apathy which snuffed out creativity and stifled the emergence of dynamism. This approach was codified in the revised Third Party Programme, which was approved by the 27th Party Congress on 1 March 1986. In this document, Developed Socialism is mentioned only cursorily, appearing only twice in the final draft. The key tasks outlined by the programme were, 'the planned and all-round perfection of socialism, for Soviet society's further advance to communism through the country's accelerated socio-economic development'. The programme also contained a passage similar to Gorbachev's indictment of Developed Socialism. As the reforms of *perestroika* got underway, Gorbachev omitted any references to Developed Socialism, and by 1987 it had disappeared from the Soviet ideological lexicon.

The final verdict on Developed Socialism, delivered by the Gorbachev leadership, recognised two things. First, the initial correctness of the decision to reinterpret the transition to communism, and to repudiate the essentials of the Khrushchevite idea of the 'full-scale construction of communism'. But, second, it also recognised its role in preventing the discussion and solution of the plethora of problems that had accumulated by the early 1980s. According to the theorists of *perestroika*, Developed Socialism had become the ideological underpinning to the era of *zastoi*. Let us review these two ideas.

Developed Socialism and Khrushchev – repudiation or continuation?

> It is . . . in its underlying significance, a credo of Soviet conservatism. It is the political expression of a ruling and possessing class which wants to project an image of a Soviet Russia on the march – and towards full communism at that – but which in actuality, is concerned most of all with the preservation, without radical change, of the existing institutional structure and its associated pattern of power, policy and privilege.[25]

This was Robert Tucker's description, in 1961, of Khrushchev's Draft Third Party Programme, although it reads like a typical assessment of Developed Socialism. It is evident that Developed Socialism was introduced to defuse the potential embarrassment of the specific timetable of Khrushchev's Third Party Programme: overtaking the United States in *per capita* production by 1970, and building communism 'in the main' by 1980, were not going to be achieved. But how far did Brezhnev's ideological innovations mark a break with the substance of the Third Party Programme? Have the essential continuities between Khrushchev and Brezhnev not been overlooked in the undue emphasis given to Khrushchev's specification of dates? To explore this in more depth, a brief review of the Khrushchev era and the Third Party programme is essential.

The early years of Khrushchev's tenure as General Secretary (1956–9, until the extraordinary 21st Congress of the CPSU) were suffused with a great deal of optimism, and an incredible sense of faith in the ability of the Soviet economy to outstrip their capitalist rivals and create the technological basis for a communist society. On this basis Khrushchev committed himself to the ideological task of ushering in the advent of the era of communism. As economic problems began to accumulate after 1960–1, and as opposition began to mount to Khrushchev's constant meddling in the working of the apparatus, so the sense of optimism began to fade somewhat. The Party Programme was framed against a background of a fierce struggle within the political elite between Stalinists and anti-Stalinists.[26] These factors were crucial in fostering an atmosphere of greater realism and pragmatism. The commitment to construct communism remained though, as the personal authority of Khrushchev, and the ideological challenge of the Chinese Communist Party to the USSR were dependent upon the achievement of this goal. This circle was squared when Khrushchev began to sketch in the *details* of what this communist society would look like.

Some recent western analyses of the Third Party Programme have tended to highlight the absurdities of Khrushchev's timescale, without delving too deeply into the details of his vision of communism.[27] Even Evans, who sets out a highly detailed account of Khrushchev's vision, concludes that '[I]t is an understatement to observe that the boldness and optimism of his expectations seem startling today.'[28] This is right. But the specifics of his vision of communism do not look anything like as bold and optimistic when judged within the context of the views and political priorities of the late 1950s. This was reflected in western writings at the time. Analysts were at one in highlighting the essentially conservative substance to the Party Programme, once the optimistic gloss and rhetoric had been peeled away.[29] A few examples will suffice to illustrate this point.

Khrushchev outlined that communism would be built in two stages. Between 1961 and 1980, the USSR would surpass the West and create the material–technical basis for communism. By 1980, communism would 'on the whole' or 'in the main' be built. Full or complete communism would be constructed in the subsequent period (although there was no timetable specified). The ultimate end-point of final communism was postponed long into the future. The immediate task set by the Third Party Programme was the construction of the material–technical basis of communism. The last line proclaimed that 'THE PRESENT GENERATION OF SOVIET PEOPLE SHALL LIVE UNDER COMMUNISM!'[30] But this was not, as we have seen, the final communist society as envisaged by Marx and Engels. So what type of communist society did Khrushchev have in mind?

The central plank of Khrushchev's vision of communism was that there would be an 'abundance of material and cultural benefits for the whole population'.[31] This would be achieved through massive increases in economic output (both industrial and agricultural) and labour productivity between 1961 and 1980. The details of this abundance included a massive increase in the availability of consumer goods, food produce and housing for the Soviet people. In addition there would be a plethora of social and economic benefits for the Soviet people, including:

> The shortest working day/week in the world;
> Free lunches in schools, offices, factories, and so on;
> Pensions and health-care extended to collective farmers;
> Free public transport.[32]

In 1961, this amounted to a massive advance in the living standards of the Soviet people. But this was not 'material abundance' as Marx and Engels would have understood it. This was not the abolition of scarcity, but the attempt to achieve a western level of consumption, ambitious by Soviet standards, but hardly akin to a utopian society. Was this a society which was functioning on the basis of the communist principle of distribution according to need? Partly. But the Programme made it clear that the definition of 'needs' would be highly circumscribed. The inculcation of a communist consciousness through extensive agitprop work would result in the population themselves moderating their demands. The full abolition of scarcity would only arrive later, the Programme itself stating that by 1980, 'Soviet society *will come close* to a stage where it can introduce the principle of distribution according to needs' (emphasis added).[33] Khrushchev appears to have redefined Lenin's dictum. Now, communism = western levels of consumption + welfare provision. This was, as Tucker, Zauberman, Tompson and others have described, a conservative, pragmatic vision of communism, little more than a more efficient version of the present. All of the radical changes – for instance, the abolition of commodity–money relations – were to be reserved for the distant future.[34]

In socio-political terms, the Programme was similarly cautious. Although the aim was to create a classless society by 1980, this was not one which had abolished inequality or social differentiation (which again was postponed until the latter phase of communism). In political terms, although the dictatorship of the proletariat was said to have fulfilled its historical mission and was now replaced by the All-People's State, there was no notion of the state withering away. The CPSU itself would continue to play a central role in guiding and directing Soviet society. The concept of popular self-government was again postponed until the final stage of communism. Khrushchev's vision does indeed appear to be rhetorically bold, but specifically pragmatic and rather conservative. Why?

The keys to understanding the ambiguous nature of the Party Programme are political power and Stalin. Domestic Soviet politics around the period 1960–1 was marked by a struggle between Stalinists and anti-Stalinists. Khrushchev, as the spokesman of the latter, wished to shift resources into consumer goods and away from heavy industry (reversing the priorities of the Stalinist faction). Arch-Stalinists wished to defend the priority accorded to heavy industry. Khrushchev also wished to bolster his own authority (and the position of the USSR *vis-à-vis* China) by arguing for embarking on the construction of communism, and so supplanting the achievements of Stalin who had 'merely' achieved the construction of socialism by 1936. Stalinists, such as Molotov, were arguing for the completion of the socialist phase (by, for example, converting the collective farms into state property). The first draft of the Party Programme outlined a radical shift towards consumer goods, but this was tempered somewhat by the time of the final draft which outlined a more balanced approach to economic development. Although there was substantial criticism of Stalin at the 22nd Congress, there was a political compromise between the two factions, as manifest in the text of the Party Programme.

When appraising the relationship between the ideological continuities and discontinuities between Khrushchev and Brezhnev, it is necessary to go beyond both the surface utopianism of Khrushchev's timetable of dates in the Party Programme, and also the debates over terminology, and instead to compare systematically the details and objectives of the two concepts. For instance, in much the same way that Developed Socialism postponed communism way over the horizon, so too did Khrushchev. In his speech to the 24th Congress, Brezhnev outlined that having built a Developed Socialist society, 'this has enabled us to tackle in practice the great task set by the Party Programme, by its latest congresses – that of building the material and technical basis of communism'.[35] There was thus a coincidence of ostensible ends: both leaders were engaged in the construction of the material and technical basis of communism. As always, though, the devil is in the detail. To what extent did Brezhnev substantially maintain the means adopted by Khrushchev as well?

In this regard, there are a number of key continuities that can be identified between Khrushchev and Brezhnev. In the same way that Khrushchev foresaw a massive growth in consumer goods and public services as a precursor of communist material abundance, so too did Developed Socialism emphasise that there would be an increased provision of goods and services available to the population. A more balanced approach to economic development (giving greater emphasis to consumer goods and agriculture) was maintained by Brezhnev. Economic growth and increases in productivity (both traditional Bolshevik touchstones) were the means by which these goals would be realised. Both approaches continued to postpone radical changes – abolition of commodity–money relations – to the communist phase. But this is where the similarities end. Khrushchev foresaw rapid increases in economic growth arising out of a combination of increased material incentives for labour, greater mass enthusiasm for the project in hand and the increased application of science and technology to the productive process. His projections were based upon extending and accelerating the rapid growth rates of the 1950s.

Brezhnev posited a process of more gradual, balanced economic growth, arising out of a shift towards intensive economic development, which rested on the application of the STR to the productive process. His more cautious projections (although still optimistic when viewed in the light of the actual growth rates of the 1980s) were a reflection on the economic downturn of the early–mid 1960s. The economic strategy underpinning Developed Socialism was a recognition that the Stalinist approach – extensive development targeting a few key areas – had to yield to a more rational, balanced, intensive approach as the Soviet Union was now a highly complex industrial economy.

In socio-political terms, similar processes can be detected. The central issue revolves around the concept of the All-People's State, as outlined in the Third Party Programme. It was described thus:

> Having brought about the complete and final victory of socialism . . . the dictatorship of the proletariat has fulfilled its historic mission and has ceased to be indispensable in the USSR . . . The state, which arose as a state of the dictatorship of the proletariat, has become a state of the entire people, an organ expressing the interests and will of the people as a whole.[36]

Why was this concept introduced by Khrushchev? The theoretical justification for its introduction rested on the claim that with the elimination of exploiting classes within the USSR, the need for the dictatorship of the proletariat had disappeared. The state now expressed the interests of the whole of the Soviet people. It was qualitatively distinct from its predecessor in a number of ways. Its activities were now said to be primarily economic and cultural, rather than coercive. Increasingly, its functions would be transferred to public organisations, drawing increasing numbers of the population directly into the administration of the system. In this way, the state was to become increasingly democratic and participative in its functioning, prefiguring the 'withering away' which would occur in the future. This would also be a crucial part of the inculcation of communist consciousness in the population. The process of administering the country would also be a process of self-education. The All-People's State was an important milestone on the road to communist self-government.[37]

So much for the theoretical rationale. The political motivation for the adoption of this new concept grew out of Khrushchev's de-Stalinisation and his desire to demonstrate a clear break with his predecessor. Increased participation by the people would unleash popular enthusiasm, legitimate the new leadership, and hopefully stabilise the system after the abandonment of Stalin's mass terror. On a personal level, it bestowed ideological kudos on Khrushchev, as he was presiding over the next phase of the USSR's evolution, extending what Stalin had achieved. On the surface this appeared to be a bold, visionary move, as the state gradually devolved more and more of its powers to the people. The details tell a different tale.

The most optimistic and bold pronouncements on this topic were outlined by Khrushchev between 1959 (at the 21st Extraordinary Congress of the CPSU) and the summer of 1961 (the preparation of the draft programme of the CPSU). In this period, Khrushchev highlighted how a whole range of functions of the state would be transferred to existing social organisations (Trade Unions, Komsomol) or voluntary organisations. By the time of the 22nd Congress and the Third Party Programme discussions, there had been a significant shift in Khrushchev's thinking, undoubtedly as a result of the ongoing struggle within the leadership. This resulted in a somewhat more conservative interpretation. The extent of activities assumed by public organisations was severely circumscribed, and instead replaced by increased participation of the masses in the work of existing state organisations (most notably the Soviets, but also the party itself). Additionally, the role of the party was also destined to grow, as this whole process required close ideological supervision to ensure that the endpoint of communism was reached. Although this was a fairly radical departure (when contrasted with the approach under Stalin), compared with Khrushchev's earlier pronouncements this was far more moderate. As communism approached, the withering away of the state entailed the withering of certain state functions (notably compulsion). The state and the party were to remain, and indeed were to increase their role. Khrushchev's innovations represented a means of bolstering the central institutions of political authority in the guise of the evolution towards communist self-government. What was the fate of the All-People's State under Developed Socialism?

In the period immediately following the removal of Khrushchev from power, the All-People's State disappeared from official discourse. It did not remain invisible for long though. Indeed it was to become a central plank of

Soviet writings on the political system of Developed Socialism. The high watermark came in 1976–7. At the 25th CPSU Congress, Brezhnev proclaimed that

> The Party and the CC [Central Committee] have always started from the premise that a developed socialist Society has been built in our country and is gradually growing into a communist society, from the premise that our state is a state of the whole people, expressing the interests and the will of the whole people.[38]

The 1977 Constitution similarly placed the All-People's State in a prominent position, signifying its importance in defining the current stage of political development of the Soviet state. But was this anything more than rhetorical continuity? What did the 'All-People's State' mean under Developed Socialism?

The radical participatory ideals which Khrushchev proposed in 1959–61 remained buried. But the underlying trend – of encouraging increased participation by the masses in the administration of the system – was sustained under Brezhnev. The general thrust of Khrushchev's moderated view of the state, as expressed in the Third Party Programme, was maintained. Developed Socialism emphasised a heightened role for both party and state. An increased role for the state administration was predicated on the notion of the growing complexity of the Soviet economy. This required a more sophisticated, technical approach to the administration of society, echoing somewhat Lenin's famous dictum about the early Soviet state requiring 'more agronomists, less politics!'[39] This required the application of technology, and the greater use of experts and expertise in policy-making. The theoretical expression of this was the concept of 'scientific management' which became the *leitmotif* of Soviet politico-administrative theory under Developed Socialism. Developed Socialism, while emphasising the growth in the level of popular involvement in the tasks of administering society, now put greater emphasis on scientific management as the means of realising a 'scientific' transition to communism. It sought to achieve this by combining the close control of social and economic processes with the introduction of the latest scientific and technical changes. Popular participation would be directed and closely controlled by the central administrative elite to ensure that it was channeled into the 'right' areas.[40]

The main shift came in regard to the character and quality of this mass participation, which embodied the underlying ethos of the Brezhnev era. Developed Socialism continued the emphasis upon popular participation in political processes. There was to be greater involvement of the population in the work of the Soviets, trade unions, Komsomol, etc. (although less so in the CPSU itself), and these bodies were also to have greater responsibilities. Formal channels were instituted to encourage participation in nation-wide discussions. But this was different from the mobilising, campaigning participation of Khrushchev. The higher educational levels of the population would enable the people to participate in a more informed, rational manner. The aim of this participation was to enhance the scientific nature of decision-making, as there would be an improved flow of information from lower levels of the system. This was portrayed as an extensive democratisation of the workings of the state. In reality it was highly controlled, highly circumscribed state-directed participation.

The essential continuities of approach between Khrushchev and Brezhnev were enshrined in the 1977 Constitution. There were substantial threads linking the Khrushchevian ideological platform with Developed Socialism. The commitment to expanded consumption, the interest in greater citizen participation, the maintenance of the central institutions of political authority and the continued postponement of the radical features of communism to the distant horizon were all common to the Marxism–Leninism of Khrushchev and Brezhnev. This should come as no surprise though. The specific functions that a new ideological concept performed – distinguish from previous leader, bolster personal authority of new leader, maintain international hegemony of USSR, enhance political authority of CPSU, demonstrate progress towards communism – were common to both Khrushchev and Brezhnev.

How then do we explain the differences? The main differences were over questions of tempo and approach, style and emphasis. Developed Socialism highlighted rational, technocratic, modernising, gradualist change. Khrushchev promised mobilising, energetic, rapid, high-tempo changes. Brezhnev's approach reflected not just his more consensual style of leadership compared to Khrushchev, but more importantly it was a reaction to Khrushchev's approach, which had ruffled so many feathers in the Soviet apparatus. The correlation of domestic political forces is also crucial in determining the emphases accorded to particular ideas within each ideological platform. The crushing of the Prague Spring gave a huge impetus to more conservative forces in the Soviet elite, which caused a retreat from some of the earlier more radical ideas within Developed Socialism.

On a wider level, the precise historical context of each leader needs to be borne in mind. Khrushchev's predictions came amidst a time of great euphoria and optimism, both in the West and the East. The commencement of the Soviet space programme and the rapid growth rates of the 1950s generated enormously enthusiastic prognoses about the future. Against this background, Khrushchev's predictions about communism seem fairly tame. Similarly, Developed Socialism emerged in an era of slowly declining economic growth. Yet its predictions about the projected performance of the Soviet economy were still optimistic and positive. The perception of Brezhnev and Developed Socialism marking a conservative rejection of Khrushchev's utopianism seems hard to sustain when the details of Khrushchev's programme are spelled out. Indeed, if Khrushchev's high-blown rhetoric and specific timetable is set to one side, a clear case can be made for seeing the technological, de-politicised, expertise-based vision of Developed Socialism as marking a much more radical break with the Stalinist approach than that of Khrushchev. So why then is it argued that Developed Socialism became the ideology of *zastoi*?

Developed Socialism and zastoi

The role of Developed Socialism in the emergence and perpetuation of the 'stagnation' of the Brezhnev years is said to lie in the ideological and intellectual atmosphere it fostered. Gorbachev's characterisation of Developed Socialism was that it became a formula for 'registering successes' and 'vindicating sluggishness'. Let us unpack these two ideas a little.

The question of 'registering successes' relates to the growing ideology–reality gap that was said to have emerged by the late 1970s and early 1980s. Official ideological pronouncements became a litany of Soviet achievements, both domestically and internationally. Each year, the progress on the road to communism was noted and celebrated. All problems and negative phenomena were ignored, and received no public airing or discussion. The official ideology became divorced from the reality of Soviet life.

At a popular level this accelerated the alienation and cynicism of the Soviet people from the party and its belief system. But the ritual incantations of Soviet leaders – progress, progress, progress! – added a deeper layer of problems. The failure to acknowledge the depth and character of the accumulating problems prevented a detailed discussion of how to resolve them. In this way, Developed Socialism became an ideological blanket, suffocating the intellectual life of the system. All pronouncements had to conform to the official line. 'Registering successes' was not just a form of complacency, it also undermined the possibility of creatively discussing solutions to the problems.

'Vindicating sluggishness' highlights how Developed Socialism began to emphasise 'gradualism' over 'change'. The imperative to proceed via gradual, moderate, measured, incremental advances overtook the imperative to realise a technocratic, efficient, rationalist variant of Soviet socialism. Indeed, so gradual was the momentum at the beginning of the 1980s that you had to look very carefully to detect any movement at all. In its opposition to the energetic, campaigning, mobilising style of Khrushchev, Developed Socialism had become a force for conservatism, a rationale for stability, a defence of the status quo. How accurate are these appraisals?

There is clearly much here to agree with. In postponing communism way over the horizon, Developed Socialism forestalled any immediate and system-wide changes. This mentality easily subsided into a preference for routine and stability, dressed up as the 'perfection' of the existing system and the prevailing distribution of power. The accent in the late 1970s and early 1980s was on consolidation, not transformation. Yet, this view is highly selective and one-sided. Developed Socialism functioned in very similar ways to other orthodox ideological concepts. Did not the official ideology constantly highlight the tremendous advances and achievements of the Soviet people and their state? How often were critical appraisals of problems in the Soviet system discussed under Stalin and Khrushchev? The role of Marxism–Leninism was to demonstrate and publicise that, at any given moment, they were on the road to communism. The present was always the best possible one, the immediate future would be rosy, the final destination perfect.

So was Developed Socialism a qualitatively distinct variation on this theme? Yes and no. Although the leadership never publicly disclosed or discussed the scale and extent of the problems within the system, shortcomings were highlighted and discussed. Solutions and reforms were proposed, right up until Brezhnev's death in 1982. The reformist potential inherent within Developed Socialism right from its emergence needs to be remembered. The whole thrust of Developed Socialism was about identifying shortcomings within socialism before embarking upon the transition to communism. This can either be seen as a postponement of transformation for reasons of political expediency, or as a greater awareness of the need for continual improvements in the nature of present system. Indeed, in its emphasis upon the application of science and technology to the productive process and to planning it appeared to offer a genuine means of overcoming scarcity and laying the basis for the material abundance of communism. In other words, the ideological framework provided by Developed Socialism continued to promote, or perhaps did not hinder, the emergence of reforms in selective areas right up until the death of Brezhnev.

The question hinges really on the appropriateness of Developed Socialism as a concept to respond to the accumulating problems. Its emphasis on the importance of measured incremental change to bring about improvements became increasingly inadequate as the problems became larger. A growing awareness existed within the Soviet politico-ideological elite that Developed Socialism could not of itself continue to maintain the hegemony and legitimacy of the CPSU. New concepts and slogans were formulated, in particular the 'socialist way of life', to address these issues. Hence, even under Brezhnev's leadership it was deemed necessary to supplement Developed Socialism with other ideas, although criticising or replacing it were never discussed. Although unofficial centres of creative and critical thought also began to flourish, only very occasionally did any of these ideas filter into the public domain and inform policy-making. Developed Socialism's explanatory framework posited that the existing institutions and practices of Soviet socialism were essentially correct. This made it inadmissible to admit to profound, systemic shortcomings or to encourage a search for radical analyses or solutions. Although it is an exaggeration to say that Developed

Socialism suffocated intellectual life, its continued defence of the status quo meant that it was increasingly dysfunctional in the search for the causes of the problems.

Most significantly perhaps, the whole tempo of Developed Socialism's view of change – measured, gradual, incremental – was increasingly at variance with the urgent need to address the slowdown in Soviet economic performance and the concomitant social problems bedevilling Soviet society. Developed Socialism was not conducive to the solution of the tasks that confronted the Soviet leadership in the mid-1980s. But as subsequent history has testified, neither was *uskorenie, perestroika, demokratizatsiya* and *glasnost'*. Sandwiched between Khrushchev's promise to build communism and Gorbachev's project to bring 'democratisation' and 'openness' to the USSR, Developed Socialism seems a staid, grey doctrine of conservatism. Yet its vision of a variant of Soviet socialism which was expertise-based, technocratic, rational, efficient and drawing upon the (directed) participation of the masses in the administration of the system was perhaps a more authentically Leninist Bolshevik vision than either its predecessor or its successor. The deaths of Brezhnev and Suslov in 1982, given the importance that new leaders placed upon ideological affairs, inevitably sounded the death-knell for Developed Socialism.

Conclusion

Developed Socialism defies easy analysis. Its meaning is difficult to grasp, its significance slippery. Appraising it depends on the context within which one situates it, and on the perspective of the appraiser. It changed and evolved over the course of the years from 1960 to 1982 and beyond. Sometimes it encouraged change, other times it fostered routine. It asserted the supremacy of the USSR in the international socialist bloc, and it cemented the political position of the post-Khrushchev leadership by providing stability for the party cadres. Analysing Developed Socialism requires us to go beyond the simplistic appraisals elaborated under Gorbachev. Understanding Developed Socialism helps us to understand the twists and turns, rhythms, values and priorities of Brezhnev and his era.

Further reading

F. Burlatskii, 'O stroitel'stve razvitogo sotsialisticheskogo obshchestva', *Pravda*, 21 December 1966.

A. Evans, *Soviet Marxism–Leninism: The Decline of an ideology* (Westport, Conn.: Praeger, 1993).

D. Kelley, 'Developed Socialism: A Political Formula for the Brezhnev Era', in J. Seroka and S. Simon (eds), *Developed Socialism in the Soviet Bloc* (Boulder, Col.: Westview Press, 1982).

R. Kosolapov, *Developed Socialism: Theory and Practice* (Moscow: Politizdat, 1982).

S. M. Terry, 'Theories of Socialist Development in Soviet–East European Relations', in S. M. Terry (ed.), *Soviet Policy in Eastern Europe* (New Haven: Yale University Press, 1984).

T. L. Thompson, 'Developed Socialism: Brezhnev's Contribution to Soviet Ideology', in T. L. Thompson and R. Sheldon (eds), *Soviet Society and Culture* (Boulder, Col.: Westview Press, 1988)

Notes

1. L. I. Brezhnev, *Report to the 24th Congress of the CPSU 1971* (Moscow: Progress 1971).
2. Various, *The Road to Communism* (Moscow: Foreign Languages Publishing House, 1961), pp. 445–590.
3. P. N. Fedoseev, 'Postroenie razvitogo sotsialisticheskogo obshchestve v SSSR: torzhestvo idei leninisma', *Kommunist*, 2, 1974, p. 18.
4. R. Kosolapov, *Developed Socialism: Theory and Practice* (Moscow: Politizdat, 1982), p. 62. See also, A. Butenko, 'O razvitom sotsialisticheskom obshchestve', in *Kommunist*, 6, 1972, pp. 48–58. F. Burlatskii, 'Politicheskaya sistema razvitogo sotsializma', in *Kommunist*, 22, 1979, pp. 62–73.
5. For details on the 1977 Constitution, see R. Sharlet, 'The New Soviet Constitution', *Problems of Communism*, 26, 1977, pp. 1–24.
6. L. I. Brezhnev, *Leninskim kursom*, Vol. 3 (Moscow: Politizdat, 1972), p. 235.
7. *Pravda*, 21 December 1966.
8. L. I. Brezhnev, *Leninskim kursom*, Vol. 3 (Moscow: Politizdat, 1972), p. 24.
9. *Pravda*, 22 December 1971, p. 2.
10. A. Butenko, 'O razvitom sotsialisticheskom obshchestve', *Kommunist*, 6, 1972, pp. 48–58.
11. R. Kosolapov, *Developed Socialism: Theory and Practice* (Moscow: Politizdat, 1982).
12. For an analysis of writings on the STR, see J. Cooper, 'The STR in Soviet Theory', in F.J. Fleron (ed.), *Technology and Communist Culture* (New York: Praeger, 1977).
13. The key works of Alfred Evans are, 'Developed Socialism in Soviet Ideology', *Soviet Studies*, 29, 1977, pp. 409–28; 'The Decline of Developed Socialism? Some Trends in Recent Soviet ideology', *Soviet Studies*, 38, 1986, pp. 1–23; 'The Polish Crisis in the 1980s and Adaptation in Soviet Ideology', *Journal of Communist Studies*, 2, 1986, pp. 263–85.
14. A. Evans, 'Developed Socialism in Soviet Ideology', *Soviet Studies*, 29, 1977, p. 426.
15. D. Kelley, 'Developed Socialism: A Political Formula for the Brezhnev Era', in J. Seroka and S. Simon (eds), *Developed Socialism in the Soviet Bloc* (Boulder, Col.: Westview Press, 1982).
16. D. Kelley, *The Politics of Developed Socialism* (New York: Greenwood Press, 1986), p. 13.
17. S. M. Terry, 'Theories of Socialist Development in Soviet–East European Relations', in S. M. Terry (ed.), *Soviet Policy in Eastern Europe* (New Haven: Yale University Press, 1984).
18. S. M. Terry, 'Theories of Socialist Development in Soviet–East European Relations', in S. M. Terry (ed.), *Soviet Policy in Eastern Europe* (New Haven: Yale University Press, 1984), pp. 224–39.
19. T. L. Thompson, 'Developed Socialism: Brezhnev's Contribution to Soviet Ideology', in T. L. Thompson and R. Sheldon (eds), *Soviet Society and Culture* (Boulder, Col.: Westview Press, 1988).
20. T. L. Thompson, 'Developed Socialism: Brezhnev's Contribution to Soviet Ideology', in T. L. Thompson and R. Sheldon (eds), *Soviet Society and Culture* (Boulder, Col.: Westview Press, 1988), pp. 215–26.

21. Yu. Andropov, 'Ucheniye Karla Marksa i nekotoriye aspekty stroitel'stva sotsializma v SSSR', *Kommunist*, (1983), 9–23.
22. Yu. Andropov, *Pravda*, 16 August 1983, p. 1.
23. *Pravda*, 10 November 1985, p. 1.
24. M. S. Gorbachev, *Report to the 27th Congress of the CPSU* (Moscow: Novosti Press, 1986), p. 114.
25. R. Tucker, 'A Credo of Conservatism', *Problems of Communism*, 10, 1961, p. 4.
26. See M. Fainsod, 'The 22nd Party Congress', *Problems of Communism*, 10, 1961, pp. i–xi.
27. See, for example, R. Hill, 'State and Ideology', in M. McCauley (ed.), *Khrushchev and Khrushchevism* (Basingstoke: Macmillan, 1987); M. McAuley, *Soviet Politics*, (Oxford University Press, 1992); R. Sakwa, *Soviet Politics* (London: Routledge, 1989).
28. A. Evans, *Soviet Marxism–Leninism: The Decline of an Ideology* (Westport, Conn.: Praeger, 1993), p. 62.
29. See L. Schapiro (ed.), *The USSR and the Future* (Munich: Institute for the Study of the USSR, 1962); W. Laqueur and L. Labedz (eds), *The Future of Communist Society* (New York: Praeger, 1962); *Problems of Communism*, 9/6, 1960.
30. Various, *The Road to Communism* (Moscow: Foreign Languages Publishing House, 1961), p. 589.
31. Various, *The Road to Communism* (Moscow: Foreign Languages Publishing House, 1961), p. 512.
32. For details of the era of communism, see Part 2 of the Programme, *The Road to Communism* (Moscow: Foreign Languages Publishing House, 1961), pp. 502–37.
33. Various, *The Road to Communism* (Moscow: Foreign Languages Publishing House, 1961), p. 512.
34. R. Tucker, 'A Credo of Conservatism', *Problems of Communism*, 10, 1961; A. Zauberman, 'The Economics of 1980', in L. Schapiro (ed.), *The USSR and the Future* (Munich: Institute for the Study of the USSR, 1962), pp. 103–13; W. Tompson, *Khrushchev: A Political Life* (London: Macmillan, 1995).
35. L. I. Brezhnev, *Report to the 24th Congress of the CPSU 1971* (Moscow: Progress 1971), p. 49.
36. Various, *The Road to Communism* (Moscow: Foreign Languages Publishing House, 1961), p. 547.
37. R. E. Kanet, 'The Rise and Fall of the All-People's State: Recent Changes in the Soviet Theory of the State', *Soviet Studies*, 20/1, 1968, pp. 81–93; G. Brinkley, 'Khrushchev Remembered: On the Theory of Soviet Statehood', *Soviet Studies*, 24/3, 1972–3, pp. 387–401.
38. L. I. Brezhnev, *Report to the 25th Congress of the CPSU 1976* (Moscow: Progress 1976), p. 99.
39. V. I. Lenin, 'Report of the All-Russia Central Executive Committee to the Eighth Congress of Soviets', *Selected Works*, Vol. 2 (Moscow: Progress, 1971), p. 517.
40. E. P. Hoffmann and R. F. Laird, *Technocratic Socialism: The USSR in the Advanced Industrial Era* (Durham, Md.: Duke University Press, 1985); V. Afanas'ev, 'Nekotorie aspekti nauchnogo upravlenie obshchestvom v SSSR', in *Sotsialniye i politicheskiye problemy razvitogo sotsializm* (Prague: Mir i sotsialisma, 1978).

9
The Roots of *Perestroika*

John Gooding

On one point, Sovietologists of the later Brezhnev period were almost unanimous: the regime would not democratise. There was, as we shall see, one leading expert who thought differently; but he was very much an exception. The conventional wisdom was that nothing short of a crisis that threatened the regime's very survival would induce it to democratise. And while economic problems were becoming grave, it was fanciful to think that they yet put the regime's existence in jeopardy. All was quiet in the streets, the dissidents had been crushed, the masses remained inert. The regime would not democratise, except under duress, because any erosion of its monopoly would go wholly against party tradition and would obviously damage the leader's interests. They, after all, knew perfectly well that, once they allowed the pillars to be weakened, the roof would sooner or later fall in upon them.[1]

In the event, of course, the Gorbachev leadership did the very thing that the experts had least expected. And democratisation, as it turned out, had even more drastic consequences than the experts might have predicted – the demise of the party, dissolution of the Union and abandonment of the socialist experiment itself. The Soviet reformers had, needless to say, anticipated an utterly different outcome. Democratisation would revitalise the economy, reduce social tensions, strengthen the party, and bring the country to a fully realised socialism. Without it, the mission on which the party had embarked in October 1917 could not be brought to a successful conclusion.

That at least had been the cardinal belief of a group of party intellectuals who during the Brezhnev years formed a kind of 'loyal opposition' and had voiced an alternative view of the path the country should take to socialism. These representatives of the Alternative Tradition, as their approach will be called, were in the main level-headed, moderate, and pragmatic; they were most certainly not intending wreckers. They accepted socialism, the CPSU, and the general Soviet framework, and while they deplored the tragedies of the Stalin period they believed that the Soviet socialist project could yet be redeemed. For that to happen, however, the party needed in their view to return to a socialism that respected the rights of the individual and set a premium on democracy. The main aim of this chapter will be to elucidate why this influential pressure-group had come to believe in the saving power of democracy and why in particular its members believed that democracy was fully compatible with the party's rule and indispensable to the fulfilment of its mission.

The Alternative Tradition and attitudes to the workers

The origins of the Alternative Tradition went back to the 1920s and early 1930s, to the struggle against Stalin's hijacking of the revolution and perversion of its purposes. Only after the Khrushchev thaw, however, did it emerge as a semi-public critique of the command economy and the Stalinist conception of socialism. Alternative thinkers of the 1960s focused first and foremost upon economic problems, and their ideas in this respect were strongly influenced by reformist theories and practices in eastern Europe.[2] The economy was performing badly; it had lost its earlier dynamism; and the principal reason for the failing, the reformers suggested, was excessive centralisation, the reliance upon commands and directives as the basic operational method. Such a system ignored economic realities; it let planners impose essentially subjective views in defiance of the objective needs and tendencies of the economy. It was both inefficient and arbitrary – inefficient because arbitrary. What was needed was to replace 'administrative' by 'economic' levers – that is to let market forces, operating through prices and profits, do the work of directives. The market, the reformers tirelessly insisted, was not alien to socialism, it was in fact intrinsic to socialist production; and the 'socialist market' – not to be confused with its capitalist counterpart – was essential if planning was to function effectively. Enterprises should be given a wide area of autonomy; they should be put on a 'cost-accounting' (*khozraschet*) basis, under which they would be responsible for covering their own costs and would be guided in their decisions above all by the criterion of profitability.

The existing system was unrealistic, and its most glaring failure of realism lay in its attitude towards the workers, whom it treated as robots or at best a 'labour resource'. Reformers were strongly critical of this tendency to dehumanise the workers and regard them as work-performing objects. Human beings were not machines. They did not work well unless stimulated, and yet, unlike machines, they were capable, once stimulated, of showing initiative and being creative. 'A machine will never replace human beings in the process of economic creativity', Alexander Birman insisted.[3] A system concerned only with what could be got out of the workers lost sight of the whole purpose of a socialist economy, which was not production for production's sake but satisfying people's material and spiritual needs, including those of the workers. The focus of attention at the workplace should therefore, Birman argued, be not so much the work done as the workers who did it. 'To what extent can they fulfil their dreams, wishes and plans, which of course are not limited to smelting more iron or making more shoes?'[4] If the workers were seen not as an undifferentiated mass of task-performers but, rather, as individuals with needs and aspirations of their own, then they would find their work more satisfying and would do it better.

The suggestion that workers had individual and group interests distinct from those of society as a whole was, however, highly contentious. The official view was that this was a society without antagonistic social relationships or serious internal divisions or conflicts of any kind, that it was a society united in its aspirations and becoming ever-more homogeneous. These conditions allowed the state to do what no capitalist state could – to define a general social interest, an interest that embraced the entire population. This interest the party represented and fully satisfied through its policies. Much of this analysis the reformers readily accepted. The socialisation of the means of production was an immense advance – without that, socialism would be unthinkable.[5] Socialism's great advantage over capitalism was that by abolishing private ownership of the means of production it had created the potential for a single, non-conflictual social interest. The restructuring of property relationships was, however, not enough by itself to remove all significant social division and conflict. The reality was less neat and more complicated than the orthodox schema suggested. Conflicting classes indeed no longer existed in the Soviet Union, but the country still had distinct social *groups*, each with its own interests, and these in turn were made up of individuals with their own needs and motivations.

Serious thinking about the importance of groups and interests within socialist society had been stimulated by Ota Sik, whose *The Economy, Interests, Politics* had been published in the Soviet Union in 1964.[6] Sik argued that workers think and act not only as a class but also, and above all, as individuals living in a particular social milieu. Only an economic system that took account of these individual interests could be effective. And it was only through their individual interests that workers would, in time, come to an awareness of their common interests. These views were fiercely combated by traditionalists, for whom any suggestion that Soviet society was less than a monolith, and that groups within it had interests of their own, was heresy.[7] The reformers nevertheless persisted. Their view, they were convinced, reflected the reality, was the key to revitalising the economy, was intrinsically socialist, and presented no threat whatsoever to the party. The revival of sociology, after years of being banned, indicated that they were making progress. And it was a sociologist, V. Shubkin, who, in 1965, put their case most explicitly: 'within classes there exist definite social groups, the differences between which are created not by forms of ownership of the means of production but by such factors as profession, level of qualification, education and income.'[8] Unless these groups were taken into account, Shubkin suggested, unless their needs, tastes, attitudes, and motives for acting as they did were given some attention, the concrete economic problems of the country could not be solved.

The cry was taken up. Interests were vital. Pay the worker decently. Pay him above all in relation to how well he worked – 'to each according to his ability, to each according to his work' was, after all, a fundamental principle of socialism. Then economic performance would improve. 'Human beings', Nikolai Petrakov pointed out, 'need to feel a direct relationship between the work they do and the satisfaction of their needs'.[9] But if workers were to be converted from passive and lacklustre performers of tasks into active and imaginative builders of socialism, more was needed than to rejig pay scales. 'The need to work', Petrakov went on, 'is linked inseparably with creativity, with a sense of participating in the decisions taken'.[10] However, for decades workers had been beaten into an inert obedience; every flicker of initiative had been stamped out in them. If the economy was to revive, there would have to be an utterly different culture at the workplace. Nothing less, it seemed, than the democratisation of the entire economic system would do.

'Democratization of management is necessary', the veteran V. V. Novozhilov urged, 'for the development of the creative activity of the popular masses. The larger the creative participation of the masses in developing the economy and culture, the quicker the rate of economic growth.'[11] The workers, then, had to be involved in day-to-day administration. The very fact of involving them would raise their level of creativity, Alexander Birman believed. It would also make their physical work 'incalculably more stimulating'.[12] Only then would they begin to show initiative. And that was indispensable. 'Workers' initiative', Otto Latsis declared, 'is an Aladdin's lamp which will solve all of the previously unsolvable economic problems'.

Democratisation beyond the workplace

That the economic system needed to be democratised was the reformers' principal argument. But their interest in democracy did not stop at the workplace. Democratisation of the economic system was inseparable, in the end, from democratisation of life in general. That democratisation at work would boost economic performance could be said openly enough. That it would also have the beneficial effect of helping to democratise the public sphere in general could not be said openly but was nevertheless a recurring theme in the reformers' writings.

The advantage of the cost-accounting (*khozraschet*) system, V. S. Nemchinov argued, was that it would create 'a reliable filter against relics of voluntarism' (that is, against arbitrary action by the authorities).[13] V. Shubkin pointed out that concern for interests and interest groups would assist 'the development and strengthening of democratic instincts and democratic methods of administering socialist society'.[14] Alexander Birman openly linked democratism at work and in the wider sphere by saying that socialism's essence lay in 'the direct participation of the labouring masses in the administration of production and of the entire country. And not just participation in administration – the word "participation" is inadequate – but administration by the masses themselves'.[15] Nikolai Petrakov turned a discussion of the pros and cons of planning into a thinly veiled criticism of the authority enjoyed by 'experts' in Soviet society. Experts were by no means infallible, he suggested, and needed to recognise that their knowledge was but relative and limited. They had the right to recommend but no right to impose their views. People had to make their own free choices; only through market preferences could mistakes by the planners be exposed and corrected.[16] Petrakov was commenting on the economic system, but the significance of his remarks for the Soviet system as a whole was obvious. What, after all, were the party leaders but 'experts' who made absolute claims for the validity of their knowledge and imposed their views upon everyone else?

Soviet reformers could not of course say outright that without general democratisation there could be no economic recovery, still less any real socialism. What many may well have wanted to say was, however, said in 1965 by a Czech who has an especial interest for us. At Moscow University in the early 1950s, Zdenek Mlynar had become a close friend of Mikhail Gorbachev. The two would remain in contact until the disaster of 1968 drove them apart.[17] Mlynar's ideas anticipate the political reform implemented in the Soviet Union from 1987. Indeed, they may be seen as a model for the within-system reformism which, after much initial success, was to be discarded in 1990 for an approach that broke with Soviet tradition entirely. Yet in the context of the 1960s, what Zdenek Mlynar had to say was nothing less than mould-breaking.

Diversity and even conflict of interests within socialist society should, he argued, be welcomed. For these group interests represented dynamic forces which should not be ignored, still less stifled, but should instead be made use of through representative institutions. In such institutions, 'the interests of society as a whole are defined in the process of a confrontation of different, and sometimes contradictory, interests and approaches'. Collisions would inevitably occur, and in the course of them 'the contradictions are resolved and proper expression is found for the real interests of society'.[18]

In suggesting that the general interest should be defined not simply by the party from above but in a process of interaction between top and bottom through representative institutions, Mlynar was saying something extremely radical. For all his radicalism, his thinking nevertheless reflected an underlying optimism about the socialist project. The group conflicts were, he was at pains to point out, *non-antagonistic*. Had he suggested otherwise, he would of course have got into serious trouble. Yet Mlynar was doing more than pay lip-service to an unavoidable dogma. For in the democratised society he envisaged, the task of 'resolving contradictions between various group interests' would fall to the party. If it was to discharge the task properly and to resist pressure from sectional interests, its leadership role, far from being diminished, would have to be strengthened.[19] The party, then, would act as an above-group arbitrating and integrating force; it would – and it alone could – subsume a mass of particular interests into a comprehensive and non-conflictual general interest.

Like Zdenek Mlynar, most Soviet alternative thinkers of the 1960s seem to have believed that, given the necessary changes, a full coincidence of interests could be achieved. Alexander Birman is a case in point. Birman argued powerfully in favour of increasing the rights of individuals and of local institutions. He emphasised in particular how important it was for soviets to be able to express local interests and even to resist the central planning authorities. The 'territorial principle' was vital 'because it creates the necessary organizational forms to involve the initiative of millions of workers'. The relationship between central and local authorities would, however, be collaborative and no serious conflicts could occur between them. 'Joint work will quickly give rise to a common language, since the disagreements will not, after all, be antagonistic and the debates will be between Soviet people, who are equally interested in the success of the common cause.'[20] There spoke the authentic voice of the Alternative Tradition!

Radicalising the Alternative Tradition

The most radical of the alternative thinkers, Roi Medvedev, came out in open opposition to the regime and advocated not democratisation but full democracy. The party should give up its monopoly and allow other parties to stand against it. Western constitutional practices should be adopted, including a clear-cut division between executive and legislature. The Supreme Soviet should become a proper parliament whose deputies were elected in free and fair competition. Medvedev's reasoning was strikingly similar to Nikolai Bukharin's of half a century before, except that it was applied to politics rather than economics. Bukharin had justified the mixed economy by arguing that in conditions of economic pluralism the virtues of the socialist economic system would shine out.[21] Almost mimicking him, Medvedev insisted that it was precisely through exposure to the ideas and policies of non-Marxist parties that people would come to appreciate Marxism and the party that embodied it. Just as Bukharin had seen a fully socialist economy being achieved by way of the market, so Medvedev argued that the practices of western democracy were necessary to bring about true socialism. Political reform would not undermine the party – quite the contrary. 'The point about open dialogue with dissidents is that it will strengthen communism and the Communist Party and facilitate adaptation to new conditions.' Socialism would always be 'the ideology of the overwhelming majority'; it enjoyed a natural majority position which nothing other than continuation of the party's monopoly could jeopardise. Once real socialist democracy had been established, then all non-Marxist parties would be 'deprived of a mass base and therefore would present no threat to the future of socialist society'.[22]

It followed that the party needed democracy and had every reason to embrace it. Given free competition, policies based on Marxism–Leninism would inevitably prevail. In such conditions, the party would revitalise itself and win the vigorous and widespread support that would enable it to accomplish its task. Much as the economic reformers argued that plan and market were complementary rather than contradictory, so Roi Medvedev had convinced himself that party domination was fully compatible with the practices of democracy.

This was alternative thinking taken to a radical extreme. Yet Medvedev shared the optimism of other alternative thinkers and even outdid them in this respect. The economy was in his view basically sound, though there was a case for some private enterprise in the service sector and small-scale industry. The social structure was and would remain basically homogeneous. The nationalities question had in essence been solved, cultural integration was taking place, and a new people 'possessing a common Soviet culture' had come into existence.[23] Thus in all conditions but one the conditions for a proper socialism existed already. Democracy alone was missing. The Prague Spring, however, was proof that a communist party could liberalise and regenerate itself without renouncing the basic values of socialism, and Medvedev was optimistic that by the end of the century the Soviet Union would have become 'a truly socialist nation'.[24]

But how would the change be brought about? How was a jealously monopolistic party to be transformed into one that accepted democracy? It would surely take more than the rationality and good sense of the democrats' arguments to prevail against such deep-rooted anti-democratism. And what was needed was sensed most clearly by someone on the other side of the Atlantic, the historian Moshe Lewin.

Like Medvedev, and unlike most American observers, Lewin viewed the early revolutionary years positively and believed that the Soviet socialist experiment might yet be redeemed. He had spent the early 1970s in writing a study of the economic reform movement which emphasised the similarity between current reformist thinking and thinking of the 1920s. And this genealogy gave him the key to the reform movement's likely success. The reformers would win not only because their arguments were more rational and sensible than their opponents'. They would win because they could relate themselves 'to important and acceptable trends in the Soviet past', because the solutions they proposed would be 'well in line with certain traditions inside the party'.[25] A case based on rationality and effectiveness would thus be reinforced and given a deep emotional resonance by an appeal to the collective memory. The party would be invited to go forward by going back, to shape its future by recovering its buried past, to complete its mission by returning to the springs of its original inspiration. And that of course meant returning to Lenin.

But which Lenin? Naturally enough, the Lenin of NEP. For in his final years the leader had been at his most emollient and un-Stalin-like, and had come closest to reconciling practical politics and the ideals of socialism. This, alternative thinkers claimed, was the true Lenin, and they attached especial importance to his very last writings – his 'political testament' – as a unique distillation of his wisdom. All of him was to be found here: 'his mind, his heart, his unusual clarity of thought, his concreteness, and the link between great theory and living reality.' With the 'testament' Lenin had 'spread out his warm and powerful wing over party and country and all of labouring mankind'.[26]

That the revolution had strayed from the Leninist path at the end of the 1920s and not yet returned to it could not be said openly. Alternative thinkers nevertheless circled endlessly around the theme of the 1920s, creating a mood of nostalgia for what they seemed to regard as a golden age before the Fall. None among them stirred nostalgia for the lost ideals of the 1920s more effectively than Mikhail Shatrov, a playwright from an Old Bolshevik family many of whose members, including his father, had fallen victim to the purges. And in 1966–7 Shatrov's play *The Bolsheviks* electrified Moscow audiences by dealing directly with the fate of the revolution and seeming to ask – 'did things have to turn out as they did?' Set in August 1918, the play showed party leaders being thrown into a panic by the news that Lenin had been struck down by a would-be assassin. 'Vladimir Ilyich can't be replaced by anyone', says Sverdlov, speaking for them all. In this crisis they rush through decrees establishing terror and concentration camps, though some endorse the decrees reluctantly, fearing how terror might get out of hand. But then comes the news that Lenin is recovering, and it leads to an explosion of joy: 'We're on our way again!'[27] With Lenin at the helm, nothing, it appears, can go wrong. The party is safe, not only from external enemies but also from the enemies lurking within its own ranks: those careerists who merely mouth socialist slogans – 'vermin' with 'red rosettes', as Lunacharsky calls them.[28] Lenin's near-miss nevertheless raises the question: what if he should die – what then? And the audience is left with the feeling that, had it not been for his premature death a few years later, the outcome would have been not Stalinism but genuine socialism.

Whereas Shatrov insinuated the idea that the Stalinist perversion had been a cruel historical accident, Roi Medvedev spent much of the 1960s writing a book that would put the idea of Stalinism's fortuity on a firm historical basis.[29] There was always of course a danger that the masses would swamp the enlightened, that peasant culture would in the end degrade the culture of socialism. Nevertheless, had Lenin not died in 1924, then 'the victory of genuinely socialist and democratic tendencies would have been more probable than the victory of Stalinism'. Stalinism's triumph, Medvedev suggested, was the outcome of two fateful historical accidents: the early death of Lenin, the genius of the revolution, and the criminal character of Stalin, 'the embodiment of all the worst elements in the Russian revolutionary movement'.[30] It followed that the Stalinist episode, however bloodstained, did not discredit the party or devalue the achievements of the early Soviet state. Stalinism – 'the negation and bloody annihilation of Bolshevism'[31] – simply made it all the more necessary that the party should return to the principles that had guided it in the 1920s, that it should resume the work so tragically broken off then, that it should lead the country from pseudo-socialism to the genuine socialism of Marx and Lenin.

Not all alternative thinkers agreed that the 'great turn' of 1929 could have been avoided. They were, however, at one in thinking that Lenin would have abhorred Stalinism and that he had been guided by an utterly un-Stalinist conception of socialism. Medvedev spoke for all in suggesting that Lenin had been a genuine democrat, even if at times he had been forced to act against his own convictions. 'Early on, Lenin envisioned Soviet power functioning as a pluralistic system, allowing for free competition within the soviets among all parties representing the workers ... Lenin, you see, was convinced the Bolsheviks would come out ahead of all other parties in any free competition.'[32] Adverse circumstances, but also their own mistakes, had then forced the Bolsheviks to flout democracy. The elections to the Constituent Assembly had been bungled; held a little later, they would have given the Bolsheviks a popular mandate. War Communism was a mistake, but Lenin had at least learned from it; and with NEP, his greatest theoretical innovation, he had laid the foundations of a truly democratic socialism.

Those who wrote in the official press had to be more cautious, but heavily emphasised the Leninist inspiration of the changes they wanted. Lenin had been pro-market and pro-peasant, had seen NEP as a long-term policy and War Communism as no more than a regrettable short-term necessity, and had tried to prevent Stalin's brutal treatment of the nationalities. Lenin as the reformers presented him in fact questioned not only the command economy and Stalinism but fundamentals of the Soviet system as it still existed. Socialism for Lenin, said Birman, had been 'not only a certain fairly high level of material production and not only the socialisation of the means of production', it had also meant direct participation by the masses in administering the state.[33]

And so, subtly and not so subtly, alternative thinkers diffused a mood of regret for the dashed hopes and unrealised ideas of the 1920s, and suggested that these ideas might yet help bring the country to socialism. But if the reformers needed to convince a ruling class that was deeply suspicious of change, they also needed to convince themselves. Lenin was both a flag of convenience and an inspiration for them. As they portrayed him, he was not only a marketeer, a democrat and an embodiment of humanity; he was, in addition, someone who had grappled successfully with the contradictions thrown up by the attempt to create socialism in a society utterly unprepared for it. This facet of Lenin's appeal was underlined by a leading reformer somewhat later: 'His ability to reconcile seemingly irreconcilable things continues to astonish one with every re-reading of his works.'[34] And that, more perhaps than anything else, was what drew the reformers to Lenin. For 'this outstanding dialectician' had reconciled the irreconcilable – on paper at least. Plan and market. Self-determination of nations and the integrity of the Soviet state. Self-determination of individuals and the leading role of the Communist Party. With NEP he had maintained centralised direction of the economy while providing wide scope for individual initiative. Battling against Stalin, he had etched a plan by which the non-Russians could be persuaded to give the Soviet state their voluntary support. And while insisting that the party dictatorship was for the time being indispensable, he had envisaged a steady convergence between party aims and popular wishes which before long would have made any 'bossing' by the party unnecessary.

Lenin had thus confronted the very dilemmas that lay at the root of the current Soviet malaise – dilemmas which the regime had side-stepped by going off into a pseudo-socialism deeply influenced by the autocratic inheritance. And, as they read him, he had indicated one and the same solution to these various dilemmas: democratisation. Carefully implemented, this would not threaten the party's hegemony. On the contrary, it would bond party and people more tightly than before. Without it, the party would never fulfil its mission; without it, socialism would remain beyond reach. This belief in the saving power of democracy was what, more than anything else, united those party intellectuals who chafed under the Brezhnev regime and rejected the ideology of 'developed socialism'.

Towards the Soviet end-game

The early 1980s saw a wave of new thinking from economists, sociologists and others who, unlike Roi Medvedev, stopped short of outright defiance of the regime. By then, the economic situation had worsened so much that the reformers' arguments had become hard to ignore. Admittedly, all was still quiet in the streets. There had, however, been disturbances in neighbouring Poland, where the government's repressiveness and its mishandling of the economy had brought workers and intellectuals into concerted opposition to it. Nothing similar to the nation-wide and cross-class Solidarity movement was likely in the Soviet Union, where dissidents were tiny in numbers and tended to be shunned by the workforce. Yet if the Polish troubles did not touch a nerve, they were not entirely irrelevant either. The policies that had led to crisis in Poland were remarkably similar to Brezhnev's. If Prague had shown the dangers of liberalising too much, Gdansk flashed a warning of the hazards of continuing with policies of economic conservatism and political repression.

Even before Brezhnev was dead, an article in the official press had come out with 1960s-type arguments for democratising the economic system but argued in addition for *political* democratisation – for 'a gradual decentralisation of authority functions'.[35] Anatolii Butenko added urgency to his plea by directly linking the current situation in the Soviet Union with the crisis in Poland. That, he suggested, had been the result of a lack of democracy within the party and in society in general; and in the Soviet Union too, he predicted, there would be social tension and even 'open political conflict' if the ordinary worker remained excluded from decision-making and if he continued to see the political and economic systems not as 'his' but as 'external and alien forces'.[36]

But was this not an increasingly homogeneous society? Had it not been purged of social conflict and 'antagonistic contradictions'? Not so, said Butenko. There was in fact a 'basic contradiction' between society's production forces and the existing system of production relationships, as a result of which the development of production forces was being held back. What he was saying in this Marxist language was that the existing political and economic systems were benefiting the ruling elite, or elements within it, at the expense of society as a whole. This was a dangerous idea even to hint at, and before long the editors of *Questions of Philosophy* would be made to grovel for having published it. That Butenko should have publicly floated such a heresy was nevertheless a remarkable sign of how the party's grip on society was weakening.

Butenko's case was developed the following year by a leading, Siberian-based economist and sociologist, Tatyana Zaslavskaya.[37] Zaslavskaya's paper was less obviously provocative since it did not argue directly for political democratisation or raise the spectre of possible Polish-type eruptions. Her paper was not in fact intended for publication at all – simply for discussion within a small circle of leading academics and functionaries. The implications of the paper were nevertheless deeply radical, and its leaking to the West caused a sensation. The failures of the Soviet economy sprang, Zaslavskaya suggested, from deficiencies that were inherent in the economic system and could not therefore be eliminated without fundamental restructuring. The system treated workers as 'cogs' and expected them to behave 'just as obediently (and passively) as machines and materials'. The result was 'low labour- and production-discipline, an indifferent attitude to the work performed and its low quality, social passivity... and a rather low level of moral discipline'. In short, the country had not yet achieved 'a genuinely socialist type of worker' or 'a genuinely socialist attitude to labour'.[38]

Zaslavskaya became more radical still when she took up Butenko's point about the conflict of interests within society. The orthodox view, she reminded her audience, held that 'under socialism there is no group interested in the preservation of outmoded production relations and therefore their perfection takes place without social conflict'. But this was wrong. There *were* divergent interests, and as a result no improvement could be achieved without conflict. The existing system suited lazy and apathetic workers because it demanded so little of them; it also, she implied, suited many in the economic hierarchy because it gave them unlimited control over a passively obedient workforce. Both elements – bosses and workers – had an interest in obstructing reform. How then might it be achieved?

Two things, Zaslavskaya suggested, were necessary. First of all, theory had to reflect reality. It had to recognise the existence of groups dedicated to keeping outmoded production relations. What was needed was a new model of production relations which took into account 'the "multi-dimensionality", and frequently even the conflict of interests, of the groups operating in the economic structure'. Changes to ideology were not, however, enough. It was necessary, in addition, to develop 'a well thought-out socialist strategy' so as 'to stimulate the activity of groups interested in changing production relations and block the actions of groups capable of obstructing this change'.[39]

The suggestion that the party, or elements within it, had interests of its own was not being aired for the first time. Back in the 1960s, the Polish economist Wlodzimierz Brus had hinted strongly that the existing system allowed the leadership to promote its own interests in ways that put it in an antagonistic relationship with society as a whole.[40] That had been implicit, too, in Nikolai Petrakov's observation that 'the planner is himself a consumer' – the planner, in other words, was likely to be influenced by subjective criteria of his own and should not be seen as a disembodied intelligence guided by an objective science. Hence the need for a market mechanism to curb him.[41] The sobering experience of the 1970s could only confirm and deepen such suspicions. The 1965 reform – which Alexander Birman had once hailed as equivalent in importance to NEP [42] – had been killed off by a leadership which saw its vital interests being threatened by it. The disjunction between the general interest as the party chose to define it (in effect the *party's* interest) and the interest of society as a whole had become glaring. The economic downturn of the late 1970s only underlined how much the wider interest was being sacrificed.

But something had at least been learned from the blighted hopes of the 1960s. Reform of the economic system in isolation from the broader power structure would be futile. Quasi-reform, as one early 1980s reformer put it, was insufficient. Nothing less than real reform would do, and that would have to be 'carried through despite the resistance of conservative and inert elements in the state apparatus'.[43] There would have, in other words, to be a planned and concerted struggle against conservative elements, who would fiercely resist any encroachment on their powers. That was why strategic thinking was vital. That was why it was necessary to build a coalition in which intellectuals joined together with reform-minded members of the governing elite.

The new realism raised a question-mark against Mlynar-type ideas of the party as an integrating force capable of acting on behalf of the general interest in a democratised, but still one-party, state. It seemed to underline instead the need for uninhibited democracy – for government based on the *majority* interest in an ideologically and socially pluralistic society. It was, however, a far cry from that to the consensual, general-interest government by a democratised but unchallenged party which had been the staple of alternative thinking. To press for complete democracy would anyway be futile and probably counter-productive. A behind-the-scenes, strategic approach suited the reformers far better. The party had been captured by self-seekers who had turned it into a sectional interest, but had this perversion been inevitable? And might not genuine socialists win back control and restore the party to its proper function? Oddly enough, the arch-democrat, Roi Medvedev, was convinced that they would.

Medvedev in fact urged those who shared his ideas to do what he himself had signally failed to do: to keep their heads down, stay in the party and work for change within it. 'Party-democrats', as he called the healthy element, were few in the 1970s, but he had no doubt that their number and influence would grow. More far-sighted people would soon enter the leadership. Once that had happened, an alliance might well emerge between the reformist leaders and 'the best of the intelligentsia', and the effect would be to restore the party to its proper role.[44] Moshe Lewin arrived, seemingly quite independently, at a similar prognosis. Before long, enlightened political leaders might join intellectuals in 'a new coalition of forces'. That coalition, taking care to relate itself to acceptable trends in the party's past, would then reform not only the economy but the whole political system, bringing it 'into accord with the growing complexity and modernity of society'.[45]

Medvedev and Lewin made their predictions in the early 1970s. A decade later, reformers like Zaslavskaya were building bridges with political leaders who might one day create a democratised and genuinely socialist Soviet Union. Each party needed the other. The reformers were of course dependent upon enlightened people in the leadership; but they in turn could only welcome 'new thinking' that promised to restore dynamism to the economy and society in general without jeopardising the party's monopoly. The *dénouement* of the Soviet tragedy thus began with a rapprochement between the leadership and 'the best of the intelligentsia', for which decades of alternative thinking had prepared the way. As the first fruits of this alliance appeared, Moshe Lewin, who had anticipated it, hailed what he saw as a return to the party's pre-Stalinist tradition, while warning that full democracy should not be expected.[46] And the General Secretary who was leading party and country into what seemed to be an auspicious new era was, of course, none other than the former Moscow University friend of Zdenek Mlynar.

Further reading

M. Lewin, *Stalinism and the Seeds of Soviet Reform* (London: Pluto Press), 1991.
R. Medvedev, *On Socialist Democracy* (London, Macmillan, 1975).
M. Shatrov, The Bolsheviks *and Other Plays* (London: Hern, 1990).
O. Sik, *The Third Way: Marxist-Leninist Theory and Modern Industrial Society* (London: Wildwood House, 1976).
P. Sutela, *Economic Thought and Economic Reform in the Soviet Union* (Cambridge University Press, 1991).
T. Zaslavskaya, 'The Novosibirsk Report', *Survey*, 28, 1984, pp. 88–108.

Notes

1. The view that the regime was unlikely to want to democratise or to come under any strong pressure to do so was expressed most cogently by Seweryn Bialer in his *The Soviet Paradox: External Expansion, Internal Decline* (London: Tauris, 1986), esp. pp. 24–37. A more liberal variant of this approach can be found in Stephen F. Cohen, *Rethinking the Soviet Experience: Politics and History since 1917* (Oxford University Press, 1985). The dissenting voice was Moshe Lewin's.
2. They were especially influenced by Janos Kornai in Hungary, Wlodzimierz Brus in Poland and Ota Sik in Czechoslovakia who, in emigration from 1968, would emerge as the leading theorist of the 'Third Way'.
3. A. Birman, 'Samaya blagodarnaya zadacha', *Novyi mir*, December 1969, p. 179.
4. A. Birman, 'Prodolzhenie razgovora', *Novyi mir*, May 1966, p. 190.
5. Though Ota Sik, for one, would soon be thinking the unthinkable!
6. O. Sik, *Ekonomika, interesy, politika* (Moscow: Progress, 1964).
7. For Sik's own comment on the controversy, see his *The Third Way: Marxist-Leninist Theory and Modern Industrial Society*, trans. Marion Sling (London: Wildwood House, 1976), p. 45.
8. V. Shubkin, 'O konkretnykh issledovaniyakh sotsial'nykh protsessov', *Kommunist*, 3, February 1965, p. 51.
9. N. Petrakov, 'Upravlenie ekonomikoi i ekonomicheskie interesy', *Novyi mir*, August 1970, p. 175.
10. N. Petrakov, 'Upravlenie ekonomikoi i ekonomicheskie interesy', *Novyi mir*, August 1970, p. 176.
11. Cited from M. Lewin, *Political Undercurrents in Soviet Economic Debates: From Bukharin to the Modern Reformers* (London: Pluto Press, 1975), p. 231.
12. A. Birman, 'Samaya blagorodnaya zadacha', *Novyi mir*, December 1969, p. 180.
13. V. Nemchinov, 'Sotsialisticheskoe khozyaistvovanie i planirovanie proizvodstva', *Kommunist*, 5, March 1964, p. 84.
14. V. Shubkin, 'O konkretnykh issledovaniyakh', sotsial'nykh protessor' *Kommunist*, 5, February 1965, p. 49.
15. A. Birman, 'Samaya blagorodnaya zadacha', *Novyi mir*, December 1969, p. 175.
16. N. Petrakov, 'Potreblenie i effektivnost' proizvodstva', *Novyi mir*, June 1971, pp. 198–9.
17. Z. Mlynar, 'Il mio compagno di studi, Mikhail Gorbaciov', *L'Unità*, 9 April 1985, p. 9.
18. Z. Mlynar, 'Problems of Political Leadership and the New Economic System', *World Marxist Review*, Vol. 8, December 1965, p. 62.
19. Z. Mlynar, 'Problems of Political Leadership and the New Economic System', *World Marxist Review*, Vol. 8, December 1965, pp. 59, 63.

20. A. Birman, 'Samaya blagodarnaya zadacha', *Novyi mir*, December 1969, pp. 179–80, 180–1.
21. N. I. Bukharin, *Put' k sotsializmu* (Novosibirsk: Nauka, 1990), pp. 28–9, 48–9, 53–4, 60–1.
22. R. Medvedev, *On Socialist Democracy* (London: Macmillan, 1975), pp. 102, 103, 106.
23. R. Medvedev, *On Socialist Democracy* (London: Macmillan, 1975), p. 84.
24. R. Medvedev, *On Soviet Dissent: Interviews with Piero Ostellino* (New York: Columbia University Press, 1980), pp. 73, 110.
25. M. Lewin, *Political Undercurrents in Soviet Economic Debates: From Bukharin to the Modern Reformers* (London: Pluto Press, 1975), pp. 352, 353.
26. Ye. Drabkina, *Zimnyi pereval* (Moscow: IPL, 1990), p. 363. The first half of this deeply 'alternative' memoir had appeared in *Novy mir*, October 1968 (pp. 3–93), but publication had then been stopped.
27. M. Shatrov, *Izbrannoe* (Moscow: Iskusstvo, 1982), p. 289.
28. M. Shatrov, *Izbrannoe* (Moscow: Iskusstvo, 1982), p. 257.
29. R. Medvedev, *Let History Judge: The Origin and Consequences of Stalinism* (London: Spokesman Books, 1976).
30. R. Medvedev, *Let History Judge: The Origin and Consequences of Stalinism* (London: Spokesman Books, 1976), pp. 360, 362.
31. R. Medvedev, *Political Essays* (Nottingham: Spokesman Books, 1976), p. 67.
32. R. Medvedev, *On Soviet Dissent: Interviews with Piero Ostellino* (New York: Columbia University Press, 1980), p. 92.
33. A. Birman, 'Samaya blagorodnaya zadacha', *Novyi mir*, December 1969, p. 176.
34. G. Lisichkin, *Socialism: An Appraisal of Prospects* (Moscow: Novosti, 1989), p. 70.
35. A.P. Butenko, 'Protivorechiya razvitiya sotsializma kak obshchestvennogo stroya', *Voprosy filosofii*, October 1982, p. 27.
36. A.P. Butenko, 'Protivorechiya razvitiya sotsializma kak obshchestvennogo stroya', *Voprosy filosofii*, October 1982, pp. 22–3.
37. 'The Novosibirsk Report', *Survey*, 28, Spring 1984, pp. 66–108.
38. 'The Novosibirsk Report', *Survey*, 28, Spring 1984, pp. 90, 106, 108.
39. 'The Novosibirsk Report', *Survey*, 28, Spring 1984, pp. 97, 102.
40. W. Brus, *The Market in a Socialist Economy* (London: Routledge, 1972), p. 6. The original was published in Poland in 1964.
41. N. Petrakov, 'Upravlenie ekonomikoi', *Novyi mir*, August 1970, p. 184.
42. A. Birman, 'Mysli posle plenuma', *Novyi mir*, December 1965, p. 194.
43. B. Kurashvili, 'Ob'ektivnye zakony gosudarstvennogo upravleniya', *Sovetskoe gosudarstvo i pravo*, October 1983, p. 44.
44. R. Medvedev, *On Socialist Democracy* (London: Macmillan, 1975), p. 313.
45. M. Lewin, *Political Undercurrents in Soviet Economic Debates: From Bukharin to the Modern Reformers* (London: Pluto Press, 1975), pp. 352, 353.
46. M. Lewin, *The Gorbachev Phenomenon: A Historical Interpretation* (London: Hutchinson, 1988), p. 134.

10
Brezhnev Reconsidered

Edwin Bacon with Mark Sandle

The question which has been asked many times by interested colleagues during the preparation of this book has been 'why?' Why publish a book on Brezhnev? Surely there is nothing new worth saying on that era? And surely an uninspiring leader presiding over a period of stagnation and decline is not the ideal subject for a new study?

Au contraire, the leadership of a superpower for nearly two decades holds inherent interest. But beyond that, there are several motivating factors behind this volume. Foremost among these are: the relative neglect of the subject in the last two decades of the twentieth century; a renewed interest in and nostalgia for the Brezhnev years in Russia itself; the desire on our part to question received wisdom concerning Brezhnev and his time in power, particularly in relation to the appropriateness of the Gorbachevian discourse of stagnation; and the hope that the present work will contribute to the opening up of research questions which might form the agenda for more detailed future studies.

Brezhnev the neglected leader

One of the chief aims of this book has been to bring to the fore again a relatively neglected figure in recent world history. Part of the motivation for pursuing this goal came from the fact that our students and colleagues would regularly ask, 'what are the best books on Brezhnev?' A surprising gap was revealed when we had to answer that no consolidated work on the era as a whole had been published in English since the time when the Brezhnev years came under the heading of 'current affairs'. Of course, academics have pursued particular aspects of the era, and the Cold War History Project at Harvard University stands out in this regard, but that the subject as a whole has been neglected is not in doubt. Why should this be the case? And what does this neglect tell us either about the Brezhnev era itself, or about the scholarly community?

A number of explanations might be posited for the relative neglect of the Brezhnev years by the scholarly community. The first explanation is that this case is simply one of many where the gap between a subject ceasing to be current affairs and becoming the preserve of historians results in an hiatus in the attention paid to it. Beguiling though the thought of some academic 'no man's land' between current affairs and history might be, there is little evidence to suggest that it exists in relation to other periods of Soviet history, and every reason to argue that it should not have existed in the case of the Brezhnev years. Books on Stalin, Khrushchev and Gorbachev have continued to be plentiful since the end of their respective periods in office, without the gap of two decades which we see in the case of Brezhnev. Furthermore, the use of the Brezhnev era as the 'other' against which the Gorbachevian reform discourse set itself up might have been expected to focus more attention on the 'era of stagnation' by the end of the 1980s. Instead, the Gorbachevian discourse, with *zastoi* (stagnation) its key signifier, seems to have been widely accepted by many observers. Why this appears to have been the case brings us to our next reasons for the relative neglect of the Brezhnev years as a subject for academic study.

Attempts to explain the widespread acceptance of the *zastoi* hypothesis can be made by using two surface arguments. Our second and third explanations for scholarly neglect of the Brezhnev era are then that the tumultuous, extraordinary events of the Gorbachev era and after took the attention and resources of the Soviet/Russian studies community to the exclusion of most other areas of research, and that the discourse of stagnation seemed to have been so self-evidently confirmed by the chaos and breakdown of the Soviet collapse that it was scarcely worth questioning.

There is truth in both of these assertions; however, neither of them has the depth to sufficiently explain the consensus on Brezhnev which became widely accepted. During Mikhail Gorbachev's period as General Secretary of the Communist Party of the Soviet Union, the Soviet studies community undoubtedly found itself with a plethora of new topics, an array of new resources, and a new focus for the funding foundations. Nonetheless, historians of other eras, particularly the Stalin years, found the late 1980s and early 1990s to be a time of renewed activity and archival access. As for the stagnation hypothesis proving to be self-evidently true, to suggest that anything is self-evident strikes at the roots of sound academic analysis, and even more so when referring to the assertions of the dominant agent in the Soviet structure, namely Mikhail Gorbachev. None of which is to say, at this stage, that the discourse did not stand on a sound factual base. Whether it did or not will be considered later on in this concluding chapter. What is more pertinent to our discussion at this point, however, is why study of the Brezhnev era was relatively neglected at the very time when the Gorbachevian reformers were laying many of the ills of the Soviet system on its back and sending it out into the historical wilderness as a scapegoat.

The fourth reason we posit then for the relative neglect of the Brezhnev era by western scholars is that the years 1964–82 were perceived as an hiatus in the normative, deterministic, modernising notion of Soviet development held by many western observers. There is a pattern of development which goes Khrushchev – Andropov – Gorbachev – democracy, and into which Brezhnev and his loyal supporter Chernenko (Soviet leader 1984–5) do not fit. Consequently, during the late 1980s and into the 1990s much was published in English on the Khrushchev years, 1953–64, but very little on Brezhnev.[1] This is not to suggest any overt 'western-centric' agenda on the part of those academics writing on Khrushchev, but rather to note that as democratisation and reform dominated in the Soviet Union and, after 1991, in Russia, so the most obvious focus of historical comparison was the reformist Khrushchev era.

Russia's renewed interest in Brezhnev

The corollary to the argument that the Brezhnev era was neglected by scholars as it did not provide a suitable historical comparison for the reformism of Gorbachev and Yeltsin, is that the long overdue renewed interest in Leonid Brezhnev becoming apparent in Russian publications since the end of the 1990s,[2] also results in part from an attempt to understand the present in an appropriate historical context.

Developments in Russian politics in the second half of the 1990s increasingly suggested parallels with the Brezhnev years. We have already noted in Chapter 1 that opinion polls repeatedly showed the affection in which Brezhnev's period as leader of the Soviet Union was held by the Russian people. In large part this was due to the fact that the reformist upheaval of the Gorbachev, and particularly the Yeltsin, years had resulted in many citizens seeing themselves as 'losers' in the reform process. Price liberalisation had inevitably brought inflation, inflation had wiped out savings, and over a third of the Russian population were living below the official poverty line by the mid-1990s. At the same time a new materialism was evident in the high street stores and shopping malls of Russia's big cities, in the visible affluence of the 'new Russians' – as the *nouveaux riches* of the Yeltsin years became known – and in the advertisements which television carried into every home. The material benefits of the Brezhnev years may have been meagre in comparison, but at least, from the point of view of many Russians and particularly the older generation, they were available more reliably, and on a more egalitarian basis.

Material well-being was not the only factor which led many Russians to hold the Brezhnev years in some esteem. That period was also remembered as a time when Russia – in the form of the Soviet Union – had a global prestige and influence which had evidently disappeared by the mid-1990s. Mike Bowker notes in Chapter 5, the assertion of Soviet Foreign Minister,

Andrei Gromyko, in 1971 that: 'there is no question of any significance which can be decided without the Soviet Union, or in opposition to her.'[3] By 1997, the old enemy NATO had expanded to the very borders of the Russian state with Poland's accession,[4] and there was a sense among more nationalist-minded observers that the West was building on its 'victory' in the Cold War to weaken Russia economically and internationally. These views found their most overt expression in the presidential election of 1996 when, despite a media campaign with a heavily pro-Yeltsin bias, the leader of the Communist Party of the Russian Federation, Gennady Zyuganov, still managed to gain over 40 per cent of the vote, against President Yeltsin's second-round majority, even after Yeltsin himself had moved to the political centre and away from the radicalism of his early years in office.

From the mid-1990s, then, we saw a dampening of Russia's initial post-Soviet, pro-western democratising fervour. After 1996, and particularly after Boris Yeltsin's quintuple heart-bypass operation which followed the presidential election, there were widespread and obvious comparisons made between an ailing and often physically incapable President Yeltsin, and the Leonid Brezhnev of the late 1970s and early 1980s. An inability to work full-time, a tendency to embarrass officials on trips abroad, and the lack of understanding of complex policy matters – none of these were features appropriate to the leader of the world's largest state, and all of these were shared by Brezhnev and Yeltsin in their later years in office.

The final major factor which suggests parallels between contemporary Russia and the Brezhnev years is that in March 2000 the Russian people elected as their president Vladimir Putin, a man who, whatever his avowed dislike of communism *per se*, has a clear respect, even nostalgia, for the achievements of the Soviet Union at the height of its powers. At various points in this volume we have noted the suppressed radicalism of the *shestidesyatniki*, as the young generation of the 1960s was known in the Soviet Union. If it was this generation that came to power in the Soviet Union and Russia in the Gorbachev–Yeltsin years (1985–99), then it could be argued that Vladimir Putin and his leadership cohort are *semidesyatniki*, or 'the generation of the 1970s'.[5] Putin himself reached adulthood in the 1970s. The years in which many of his attitudes and beliefs consolidated themselves were the Brezhnev years of stability, superpower status, and stagnation. Certainly the first two of this *troika* seem to be aims of President Putin for Russia in the twenty-first century.

Reconsidering Brezhnev

The aim of this volume has never been revisionism for revisionism's sake. Reconsidering Brezhnev always allows for the possibility that perhaps the central conclusion after reconsideration will be that the consensus view on the Brezhnev years has become widely accepted simply because it's true.

What is clear from the outset, however, is that even if one broadly accepts the Gorbachevian discourse of stagnation, taken on its own it is a shallow conceptualisation of what is a far more complex issue. The chapters of this volume have gone some way towards a deeper interrogation of the Brezhnev era, focusing on specific areas of policy and providing context for the evidence.

Two basic points need establishing before we consider in more detail the extent to which we might want to reconsider the standard approach to the Brezhnev years. The first is that of course the Brezhnev era did not appear from nowhere and disappear into nothing. It was part of a process, be that the attempt to build communism, or simply the attempt to strengthen the Soviet superpower. Whatever story we choose to tell about this period in time, a fuller understanding will come from an acknowledgement of the constraints within which Brezhnev was working. He came to power with a given set of circumstances, the structural legacy of not just the Khrushchev regime, but particularly the Stalin years and even before. The choices he made were constrained by the structure within which he made them. Equally when he died, he left a legacy, a foundation on which his successors built. That the Soviet Union would no longer exist a decade after his death would have seemed inconceivable at the time.

To reconsider Brezhnev and his era requires appropriate awareness then of what Brezhnev was working with, in terms of systemic norms and structural constraints, as well as of the decisions he made within this framework. Of all the chapters in this volume, that by Ian Thatcher (Chapter 2) takes the most apparently revisionist line. His central thesis is that Brezhnev had many attributes as a leader which were suited to the specific context in which he operated. According to Thatcher, Brezhnev's leadership was marked by:

- The ability to know what to prioritise
- The avoidance of extremism
- A predisposition for teamwork and consultation
- A populist touch, for example in the introduction of the five-day working week and the reduction of the pension age
- The projection of a strong image abroad where, in contrast to the erratic behaviour of his predecessor Khrushchev, Brezhnev was perceived as a shrewd but reliable interlocutor.

In short, Ian Thatcher argues that '[r]ather than deserving a reputation as the most vilified of all Soviet leaders, Brezhnev should be praised as one of the most successful exponents of the art of Soviet politics'. The key to accepting this view – whether in part or in whole – must surely be to note Thatcher's contextualisation. His argument, that *given the Soviet system* Brezhnev was more adept than most at operating within it, requires critics to consider the leadership of Brezhnev without imposing on him criticisms of the Soviet state as a whole. Clearly such a separation is not entirely achievable – for example, if one takes exception to religious persecution in the Brezhnev years, one cannot ignore the role of a man who could have, within certain ideological limits, alleviated this persecution. Nonetheless, Thatcher is himself not uncritical of Brezhnev – seeing him as a far more successful Party leader than head of state – but seeks rather to assess him within the context in which he operated.

Periodisation

An approach used by many to try and reconcile the contradictions of the Brezhnev years which we have noted throughout this volume is the adoption of a clear periodisation. That there is a division between 'early' and 'late' Brezhnev is a widely accepted view. Put simply, the construct is that the positive features of the Brezhnev era for the Soviet Union (economic stability, growth in consumer well-being, an increased role on the global stage, technological prowess) were largely achieved in the early part of his time in power, and that decline set in some time in the 1970s. Ian Thatcher's most straightforward criticism of Leonid Brezhnev is that he failed to retire once ill-health clearly began to impinge on his effectiveness. There is little doubt that had Brezhnev stepped down voluntarily some time in the second half of the 1970s – after the adoption of the 'Brezhnev constitution' in 1977, for example, would seem an appropriate time – his historical reputation would be more favourable. He would have been the only Soviet leader to voluntarily leave office and the damaging picture of an increasingly decrepit General Secretary, which so doggedly remains the lingering image of Leonid Brezhnev, would have been avoided. In line with a number of other contributors to this volume then, Thatcher supports the view that a clear periodisation of the Brezhnev years is possible. As he puts it:

> there is a division between an 'early', 'good' Brezhnev and a 'bad', 'late' Brezhnev...The emergence of the 'bad' Brezhnev is normally linked to the onset of illness, which depending upon the source, paralysed Brezhnev as leader from the last eight to the final two years of his rule.

Quite when the downturn in the fortunes of the Soviet Union under Brezhnev is to be dated from is a matter of dispute. The most widely accepted periodisation has long been based on Brezhnev's health, and precise dates are difficult to come up with. Volkogonov opts for a vague, 'from the middle of the 1970s Brezhnev took no active part in either Party or state activity'.[6] Gorbachev is no more precise, only a little later in his vagueness, 'The removal of Podgorny in 1977 and of Kosygin in 1980 finally sealed the personal power of Brezhnev. The irony was that this happened when his capacity for work was already ebbing. His grip on power had by then become ephemeral.'[7]

Mark Sandle discusses in some detail in Chapter 7 the differing periodisations offered by some of the key intellectuals of the Brezhnev years. Georgii Arbatov's view was that both the character and the physical well-being of Leonid Ilyich played a part in the temporal division of the Brezhnev era, with the dividing line coming in 1974 after Brezhnev's first serious illness. Before that time, the Arbatov line has it, the non-conflictual nature of Brezhnev, which sought to keep as many people on-side as possible, coupled with his relatively limited intellectual capacity, led to a struggle over Brezhnev's 'soul', as both conservative and reformist *apparatchiki* sought to influence the party leader. Consequently, there was a deal of reformism evident in Soviet policy in the 1960s, which gradually faded along with Brezhnev's health and the rise of the conservatives.

Burlatskii rejects Arbatov's view so far as it concerns the character of Brezhnev himself, seeing him as a convinced opponent of reform from the start; after all, was it not to bring an end to the constant reforming 'schemes' of the Khrushchev era that Brezhnev and his co-plotters engineered Khrushchev's dismissal in 1964? Even so, Burlatskii acknowledges that reforms did continue into the second half of the 1960s, seeing these, like Arbatov, as an indication of the struggle between different factions within the leadership. Mark Sandle himself concludes that a notable temporal division in this struggle for hegemony within the Soviet regime came in 1968, with the invasion of Czechoslovakia and the crushing of the Prague Spring. Although the final outcome of the factional dispute took a few years to become fully apparent, events in Czechoslovakia ushered a change of approach and atmosphere into the debates of the Soviet elite. After 1968, Sandle argues, '[d]ogmatism, conformism, ideological hairdressing, and intellectual mediocrity seem to have held sway'.

What then do we make of the differing views of such participants and observers? A survey of intellectual life provides us with observations about the Brezhnev era, the man and the system. As a narrative of these years, the history of the intellectual sphere raises questions about the correct periodisation of the years 1964–82. The Brezhnev era was a complex, transitional one: de-Stalinisation and re-Stalinisation, dissent and obedience, creativity and conformity. Any attempt to divide it up into a pre-1968 (essentially reformist) and post-1968 (conservative) system is too simplistic, and yet there is no doubt that the latter years of the Brezhnev leadership were more conservative than the earlier years. A picture of Brezhnev emerges which tends to reinforce the view of his leadership style: cautious, centrist, non-interventionist. Around him, many groups struggled and vied for influence. Such a survey also highlights the paradoxes of this era. As the state grew weaker so it applied more and more coercion. While it grew increasingly intolerant of dissent, it was also becoming more and more heavily dependent on the intelligentsia in order to cope with the complexity of governing a complex modern industrial society. To make informed and effective policy decisions required a broader, more flexible, and more specialised intellectual sector than that offered by the official ideology and its guardians.

As we consider the periodisation of the Brezhnev years from the viewpoint of intellectual life, it is apparent that the health of Leonid Ilyich is not the only factor to decide the location of temporal dividing lines. Several other chapters in this volume also offer a periodisation on a thematic basis. In the arena of international affairs, Mike Bowker notes in Chapter 5 that a disillusionment with détente set in during 1973 and 1974, and led to a hardening of Soviet foreign policy after the Central Committee plenum of December 1974. Bowker's argument is that although the policies of détente continued for a while in relation to the restraint of Soviet rhetoric with regard to the Third World, US actions in supporting Pinochet's coup in Chile in 1973 and increasingly working to diminish Soviet influence in the Middle East contributed to a strengthening of the hand of the 'hawks' in the Politburo, who were then able to argue more successfully for an increasingly firm line against the West. One might even take this argument further than Bowker does, and suggest that the downturn in relations between the United States and the Soviet Union from the mid-1970s onwards contributed to the maintenance of military priority in the Soviet budget, to the increasing pace of the arms race, to the rise of the resurgent Republicanism of Ronald Reagan in the United States, and to the near meltdown in US–Soviet relations in the early 1980s. From this point of view, the Central Committee plenum of December 1974 becomes a key division in the periodisation of the Brezhnev era.

From the economic point of view, Mark Harrision (Chapter 3) argues for a precise periodisation of the Brezhnev years. In fact, he shows the mid-point of the Brezhnev era to represent not just a clear downturn in its own temporal context, but also to mark a long-run downturn in the economic progression of the Soviet state:

> The long-run context shows that from 1928 until 1973 the Soviet economy was on a path that would catch up with the United States one day. This was in spite of a huge US advantage: it did not suffer the severe capital losses inflicted on the Soviet economy first by Stalin through his policy of farm collectivisation, then by Hitler's war of aggression. However, in 1973, half-way through the Brezhnev period, the process of catching up came to an abrupt end. This year is widely recognised as marking a downturn in the post-war growth of the whole global economy. But the growth rates of the Soviet Union and the Central and East European socialist states turned down much more severely than those of western Europe or the United States.

1973 is also suggested as a clear division in the periodisation of the Brezhnev years in Chapter 1 of this volume. It was in this year that the representation of the 'power ministries' in the Politburo was increased. Minister of Defence Andrei Grechko, Minister of Foreign Affairs Andrei Gromyko and KGB Chairman Yurii Andropov were all elected voting members of the Politburo at the Central Committee plenum in April 1973. This was a shrewd move by Brezhnev, carried out in order to balance the influence of the Party apparatus, and decrease his own vulnerability to opposition from that source These appointments marked the end of the collective leadership of the first half of Brezhnev's term as General Secretary, as demonstrated by Brezhnev's name being placed at the head of the list of otherwise alphabetically ordered Politburo members. In terms of his period in office as a whole, it was only after this proportionally large increase in the number of his own supporters within the Politburo that Brezhnev felt free of the fear of meeting the fate that he himself had visited on his predecessor, Khrushchev, when he engineered the latter's removal from power in 1964. The subsequent removals of Podgorny in 1977 and of Kosygin in 1980 were comparatively less significant serving, as Gorbachev stated in his memoirs, to seal the personal power of Brezhnev, confirming that he was in a position to control the highest level appointments and resignations, rather than actually establishing that position.

If periodisation is one way of reconciling the apparent contradictions of the Brezhnev years, then an extension of this is to argue that the achievements of the Brezhnev years were gained despite his leadership, whereas the failures were all his own work. Such a view would start from the fact that in the first years of the Brezhnev era, the Soviet Union was seen as having a collective leadership. Furthermore, as pointed out in a number of memoirs and discussed in Chapter 1 of this volume, Brezhnev was clearly willing to leave many areas of policy in the hands of the specialists in the Party and the state structures. Consequently then, in almost any area of achievement it could be argued that Brezhnev's own role was minimal. However, clearly, as *de facto* leader of the Soviet Union, ultimate responsibility for the well-being of the Soviet state and people rested with him, and therefore policy failures were to be identified and corrected by him. It might have been the case that he was by and large content to delegate responsibilities to his subordinates, so long as his position of power was not challenged, but it ultimately ought not to have been the case.

From Brezhnev to Gorbachev

The links between the Brezhnev years (1964–82) and the Soviet collapse under Gorbachev (1985–91) have been the subtext to much of the discussion in this volume. The question of how a superpower with global influence could not only decline but disappear within a decade of Brezhnev's passing is of course the stuff of many volumes. In this volume, though, the linkage has been investigated through two main approaches. First, to what extent did the Brezhnev years create the crisis of the later 1980s, building a Potemkin superpower of nuclear weapons and military might, client states and communist double-speak, behind whose façade the economy crumbled, the people grumbled and the ideology struggled to keep up with a changing world? Second, where did the Gorbachev team, with its radical but flawed approach, spring from? And what did they bring with them from their years as, at the least, loyal lip-servants to the regime of Leonid Ilyich Brezhnev?

We noted in Chapter 1 Mikhail Gorbachev's assertion that when he came to power in 1985 he inherited a 'pre-crisis situation'.[8] A more pertinent evaluation might be that found in a Soviet joke of the late 1980s: 'When Gorbachev came to power, the Soviet Union stood on the edge of a precipice. Under his leadership we have taken a great step forward.' In other words, whatever the difficulties facing the Soviet Union after Brezhnev's death – and they were surely legion – to lay at his door the blame for the manner in which the crisis developed to eventually lead to the system's collapse is at best a matter of pure conjecture.

In Chapter 4 in this volume, Ben Fowkes discusses the single issue which by definition brought about the break-up of the Soviet Union, that of the national question:

> But was Brezhnev responsible for the disintegration of the USSR? Did he 'prepare the way for the demise of the Soviet state'.[9] This claim, which is often made, is as absurd as the claim that the Emperor Francis Joseph was responsible for the fall of the Austrian Empire in 1918. In both cases the measures they were asked to undertake by radical nationalists would have led to piecemeal disintegration in any case.

Fowkes' argument is rather that Brezhnev managed to hold the Soviet Union together by taking the line of least resistance. He rejects the view that somehow the Brezhnev years sowed the wind, and that it was the lot of Gorbachev to reap the whirlwind. In other words, with regard to the national question at least, it is too glib to say that the Brezhnevian emphasis on stability – which unquestionably became a hallmark of his regime in many policy areas – stored up problems with which it was impossible for his successors to deal.

Brezhnev resisted the actions for which Gorbachev would later opt, for fear of the very consequences which eventually did occur in the worst-case scenario of both leaders, namely, the disintegration of the Soviet state. Whether holding the Soviet Union together was in itself a laudable aim is another matter altogether, and Gorbachev is surely to gain credit for the largely bloodless nature of the eventual break-up. However, within their own terms, within the framework of the Soviet Union's national interest and ideological commitment, Brezhnev's achievements in relation to the national question are perhaps the more impressive when set against those of his erstwhile Politburo colleague, Mikhail Gorbachev.

Similar conclusions are reached by Mark Harrison (Chapter 3) with regard to the Soviet economy:

> When Gorbachev came to power in 1985 he claimed to have inherited a 'pre-crisis situation'...Had an overwhelming economic disaster become inevitable by the early 1980s? Almost certainly not. At the end of the Brezhnev years most Soviet citizens lived adequately and there was relatively full or overfull employment. The economy was still just growing, although its sluggishness was certainly alarming...Andropov and Chernenko both took determined steps to correct the crisis by traditional means, intensifying centralisation, work discipline and the policing of state property. Moreover, the statistical evidence...shows that these measures paid off: in 1983 the growth slowdown stopped. Thus the situation that Andropov and Chernenko passed on to Gorbachev was no worse than that which they had inherited from Brezhnev, and in some respects better. The Soviet economy was not already a lost cause; indeed Gorbachev's intention in declaring an emergency was not to predict a crisis but to galvanise the efforts necessary to avert one, and he clearly believed that this was still possible. That a crisis resulted, and proved terminal, does not mean that collapse was already inevitable.

Again, a detailed analysis in the light of new material available from the late 1980s onwards undermines the broadly accepted view that Brezhnev's emphasis on stability and the preservation of the existing Soviet system – while, in Gorbachev's words, 'they ignored the transformations that were occurring in other countries',[10] – meant that he bequeathed his successors a basket-case. This was far from the whole story. No one would pretend that Brezhnev's record was unblemished, and indeed there is no doubt on the economic side at least that decline had set in. Nonetheless, that stability and stagnation were one and the same is clearly not always the case.

In the sphere of international relations we are dealing with a multi-faceted complex of issues without the same clear sense of outcome which is apparent in the break-up of the Soviet Union or the collapse of the centrally planned economy. The international relations of any state, but the Soviet Union and Russia more than most, encompass many issues and many interlocutors. Furthermore, the international relations of the Russian Federation today maintain a degree of continuity with those of the USSR, in contrast to the finality which was the collapse of the Soviet state and its economic system. Nonetheless, there is one particularly evident specific outcome of the Soviet Union's international relations under Gorbachev which can be identified, namely the end of the Cold War.

The end of the Cold War differs from our two other examples of policy outcomes in the Gorbachev years in one fundamental fact, specifically that it is widely perceived, both in the USSR/Russia and in the West, to have been a positive achievement. If the Brezhnev regime is to receive some of the blame for later failures in nationalities policy and the economy, should it not then be apportioned a little praise for the positive turn taken in East–West relations in the Gorbachev years? Some of the same problems arise in giving credit to the Brezhnev regime for the end of the Cold War as in laying blame at its feet for the collapse of the Soviet system.[11] In particular, too much of what happened in the Soviet polity, society and economy in the late 1980s can be readily identified with the decisions of individuals (particularly Gorbachev and Yeltsin) rather than with the systemic and structural faults within which they operated.[12] Nonetheless, as in the other policy areas discussed above, there are inevitably elements within Brezhnevian policy which can be argued to have had clear impact in the Gorbachev years.

Mike Bowker (Chapter 5) identifies several ways in which the Brezhnev era, and in particular the policy of détente, might be said to have contributed to the end of the Cold War. He notes first of all though that 'there are limits to how far it is possible to attribute the end of the Cold War to détente' – a similar point to that made by Harrison and Fowkes with regard to the direct impact Brezhnev's policy had on the Gorbachev era in terms of the economy and nationalities policy, respectively. With this caveat in place, Bowker argues that détente laid the groundwork for the end of the Cold War in two particular ways.

First, détente was a learning process, the apparent failure of which taught both sides lessons which they then applied in the second half of the 1980s. For example, in the Brezhnev years the Soviet position in arms negotiations had been wedded to the concept of nuclear parity. Under Gorbachev the replacement of this emphasis on parity with an insistence that the USSR maintain a 'reasonable sufficiency' of nuclear missiles was a tacit acknowledgement that the earlier stance had tied the hands of Soviet negotiators too much in the years of détente. A similar argument could perhaps be made with regard to Soviet policy towards the Third World. As Mark Webber notes in Chapter 6, under Gorbachev there was a decisive break with the Brezhnevian strategy of competitive interventionism and military support for Third World clients. Again, this could be couched in terms of lessons learnt from détente, the eventual failure of which can in no small part be explained by tit-for-tat responses to competitive interventionism.

Second, according to Mike Bowker, détente contributed to the end of the Cold War by playing a role in the lowering of socio-cultural barriers between East and West, for example, in the slow trickle of Western consumer products, information and youth culture into the Soviet Union and in the increased awareness of life in the West on the part of members of the Soviet élite (notably Gorbachev himself, who had spent time travelling in France and Italy at the height of détente).

Having considered then the extent to which the policies of Brezhnev contributed to the successes and failures of the Gorbachev era, let us turn to a second point of enquiry arising from this volume – what contribution did the Brezhnev era make to the Soviet Union under Gorbachev in the form of the intellectuals who came to prominence in the second half of the 1980s? What role, if any, did these intellectuals play in bringing about political change? Can a direct causal link between the reformist intelligentsia of the Brezhnev years and the policies of *perestroika* be identified?

Theorists of the origins of *perestroika* divide over whether to privilege politics – the state, or society–social forces (including education, professionalisation, urbanisation and generational change) in explanations for the emergence of *perestroika*.[13] One of the problems, identified by Schroeder, with societally privileged causal explanations, has been their inability to explain how a set of attitudes and values commensurate with a rapidly evolving social milieu enter and affect the political process. In Schroeder's words:

> Analyses that focus on learning or generations beg the question how, in the presence of diverging lessons and heterogenous generations, one point of view or one part of a generation came to shape policy. Because they do not develop a model of political institutions, the emphases on ideas and generations ultimately rest on a dubious democratic metaphor. They get close to positing a majoritarian process in which prevailing attitudes, or the shifting weight of attitudes within a generation, are translated automatically into policy orientations.[14]

The following analysis may provide some more insights into this process. The group of liberal party intellectuals – identified by Mark Sandle in Chapter 7 as those who occupied the 'space' between conformity and dissent – can perhaps be conceived as the agents or bearers of this set of attitudes and values commensurate with a 'modernising', educated society. Their existence within the politico-intellectual hierarchy, their shared sense of values, the network of supports and contacts they built up and their contacts with, and influence over, key political figures, provides evidence of a mechanism by which policy was shaped by forces from below. It would, of course, be absurd to deny or downplay the role played by politics, or the state (or indeed economic and international factors) in this process. Without the existence of political figures sympathetic to these new values, then the opportunity for participation in the policy process would have been non-existent. Yet this does not invalidate the point that privileging politics in an explanatory framework may be difficult to sustain in the light of the above.

There were clearly avenues for the intelligentsia to influence the policy process. The growing complexity of Soviet economic and social policy forced the party leadership and its apparatus under Brezhnev into a dependence upon the expertise of the intelligentsia. In particular, in the fields of international relations/national security and social policy, many of the research institutes were able to play an important role in influencing the policy process. The roles of IMEMO (the Institute for the World Economy and International Relations) and ISKAN (the US and Canada Institute) in the development of Soviet foreign and defence policy appear to have been fairly significant. Many researchers were part of the *nomenklatura*, and diplomats and officials from the Ministry of Foreign Affairs often went there to study. Most importantly, the heads of these institutes – Inozemtsev and Arbatov – were full members of the Central Committee of the Communist Party, giving them access to the political leadership, and also to western information and classified material. The extent of the influence was dependent upon a number of variables – the wider political and international context, the relationships between individuals, the correlation of political forces and the specific area of research – but those institutes (and hence the individuals within them) that had the most significant input into the policy process were those that:

- Were concerned with ideologically less sensitive areas
- Enjoyed close links between sector heads and the political leadership
- Were able to demonstrate ideological orthodoxy and analytical innovation simultaneously.

The network of relationships between the political elite, the intelligentsia and the apparat under Brezhnev created an environment in which the intellectuals were able to resist conservative pressures in some areas, and to influence the orientation of policy in others. However, in keeping with the aim of this volume to contribute to the opening up of the research agenda on the Brezhnev years, more needs to be discovered about the precise relationships that developed between reformist politicians and the liberal intellectuals, and the impact the latter had in bringing about the wider political, economic and social changes after 1985. How close was the contact between the two groups? How influential was the empirical research – in the field of labour productivity, or agricultural sociology, or on the nature of capitalism – in shaping the views of Gorbachev, Yakovlev, Medvedev, *et al.*?

All of these issues require more research, research beyond the scope of a volume which deals in broad brushstrokes with the Brezhnev era, and with Brezhnev the leader. This volume has raised a number of potential research issues, and has reconsidered Brezhnev in an attempt to reclaim a more rounded assessment of his eighteen-year leadership of the Soviet

Union. It has argued for a deeper analysis of Brezhnev than the stagnation hypothesis allows, while not decisively rejecting all of the charges of this approach. 'Stagnation' there was by the end of the 1970s and into the 1980s in many areas – for example, in the leadership cohort, in the economy, in much that passed for intellectual life – but this is only one aspect of a far more multi-faceted situation than the stagnation discourse allows. Few would argue that academic analysis of nearly two decades in the history of a superpower must continue to interrogate these years in the light of new sources, with a range of approaches, and in appropriate disciplinary contexts.

Notes

1. See, for example, W. Tompson, *Khrushchev. A Political Life* (Basingstoke: Macmillan, 1997); S. N. Khrushchev, *Nikita Khrushchev and the Creation of a Superpower* (Pennsylvania State University Press, 2000).
2. V. Shelud'ko (ed.), *Leonid Brezhnev v vospominaniyakh, razmyshlenniyakh, suzhdeniyakh* (Rostov on Don: Feniks, 1998); Lyudmilla Brezhneva, *Plemyannitsa genseka* (Moscow: Tsentropoligraf, 1999).
3. M. Bowker and P. Williams, *Superpower Détente: A Reappraisal* (London: Sage, 1988), p. 38.
4. Poland has a common border with the Russian enclave of Kaliningrad.
5. I am grateful to Richard Sakwa for first suggesting this nomenclature.
6. D. Volkogonov, *The Rise and Fall of the Soviet Empire* (London: HarperCollins, 1998), p. 324
7. M. Gorbachev, *Memoirs* (London: Doubleday, 1995), p. 113
8. Gorbachev report to the 27th Party Congress, 25 February 1986.
9. R. Brubaker, *Nationalism Reframed* (Cambridge University Press, 1996), p. 23.
10. M. Gorbachev, *Memoirs* (London: Doubleday, 1995), p. 138.
11. We leave aside, for the sake of clarity of argument, the fact that many observers, particularly in the West, would classify the Soviet collapse as a positive outcome. The categories of 'blame' and 'praise' are not meant here to be definitive assertions. Rather, the aim is to interrogate the usual discourse of the Brezhnev–Gorbachev linkage by applying it to policy areas often excluded from the discourse.
12. For a detailed argument of this case, see, J. Hough, *Democratization and Revolution in the USSR, 1985–1991* (Washington, DC: Brookings Institution, 1997).
13. Among those who tend to privilege social factors, see M. Lewin, *The Gorbachev Phenomenon* (Berkeley: University of California Press, 1988); G. Hosking, *The Awakening of the Soviet Union* (Cambridge, Mass.: Harvard University Press 1991); T. J. Colton, *The Dilemma of Reform in the Soviet Union* (New York: Council on Foreign Relations, 1986). For state-centred ones, see P. Schroeder, *Red Sunset: The Failure of Soviet Politics* (Princeton University Press, 1993), esp. Chapter 1. See also, M. R. Beissinger, 'In Search of Generations in Soviet Politics', *World Politics*, 38, January 1986.
14. P. Schroeder, *Red Sunset: The Failure of Soviet Politics* (Princeton University Press, 1993), p. 7.

The Brezhnev Bibliography

General works on the Brezhnev era

Amalrik, A., *Will the Soviet Union Survive Until 1984?* (London, 1970).

Bialer, S., *Stalin's Successors* (Cambridge, 1980).

Bialer, S., *The Soviet Paradox; External Expansion, Internal Decline* (London, 1986).

Bialer, S. and T. Gustafson (eds), *Russia at the Crossroads: The 26th Congress of the CPSU* (London, 1982).

Breslauer, G., *Khrushchev and Brezhnev as Leaders* (London, 1982).

Brezhnev, L. I., *Leninskim kursom*, 7 vols (Moscow, 1970–9).

Brezhnev, L. I., *Ob osnovnykh voprosakh ekonomicheskoi politiki KPSS na sovremennom etape*, 2 vols (Moscow, 1975).

Brezhnev, L. I., *Malaya zemlya* (Moscow, 1978).

Brezhnev, L. I., *Ob osnovnykh voprosakh ekonomicheskoi politiki KPSS na sovremennom etape: rechi i doklady*, 2 vols, expanded edn (Moscow, 1979).

Brown, A. and M. Kaser (eds), *The Soviet Union Since the Fall of Khrushchev*, 2nd edn (London, 1978).

Cohen, S., *Rethinking the Soviet Experience* (Oxford, 1985).

Cohen, S., A. Rabinowitch and R. Sharlet (eds), *The Soviet Union Since Stalin* (London, 1980).

Colton, T., *The Dilemma of Reform in the USSR* (New York, 1986).

Conquest, R., *Russia after Khrushchev* (New York, 1965).

Dallin, A. (ed.), *The Khrushchev and Brezhnev Years* (New York, 1992).

Dallin, A. (ed.), *The 25th Congress of the CPSU* (Stanford, 1977).

Dallin, A. and G. Lapidus (eds), *The Soviet System in Crisis* (Boulder, Col., 1991).

Dornberg, J., *Brezhnev. The Masks of Power* (London, 1974).

Fleron, F. J. (ed.), *Technology and Communist Culture* (New York, 1977).

Hosking, G., *A History of the Soviet Union*, final edn (London, 1994).

Hough, J., 'The Brezhnev Era: The Man and the System' *Problems of Communism*, 25(4), 1976.

Hough, J., *Russia and the West* (New York, 1988).

Hoffmann, E. P., *The Politics of Economic Modernisation* (Ithaca, 1982).

Hoffmann, E. P. and R. Laird, *The Soviet Polity in the Modern Era* (Hawthorne, NY, 1984).

Hoffmann E. P. and R. Laird. *Technocratic Socialism: The USSR in the Advanced Industrial Era* (Durham, Md., 1985).

Keep, J., *Last of the Empires* (Oxford, 1996).

McCauley, M., *The Soviet Union after Brezhnev* (London, 1983).

McNeal, R. H., *The Bolshevik Tradition* (Englewood Cliffs, 1975).

Medvedev, Zh., 'Russia Under Brezhnev', *New Left Review*, 117 (September–October 1978).

Murphy, P. J., *Brezhnev. Soviet Politician* (Jefferson, NC, 1981).

Nove, A., *Stalinism and After*, 3rd edn (London, 1989).

Rigby, T. H., A. Brown and P. Reddaway (eds), *Authority, Power and Policy in the USSR* (London, 1980).

Smith, H., *The Russians* (London, 1976).
Strong, J. (ed.), *The Soviet Union Under Brezhnev and Kosygin* (New York, 1971).
Tucker, R. (ed.), *Political Culture and Leadership Since Stalin* (Brighton, 1987).
Various, *Leonid Brezhnev: The Period of Stagnation* (Moscow, 1989).
Volkogonov, D., *The Rise and Fall of the Soviet Empire: Political Leaders from Lenin to Gorbachev* (London, 1998).

Memoirs

Aksyutin, Yu. (ed.), *L. I. Brezhnev: materialy k biografii* (Moscow, 1991).
Aleksandrov-Agentov, A., *Ot Kollontai do Gorbacheva* (Moscow, 1994).
Arbatov, G., *Zatnayuvsheesya vyzdorovlenie (1953–85gg.): svidetel'stvo sovremennika* (Moscow, 1991).
Burlatskii, F., *Khrushchev and the First Russian Spring* (London, 1991).
Burlatskii, F., *Vozhdi i sovetniki: o Khrushcheve, Andropove i ne tol'ko o nikh* (Moscow, 1990).
Dobrynin, A. F., *Sugubo doveritel'no: Posol v Vashingtone pri shesti prezidentakh SshA (1962–1986)* (Moscow, 1997).
Gorbachev, M. S., *Zhizn' i reformy* (Moscow, 1995).
Grishin, V. V., *Ot Khrushcheva do Gorbacheva. Politicheskie portrety pyati gensekov i A. N. Kosygina* (Moscow, 1996).
Medvedev, R., *Lichnost i epokha. Politicheskii portret L. I. Brezhneva* Vol. 1 (Moscow, 1991).
Shelud'ko V. (ed.), *Leonid Brezhnev* (Rostov-on-Don, 1998).

Domestic politics

Amann, R., 'Searching For An Appropriate Concept of Soviet Politics: The Politics of Hesitant Modernisation?', *British Journal of Political Science*, 16/4, 1986.
Blackwell, Robert, Jr, 'Cadres Policy in the Brezhnev Era', *Problems of Communism*, 28, March–April 1979.
Brzezinski, Z. (ed.), *Dilemmas of Change in Soviet Politics* (New York, 1969).
Bunce, V. and J. M. Echols, III, 'Soviet Politics in the Brezhnev Era: "Pluralism" or "Corporatism?"', in D. R. Kelley (ed.), *Soviet Politics in the Brezhnev Era* (New York, 1980).
Cocks, P., R. V. Daniels and N. W. Heer (eds), *The Dynamics of Soviet Politics* (Cambridge, Mass., 1976).
Connor, W. D., 'Generations and Politics in the USSR', *Problems of Communism*, 24, September–October 1975.
Cook, L. J., *The Soviet Social Contract and Why It Failed* (Cambridge, Mass., 1994).
Dallin, A. and T. B. Larson (eds), *Soviet Politics Since Khrushchev* (Englewood Cliffs, 1968).
Friedgut, T., *Political Participation in the USSR* (Princeton, 1979).
Gustafson, T., *Reform in Soviet Politics* (Cambridge, 1981).
Hammer, D., *USSR: The Politics of Oligarchy* (Hinsdale, 1974).
Hough, J. and M. Fainsod, *How the Soviet Union is Governed* (Cambridge Mass., 1979).
Hough, J., 'The Soviet Union: Petrification or Pluralism?, *Problems of Communism*, 22, 1972.
Hough, J., *The Soviet Union and Social Science Theory* (Cambridge, Mass., 1977).

Hough, J., *Soviet Leadership in Transition* (Washington, 1980).
Kelley, D. R., *The Politics of Developed Socialism* (Westport, Conn., 1986).
Kelley, D. R. (ed.), *Soviet Politics in the Brezhnev Era* (New York, 1986).
Lewin, M., *Political Undercurrents in Soviet Economic Debates* (Princeton, 1974).
McAuley, M., *Politics and the Soviet Union* (Harmondsworth, 1979).
McAuley, M., *Soviet Politics, 1917–91* (Oxford, 1992).
Millar, J. R. (ed.), *Cracks in the Monolith: Party Power in the Brezhnev Era* (New York, 1992).
Osborn, R., *The Evolution of Soviet Politics* (Homewood, Ill., 1974).
Parker, J., *Kremlin in Transition*, 2 vols (London, 1992).
Rigby, T. H., 'The Soviet Leadership: Towards a Self-Stabilising Oligarchy?', *Soviet Studies*, 22/2, October 1970.
Rigby, T. H., 'The Soviet Regional Leadership: The Brezhnev Generation', *Slavic Review*, March 1978.
Schapiro, L., *The Communist Party of the Soviet Union* (London, 1970).
Sharlet, R., 'The New Soviet Constitution of 1977', *Problems of Communism*, 26, September–October 1977.
Skilling, H. Gordon and F. Griffiths (eds), *Interest Groups in Soviet Politics* (Princeton, 1971).
Terry, S. M., 'Theories of Socialist Development in Soviet–East European Relations', in S. M. Terry (ed.), *Soviet Policy in Eastern Europe* (New Haven, 1984).
Willerton, J. P., 'Patronage Networks and Coalition-Building in the Brezhnev Era', *Soviet Studies*, 40, April 1989.
Willerton, J. P., *Patronage and Politics in the USSR* (Cambridge, 1992).
Zaslavsky, V., 'The Rebirth of the Stalin Cult in the USSR', *Telos*, Summer 1979.

Economics

Arnot, B., *Controlling Soviet Labour* (London 1988).
Åslund, A., 'How Small is Soviet National Income?', in H. S. Rowen and C. Wolf (eds), *The Impoverished Superpower: Perestroika and the Soviet Military Burden* (San Francisco, Cal., 1990).
Bergson, A., *Planning and Performance in Socialist Economies: The USSR and Eastern Europe* (Boston, Man., 1989).
Bergson, A., 'Neoclassical Norms and the Valuation of National Income in the Soviet Union: Comment', *Journal of Comparative Economics*, 21/3, 1995.
Berliner, J. S., *The Innovation Decision in Soviet Industry* (Cambridge, Mass., 1976).
Birman, Igor, 'The Financial Crisis in the USSR', *Soviet Studies*, 32/1, 1980.
Birman, Igor, *Personal Consumption in the USSR and the USA* (London, 1989).
Bornstein, M., 'Improving the Soviet Economic Mechanism', *Soviet Studies*, 37/1, 1985.
Brus, W., '1950 to 1953: The Peak of Stalinism', '1953 to 1956: The "Thaw" and the "New Course"', '1956 to 1965: In Search of Balanced Development', and '1966 to 1975: Normalization and Conflict', in M. Kaser (ed.), *The Economic History of Eastern Europe 1919–75*, Vol. 3, *Institutional Change Within a Planned Economy* (Oxford, 1986).
Davies, R. W., *Soviet Economic Development from Lenin to Khrushchev* (Cambridge, 1998).
Easterly, W. and S. Fischer, 'The Soviet Economic Decline', *World Bank Economic Review*, 9, 1995.

Ehrlich, É., 'Contest between Countries: 1937–1986', *Soviet Studies*, 43, 1991.
Ellman, M. and V. Kontorovich (eds), *The Disintegration of the Soviet Economic System* (London, 1992).
Ellman, M. and V. Kontorovich (eds), *The Destruction of the Soviet Economic System: An Insider's History* (London, 1998).
Goskomstat SSSR, *Narodnoe khoziaistvo SSSR za 70 let* (Moscow, 1987).
Goskomstat SSSR, *Narodnoe khoziaistvo SSSR v 1988 godu* (Moscow, 1989).
Gregory, P. R., 'Productivity, Slack, and Time Theft in the Soviet Economy', in J. R. Millar, (ed.), *Politics, Work, and Daily Life in the USSR: A Survey of Former Soviet Citizens* (Cambridge, 1987).
Grossman, G., 'The "Second Economy" of the USSR', *Problems of Communism*, 26, 1976.
Grossman, G., 'Subverted Sovereignty: the Historic Role of the Soviet Underground', in S. S. Cohen, A. Schwartz and J. Zysman (eds), *The Tunnel at the End of the Light: Privatization, Business Networks, and Economic Transformation in Russia* (Berkeley, 1998).
Hanson, P., 'Success Indicators Revisited: The July 1979 Decree on Planning and Management', *Soviet Studies*, 35/1, 1983.
Harrison, M., 'Soviet Economic Growth since 1928: The Alternative Statistics of G. I. Khanin', *Europe–Asia Studies*, 45/1, 1993.
Harrison, M., 'Trends in Soviet Labour Productivity, 1928–1985: War, Postwar Recovery, and Slowdown', *European Review of Economic History*, 2/2, 1998.
Knorr, H., 'Shchekino: Another Look', *Soviet Studies*, 38/2, 1986, pp. 141–69.
Kontorovich, V., 'Soviet Growth Slowdown: Econometric vs Direct Evidence', *American Economic Association Papers and Proceedings*, 1986.
Kontorovich, V., 'Discipline and Growth in the Soviet Economy', *Problems of Communism*, 34/6, 1986.
Kontorovich, V., 'Lessons of the 1965 Soviet Economic Reform', *Soviet Studies*, 40/2, 1988.
Kudrov, V. M., *Sovetskaya ekonomika v retrospektive. Opyt Pereosmysleniya* (Moscow, 1997).
Millar, J. R., 'The Little Deal: Brezhnev's Contribution to Acquisitive Socialism', *Slavic Review*, 44/4, 1985.
Nove, A., *An Economic History of the USSR, 1917–1991*, 4th edn (Harmondsworth, 1992).
Ofer, G., 'Soviet Economic Growth: 1928–1985', *Journal of Economic Literature*, 25/4, 1987.
Rosefielde, S., 'The Illusion of Material Progress: The Analytics of Soviet Economic Growth Revisited', *Soviet Studies*, 43/4, 1991.
Rutland, P., 'The Shchekino Method and the Struggle to Raise Labour Productivity in Soviet Industry', *Soviet Studies*, 36/3, 1984.
Schroeder, G. E., 'The 1966–67 Soviet Industrial Price Reform: A Study in Complications', *Soviet Studies*, 20/4, 1969.
Schroeder, G. E., 'The "Reform" of the Supply System in Soviet Industry', *Soviet Studies*, 24/1, 1972.
Schroeder, G. E., 'The Soviet Economy on a Treadmill of 'Reforms'', in US Congress, Joint Economic Committee, *Soviet Economy in a Time of Change*, Vol. 1 (Washington, DC, 1979).
Schroeder, G. E., 'Soviet Economic "Reform" Decrees: More Steps on the Treadmill', in US Congress, Joint Economic Committee, *Soviet Economy in the 1980s: Problems and Prospects*, Part 1 (Washington, DC, 1982).
Schroeder, G. E., 'The Slowdown in Soviet Industry, 1976–1982', *Soviet Economy*, 1/1, 1985.

Schroeder, G. E., 'Reflections on Economic Sovietology', *Post–Soviet Affairs*, 11/3, 1995.

Treml, V. G., and M. Ellman, 'Debate: Why Did the Soviet Economic System Collapse?', *Radio Free Europe/Radio Liberty Research Report*, 2/23, 1993.

Nationalities

Allworth, E. (ed.), *Soviet Nationality Problems* (New York, 1971).

Azrael, J., *Soviet Nationality Policies and Practices* (New York, 1978).

Besançon, A., 'The Nationalities Issue in the USSR', *Survey*, 30/4, 1989, pp. 113–30.

Carrère D'Encausse, H., *Decline of an Empire. The Soviet Socialist Republics in Revolt* (New York, 1979).

Conquest, R., *The Last Empire* (Stanford, 1986).

Conquest, R. (ed.), *Soviet Nationalities Policy in Practice* (London, 1967).

Denber, R. (ed.), *The Soviet Nationality Reader* (Boulder, Col., 1992).

Dzyuba, I., *Internationalism or Russification* (London, 1968).

Fowkes, B., *The Disintegration of the Soviet Union* (Basingstoke, 1997).

Gitelman, Z., 'Are Nations Merging in the USSR?', *Problems of Communism* 32/5, 1983.

Gleason, G., *Federalism and Nationalism. The Struggle for Republican Rights in the USSR* (Boulder, Col., 1990).

Goble, P., 'Ethnic Politics in the USSR', *Problems of Communism* 38/4, 1989.

Hajda, L. and M. Beissenger (eds), *The Nationalities Factor in Soviet Politics and Society* (Boulder, Col., 1990).

Hodnett, G., 'The Debate over Soviet Federalism' *Soviet Studies* 18/4, 1966–7 pp. 458–81.

Huttenbach, H. (ed.), *Soviet Nationality Policies. Ruling Ethnic Groups in the USSR* (London, 1990).

Jones, E. and F. Grupp., 'Modernisation and Ethnic Equalisation', *Soviet Studies*, 36/2, 1984.

Jones, E. and F. Grupp., *Modernization, Value Change and Fertility in the Soviet Union* (Cambridge, 1987).

Kaiser, R. J., *The Geography of Nationalism in Russia and the USSR* (Princeton 1994).

Karklins, R., *Ethnic Relations in the USSR. The Perspective from Below* (London, 1985).

Katz, Z. (ed.), *Handbook of Major Soviet Nationalities* (New York, 1975).

Kozlov, V., *The Peoples of the Soviet Union* (London, 1988).

Kreindler, I. T. (ed.), *Sociolinguistic Perspectives on Soviet National Languages* (Berlin, 1985).

Kux, S., 'Soviet Federalism', *Problems of Communism*, 39/2, 1990.

McAuley, M., 'Nationalism and the Soviet Multi-Ethnic State', in N. Harding (ed.), *The State in Socialist Society* (London, 1984).

Motyl, A., *Will the Non-Russians Rebel? State, Ethnicity and Stability in the USSR* (Ithaca, 1987).

Motyl, A. (ed.), *Thinking Theoretically About Soviet Nationalities* (New York, 1992).

Nahaylo, B. and V. Swoboda, *Soviet Disunion. A History of the Nationalities' Problem in the USSR* (London, 1990).

Newth, J., 'The 1970 Soviet Census', *Soviet Studies*, 24/2, 1972–3.

Rakowska-Harmstone, T., 'The Dialectics of Nationalism in the USSR', *Problems of Communism*, 23/3, 1974.

Simmonds, G. W. (ed.), *Nationalism in the USSR and Eastern Europe in the Era of Brezhnev and Kosygin* (Detroit, 1977).

Simon, G., *Nationalism and Policy towards the Nationalities in the Soviet Union* (Boulder, Col., 1991).
Smith, G. (ed.), *The Nationalities Question in the Soviet Union* (London, 1990).
Suny, R. G., *Revenge of the Past. Nationalism, Revolution and the Collapse of the Soviet Union* (Stanford, 1993).
Zaslavsky, V., 'The Ethnic Question in the USSR', *Telos*, 45, 1980, pp. 45–76.
Zaslavsky, V., *The Neo-Stalinist State. Class, Ethnicity and Consensus in Soviet Society* (Armonk, N. Y, 1982).

Society

Bahry, D., 'Society Transformed? Rethinking the Social Roots of Perestroika', *Slavic Review*, 52/3, 1993.
Bialer, S. and J. Afferica., 'The Genesis of Gorbachev's World', *Foreign Affairs*, 3, 1986.
Hosking, G., *Beyond Socialist Realism: Soviet Fiction since Ivan Denisovich* (London, 1980).
Hosking, G., *The Awakening of the Soviet Union* (London, 1991).
Kerblay, B., *Modern Soviet Society* (London, 1983).
Lane, D., 'The Roots of Political Reform: The Changing Social Structure of the USSR' in C. Merridale and C. Ward (eds), *Perestroika: The Historical Perspective* (London, 1991).
Lapidus, Gail, W., *Women in Soviet Society* (Berkeley, 1978).
Lewin, M., *The Gorbachev Phenomenon* (London, 1988).
Matthews, M., *Soviet Social Structure* (London, 1972).
Matthews, M., *Privilege in the Soviet Union* (London, 1979).
Ruble, B., 'Stepping Off The Treadmill of Failed Reforms', in H. D. Balzer (ed.), *Five Years That Shook The World* (Boulder, Col., 1991).
Tokes, R. L. and H. W. Morton (eds), *Soviet Politics and Society in the 1970's* (New York, 1974).
Voslensky, M., *Nomenklatura* (London, 1984).
Yanov, A., *Essays on Soviet Society*, Special issue of *International Journal of Sociology*, Summer–Fall 1976.

Ideology and intellectual life

Churchward, L., *The Soviet Intelligentsia* (London, 1973).
Cohen, S. F. and K. vanden Heuvel (eds), *Voices of Glasnost: Interviews with Gorbachev's Reformers* (New York, 1989).
Evans, A. B., 'Developed Socialism in Soviet Ideology', *Soviet Studies*, 29, 1977.
Evans, A. B., 'The Decline of Developed Socialism? Some Trends in Recent Soviet Ideology', *Soviet Studies*, 38, 1986.
Evans, A. B., 'The Polish Crisis in the 1980's and Adaptation in Soviet Ideology', *Journal of Communist Studies*, 2, 1986.
Evans, A. B., *Soviet Marxism–Leninism. The Decline of an Ideology* (Westport, Conn., 1993).
Garrard, J. and C. Garrard., *Inside the Soviet Writers' Union* (New York, 1990).
Heer, N. W., *Politics and History in the Soviet Union* (Cambridge, Mass., 1971).
Kagarlitsky, B., *The Thinking Reed* (London, 1988).
Kanet, R. E., 'The Rise and Fall of the All-People's State: Recent Changes in the Soviet Theory of the State', *Soviet Studies*, 20, 1968.

Kelley, D. R, 'Developed Socialism: A Political Formula for the Brezhnev Era', in J. Seroka and S. Simon (eds), *Developed Socialism in the Soviet Bloc* (Boulder, Col., 1982).
Kosolapov, R., *Developed Socialism: Theory and Practice* (Moscow, 1982).
Kux, E., 'Contradictions in Soviet Socialism', *Problems of Communism*, 33/6, 1984.
Lewin, M., *Stalinism and the Seeds of Soviet Reform* (London, 1991).
Markwick, R., 'Catalyst of Historiography, Marxism and Dissidence: The Sector of Methodology of the Institute of History, Soviet Academy of Sciences 1964–68', *Europe–Asia Studies*, 46/4, 1994.
McClure, T., 'The Politics of Soviet Culture 1964–67', *Problems of Communism*, Vol. 17, March–April 1967.
Sandle, M., *A Short History of Soviet Socialism* (London, 1999).
Seroka, J. and S. Simon (eds), *Developed Socialism in the Soviet Bloc* (Boulder, Col., 1982).
Shatrov, M., The Bolsheviks *and Other Plays*, trans. and introd. by Michael Glenny (London, 1990).
Shlapentokh, V., *Soviet Intellectuals and Political Power* (London, 1990).
Sik, O., *The Third Way: Marxist–Leninist Theory and Modern Industrial Society* (London, 1976).
Sutela, P., *Economic Thought and Economic Reform in the Soviet Union* (Cambridge, 1991).
Thompson, T. L., 'Developed Socialism: Brezhnev's Contribution to Soviet Ideology', in T. L. Thompson and R. Sheldon (eds), *Soviet Society and Culture* (Boulder, Col., 1988).
Thompson, T. L., *Ideology and Policy: The Political Uses of Doctrine in the Soviet Union* (Boulder, Col., 1989).
Yanov, A., *The Drama of the Soviet 1960s: A Lost Reform* (Berkeley, 1984).
Yanowitch, M., *Controversies in Soviet Social Thought: Democratisation, Social Justice, and the Erosion of Official Ideology* (Armonk, NY, 1991).
Zaslavskaya, T., 'The Novosibirsk Report', *Survey*, 28, 1984.

Dissent

Alekseeva, L., *Soviet Dissent: Contemporary Movements for National, Religious and Human Rights* (Middleton, Conn., 1985).
Amalrik, A., *Involuntary Journey to Siberia* (Newton Abbott, 1971).
Barghoorn, F. C., *Détente and the Democratic Movement in the USSR* (New York, 1976).
Brumberg, A. (ed.), *In Quest of Justice* (New York, 1970).
Bukovsky, V., *To Build A Castle* (London, 1978).
Chornovil, V., *The Chornovil Papers* (New York, 1968).
Cohen, S. F. (ed.), *An End to Silence: Uncensored Opinion in the Soviet Union* (New York, 1982).
Hayward, M. (ed.), *On Trial* (New York, 1966).
Hopkins, M., *Russia's Underground Press: The Chronicle of Current Events* (New York, 1983).
Lakshin, V., *Solzhenitsyn, Tvardovsky and Novyi Mir* (Cambridge, Mass., 1980).
Medvedev, R., *On Socialist Democracy* (London, 1975).
Medvedev, R., *Political Essays* trans. by Tamara Deutscher (Nottingham, 1976).
Medvedev, R., *On Soviet Dissent. Interviews with Pierro Ostellino*, trans. by William A. Packer (New York, 1980).
Rothberg, A., *The Heirs of Stalin* (Ithaca, 1972).

Rubenstein, J., *Soviet Dissidents: Their Struggle for Human Rights* (London, 1980).
Sakharov, A., *Progress, Co-Existence and Intellectual Freedom* (New York, 1968).
Sakharov, A., *Sakharov Speaks* (London, 1974).
Sakharov, A., *My Country and the World* (New York, 1975).
Sakharov, A., *Alarm and Hope* (New York, 1978).
Saunders, G. (ed.), *Samizdat: Voices of Opposition* (New York, 1974).
Shatz, M., *Soviet Dissent in Historical Perspective* (Cambridge, 1980).
Spechler, D. R., *Permitted Dissent in the USSR: Novyi Mir and the Soviet Regime* (New York, 1982).
Tokes R. L. (ed.), *Dissent in the USSR* (Baltimore, Md., 1975).

Foreign policy

Anderson, R. D. Jr, *Public Politics in an Authoritarian State. Making Foreign Policy During the Brezhnev Years* (Ithaca and London, 1993).
Aspaturian, V. V., *Process and Power in Soviet Foreign Policy* (Boston, 1971).
Aspaturian, V. V., 'Soviet Global Power and the Correlation of Forces', *Problems of Communism*, 29/3, 1980.
Bialer, S. (ed.), *The Domestic Context of Soviet Foreign Policy* (Boulder, Col., 1980).
Bowker, M. and P. Williams, *Superpower Détente: A Reappraisal* (London, 1988).
Breslauer, G. W., 'Ideology and Learning in Soviet Third World Policy', *World Politics*, 34/3, 1987.
Brezhnev, L. I., *Peace, Détente and Soviet–American Relations* (New York and London, 1979).
Brzezinski, Z., *The Soviet Bloc: Unity and Conflict* (Boston, 1967).
Casey, F. M., 'The Theory and Tactics of Soviet Third World Strategy', *Journal of Social, Political and Economic Studies*, 12/3, 1987.
Cobb, T. W., 'National Security Perspectives of Soviet "Think-Tanks"', *Problems of Communism*, Vol. 31, November–December 1981.
Dawisha, K., 'Soviet Decision-Making in the Middle East: The 1973 October War and the 1980 Gulf War', *International Affairs*, 57/1, 1980–1.
Dawisha, K and A. Dawisha (eds), *The Soviet Union in the Middle East: Policies and Perspectives* (London, 1982).
Dawisha, K and P. Hanson (eds), *Soviet–East European Dilemmas* (London, 1981).
Dobrynin, A., *In Confidence* (New York, 1995).
Donaldson, R. H., (ed.)., *The Soviet Union in the Third World: Successes and Failures* (Boulder, Col., 1980).
Duncan, P. J. S., *The Soviet Union and India* (London, 1989).
Duncan, W. R., *The Soviet Union and Cuba. Interests and Influence* (New York, 1985).
Edmonds, R., *Soviet Foreign Policy, 1962–73: The Paradox of Superpower* (New York, 1975).
Fogarty, C. and K. Tritle, 'Moscow's Economic Aid Programs in Less Developed Countries: A Perspective on the 1980s', in *Gorbachev's Economic Plans. Volume 2, Study Papers Submitted to the Joint Economic Committee, Congress of the United States, November 1987* (Washington, DC, 1987).
Garthoff, R. L., *Détente and Confrontation: American–Soviet Relations from Nixon to Reagan* (Washington, DC, 1985).
Gati, C. (ed.), *Caging the Bear: Containment and the Cold War* (Indianapolis, 1974).
Gati, C. (ed.), *The International Politics of Eastern Europe* (New York, 1976).
Gelman, H., *The Brezhnev Politburo and the Decline of Détente* (Ithaca: Cornell, 1984).

Golan, G., *The Soviet Union and National Liberation Movements in the Third World* (Boston, 1988).
Goldgeier, J. M., *Leadership Style and Soviet Foreign Policy. Stalin, Khrushchev, Brezhnev, Gorbachev* (Baltimore, Md. and London, 1994).
Gorodetsky, G. (ed.)., *Soviet Foreign Policy 1917–91: A Retrospective* (London, 1994).
Gromyko, A. A. and B. N. Ponomarev (eds), *Soviet Foreign Policy, 1917–1980*, 2 Vols. 4th edn (Moscow, 1981).
Gupta, S. K., 'Indo-Soviet Relations', *Problems of Communism*, 22/3, 1974.
Halliday, F., 'Soviet Foreign Policymaking and the Afghanistan War: from "Second Mongolia" to "Bleeding Wound"', *Review of International Studies*, 25/4, 1999.
Hoffmann, E. P. and F. J. Fleron (eds), *The Conduct of Soviet Foreign Policy* (New York, 1980).
Holloway, D., *The Soviet Union and the Arms Race* (New Haven, 1983).
Jones, C. D., *Soviet Influence in Eastern Europe: Political Autonomy and the Warsaw Pact* (New York, 1981).
Israelyan, V., *Inside the Kremlin During the Yom Kippur War* (Pennsylvania, 1995).
Kennedy-Pipe, C., *Russia and the World, 1917–1991* (London, 1998).
Khalilzad, Z., 'Soviet-Occupied Afghanistan', *Problems of Communism*, 29/6, 1980.
Laird, R. F. and E. P. Hoffmann (eds), *Soviet Foreign Policy in a Changing World* (New York, 1986).
Levgold, R., 'The Super Rivals: Conflict in the Third World', *Foreign Affairs*, 57/4, 1979.
MacFarlane, S. N., 'The Soviet Conception of Regional Security', *World Politics*, 37/3, 1985.
McConnell, J. M. and B. Dismukes, 'Soviet Diplomacy of Force in the Third World', *Problems of Communism*, 28/1, 1979.
Menon, R., *Soviet Power and the Third World* (New Haven, London, 1986).
Nation, R. C., *Black Earth, Red Star. A History of Soviet Security Policy, 1917–1991* (Ithaca, London, 1992).
Papp, D. S., 'National Liberation during Détente: The Soviet Outlook', *International Journal*, 32/1, 1976–7.
Parrot, B., 'Soviet Foreign Policy, Internal Politics and Trade With the West', in B. Parrot, *Trade, Technology and Soviet–American Relations* (Bloomington Ind., 1985).
Porter, B. D., *The USSR in Third World Conflicts: Soviet Arms and Diplomacy in Local Wars, 1945–1980* (Cambridge, 1984).
Ramet, P., 'The Soviet–Syrian Relationship', *Problems of Communism*, 35/5, 1986.
Rubinstein, A. Z., *Moscow's Third World Strategy* (Princeton, 1988).
Rubinstein, A. Z., (ed.)., *Soviet and Chinese Influence in the Third World* (New York, 1975).
Saivetz, C. R. and S. Woodby., *Soviet–Third World Relations* (Boulder, Col., London, 1985).
Schmid, A. P., *Soviet Military Interventions since 1945* (London, 1985).
Shevchenko, A., *Breaking With Moscow* (New York, 1985).
Szporluk, R. (ed.)., *The Influence of Eastern Europe and the Soviet West on the USSR* (New York, 1976).
Ulam, A., *Dangerous Relations: The Soviet Union in World Politics 1970–82* (Oxford, 1983).
Ulam, A., *The Communists: The Story of Power and Lost Illusions 1948–91* (New York, 1992).
Valenta, J., *Soviet Intervention in Czechoslovakia, 1968* (Baltimore, Mo., 1979).

Valenta, J. and W. Potter (eds)., *Soviet Decisionmaking for National Security* (Hemel Hempstead, 1984).

Valkenier, E. K., *The Soviet Union and the Third World. An Economic Bind* (New York, 1983).

Valkenier, E. K., 'Revolutionary Change in the Third World: Recent Soviet Assessments', *World Politics*, 38/3, 1986.

Volten, P., *Brezhnev's Peace Programme* (Boulder, Col., 1982).

Westad, O. A., 'Prelude to Invasion: the Soviet Union and the Afghan Communists, 1978–1979', *The International History Review*, 16/1, 1994.

Westad, O. A., 'Moscow and the Angolan Crisis, 1974–1976: A New Pattern of Intervention', *Bulletin (Cold War International History Project)*, Issues 8–9, Winter 1996–7.

Westad, O. A., 'Concerning the Situation in "A": New Russian Evidence on the Soviet Intervention in Afghanistan', *Bulletin (Cold War International History Project)*, Issues 8–9, Winter 1996–7.

Yanov, A., *Détente after Brezhnev* (Berkeley, 1977).

Index